Power Visual Basic with Developer's Library

Frank J. Engo

boyd & fraser publishing company
I(T)P An International Thomson Publishing Company

Danvers • Albany • Bonn • Boston • Cincinnati • Detroit • London • Madrid • Melbourne
Mexico City • New York • Paris • San Francisco • Singapore • Tokyo • Toronto • Washington

Production Manager: Patty Stephan
Production Editor: Jean Bermingham
Composition: Gex, Inc.
Interior Design: Maria Karkucinski
Cover Design: Diana Coe
Manufacturing Coordinator: Brian Harvey

Printed in the United States of America

For more information, contact boyd & fraser publishing company:

boyd & fraser publishing company
One Corporate Place • Ferncroft Village
Danvers, Massachusetts 01923, USA

International Thomson Publishing Europe
Berkshire House 168-173
High Holborn
London WCIV 7AA, England

Thomas Nelson Australia
102 Dodds Street
South Melbourne 3205
Victoria, Australia

Nelson Canada
1120 Birchmount Road
Scarborough, Ontario
Canada M1K 5G4

International Thomson Editores
Campose Eliseos 385, Piso 7
Col. Polanco
11560 Mexico D.F. Mexico

International Thomson Publishing GmbH
Konigswinterer Strasse 418
53227 Bonn, Germany

International Thomson Publishing Asia
221 Henderson Road
#05-10 Henderson Building
Singapore 0315

International Thomson Publishing Japan
Hirakawacho Kyowa Building, 3F
2-2-1 Hirakawacho
Chiyoda-ku, Tokyo 102, Japan

1 2 3 4 5 6 7 8 9 10 BN 9 8 7 6 5

ISBN: 0-87709-987-1

To my parents for their support and understanding.
Very special thanks to John Maolucci, Patty Lamond, and
Vivien Lichter for all their additional help and support.

In memory of my brother Ken.

CONTENTS

PREFACE

Microsoft's Visual Basic for Windows is the quickest and easiest method available today for creating powerful Windows-based applications. Even relatively novice programmers can create attractive and efficient applications simply by designing windows and menus, customizing buttons and textboxes, and writing the short lines of code that respond to events.

The purpose of this book is to go beyond the basics, to explore the enormous number of resources and tools that exploit Visual Basic's graphical user interface (GUI) in building professional-quality, full-featured applications. Students will learn advanced techniques for data and control handling, object linking and embedding (OLE), incorporating dynamic data exchange (DDE), and using dynamic-link libraries with custom controls and calling procedures.

This book is for potential programmers and serious students with some prior experience in Basic or another upper-level programming language (such as Turbo Pascal or C), who want to make a smooth transition from writing introductory programs to creating practical applications.

Part I, Fundamentals, reinforces and expands the essential tools of the language and programming environment. Topics include creating interfaces, programming fundamentals, designing menus, and using common dialogs. Part II, Power Programming, shows how to apply Visual Basic to professional system development. Students learn how to save and restore grids, determine if an application is running, create powerful memo editors, link Visual Basic projects, work with objects, produce charts and graphs, design reports, achieve animation, incorporate professional features and third party extensions into applications, work with DLLs, and install programs.

Part III, The Library, shows students how to create polished, professional applications using the Developer's Library that extends Visual Basic with over 80 reusable routines. The general topics include database, date and time, environment, graphic and sound, grid, memo handling, screen and printer, security, statistical, utility and data validation. Each function has a standardized description listing its name, purpose, parameters, defaults and return values. There is also a list of related functions, a discussion of each routine, and at least one coding example. Hints, warnings, and notes appear as needed.

The appendices contain additional information to help users get up and running with Visual Basic. Appendix A shows how to install the library. Appendix B provides instructions on how to create executable programs. Appendix C contains the answers to the odd-numbered review questions. Appendix D covers sequential access, random access, and binary access.

The examples and routines in this book are real-life applications that go beyond the limits of most CIS books, providing both experiential learning tools and building blocks for later development. By exploring and expanding the full potential of Visual Basic, this book shows programmers how to become full-fledged Windows applications developers.

HOW TO USE THIS BOOK

Power Visual Basic is a practical guide to learning Visual Basic. Parts I and II discuss how to program in the language. Each chapter includes:

- Discussions of topics
- Steps for performing operations ("To Do..." lists—these steps are for reference but can also be done at the computer)
- Hands-on exercises
- Review Questions (short answers and coding exercises)
- Class Projects (problem solving exercises that demonstrate the real life application of topics covered in that section)

Power Visual Basic also includes a Developer's Library with more than 80 reusable routines. The hands-on exercises, class projects, and coding examples will show you how to apply these functions. By working through the exercises and studying the examples, you will learn how to develop professional applications using reusable code modules.

READING ASSIGNMENTS

Chapters 1 and 2 are particularly comprehensive and provide a strong foundation for programming in Visual Basic. If you are new to the language, it is recommended that you read these chapters twice. Experienced Visual Basic programmers may wish to perform the Quick Start and proceed directly to Part II, Power Programming.

ACKNOWLEDGMENTS

I would like to thank the staff of boyd & fraser, Joe Trovato, and Richard Smith for all their help and technical assistance. Thanks to Maria Karkucinski for her work on the interior design. The following reviewers provided valuable input and suggestions:

Pat Fenton	West Valley College
Ira Lustman	Franklin Pierce College
Munir Mandiviwalla	Temple University
David Rosseu	Essex County Community College

Frank Engo

TEXT CONVENTIONS

Example	Description
`MAXELEMENT`	Capitalized words indicate constants
`<filename>`	Items in angle brackets are user-defined variables or parameters
`[Else If expression2]`	Items in square brackets are optional
`instance`	Italics indicate key words or emphasized text
`Sub`	Words appearing in boldface are reserved by Visual Basic—these include commands, statements, logical operators, mathematical operators, and methods
`Text, Caption`	Words beginning with the initial letter capitalized are properties or function names

PROGRAMMING CONVENTIONS

Example	Description
`MAXELEMENT`	Capitalized words indicate constants
`Print name, age, sex`	Lowercase words are user-defined variables or Visual Basic controls
`Text, Caption`	Words beginning with the initial letter capitalized are custom controls or reserved by Visual Basic
`' Draw shadow box`	Apostrophes indicate comments
`Fileexists_err:`	Words ending in semicolons indicate line labels for error routines

`Sub Setdate`
`  Call setdate`
`End Sub`
	Executable statements are indented from procedure definitions

`MsgBox "Invalid file handle"` `      ⇨ 0,"Run Time Error"`	Parameter lists and long commands are indented after the first line and are marked with an arrow (but must appear on one line in code)

ACRONYMS LIST

DDE	Dynamic Data Exchange
DLL	Dynamic Link Library
MCI	Media Control Interface
OLE	Object Linking and Embedding
GUI	Graphical User Interface
hDC	handles to Device Contexts
hWnd	handles to Windows
MDI	Multiple Document Interface
SQL	Structured Query Language
VBX	Visual Basic Extension file
Windows API	Windows Application Programming Interface

LIBRARY ROUTINES

DATABASE & FILE ACCESS

- DBEngine—adds, updates or removes records using the database engine
- Deleterec—removes a record from a random access file
- Delnull—removes inaccessible records at the end of a random access file
- Initscroll—initializes a scroll bar for browsing records in a random access file
- Lastrec—calculates the total number of records in a random access file
- OLERead—reads a previously saved OLE object from disk
- OLESave—saves an OLE object to a file
- Replacerec—updates the contents of a record from a file opened for random access
- Saverec—adds a record to a file
- Scrollupdate—reads a record into memory each time the scroll bar is clicked

DATE AND TIME

- Begmonth—returns first day of month formatted as a string
- Begweek—returns beginning of work week formatted as a string
- Dateformat—changes the date format
- Endmonth—returns last day of month formatted as a string
- Setdate—sets system date
- Settime—sets system time
- Showday—returns the day of the week for any date
- Timediff—returns the difference between two time arguments

ENVIRONMENT

- Chgdrive—attempts to change drive and returns error number if unsuccessful
- Copylist—copies a list of files and displays bar graph showing progress of operation
- Direxists—checks if a directory exists
- Fileexists—checks if a file exists
- Filelist—returns a list of files in a directory with their dates of last modifications and sizes in bytes

- Fileschanged—returns a list of files in a directory recently updated
- Filestatus—checks if a file is open
- Is_active—checks if a program is currently running
- Runapp—runs a Windows application
- Sysconfig—returns the system configuration (CPU type, available memory, and whether a match coprocessor and network are installed)

GRAPHICS AND SOUND

- Drawcard—creates a card deck
- Mouseset—sets the position of the mouse pointer
- Soundeffects—plays one of several pre-defined sound effects through the PC speaker
- Swapimages—swaps two bitmaps in a picture box or image control

GRID

- Cleargrid—clears a grid
- Gridfill—restores contents of a grid previously saved
- Gridsave—saves contents of a grid to a file
- Initgrid—sets the total number of rows and columns and the column width of a grid
- Timesched—prints a 60-minute time schedule on a grid

MEMO HANDLING

- Edittext—text file handler for cut, copy and paste operations
- Findtext—finds a string in a text box
- Memowrite—saves contents of text file to disk
- Mergetext—merges two text files
- Readmemo—reads contents of text file into a variable for editing
- Upperword—capitalizes the first letter of each word in a string (used to format proper names)
- Undolast—reverses the last edit operation in a text box

SCREEN AND PRINTER

- Bargraph—displays a bar graph
- Centerstr—centers a string on a form in large characters
- Checkfont—Returns **True** if a font is installed
- Colorstr—shows a message with each letter in a different color
- Delaywin—shows a pop-up window with a delay effect (window increases in size as it is drawn and then a message is printed inside it)
- Delaytext—shows a message with a delay effect and an optional shadow border
- Fontlist—creates a list of fonts available for the current display device and printer

- Introscr—shows a custom introductory screen
- Shadowbox—displays a shadow box on a form
- Shadowtext—shows a message with a shadow effect
- Strwalk—scrolls a message in a picture box
- Text3D—displays a message with a 3D effect
- Textblur—displays a message with a blur effect
- Textgrow—shows a message growing on a form

SECURITY

- Decrypt—decrypts a string
- Decryptfile—decrypts a file
- Encrypt—encrypts a string
- Encryptfile—encrypts a file

STATISTICAL

- Arravg—returns the average of the numbers in an array
- Arrmax—returns the maximum value in an array
- Arrmedian—returns the median value in an array
- Arrmin—returns the minimum value in an array
- Arrmode—returns the mode of the values in an array
- Arrneg—counts negative elements in an array
- Arrnonzero—counts non-zero elements in an array
- Arrpos—counts positive elements in an array
- Arrstdv—returns the standard deviation of a list of numbers stored in an array
- Arrsort—sorts an array
- Arrsum—sums an array of values
- Arrvar—returns the variance of a list of numbers stored in an array

UTILITY

- ChgFrac—converts decimals to fractions
- Moveto—moves cursor to the next or previous control on a form when the user presses Enter or the up or down arrow keys
- Scrblanker—prevents burn-in by showing one of three pre-defined screen blankers
- Showcalend—displays a calendar
- Showclock—displays a digital clock

VALIDATION

- Valentry—validates input in a text box by filtering out non-numeric characters
- Valfile—validates a file name
- Valtime—validates a time argument

Q POWER VISUAL BASIC

This book contains examples and instructions that show you how to get the most out of Visual Basic. For example, there is particular emphasis on file management, techniques for linking together Visual Basic projects, saving and restoring grids, creating enhanced security systems, detecting whether other Windows applications are running (important in DDE), working with memos, handling objects, using custom controls, interfacing with the Windows API, performing animation, writing setup programs and more.

On the sample disks, you will find the source code for several complete applications, many short code listings, and the developer's library. The longer program examples demonstrate the practical application of various library procedures. The shorter program examples show you how to get up and running quickly with Visual Basic.

You also will learn how to develop powerful Windows-based applications using reusable code modules such as those contained in the developer's library. You can use any of the procedures in the developer's library for the professional development of applications.

Q.1 CREATING A PROGRAM

The quickest way to tap into the power of Visual Basic is to write your own program. This Quick Start shows you how to write a custom screen saver application using a routine from the developer's library included with this book. If you have experience with other developer's libraries or are familiar with Visual Basic, you should have no problem with this section.

You can install the library to the hard drive (using the steps outlined in Appendix A) or you can access these files from a floppy. Since the developer's library takes up only about 100K disk space, it is recommended that you install these files onto the system you will be using.

Exercise: Creating a Screen Blanker Program

1. From the Program Manager, start Visual Basic by double clicking on the Visual Basic icon in the program group by the same name.
   A blank form will appear. On the left, you will see another dialog known as the Toolbox (see Figure Q.1). The Toolbox contains many small icons known as controls. You use these controls to create the front-end or *interface* of a program.
2. From the Toolbox, select the timer control by double clicking on the clock icon.
   An image of the control will appear centered on the form. You use this control to keep track of events in your program. At *run time,* the timer control is always invisible.

NOTE: Chapter 1 will provide a more detailed explanation of the Toolbox and Visual Basic controls.

3. Click on the timer control to give it *focus.*
4. Press the F7 key to create an *event procedure* for this control.
   The Code Window will appear. Inside this window, you insert the commands that will be performed each time the timer executes (between the **Sub** and **End Sub** statements). Visual Basic automatically names the procedure as Timer1_Timer. This is where the instructions for the timer must be entered.
5. In the Timer1_Timer procedure, type:

```
Const BLOCKS = 1, LINES = 2, CIRCLES = 3, INFO_ICON = 64

Dim blanker_option As Integer
```

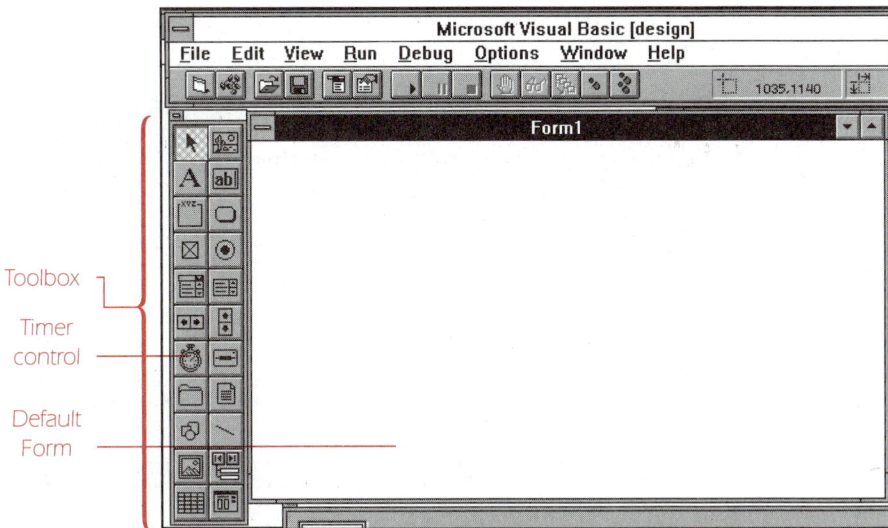

FIGURE Q.1 Starting Visual Basic

```
blanker_option = BLOCKS

' Show moving blocks screen blanker

If show_blanker = True Then
   Call Scrblanker(Form1, blanker_option,
             ⇨ startblanker)
Else
  Call ShowCursor(True)
  MsgBox "Custom Screen Blanker", INFO_ICON,
      ⇨ "Program Information"
  End
End If
```

6. On the top left-hand side of the Code Window, you will see a drop-down list that reads Object: Timer1 (see Figure Q.2). Click on the downward pointing arrow to open the list.
   This window shows all the objects available in your program. In Visual Basic, each part of the screen is considered a separate *object*. The timer control, for example, is actually a pre-defined object requiring only the instructions that tell Visual Basic what to do when the timer executes.
7. From the Object drop-down list, choose the Form object.
   A new window containing the Form_Load procedure will appear. When you run the program, the code in this procedure always executes first.
8. In the Form_Load procedure, type:

```
startblanker = 0: show_blanker = True

Call ShowCursor(False)

' Set timer interval to activate screen blanker

timer1.Interval = 50
```

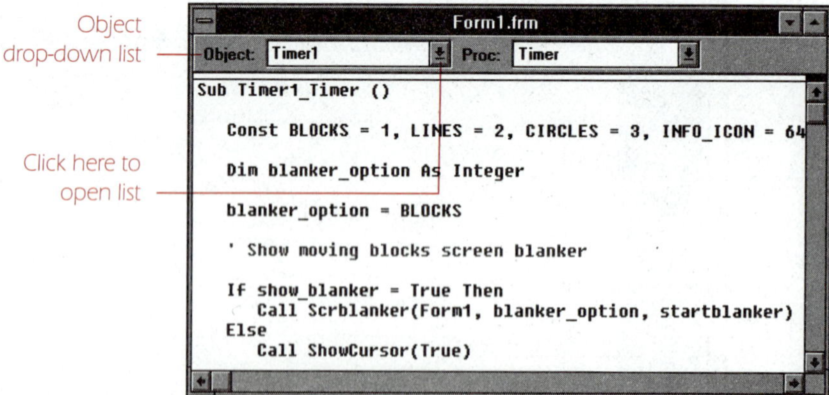

FIGURE Q.2 The Object drop-down list

9. Towards the right of the Object drop-down list, is another window called the Procedures drop-down list (abbreviated as Proc.). Open this window by clicking on the downward pointing arrow.
10. From the Procedures drop-down list, choose the KeyPress procedure.

NOTE: You will have to scroll up through the list to see this option.

The KeyPress procedure monitors keyboard activity on the form. You will use it in this exercise to detect when a key has been pressed while the screen blanker is running.

11. In the Form_KeyPress procedure, type:

```
' Restore normal mouse pointer

Call ShowCursor(True)

' Set flag to end run

show_blanker = False
```

12. From the Object list, choose (general).
A new window will appear. The Declarations section of this form is where you declare variables that are local to the form and retain their values between procedure calls.
13. In the Declarations section of the form, type:

```
Dim startblanker As Integer, show_blanker As Integer
```

14. From the File menu, choose Add File...
15. For the file specification, type: **C:\VB_LIB\SCR.BAS.**

NOTE: This step assumes you installed the library in the default VB_LIB directory. If you are accessing these files from a floppy, be sure to specify the correct path.

16. Click on OK.
17. Open the Window menu (by pressing Alt-W) and select Project.
18. In the Project Window, click on View Form.
19. Click on the form (not the timer) to give the form focus.

NOTE: You give focus to a form by clicking on the internal area or white part of the form.

20. Press F4 to call up the Properties window.
You use the Properties window to specify the custom settings of each object in the program.
21. Set the BorderStyle property of the form to 0 - None.
22. Click on the form to save the new property setting.
23. Press F5 to run the program.
When the program is running, the screen becomes black and colored blocks move in various directions.
24. After observing the screen blanker pattern, press any key to end the run.

NOTE: Certain keys, like the Shift key, produce no return code by themselves and thus you will have to press another key to end the blanker.

25. In the Program Credits dialog, press Enter to close the dialog.

Exercise: Modifying the Screen Blanker Program

1. Click on the timer control to give it focus.
2. Press the F7 key to view the event procedure for this control.
3. Change the line that reads *blanker_option = BLOCKS* to *blanker_option = LINES*.
4. Execute the screen blanker again by pressing F5.
   A new pattern appears showing random colored lines at various screen coordinates.
5. After observing the new pattern, press any key to stop the screen blanker.
6. Press Enter to close the Program Credits dialog.

Exercise: Creating Circles in the Screen Blanker Program

1. Using the method described in Exercise 2, change the <blanker_option> in the program from LINES to CIRCLES.
2. Run the program again by pressing either Alt-R or using the F5 shortcut key.
   Balls appear at random points on the screen.
3. Press any key to quit.

PART I

FUNDAMENTALS

There is nothing extraordinarily difficult about Visual Basic. Underlying its simplicity, however, is a rich and powerful programming language combined with a graphical environment that allows programmers to create dynamic, attractive, and professional programs. Part I is both a review of Visual Basic fundamentals as well as an example-driven exploration of working programs.

After completing this section, you should be able to create programs quickly and easily.

1 CREATING INTERFACES

Creating an interface in Visual Basic for Windows is as easy as drawing the windows and forms that you need. Once you have designed the application screen, you turn your design into a working program by setting the properties of controls such as text boxes and buttons and then writing the short chunks of code that respond to user-initiated events. These three steps—create, customize, and code—can be summarized as:

1. Design and paint an interface window.
2. Customize the interface by setting the properties of each control.
3. Create event procedures for user and system interaction.

1.1 DESIGNING AN INTERFACE

You create an interface when you draw controls on a form. A *control* is a graphical object that responds to a user or system event. The sample interface shown in Figure 1.1 illustrates a number of different controls—six labels, six text boxes, two command buttons and a frame. Table 1.1 summarizes the functions of these controls.

The Toolbox, which Visual Basic automatically loads when you begin a new session, is used to place objects on a form. You can also open this window by selecting the Toolbox command from the Window menu. Figure 1.2 shows what the Toolbox looks like and what each of its buttons does.

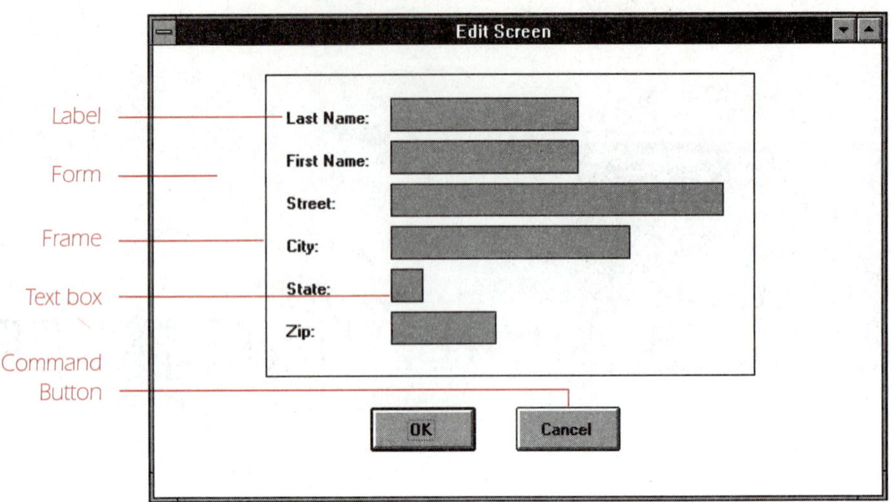

FIGURE 1.1 A sample interface

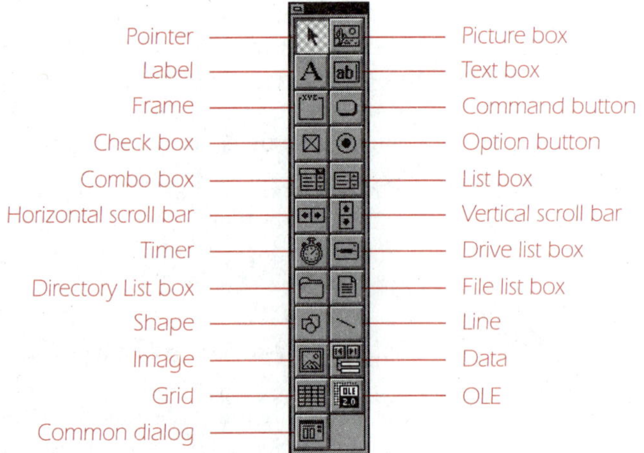

FIGURE 1.2 The Toolbox

To Draw a Control

1. From the Toolbox, click on the associated icon of the control. The mouse pointer will change to a cross hair.
2. Move the mouse pointer onto the form at the position you want the control to appear.
3. Draw the control on the form by holding the left mouse button down while dragging the mouse.

Another way to draw a control is to double click on its associated button in the Toolbox. When you select a control this way, Visual Basic automatically centers the object on the form. Afterwards, you can move the control using a mouse the same way you would move an icon in Windows.

Control	Description
Label	Displays headings and messages.
Text box	Multipurpose control used for accepting input, editing fields and displaying information.
Command button	A push button.
Frame	A control separator.

TABLE 1-1 CONTROLS IN THE SAMPLE INTERFACE

SETTING PROPERTIES

The pre-defined objects in Visual Basic have properties that can be set to control their appearance and behavior. Although Visual Basic automatically sets property values, it is sometimes necessary to change these default settings. For example, when you draw a label on a form, Visual Basic uses the name of the control as a caption. To change this value to something more user friendly, set the Caption property to display a field heading, short message or prompt to the user.

You use the Properties window to change the property settings of controls. Figure 1.3 shows how this window appears.

To Change the Property Settings of an Object

1. Click on the control (to give it focus).
2. Choose either the Properties command from the Window menu or Press F4.
3. In the Properties window, double click on the property you wish to edit (e.g., Name, Caption, Size, etc.).
4. Type the new property value.

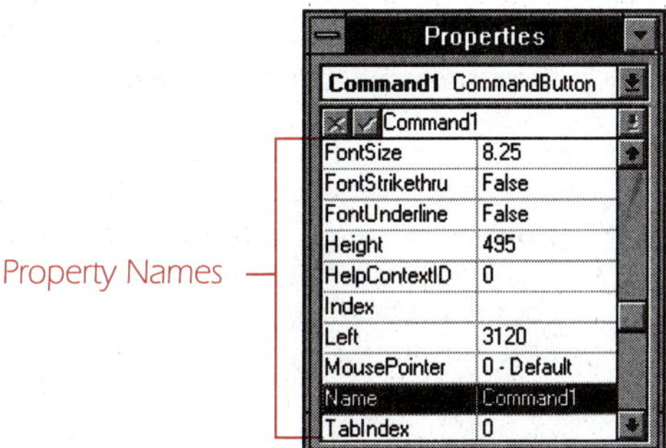

FIGURE 1.3 The Properties window

NAMING CONTROLS

Although Visual Basic automatically labels objects, its naming conventions are strictly utilitarian. While there is nothing wrong with having three text boxes in a program named text1, text2 and text3, it is hard to differentiate objects this way. For the sake of clarity, it is usually better to rename each control before writing code.

To Change the Name of a Control

1. Click on the control (to give it focus).
2. Press F4 or select Properties from the Window menu.
3. Click on the Name property.
4. Type the new name.

Although this is not mandatory, you should use control prefixes when labeling objects. By applying standard naming conventions in programs, your source code will be easier to read and maintain. Table 1.2 shows some common prefixes that many programmers use.

CHANGING THE SIZE OF CONTROLS

The Size property is another common property that is often changed at design time. Unlike other properties, this one can be altered using a mouse.

To Change the Size of a Control

1. Click on the control (to give it focus).
   The outer perimeters of the object reveals several rectangular blocks known as size handles.
2. Click on any of these size handles and drag the mouse while holding down the left button.

CREATING EVENT PROCEDURES

To use the objects on a form, each one must be linked to an *event procedure*. An event procedure is a block of code associated with a control that executes when the object receives *focus* or attention.

Control	Prefix	Example
command button	cmd	cmdOK
option button	opt	optSave
check box	chk	chkPrintScr
picture box	pic	picHouse
menu item	mnu	mnuFileOpen

TABLE 1-2 CONTROL PREFIXES

To Create an Event Procedure

At design time, double click on the control and Visual Basic will automatically open the Code window. Alternately, you can create an event procedure by choosing Code from the View menu or by pressing F7 while the control has focus.

NOTE: If a form has focus when you create an event procedure, Visual Basic puts you in the Form_Load procedure. This procedure always executes first when the form loads.

When an event procedure is created, its name and any parameters it uses appears with it. For example, assuming the default name for a command button is used, the following procedure will appear:

```
Sub Command1_Click ()
End Sub
```

It is here, between the **Sub** and **End Sub** statements, that code can be inserted. The following code fragment, for example, displays a message in a dialog box:

```
MsgBox ("This is a test")
```

1.2 WORKING WITH DIALOGS

MsgBox is a pre-defined function in Visual Basic that displays text output in a window. You can also get input using the **InputBox** function (see example below). The dialogs these functions display are *modal* — that is, they must be closed before another process can begin.

```
response = InputBox ("Enter name")
```

The pre-defined dialogs that **MsgBox** and **InputBox** show are less versatile and elegant than the custom dialog boxes you create by drawing your own controls on a form, but they can be very useful. The following procedure, for example, shows how to display a file not saved warning with a question mark in it. Figure 1.4 shows how the dialog appears.

```
Sub Command1_Click ()

  Const ICON_QUESTION = 33 ' Question mark

  Dim message As String

  message = "File not saved - update"
  MsgBox message, ICON_QUESTION, "Warning"

End Sub
```

In the preceding example, <message> is declared as a *string* — that is, a string of characters. ICON_QUESTION is a constant. This value remains the same throughout the program. The apostrophe on line 3 is a comment. When Visual Basic encounters this mark, it simply ignores the rest of the line.

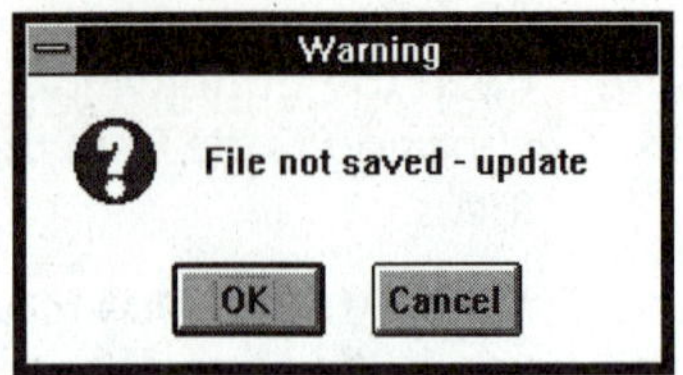

FIGURE 1.4 Displaying a modal dialog with a question mark icon

THE LABEL CONTROL

Label controls are pre-defined objects in Visual Basic that display headings and messages on forms. Since they are read-only, the user cannot edit them at run time. The following procedure shows how to assign a value to a label:

```
Sub Command1_Click ()
  label1.Caption = "Employee Record Screen"
End Sub
```

Notice how the string or message is assigned to the label's Caption property. The same assignment could have also been done at design time using the Properties window. The period between label1 and Caption is a separator. Visual Basic uses this symbol to separate controls from property names (and as you will see later, also *methods*).

By default, a label appears on a form with its Border property set to 0 (no border). When this property is assigned a value of 1, the label is framed with a single line border (see Figure 1.5).

THE TEXT BOX CONTROL

Text boxes are pre-defined objects in Visual Basic that get information from users. You can place a text box anywhere on a form.

FIGURE 1.5 The label control

Although text boxes are often used to get input, you also can assign output to them. Caution must be taken, however, since headings appearing in a text box can be edited at run time by users. If you wish to display text on a form that is read-only, use a label control instead.

READING TEXT BOXES

To read input from a text box, assign the Text property of the control to a variable. For example, to accept a customer's name, the following code can be used:

```
custname = cust.Text
```

NOTE: This example assumes that the Name property of the control has been set to *cust*.

To assign output to the text box, simply reverse these statements. For instance, assuming that it is all right to edit the contents of the text box, you could type:

```
cust.Text = "Susan Smith"
```

This technique is useful if you need to display a value that the user can edit. For example, at run time, the program can display a default path for a file transfer in a text box. The user can then modify the string to indicate a new drive and directory specification.

Note that in Visual Basic, you do not always have to explicitly declare the data type of a variable since the default type is a variant. However, the assignment could have also been done this way:

```
Dim custname As String

custname = cust.Text
```

Although you do not always have to explicitly declare data types, Visual Basic can often process code more efficiently when the type is declared. Thus, it is generally considered good programming style to declare all variables.

Sometimes a type declaration leads to an invalid operation when a program runs. The following assignment, for example, causes a run time error:

```
Sub cmdGetInput_Click ()

 Dim custID As Integer

 custID = custno.Text

End Sub
```

This error occurs because the Text property of a text box assumes the input is a string. To convert the string to a numeric value, use the **Val** function:

```
Dim CustID As Integer

custID = Val(custno.Text)
```

CREATING MEMOS

Text boxes are not limited to small strings. You can also assign entire files of text to them. When a text box's MultiLine property is set to **True**, word wrapping and full screen editing are enabled. You use this technique to create memo handlers (see Chapter 8).

CREATING PASSWORDS WITH TEXT BOXES

By setting the PasswordChar property of a text box to a specific value, you create a password. When this is done, place holders appear instead of character input. For example, if the property is set to an asterisk, each key entered displays an asterisk.

The MaxLength property specifies the maximum number of characters that the user can type in a text box. If the user tries to enter more than the limit, the program beeps. This technique is useful for passwords but also works well for validating other string input.

Exercise: Creating an Interest Rate Calculator

1. From the Program Manager, start up Visual Basic.
2. Once the program is loaded, draw the following controls on the form using the Toolbox. Place and size each object as they appear in Figure 1.6.

```
label1  text1
label2  text2
label3  text3
label4  command1
label5  command2
```

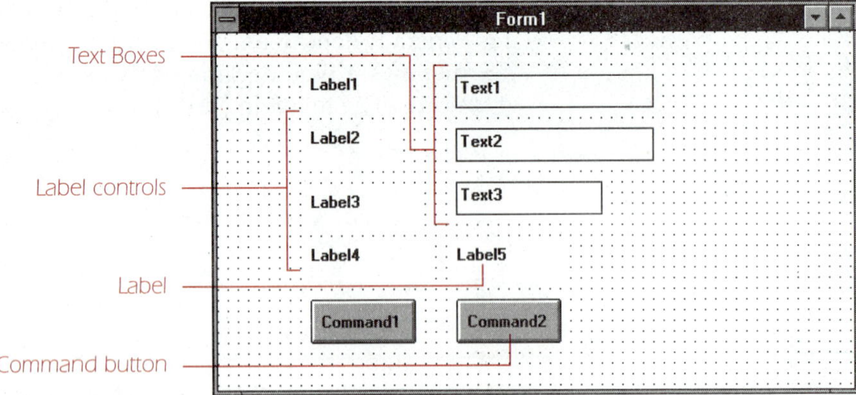

FIGURE 1.6 Controls for interest rate calculator

3. Set the properties of each control as follows:

Control	Property	Value
label1	Caption	Future Value:
label2	Caption	Present Value:
label3	Caption	Periods:
label4	Caption	Interest Rate:
label5	Caption	null value
text1	Text	null value
text2	Text	null value
text3	Text	null value
command1	Caption	OK
command2	Caption	Exit
Form1	Caption	Interest Calculator

4. Rename each control as:

Old Name	New Name
text1	future
text2	present
text3	periods
label5	inter
command1	cmdOK
command2	cmdExit

5. Double click on the command button labeled OK to open the Code window.
6. In the cmdOK_Click procedure, type:

```
'Read text boxes

present_value = present.Text
future_value = future.Text
periods = periods.Text

'Compute interest rate needed

temp = (future_value / present_value) ^ (1 / periods)
investrate = temp - 1

'Print interest rate

inter.Caption = Format(investrate, "###%")
```

NOTE: This expression will compute the interest rate required to reach a goal of an investment. In Chapter 2, you will learn how to write expressions.

7. From the Window menu, choose the Project command.

8. From the Project window, click on View Form.

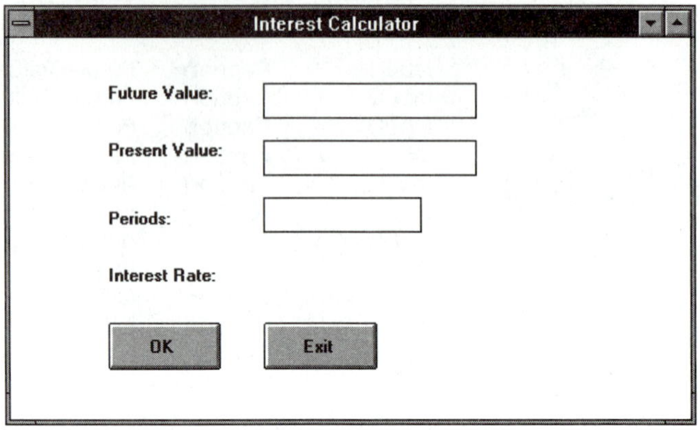

FIGURE 1.7 The completed interest rate calculator form

9. Double click on the command button labeled Exit.
10. In the cmdExit procedure, type:

```
'End session

End
```

When you are done, use the F5 shortcut key to run the project. If you have made any errors while coding the program, you will have to fix them before it will run successfully. In any case, Visual Basic will point out these mistakes and even give you help if you press F1 while it shows the error message. Once you have the program running, use the following test data to check the interest rate:

Future Value: 20000
Present Value: 7000
Periods: 10

If you coded the cmdOK_Click procedure correctly, the answer should be .11 or 11%. Figure 1.7 shows how the completed form should look.

1.3 CREATING LISTS

The *List box control* displays a list of entries that the user scrolls through at run time to make a selection. Figure 1.8 shows an example of a list box.

If there are more options in the list than will fit on one screen, scroll bars appear automatically. To add items to the list, use the **AddItem** method. Its syntax is:

```
listcontrol.AddItem [,<item no.>]
```

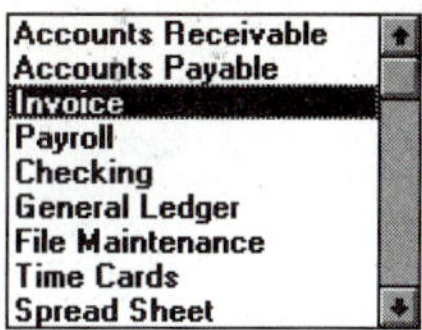

FIGURE 1.8 A sample list box

A *method* is a keyword that causes an action to occur on an object. In this case, the **AddItem** method adds entries to the list. The following procedure shows how this is done:

```
Sub Form_Load ()

  list1.AddItem "Northern Division"
  list1.AddItem "Southern Division"
  list1.AddItem "Western Division"

End Sub
```

The <index> argument determines where the item is added in the list. The first element contained in the list always begins at position 0. If the <index> argument is omitted, the end of the list is assumed.

SORTING LISTS

The Sorted property of a list box permits the organization of its elements. The sort is not case sensitive. Therefore the items "services rendered" and "SERVICES RENDERED" are treated the same.

To Sort a List

1. Click on the list box control (to give it focus).
2. Press F4 or select Properties from the Window menu.
3. Set the Sorted property to **True**.

THE COMBO BOX CONTROL

A closely related function in Visual Basic is the *combo box*. Like list boxes, combo boxes permit users to select items from lists. Combos are more versatile, however, and come in three styles. Figure 1.9 shows the function of each one and what they look like.

Although combo boxes have similar features, there are some exceptions. Except for Style 1, combo boxes save space on forms since the list is not actually displayed until the box is opened. With exception of Style 2, users also may type the name of the entry to make a selection.

Combo boxes share many of the same properties, methods and events as list boxes. The **AddItem** method, for example, appends new entries to a list.

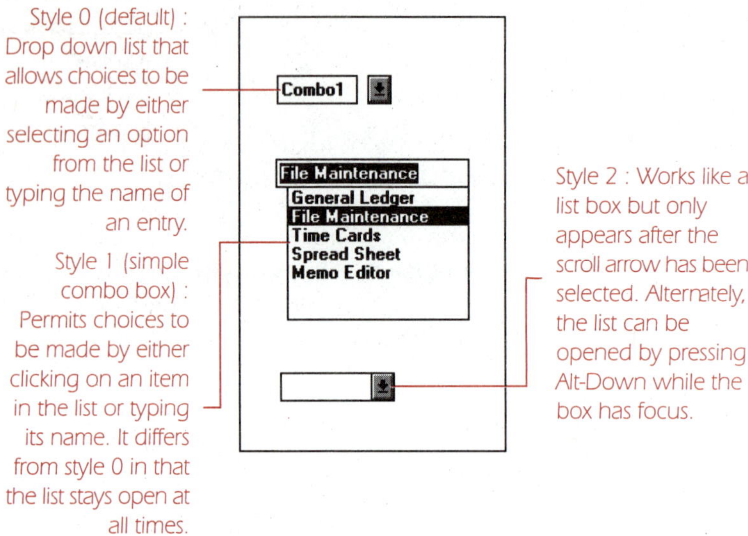

Style 0 (default) : Drop down list that allows choices to be made by either selecting an option from the list or typing the name of an entry.
Style 1 (simple combo box) : Permits choices to be made by either clicking on an item in the list or typing its name. It differs from style 0 in that the list stays open at all times.
Style 2 : Works like a list box but only appears after the scroll arrow has been selected. Alternately, the list can be opened by pressing Alt-Down while the box has focus.
Combo1
File Maintenance
General Ledger
File Maintenance
Time Cards
Spread Sheet
Memo Editor

FIGURE 1.9 Combo box styles

SPECIAL CONSIDERATIONS FOR INTERPRETING LIST EVENTS

Visual Basic automatically creates event procedures when you double click on an object at design time. From there, you can either write code or select another event procedure using the Procedures drop down list (see Figure 1.10). The procedures shown contain every possible combination of events that can occur for the current object.

When a selection is made from a list at run time, a Click event occurs. Similarly, double-clicking an entry in a list generates a DblClick event. The code to interpret these events must be placed in the right procedures. The Text property of a list box control shows the item the user selects at run time. If the code needed to read the entry is placed in a command button's Click procedure, this code is not actually executed until the command button is selected. However, if you want a program to respond immediately after a choice is made, put the statement in the list's Click or DblClick procedures.

Example

```
Sub List1_Click ()

    selection = mylist.Text

    MsgBox (selection)

End Sub
```

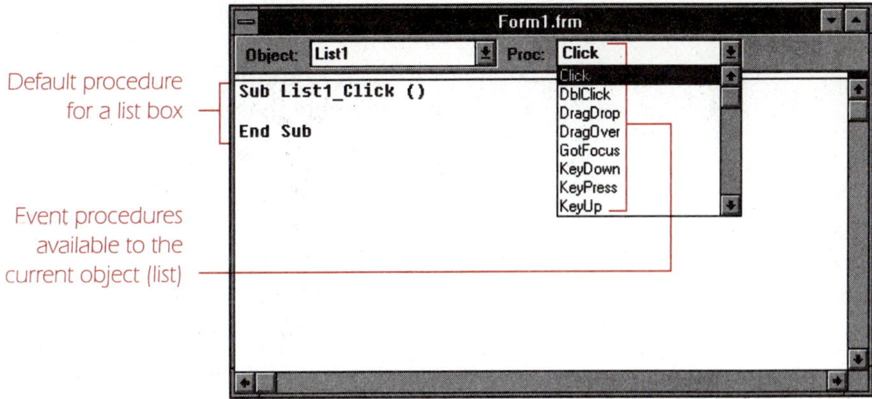

FIGURE 1.10 The Procedures drop-down list

In the preceding example, the Text property of the list item is assigned to a variable. The choice is then displayed using **MsgBox**.

Another way to get the user's choice is to use the List property. The syntax for the List property is:

```
listcontrol.List (<index>)
```

<Index> is the number of the item in the list. To read this value, you assign the element to a string:

```
Sub cmdOK_Click ()
  Dim choice As String
  choice = mylist.List(5)
  'Show choice selected
  MsgBox ("Choice: " & choice)
End Sub
```

Since the list begins with 0, this code returns the sixth element (not the fifth). To determine which item is the current entry, you write a routine like this:

```
current_item = mylist.ListIndex
text1.Text = mylist.List (current_item)
```

The ListIndex property returns either the number of the item selected or –1 if no choice is made. It also returns –1 if the user types the name of the entry in a combo box.

COUNTING ELEMENTS IN A LIST

The ListCount property returns the total number of list elements. The following code fragment shows how it is applied:

```
text1.Text = "Total list elements: " & mylist.ListCount
```

REMOVING ITEMS FROM A LIST

To remove an entry from a list, use the **RemoveItem** method. This example shows how to delete the current element:

```
current_item = mylist.ListIndex
If current_item >= 0 Then
   mylist.RemoveItem current_item
End If
```

In this case, the **If Then** block is a decision structure that tests whether the current item is selected. If it is, the program removes the current entry from the list.

CLEARING A LIST

Occasionally, it is necessary to clear all the elements in a list. For example, you may wish to clear a list box so that other items can be displayed. The fastest way to reinitialize a list is to use the **Clear** method.

Example

```
mylist.Clear
```

CREATING MULTIPLE-COLUMN LIST BOXES

One of the more interesting type of list boxes is one that automatically scrolls to multiple columns. Figure 1.11 shows such an example. The following options are available:

Columns Property	Description
0	Single column scrolling (default)
1	Single column with group scrolling
2	Multiple columns with horizontal scrolling

In order for the entries to appear in multiple columns, the list box must be drawn wide enough to hold all the items it contains. If the list is drawn too wide, however, the entries may appear in one column rather than multiple columns. In any case, Visual Basic automatically adds scroll bars if necessary.

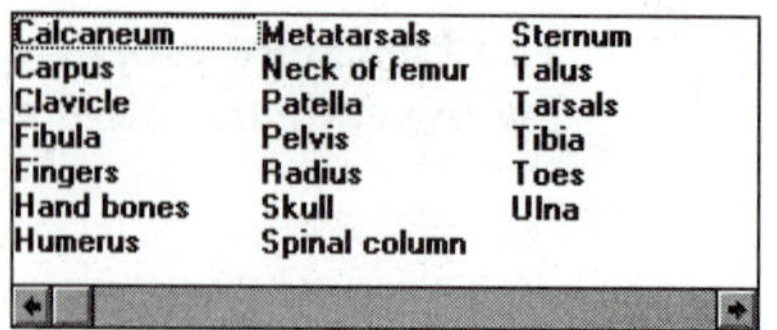

FIGURE 1.11 A multiple-column list box

1.4 USING CHECK BOXES AND OPTION BUTTONS

Check boxes and *option buttons* present choices to users. They are easy to implement and provide alternatives to combo and list boxes. Figure 1.12 shows what these controls look like.

A *check box* is a graphical object with a Caption property that permits choices to be made. The label serves to identify the control. At run time, the user selects a check box by clicking on the control or by tabbing over to the box and pressing Enter. Afterwards, a check will appear in the box. The benefit of these controls is that the user can pick any number of options such as multiple boxes. The following code shows how to test if a check box is selected:

```
Sub chkRep_Click ()

 If chkrep.Value = 1 Then ' Item selected
   Call print_routine
 End If

End Sub
```

Like check boxes, *option buttons* are used to select among various program options. Option buttons differ from check boxes, however, in that the user is restricted to choosing only one button at a time.

By default, Visual Basic treats all the option buttons on a form as a group. Therefore, only one item can be selected at any given time. To over-ride this default, use the *frame control* to create subgroups of options. Figure 1.13 shows how this can be done.

When controls are organized this way, a *parent/child relationship* is established. The frame, being the parent, controls the way the option buttons behave. For example, if you move a frame using a mouse, the controls in it also move.

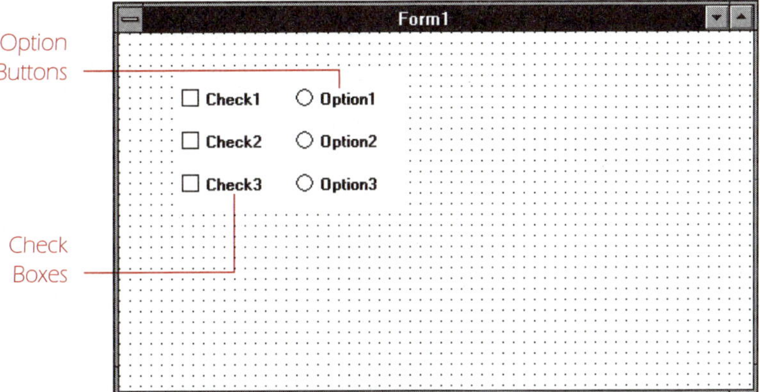

FIGURE 1.12 Check boxes and option buttons

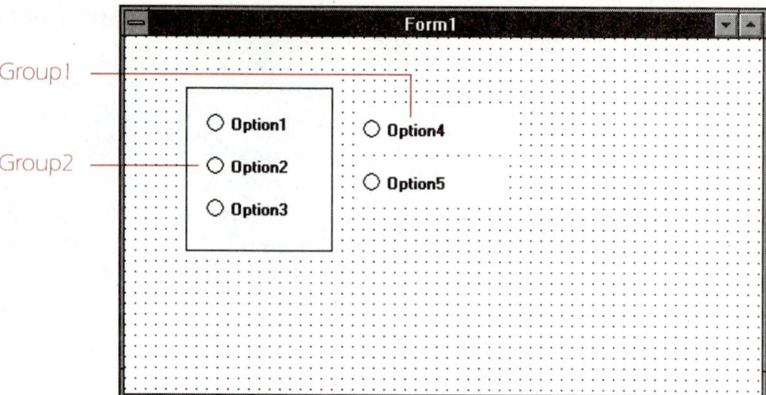

FIGURE 1.13 Grouping controls with a frame

NOTE: In order to establish a parent/child relationship, the controls must be cut and pasted into the frame using the Edit menu commands. Dragging the objects into the framed area does not constitute a parent/child relationship.

The following code shows how you can test whether an option button has been selected or not. Notice the use of the **Else** clause in the **If Then Else** block. If the first option button is not chosen, the program automatically sends output to the printer device.

```
Sub cmdOK_Click ()

 If opt_prtscreen.Value = True Then
   Call PrtScreen
 Else
   Call PrtPrinter
 End If

End Sub
```

This system works fine for small groups of options, but what if there are 12 buttons on a form? You would have to name each control individually and keep track of a dozen different buttons in the program. Fortunately there is an easier way.

1.5 CREATING CONTROL ARRAYS

A *control array* is a group of controls that share the same name and event procedure. By creating a control array, a procedure can reference several instances of an object at the same time. An *instance* is an occurrence of an object. If there are 10 buttons on a form, for example, each one is a separate instance. Therefore, instead of having to name each control and explicitly test their values, you could write code this way:

```
Sub Option1_Click (index As Integer)
```

```
 'Branch to appropriate routine

 Select Case index
  Case 0
   Call CalcCur
  Case 1
   Call FValue
  Case 2
   Call DDeclin
  Case 3
   Call RateCalc
  Case 4
   Call CalcPmt
  Case 5
   Call CalcStrLine
  Case 6
   Call CalcSumOfYrs
 End Select

End Sub
```

This example, taken from the sample financial application, FIN.MAK, uses a control array to branch to the appropriate routine (see Figure 1.14). The program disk contains the source code for this example.

On the form, there are seven options buttons. Each button is a separate instance or element of the control array. As with standard controls, the index of a control array starts at 0, not 1. The **Select Case** block, in the preceding example, is a decision structure. It is often used as an alternative to the **If Then Else** decision structure. For more information on using **Select Case**, refer to Chapter 2 Programming in Visual Basic.

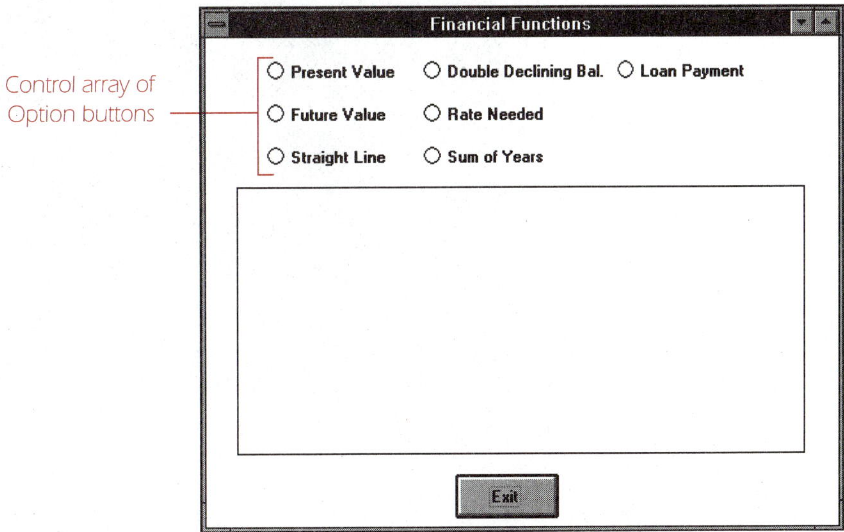

FIGURE 1.14 The FIN.MAK application

To qualify as a control array, each object (or button in this case) must share a common Name property. Visual Basic automatically creates control arrays when you try to save two controls under the same name.

NOTE: Once a control array is created, subsequent objects drawn on the form are automatically added to it if they are of the same object type.

1.6 USING SCROLL BARS

A *scroll bar* is a vertical or horizontal bar that has two arrows pointing outward on either end. They are often used to set the speed of timers, retrieve records from files and move the mouse pointer within windows.

Some of the controls in Visual Basic such as list boxes already have scroll bars attached. You can also define your own scroll bars. The following code, for example, sets the speed of a timer for a delayed welcome screen. The graphics for this example were created in Microsoft Paintbrush (supplied with Windows). Figure 1.15 shows what the screen looks like.

```
Dim timerspeed As Integer
Dim countpict As Integer

Sub Form_Load ()

 'Set range of scroll values
 hscroll1.Min = 20 ' Milliseconds
 hscroll1.Max = 1000

End Sub
```

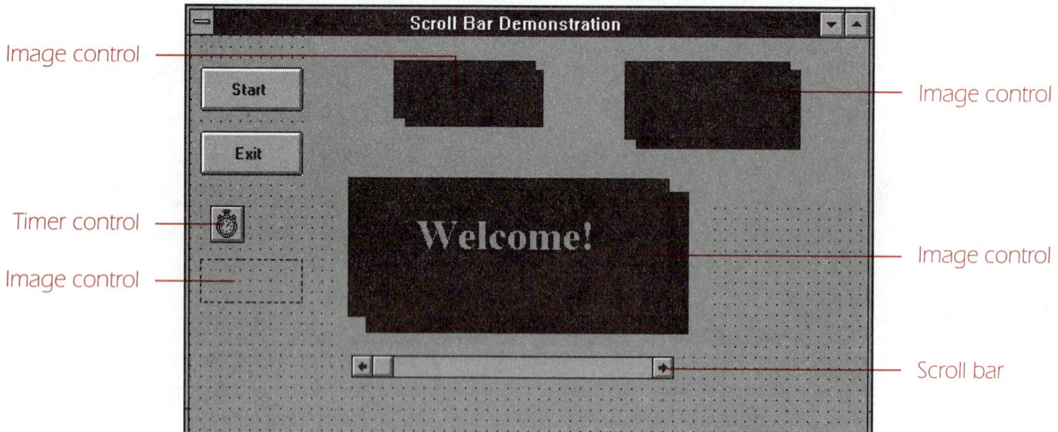

FIGURE 1.15 The welcome screen

```
Sub cmdStart_Click ()
 'Set default timer speed

 timer1.Interval = hscroll1.Min
End Sub


Sub Timer1_Timer ()

 'Swap pictures

 countpict = countpict + 1
 Select Case countpict
   Case 1
    current_image.Picture = window1.Picture
   Case 2
    current_image.Picture = window2.Picture
   Case 3
    current_image.Picture = window3.Picture
 End Select

End Sub
```

The Form_Load procedure contains the necessary code to initialize the scroll bar. By default, the scroll bar uses the Min property to determine the speed of the *timer* (in milliseconds). At run time, the timer is invisible. Upon each call to the Timer1_Timer procedure, the program displays a different bitmap. By clicking on the scroll bar, you can increase/decrease the speed of the presentation.

Dragging the scroll box causes the scroll bar value to change in large increments and generate a Change event. The same event also happens when you click on one of the arrows or the bar itself:

```
Sub HScroll1_Change ()

 'Set timer speed according to scroll bar's current
 'value

 timerspeed = hscroll1.Value

End Sub
```

1.7 FINE TUNING APPLICATIONS

After designing an interface and testing the initial events, many programmers fine tune a program to make it easier to use. Fine-tuning techniques include assigning hot keys, changing the tab order and enabling or disabling controls.

ASSIGNING HOT KEYS

Controls that have a Caption property can be programmed to work with hot keys. A *hot key* is a key that provides quick access to an object.

Label controls have a Caption property. However, labels cannot receive focus. When a hot key is set to a label control, Visual Basic automatically moves focus to the next control on a form. Typically, this would be a text box which does not have a Caption property. You can use this technique to give input boxes focus.

To Assign a Hot key

Use an ampersand (&) in the Caption property of the control to set the access key. The key immediately after the ampersand is the hot key.

CHANGING THE TAB ORDER

When a control is drawn on a form, Visual Basic records the order in which it was created by setting the TabIndex property. The TabIndex property determines which control will receive focus when the Tab key is pressed.

The TabIndex of the first control begins with 0. Subsequent objects appearing on a form are listed in the order in which they were drawn.

To Reset the TabIndex

Set the TabIndex property of each control on the form. Note that Visual Basic automatically renumbers the tab order when the index of one object is changed. In many cases, however, you will still have to fine tune this.

ENABLING/DISABLING & HIDING CONTROLS

By default, controls in Visual Basic are enabled at run time. This simply means that the controls can be used in an application. In some cases, this is not always advantageous. For example, if a user tries to remove a record from a file before it is open, the program will crash. To prevent this from happening, the delete option can be disabled until the file is opened.

To Enable or Disable a Control

- At design time, set the control's Enabled property to **True** or **False**.

or

- Make the same assignment in the program.

```
e.g., Command1.Enabled = False
```

NOTE: When a control is disabled, it appears grayed-out.

Another way to prevent users from selecting controls at inappropriate times is to set the Visible property to **False**. You can also use this technique to hide invalid or irrelevant program options until they are needed.

1.8 MAINTAINING PROJECTS

Visual Basic saves all the forms and other associated files of an application as a project in files with a .MAK file extension. Forms have a .FRM file extension. If the extension is not included, Visual Basic automatically adds the correct extension.

To Save a Project

1. Select Save Project from the Project menu or click on the Save Project button from the toolbar (see Figure 1.16).
2. Type the name of the project.
3. Click on OK.

NOTE: Visual Basic will prompt you first to name any files that have been created before saving the project.

PROJECT FILE TYPES

A typical project contains forms, modules and Visual Basic extension files. You use forms to create an interface for a program, modules to store global definitions and extension files to gain access to custom controls. Table 1.3 shows the extensions these files use.

ADDING FILES TO PROJECTS

There are two ways to add a file to a project. First, you can create the file by choosing either the New Form or New Module command from the File menu or the toolbar. Alternatively, you can borrow code from other projects by selecting the Add File... command from the File menu.

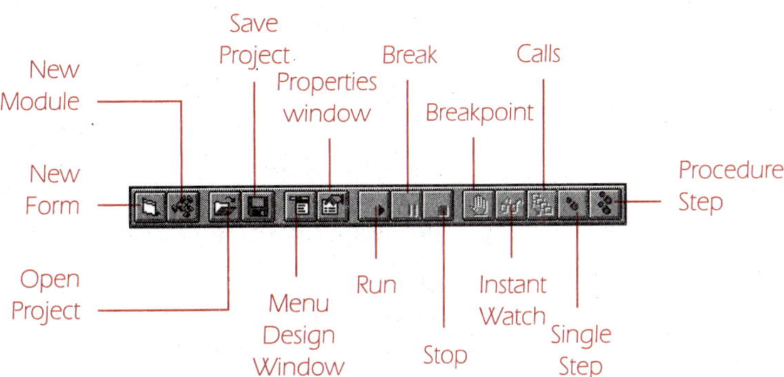

FIGURE 1.16 The toolbar containing the Save Project button

File Type	Extension
Forms	.FRM
Modules	.BAS
Custom controls	.VBX

TABLE 1-3 FILE TYPES IN PROJECTS

SUMMARY

Visual Basic is a complete developers system for producing graphical applications in Windows. Its visual design tools are used to create text boxes, labels, command buttons, list boxes, combo boxes, option buttons, check boxes, scroll bars and other controls. In this chapter, you have learned how to create an interface, work with properties, write event procedures, fine tune applications and maintain projects.

REVIEW QUESTIONS

1. Why is it important to rename controls on a form before writing code?
2. How do you create an event procedure?
3. Define the following terms:

   control
   event procedure
   focus
   property
   method

4. To create a password, what text box property do you set?
5. How can you restrict the number of characters entered into a text box at run time?
6. What are the advantages and disadvantages of modal dialog boxes?
7. Code a routine to display a modal dialog box when a command button is selected.
8. What is the difference between a text box and a label control? When would you use each?
9. Write a routine to display a message in a text box.

HINT: Put the code for the assignment in either the Form_Load procedure or in a command button's Click procedure.

10. How can you modify the preceding example so that the programs reads input from the text box? Use **MsgBox** to display the value after the program reads the input.
11. Code a procedure to display a string in a label control.
12. To add an item to a list box or combo box, what method do you use? Show examples of each.

13. What list box property returns the total number of list elements?
14. How can you sort a list box, remove a list item and clear a list at run time?
15. What is the difference between a check box and an option button? How can you test if these controls are selected at run time?
16. To initialize a scroll bar, what properties do you set?
17. To display a bitmap in an image control, what property do you set?
18. How can you create a control array?
19. To change the tab order of a control, what property do you set?
20. What Visual Basic properties allow you to enable/disable and show/hide controls?

NOTE: The answers to odd-numbered review questions are listed in Appendix C.

CLASS PROJECTS

1. Create a program to display three bitmaps created in Paintbrush. Use the Visual Basic **LoadPicture** function, an image control and three option buttons to display the painted images. The program should show a different bitmap each time an option button is selected.

NOTE: To indicate the file name, you must include a complete path enclosed in quotes. For example:

```
picture1.Picture = LoadPicture("C:\WINDOWS\PARTY.BMP")
```

2. Write a program to read and validate a password. The user should not see the password as it is typed. Use **MsgBox** to inform the user if the password is correct.

HINT: Set the PasswordChar property to a null string to suppress the display of keys entered.

3. Write a simple program to initialize a list. Use the **AddItem** method to fill the list and **MsgBox** to display the user's choice at run time.

2 PROGRAMMING IN VISUAL BASIC

Visual Basic supports most of the basic constructs found in other programming languages including loops, decision structures, procedures and arrays. In this chapter, you will learn how to apply these constructs in creating your own programs and projects.

2.1 SEQUENTIAL VRS. EVENT-DRIVEN PROGRAMMING

A sequence is a group of commands that the computer performs in order. In traditional programming, an application would run until each statement in the program finished executing. In Visual Basic, the code in a program remains idle until an event occurs. This style of programming is known as *event driven programming*.

An event may occur for any number of reasons: a timer executing or a user clicking on a list entry, selecting a command button or menu item, or choosing an option. When such events occur, Visual Basic executes the code block or event procedure associated with the control.

CODING EVENT PROCEDURES

When an event procedure is executing, its commands are generally performed in order. However, an event procedure can also contain decision structures and loop structures. The following sections examine each possibility.

WRITING EXPRESSIONS

In Visual Basic, you write expressions the same way you would in QuickBASIC or QBasic. For example, the following expression adds two variables and assigns the result to a third:

```
cust_bal = prev_bal + cur_bal
```

In the preceding example, <cust_bal> is set to the total of <prev_bal> + <cur_bal>. Multiplication and division also use the same mathematical operators. The following example shows how to compute the cost of an item with sales tax:

```
' Compute cost of item with tax

sales_tax = .07
unit_price = 5

total_due = unit_price * sales_tax + unit_price

MsgBox ("Total Due: " & total_due)
```

Expressions are always evaluated from left to right with operators and parenthesis having precedence. For example, multiplication and division are performed before addition and subtraction. If you want a particular part of the formula to be performed first, add parentheses like this:

```
strline = (cost - salvage) / life
```

THE ^ OPERATOR

The exponential (^) operator raises a value to a power. The following example shows how the exponential operator can be used:

```
futureval = present_value * (1 + interest) ^ periods
```

In this example, the future value of an investment is calculated by multiplying the present value by (1 + interest) ^ periods.

THE PRINT METHOD

With the **Print** method, you send the results of an expression to a form, picture box or the **Printer** object. When using this method, it is important to remember that the default printing style is not a fixed pitch font. For example, columns in reports will not line up unless you use a font like Courier that is proportionally fixed.

Syntax

```
[Object.]Print {[Spc(n)] | [Tab(n)]} <expression list>
```

The expression list can be any numeric or string expression, or optionally, the **Spc()** or **Tab()** functions. **Spc()** separates items in <expression list> with blank spaces. **Tab()** measures the distance between items by columns. For example, Tab(5) skips 5 columns before printing <expression list>.

Alternatively, you use the semicolon (;) and comma separators to format the output. When a colon is used with the **Print** method, the next character will appear immediately after the last character printed. If a comma is used to separate the items, the next character will be printed 14 columns from the previous character (in the next print zone).

NOTE: If the Form_Load procedure contains references to the Print **method, the output will not appear on the form unless the** Show **method precedes it in code.**

The sample time and billing application, TIME.MAK, demonstrates the use of the **Print** method. You can find the source code for this example on the program disk.

Prt_headings uses the **Print** method to show headings in a picture box. Each item printed is separated by the amount of space indicated by **Spc()**. To keep groups of items together on the same line, the ";" option is used during each print. Figure 2.1 shows what the report looks like.

Time Report

```
Client          Employee        Hours   Rate   Total
======          ========        =====   ====   =====

John Smith      Sara Adoms          3     75     225
John Smith      Sara Adoms          4     75     300
John Smith      Sara Adoms          2     75     150

                    Total Hours:    9   Total Due:   675

Mary Jones      Tom Johnson         4     75     300
Mary Jones      Bob Anderson        4     75     300

                    Total Hours:    8   Total Due:   600

Ron Mathews     Laura Swan          6     75     450

                    Total Hours:    6   Total Due:   450
```

OK

FIGURE 2.1 A sample report

```
Sub Prt_headings ()

 ' Print headings for detail report

 ReportForm.Caption = "Time Report"

 ReportForm.Picture1.FontName = "Courier"

 ReportForm.Picture1.Cls
 ReportForm.Picture1.Print Spc(2); "Client";
 ReportForm.Picture1.Print Spc(13); "Employee";
 ReportForm.Picture1.Print Spc(7); "Hours";
 ReportForm.Picture1.Print Spc(5); "Rate";
 ReportForm.Picture1.Print Spc(4); "Total"

 ReportForm.Picture1.Print Spc(2); "======";
 ReportForm.Picture1.Print Spc(13); "========";
 ReportForm.Picture1.Print Spc(7); "=====";
 ReportForm.Picture1.Print Spc(5); "====";
 ReportForm.Picture1.Print Spc(4); "====="
 ReportForm.Picture1.Print

End Sub
```

After printing the headings, PrtRecs shows the detail lines of the report. The program then calls Prt_footer and displays the total hours and balance due for each customer:

```
Sub PrtRecs (timerec As Struct1)

 ' Print records for Detail report

 ReportForm.Picture1.Print Spc(2); timerec.client_name;
 ReportForm.Picture1.Print timerec.last_name;
 ReportForm.Picture1.Print Spc(6); timerec.hours;
 ReportForm.Picture1.Print Spc(5); timerec.rate;
 ReportForm.Picture1.Print Spc(4); timerec.tot_due

End Sub


Sub Prt_footer (tothours As Single, totbill As
           ⇨ Currency)

 ' Print group footer for detail report

 ReportForm.Picture1.Print
 group_footer = " Total Hours: " + Str(tothours) +
        ⇨ Space(5) + "Total Due: " + Str(totbill)
```

```
 ReportForm.Picture1.Print Tab(28); group_footer
 ReportForm.Picture1.Print

End Sub
```

SENDING OUTPUT TO A PRINTER

To send output to a printer, use the **Printer** object. By default, Visual Basic sends output to the standard printer device. The following example demonstrates how this is done:

```
Sub cmdPrint_Click ()

 ' Send string to printer device

 Printer.Print "This is a test"
 Printer.EndDoc

End Sub
```

Note that before output is actually sent to the printer device, you must use the **EndDoc** method to inform the Print Manager when to start printing.

2.2 USING DECISION STRUCTURES

Sometimes a program must provide choices to the user. For example, a print routine can direct output to the screen, printer or disk devices. To ask a question in Visual Basic, you use either the **If Then** or **If Then Else** decision structures. Alternately, you can use the **Select Case** decision structure to simplify decisions.

THE IF THEN/IF THEN ELSE DECISION STRUCTURES

With **If Then** and **If Then Else**, you can perform operations conditionally in an application. These programming constructs use the following syntax:

Syntax 1

```
If<condition> Then
  <block>
End If
```

Syntax 2

```
If<condition-1> Then
  <block-1>
[ElseIf <condition-2> Then
  <block-2>
```

```
    .    .    .
    .    .    .]
[Else
  <block-n>]
End If
```

If the value of <condition–1> evaluates to be **True**, the statements immediately after the **Then** clause are performed. Otherwise, if the value of <condition–2> evaluates to be **True**, the statements in the **ElseIf** path are executed. If neither <condition–1> or <condition–2> are **True**, the **Else** path is performed instead.

Example

```
trans_date = InputBox("Enter date of transaction")

If IsDate(trans_date) <> True Then
   MsgBox ("Invalid date")
End If
```

Example 2

```
If gross_sales >= 50000 Then
   bonus = 5000
ElseIf gross_sales >= 35000 Then
   bonus = 2500
Else
   bonus = .25
End If
```

THE SELECT CASE STRUCTURE

The **Select Case** structure is a decision structure used as an alternative to the **If Then Else** decision structure. When an **If Then Else** block has multiple **ElseIf** clauses, it becomes cluttered and hard to read. By using **Select Case**, your programs will be not only easier to read, but will perform more optimally as well.

Syntax

```
Select Case <test expression>
 Case [Is] <expression group>
  <block-1>
 [Case [Is] <expression group>
  <block-2>]
[Case Else
  <block-n>]
End Select
```

Select Case evaluates the value of <test expression> and compares this value with each **Case**. If more than one value is contained in <expression group>, the values must be separated by commas. **Select Case** continues to compare expressions until a match is found. If no match occurs, the optional **Case Else** path is performed.

Example

```
Select Case quarter

 Case 1
    quarter_str = "March 31, "
 Case 2
    quarter_str = "June 30, "
 Case 3
    quarter_str = "September 30, "
 Case 4
    quarter_str = "December 31, "
 Case Else                  ' Default to first quarter
    quarter_str = "March 31, "

End Select
```

Example 2

```
' Return closest decimal to a fraction

Select Case dec

  Case Is <= .03125   ' 1/32
    frac = "1/32"
  Case Is <= .0625    ' 1/16
    frac = "1/16"
  Case Is <= .125     ' 1/8
    frac = "1/8"
  Case Is <= .25      ' 1/4
    frac = "1/4"
  Case Is <= .33      ' 1/3
    frac = "1/3"
  Case Is <= .5       ' 1/2
    frac = "1/2"
  Case Is <= .66      ' 2/3
    frac = "2/3"
  Case Is <= .75      ' 3/4
    frac = "3/4"
  Case Is <= .8125    ' 13/16
    frac = "13/16"
  Case Is <= .875     ' 7/8
    frac = "7/8"
```

```
  Case Is <= .9375    ' 15/16
    frac = "15/16"
End Select
```

2.3 WORKING WITH LOOP STRUCTURES

Sometimes a group of commands must be performed repeatedly in the same procedure. Visual Basic provides three structures that are used to implement loops; **For...Next**, **While** & **Do...Loop**.

USING FOR...NEXT

The **For...Next** loop executes a block of statements a fixed number of times.

Syntax

```
For <count> = <start> To <end> [Step <amount>]
   [block-1]
   [Exit For]
   [block-2]
Next [<count>]
```

Each time the **For...Next** loop executes, the value of <count> is either increased or decreased by <amount>. If the **Step** clause is omitted, <count> is incremented by 1. The loop continues until the value of <start> reaches the value of <end>. If the **Step** amount is a negative value, <start> must be initialized greater than <end> or the loop will never perform. The optional **Exit For** clause terminates the loop. Typically, the program would use an **If Then** decision structure to determine when to break from the loop. The following example uses a **For...Next** loop to add part numbers to a list:

```
Sub Command1_Click ()

 ' Fill list with part numbers

 Static Parts_no(5) As String

 Parts_no(1) = "L571444-5456"
 Parts_no(2) = "J206905-4543"
 Parts_no(3) = "E276457-7611"
 Parts_no(4) = "L647435-2318"
 Parts_no(5) = "E979653-2900"

 For i = 1 To 5
   list1.AddItem Parts_no(i)
 Next

End Sub
```

In the preceding example, an array initializes the list. Arrays organize groups of related information. For more information on the proper usage of arrays, refer to section 2.7 Using Arrays at the end of this chapter.

THE WHILE...LOOP

Syntax

```
While condition
 [block]
Wend
```

The **While** loop continues until a certain condition is met. Use **While** when you do not know how many times the loop will execute. In this next example, **While** is used to read records from a file until the end of the file is reached:

```
Sub cmdOpen_Click ()

 Dim filename As String
 Dim fileno As Integer

 filename = "vendor.dat"
 fileno = 1

 Open filename For Input As #fileno

 picture1.Cls

 ' Print vendor names and numbers

 While Not EOF(fileno)
  Input #1, vendor, phone
  picture1.Print vendor, phone
 Wend
 Close #fileno

End Sub
```

THE DO...LOOP

Syntax 1

```
Do [{While | Until} condition]
 [block-1]
 [Exit Do]
 [block-2]
Loop
```

Syntax 2

```
Do
 [block-1]
 [Exit Do]
 [block-2]
Loop [{While | Until} condition]
```

Like **While**, the **Do...Loop** executes a code block while a condition is **True** or until it becomes **True**. The **Do...Loop**, however, is more flexible than **While** and offers greater control over program execution. The following procedure uses a **Do...Loop** to retrieve a text file for editing:

```
Sub Read_Click ()

 ' Open text file for editing

 fileno = 1

 Do While found <> True

  filename = InputBox("Enter file name:", "File Open")

  retval = Valfile(filename)

  If retval = True Then
    found = True
  End If

  If filename = "" Then
    Exit Sub
  End If

  Loop

  ' Read file into text box

  text1.Text = Readmemo(fileno, filename)
  Form1.Caption = filename

End Sub
```

In this example, the Valfile function validates a file name. To be valid, the file must exists. If Valfile returns **True**, the loop ends. Otherwise, the program continues to prompt for a name until either a valid one is entered or the Cancel button is selected—in which case, <filename> is set to a null string.

Exercise: Creating a Time Clock Program

1. From the File menu in Visual Basic, choose New Project.
2. Draw the following controls on the form. Place each object as it appears in Figure 2.2.

Control	Property	Value
text1	Text	null string
text2	Text	null string
label1	Caption	Time In:
label2	Caption	Time Out:
label3	Caption	Hours Worked:
label4	Caption	null string
command1	Caption	OK

3. Rename each control as follows:

Old Name	New Name
text1	time_in
text2	time_out
label4	timeworked
command1	cmdOK

4. Double click on the command button. This will put you in the Code window.

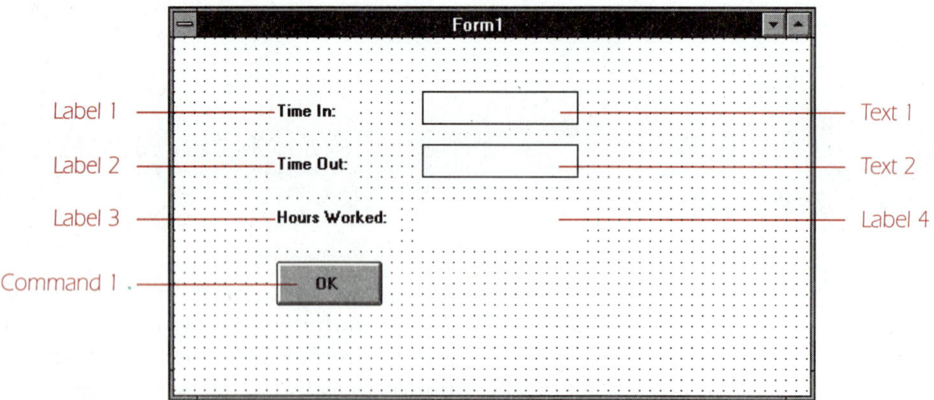

FIGURE 2.2 Controls for the time clock

NOTE: Alternatively, you can press F7 while the control has focus to create the event procedure.

5. In the cmdOK_Click procedure, type:

```
Dim time1 As String, time2 As String

' Get beginning and ending times

time1 = time_in.Text
time2 = time_out.Text

' Calculate and show time difference

timeworked.Caption = Timediff(time1, time2)
```

6. From the File menu, choose Add File...
7. Insert the disk with the library modules in drive A:\.
8. Type A:\DATEFUNC.BAS. This file contains the definition for the Timediff library function which will be used in the example.

NOTE: Appendix A shows how to install the library modules to a hard drive if amenable to your system.

9. Click on OK to add the file to the project.
10. Save the program and run it.
    Timediff calculates the difference between two time arguments. The times must be entered in 24 hour format.
    To check the program, use the following test data:

    Time In: 09:00
    Time Out: 17:30

    After entering the times, click on OK to compute the time difference (8 hrs. 30 min.).

2.4 WORKING WITH PROCEDURES

A *procedure* is a block of instructions that performs a particular task. Procedures come in two classes, **Sub** procedures and **Function** procedures. The basic difference between a **Sub** procedure and a **Function** procedure is that a **Function** procedure returns a value but a **Sub** procedure does not.

In Chapter 1, you learned how to create event procedures. In Visual Basic, you also can create your own functions. These kinds of procedures are known as *general procedures*.

Organizing code into different functions makes an application easier to read and maintain. Another advantage of organizing programs this way is that you can reuse code that would otherwise not be reusable. This book includes a developer's library with more than eighty pre-defined routines that perform many common operations including database access, date and time, environment, grid, memo handling, screen effects, security, statistical, utility and validation operations. All of this code is reusable.

USING THE LIBRARY

To use the library, add the appropriate module to the current project. The files have a .BAS file extension. Part III of this book lists each routine and shows which modules must be included in a project to call each function. To keep the size of an application smaller, the library is organized categorically by function purpose.

CALLING THE LIBRARY

To call a routine in the library, two methods are used. For **Sub** procedures, you place a call to a routine simply by naming the procedure in your program. For example, assuming the ENVIR.BAS module has been added to the current project, you get information about the system by placing a call to Sysconfig.

Example

```
Sub cmdOK_Click ()
  ' Show system configuration
  Sysconfig
End Sub
```

...or use the **Call** keyword to invoke the function:

```
Sub cmd_OK ()
  ' Show system configuration
  Call Sysconfig
End Sub
```

To call a function, an alternate syntax is used:

```
<return value> = FunctionName ([<parameter list>])
```

Example

```
file_OK = Valfile("MYFILE.DAT")
```

The *return value* is a variable of the return type (see Section 2.5, Working with Data Types). The function name is the name of the library routine. The *parameters list* is any information that the function needs to complete the operation. Part III of this book shows the proper syntax for calling each function. You can use these routines to develop your own applications provided that you agree to the terms in the licensing agreement.

CREATING GENERAL PROCEDURES

Visual Basic supports user-defined functions or general procedures. To create a new general procedure, select the New Procedure option from the View menu. A dialog box appears (see Figure 2.3). In this box, type the name of the procedure. By default, Visual Basic creates a new **Sub** procedure. If you wish to code a **Function** procedure instead, select the Function option button. Then click on OK.

Creating a new procedure opens the Code window with the function heading already declared. For example, when creating a **Sub** called ShowBalance, the Code window appears as:

```
Sub ShowBalance ()
End Sub
```

Between the **Sub** and **End Sub** statements, insert code. If the procedure needs information from another part of the program to complete the operation, pass variables as parameters to the procedure by adding the parameter declarations to the **Sub** or **Function** header. For example, to pass two variables, <cust_name> and <cust_ID>, you type:

```
Sub ShowBalance (cust_name As String, cust_ID As
             ⇨ Integer)
End Sub
```

This assumes that <cust_name> and <cust_ID> are defined in the calling procedure. For example, if you called ShowBalance from an event procedure, the following declarations must be made:

```
Sub cmdOK_Click ()

 Dim cust_name As String
 Dim cust_ID as Integer
 .      .      .
 .      .      .
 Call ShowBalance(cust_name, cust_ID)

End Sub
```

In this example, the call to ShowBalance is made from a command button's Click procedure. You can also call general procedures from other event procedures as well.

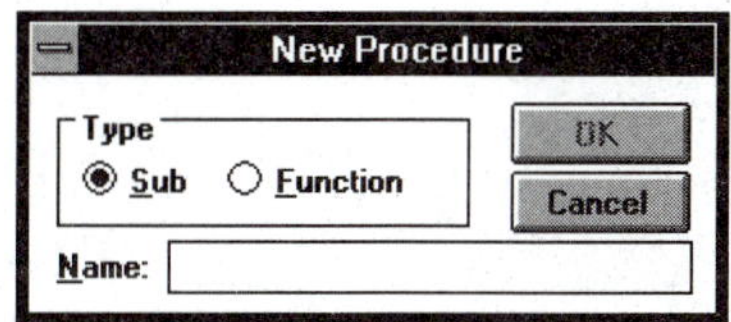

FIGURE 2.3 The New Procedure dialog box

Once a parameter is passed to a procedure, it becomes local to it (as an argument). Thus, any value it holds is lost after the procedure is finished executing. If you wish to preserve the value of a parameter between procedure calls, the variable must be declared as either **Global** throughout the application or local to the form. Alternatively, declare a **Static** variable in the procedure itself.

To Declare a Global Variable

- Use the **Global** statement to define a variable in the Declarations section of a module (.BAS File). Once a global variable has been declared, it is available throughout the application (and can be shared among forms).

Example

```
Global myvar As String
```

To Declare a Variable Local to a Form

- Use the **Dim** statement to define the variable in the Declaration section of the form (see Figure 2.4).

To Declare a Static Variable

- Use the **Static** statement to define the variable in a procedure.

Example

```
Static testvar As Integer
```

RETURNING VALUES FROM FUNCTIONS

Since functions return values, you do not need to declare a **Global** variable to preserve its value. Instead, assign the return value to the name of the function:

Example

```
Sub Command1_Click ()
 ' Call function to square number
 Dim value As Integer
 value = 12
 squared_value = Sqr_Val(value)
End Sub

Function Sqr_Val (value As Integer)
 ' Return answer
 Sqr_Val = value * value
End Function
```

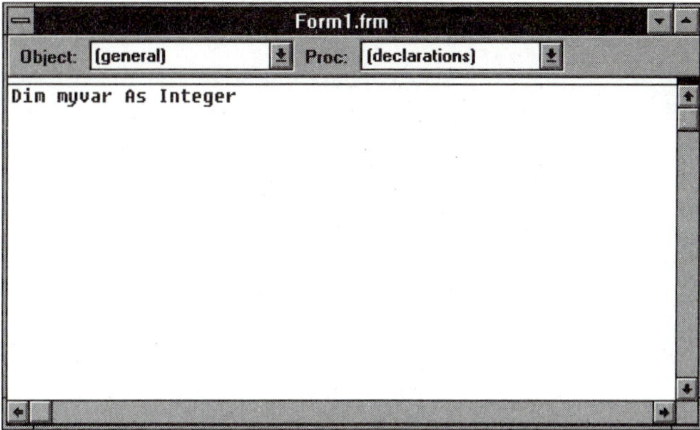

FIGURE 2.4 The Declarations section of a form

2.5 WORKING WITH DATA TYPES

The default data type in Visual Basic is a variant; you do not always have to explicitly declare data types when working with variables. However, Visual Basic can often process code more efficiently when it knows what type a variable is. In Chapter 1, you worked with the **String** and **Integer** types. Table 2.1 lists additional types supported by Visual Basic.

You can also declare the return type of a **Function** procedure. For example:

```
Function Sqr_Val (value As Integer) As Integer
  ' Return answer
 Sqr_Val = value * value
End Function
```

By adding **As Integer** after the parameter list, Visual Basic returns an integer value to the calling procedure. If the return type is not specified, Visual Basic treats the argument as a variant.

Data Type	Type Suffice	Storage
Long	&	4 Bytes
Single	!	4 Bytes
Double	#	8 Bytes
Currency	@	8 Bytes
Variant	N/A	Size of current type

TABLE 2-1 VISUAL BASIC DATA TYPES

VARIABLE STANDARDS

You can also change the default way Visual Basic handles variable so that each variable must be declared before it is used. By adding the **Option Explicit** statement to the Declaration section of a form or module, all variable must be explicitly declared before they can be used. This technique is particularly useful if you are accustomed to Turbo Pascal or C, which require that all variables be formally declared in an application. Through **Option Explicit**, you can detect misspelled variables or variables not initialized before logical flaws can occur in your programs.

Visual Basic also permits you to specify the default data type for an application. The following code, for example, shows how to specify that all undeclared variables be treated as type **Integer**:

```
DefInt A-Z
```

The A–Z argument specifies the scope of the variables—that is, all variables beginning with the letters A–Z are assumed to be integers. You can also set other default types using any of the following statements:

```
DefLng <range>      Set all variables to Long
DefSng <range>      Set all variables to Single
DefDbl <range>      Set all variables to Double
DefCur <range>      Set all variables to Currency
DefStr <range>      Set all variables to String
DefVar <range>      Set all variables to Variant
```

USER-DEFINED TYPES

You can even declare your own user-defined data types by using the **Type** statement. The syntax for this statement is:

```
Type <TypeName>
      <element> [(subscripts)] As Datatype
      .           .             .
      .           .             .
End Type
```

The data type can be any Visual Basic type (**Integer**, **Long**, **Single**, **Double**, **Currency** or **String**). If the type is used to define the structure of a record in a random access file, all string elements must be fixed in length—for example, item_name As String * 25.

Example

```
Type Struct1
  valid_add As Integer
  last_name As String * 18
```

```
  first_name As String * 18
  phone_no As String * 13
End Type

Global client As Struct1

Sub cmdSave_Click ()

  ' Save record to disk

 client.valid_add = True
 client.last_name = last_name.Text
 client.first_name = first_name.Text
 client.phone_no = phone.Text

 Call Saverec(fileno, filename, client)

End Sub
```

The cmdSave_Click procedure of ADD.MAK uses the library routine Saverec to add records to a random access file. The user type for this example is defined in DB_DEFIN.BAS. Notice that the **Global** variable <client> is of type Struct1.

2.6 USING PRE-DEFINED FUNCTIONS

In previous sections, you learned how to create procedures and work with data types. Visual Basic also includes its own standard set of procedures. These routines are used to perform anything from rounding a value to formatting a string. The online Help in Visual Basic and *Language Reference* include a listing and discussion of each function. This section describes some commonly used procedures in version 4.0.

THE CHR$ FUNCTION

The **Chr$** function prints an ANSI character to a form, picture box or the **Printer** object. CHRDEMO.MAK, shows how to display special characters in Visual Basic. When the form loads, the program prints a copyright notice, trademark, registered trademark, carriage return symbol, check mark and four arrows. Figure 2.5 shows how the output appears. Notice that the **Show** method is used at the beginning of the Form_Load procedure (so the output will appear in the picture box when the form loads).

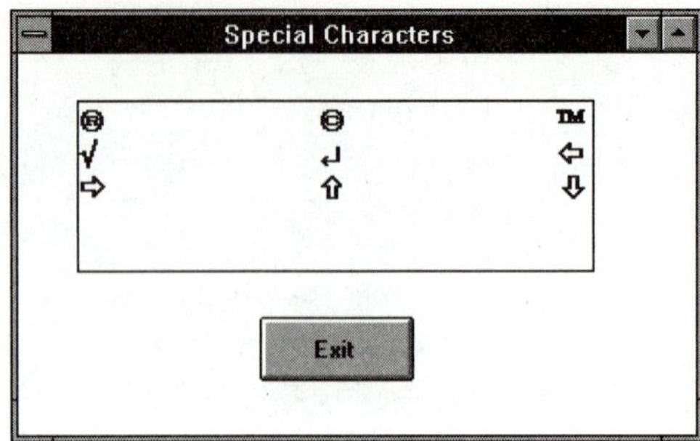

FIGURE 2.5 Printing special characters with the Chr$ function

Syntax

```
Chr[$] (<character code>)
```

Example

```
Sub Form_Load ()

 Show

 picture1.FontName = "Symbol"
 picture1.FontSize = 12

 picture1.Print Chr$(Val("0210")) + Space(5),   ' Registered trademark
 picture1.Print Chr$(Val("0227")) + Space(5),   ' Copyright notice
 picture1.Print Chr$(Val("0212"))               ' Trademark
 picture1.Print Chr$(Val("0214")) + Space(5),   ' Check mark
 picture1.Print Chr$(Val("0191")) + Space(5),   ' Enter key

 picture1.FontName = "Wingdings"

 picture1.Print Chr$(Val("0239")) + Space(5)    ' Left arrow
 picture1.Print Chr$(Val("0240")) + Space(2),   ' Right arrow
 picture1.CurrentX = 1875
 picture1.Print Chr$(Val("0241")),              ' Up arrow
 picture1.CurrentX = 3825
 picture1.Print Chr$(Val("0242")) + Space(5)    ' Down arrow

End Sub
```

Although **Chr$** returns a string and **Chr** returns a variant, both forms produce identical results. When using **Chr** or **Chr$**, be aware that each font contains its own character set. Therefore, you must indicate the correct font in your program before calling **Chr/Chr$**.

NOTE: The Character Map Accessory supplied with Windows version 3.1 shows the character set for each font.

THE FIX AND INT FUNCTIONS

Both **Fix** and **Int** convert numbers to integers. The **Fix** function, however, rounds values up when negative whereas **Int** rounds them down. For example, Fix(–6.3) returns –6 and Int(–6.3) returns –7.

Syntax

```
Fix (<value>)

Int (<value>)
```

Example

```
n = Fix(-4.7)
MsgBox ("The value of n is " & n)
```

THE INSTR FUNCTION

Syntax

```
InStr ([<start>],<searchstring>,<comparestring>)
```

The **InStr** function returns the position of a character pattern within another string. If no match is found, **InStr** returns 0. The following example uses **InStr** to determine if a user entered a valid return authorization code for an exchange credit:

```
Sub cmdOK_Click ()

 Dim code As String

 ' Read return authorization code

 code = returncode.Text

 ' Validate code string
```

```
If InStr(code, "A15") <> 0 Then
 MsgBox ("Code is valid")
Else
 MsgBox ("Code is invalid")
End If

End Sub
```

THE MID, MID$ FUNCTIONS

Syntax

```
Mid[$] (<strexpr>, <startpos>, <length>)
```

The **Mid** function returns a sub-string of characters contained in another string. If no match is found, <strexpr> returns 0. <Strexpr> can be any string value. The difference between **Mid** and **Mid$** is that only **Mid** can accept a null string. If <strexpr> is a null value, then **Mid** returns a null value as well. The <startpos> argument indicates where the search should begin in the string. The <length> argument specifies how many characters should be returned.

Example

```
' Extract drive name

Dim filespec As String, start As Integer, length As
  ⇨ Integer

filespec = "C:\VB\MYFILE.DAT"
start = 1: length = 2

MsgBox (Mid(filespec, start, length))
```

USING OTHER PRE-DEFINED FUNCTION

Table 2.2 shows a listing of some other commonly used functions in version 4.0. Many of the examples in this book use Visual Basic functions to perform operations. You can get additional information on these and other topics by using the online Help Search command.

Function	Description
Abs	Returns absolute value of a number
Atn	Returns the arctangent of a numeric value
Asc	Returns the ANSI code of the first character in an expresion
CCur	Converts an expression to a currency value (see also **CDbl**, **CInt**, **CLng**, **CSng**, **CStr** and **CVar**)
Command	Returns the command string used to launch a Visual Basic program
Cos	Returns cosine of an angle
CVDate	Converts an expression to a date value
Day	Returns the day of the month as an integer value
EOF	Returns **True** if End Of File
Err	Returns the error number of an error
Error, Error$	Returns the error message of an error
Exp	Returns an exponent of a number
FileLen	Returns the file length of a file in bytes
Format, Format$	Formats an expression
FreeFile	Returns the next available file number
GetAttr	Returns the attribute status of a file, directory or volume label
Hour	Returns a value between 0 and 23 representing the hour of the day
Input, Input$	Returns character input from a file opened for sequential access
IsDate	Returns **True** if a variable can be converted to a date value
IsEmpty	Returns **True** if a variant is a null value
IsNumeric	Returns **True** if a variable can be converted to a numeric type
LCase, LCase$	Converts a string to lowercase
Left, Left$	Returns a specified number of characters from the leftmost part of a string
Len	Returns the length of a string
LoadPicture	Loads a graphic image into a form, picture box or image control
Log	Returns the natural logarithm of a numeric value
LTrim, LTrim$	Removes leading spaces from a string (see also RTrim, RTrim$)
Month	Returns the month of the year as an integer value
Now	Returns the current date and time
QBColor	Returns the **RGB** color code equivalent of a QuickBASIC color number
RGB	Returns an **RGB** color value
Rnd	Returns a random value
Seek	Returns the position of the file pointer
Shell	Executes a program
Sin	Returns the sine of an angle
Sqr	Returns square root of n
Str, Str$	Converts a numeric value to a string
Tan	Returns the tangent of an angle
Time, Time$	Returns current time
UBound	Returns the upper bound of an array subscript
UCase, UCase$	Converts a string to uppercase
Val	Converts a string to a numeric value
Year	Returns year of a date argument

TABLE 2-2 COMMONLY USED FUNCTIONS IN VISUAL BASIC

2.7 USING ARRAYS

In Visual Basic, as in other programming languages, you declare an array in order to reference groups of related information. An *array* is an organized collection of variables that uses an index to access its elements. The following procedure shows how to declare and initialize a one-dimensional array:

```
Function GetDay (dayno As Variant)

 ' Returns day of week (called from Showcalend)

 Static WeekDays(7)

 WeekDays(1) = "Sun": WeekDays(2) = "Mon"
 WeekDays(3) = "Tue": WeekDays(4) = "Wed"
 WeekDays(5) = "Thr": WeekDays(6) = "Fri"
 WeekDays(7) = "Sat"

 GetDay = WeekDays(dayno)

End Function
```

After initializing an array, you can display the values it contains in a loop like this:

```
' Print days of week

Const DAYS_PER_WEEK = 7

For current_day = 1 To DAYS_PER_WEEK
  picture1.Print WeekDays(current_day) & Space(3);
Next
```

If you need to access a particular element of an array, use an index to read its value. The following example shows how this is done:

```
' Print fifth element of array

Dim my_index As Integer

my_index = 5
MsgBox (WeekDays(my_index))
```

Several rules are important to observe when declaring arrays. If the array is declared as **Global**, its definition must appear in the Declaration section of a module (.BAS file). Similarly, if the array is declared local to a form, the **Dim** statement must be in the Declaration section of that form. If the array is declared as **Static**, the definition must be in a procedure.

NOTE: The Dim **statement can also be used to declare an array in a procedure if the procedure itself is declared as** Static.

MULTIDIMENSIONAL ARRAYS

In Visual Basic, you can declare an array up to sixty dimensions. The sample statistical application included with this book, STAT.MAK, uses a two-dimensional array to graph sales for a company that sells marine products such as lorans, generators and depth finders. Subscript 1 contains the numbers of each category. Subscript 2 holds the actual data. For more information on this example, refer to the discussion of Bargraph in Part III, Array Functions.

```
Sub GraphStat_Click ()

 ' Show bar graph

 Const SCALEMAX = 10000: Const SCALES = 5
 Const BARS_PERCAT = 3: Const BARGROUPS = 3
 Const BAR1 = 1: BAR2 = 2: BAR3 = 3

 Static Graph_data(BARGROUPS, BARS_PERCAT)

 fileno = 1
 filename = "sample.dat"

 Open filename For Input As #fileno

 ' For each group, read values into array

 For i = 1 To BARGROUPS

    Input #fileno, east, west, south

    Graph_data(i, BAR1) = east
    Graph_data(i, BAR2) = west
    Graph_data(i, BAR3) = south

 Next

 Close #fileno

 ' Show bar graph

 picture1.Cls
 Call Bargraph(Form1, picture1, SCALES, SCALEMAX, BAR
           ⇨ GROUPS, BARS_PERCAT, (( Graph_data())

 ' Show bar graph labels

 Form1.Caption = "U.S. Sales Divisions"
 Call ShowCtrls
```

```
 ' Temporarily hide other controls on form

 Loran_option.Visible = False
 Gener_option.Visible = False
 Depthfinder_option.Visible = False

End Sub
```

CREATING DYNAMIC ARRAYS

Fixed size arrays have one disadvantage. When a fixed size array is declared, the application must reserve enough space in memory to initialize all its elements. *Dynamic arrays*, on the other hand, save space by allocating memory while the program is running.

To Declare a Dynamic Array

- Use the **Global**, **Dim** or **Static** statements to declare a global, module level or static array. Note that with dynamic arrays, it is permissible to use a **Dim** statement within a procedure.

  ```
  e.g., Dim CustList()
  ```

- Allocate space for the array using **ReDim Preserve**:

  ```
  ReDim Preserve CustList(elements + 1)
  ```

The following example shows how to declare a dynamic array. Notice that each time an element is added to the array, the **Preserve** statement saves the values of other elements in the array:

```
Sub Form_Load ()

 Show

 ' Declare dynamic array

 Dim Arr()

 ' Add new array elements

 For totelem = 1 To 5
   ReDim Preserve Arr(totelem)
 Next

 ' Fill array

 Arr(1) = 7: Arr(2) = 3
 Arr(3) = 5: Arr(4) = 2
 Arr(5) = 6

 ' Print each element
```

```
  For i = 1 To 5
    Form1.Print Arr(i)
  Next

End Sub
```

2.8 CREATING LARGE PROJECTS

PROJ1.MAK demonstrates how to create large projects in Visual Basic. Although its source code is brief, the example identifies guidelines for the creation of full scale applications.

At run time, the Form_Load procedure of the start up form (INTROSCR.FRM), displays information about the program. Figure 2.6 shows how the screen appears.

To display the message, the program builds a large string from several smaller ones:

```
Sub Form_Load ()

  ' Show intro. screen

  Show

  newline = Chr(13) + Chr(10)

  str1 = Space(16) + "This program demonstrates how to"
  str2 = Space(10) + "manage multi-form applications. It
          ⇨ shows how "
  str3 = Space(12) + "to share information between forms
          ⇨ and "
  str4 = Space(21) + "how to use dialog boxes."
```

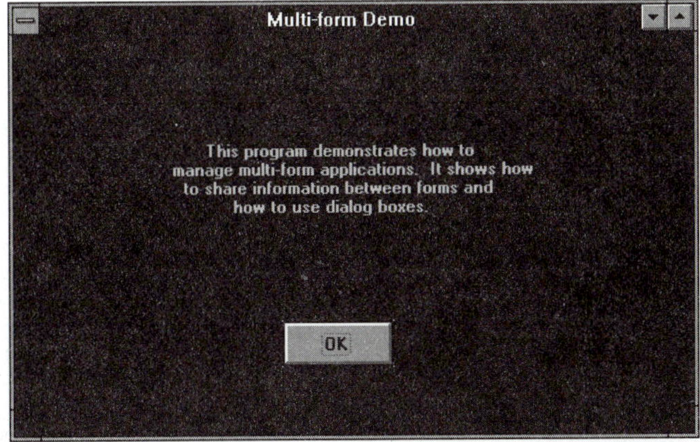

FIGURE 2.6 The introductory screen of PROJ1.MAK

```
    message = str1 + newline + str2 + newline + str3 +
              ⇨ newline + str4

    IntroScr.Picture1.Print
    IntroScr.Picture1.Print
    IntroScr.Picture1.Print message

End Sub
```

NOTE: To change the start up form for an application, select the Project command from the Options menu.

When the user clicks on the OK button, the program switches to the record viewing form (ViewScr). To accomplish this, the cmd_OK_Click procedure uses the **Show** method:

```
Sub cmd_OK_Click ()

    ' Switch to main screen

    ViewScr.Show

End Sub
```

To demonstrate how information can be shared among forms, the program copies the contents of three label controls to the employee edit form (EditScr) so the record can be edited. At design time, the labels are initialized as:

Control	Property	Value
Employee	Caption	Tom Jones
Title	Caption	Salesman
Rate	Caption	100.00

For the purpose of demonstration, the test record is copied to EditScr so it can be modified. To accomplish this, the following code is needed:

```
Sub cmd_Edit_Click ()

    ' Copy record to employee edit screen

    EditScr.Employee.Text = Employee.Caption
    EditScr.Title.Text = Title.Caption
    EditScr.Rate.Text = Rate.Caption

    EditScr.Show

End Sub
```

PROJ1.MAK allows the user to edit the record by copying its contents to three text boxes (where each field can be changed). After making the alterations, clicking on the Save button copies the record back to the view screen (VIEWSCR.FRM):

```
Sub cmd_Return_Click ()

 ' Copy record back to view form

 ViewScr.Employee.Caption = Employee.Text
 ViewScr.Title.Caption = Title.Text
 ViewScr.Rate.Caption = Rate.Text

 ' Return to view form

 Unload EditScr

End Sub
```

As a design consideration, PROJ1.MAK unloads forms when they are not in use. By doing this, the program conserves memory. Alternatively, the **Hide** method could be used to swap the forms faster. The tradeoff is that the extra overhead will mean heavier system requirements.

To Hide or Display a Form

- Use the **Hide** method to hide the form and the **Show** method to redisplay it.

Example

```
Form2.Hide
Form1.Show
```

The About menu of ViewScr, shows credits for PROJ1.MAK. To display the message, the program builds a string by concatenating several smaller strings (using the plus operator and **Chr** function). Figure 2.7 shows how the dialog appears.

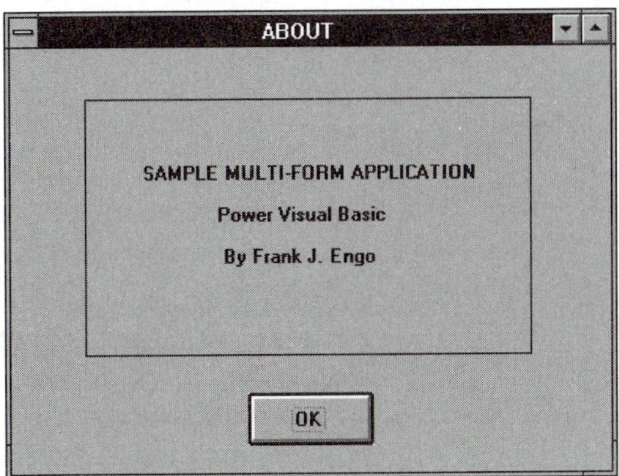

FIGURE 2.7 The program credits screen of PROJ1.MAK

```
Sub AboutScr_Click ()

 ' Show program credits screen

 newline = Chr(13) + Chr(10)

 doublespace = newline + newline

 line1 = doublespace + newline

 pad = Space(10)
 line2 = pad + "SAMPLE MULTI-FORM APPLICATION" +
    ⇨ doublespace

 pad = Space(20)
 line3 = pad + "Power Visual Basic" + doublespace

 pad = Space(24)
 line4 = pad + "By Frank J. Engo" + newline

 ' Concatenate strings to create message

 AboutForm.Label1.Caption = line1 + line2 + line3 +
                              ⇨ line4
 AboutForm.Show

End Sub
```

SUMMARY

Visual Basic is an event-driven programming language that supports many programming constructs such as decision structures, loop structures, user-defined types, procedures and arrays. In this chapter, you learned how to write expressions, use the **Printer** object, work with **Sub** procedures and **Function** procedures, apply programming constructs and manage large projects.

REVIEW QUESTIONS

1. Code a routine to print a message in a picture box. Put an option in the program to send output to the **Printer** object.
2. Create a function to add two numbers and return the sum.
3. Write a routine to add 10 numbers in a loop. Use **For...Next** and a **Do...Loop**.
4. What statements are used to declare global, local and static variables? Where must these definitions appear in a program?

5. Declare the following array:

Scope	Name	Elements	Type
Static	Products	3	String

6. Fill the array with test data and print the output to a picture box.
7. What statements are needed to declare and initialize a dynamic array?
8. What methods are used to show, hide and unload forms?
9. How can you copy the contents of a label control to a text box on another form?
10. What library routines allow you to get information about the system, display a bar graph and calculate the difference between two time arguments? To call these routines, what modules must you add to a project?

NOTE: Part III, The Library, contains the necessary module listings for each procedure of the library.

CLASS PROJECTS

1. Generate a program to accept an employee's name, ID and salary using three text box controls. Assign the values of the text boxes to three variables. Use descriptive names to indicate the purpose and function of each. Be sure to convert string input to numeric values and to use comments. Once you have read the input, use **MsgBox** to display the employee's name.
2. Using the Visual Basic **InStr** function, modify the password program you created in Chapter 1 to have the following security feature:
   Determine if a password is contained in a string that contains other characters. For example, if the password is *apples* then the user should be able to type any of the following passwords and be accepted:

   ```
   grapespearsapplesbannanas
   ```

   or

   ```
   CPUdatabasekeyboardapplesrockets
   ```

   or

   ```
   carstrucksapples
   ```

   How can this be used to your advantage?
3. Code a procedure using the library function Upperword to format a proper name. For example, if the user types john smith, the program should change the string to appear as John Smith (see Part III, String and Memo Handling Functions).
4. Using the Showcalend function of the library (covered in Part III, Security, Validation and Utility Functions), write a program to display a calendar. The user should be able to view previous and subsequent months at the press of a button.

3 CREATING MENUS

The *Menu Design window* tools provide support for enabling/disabling menu items, assigning shortcut and access keys, creating separator bars, adding menu controls at run time and displaying submenus. In this chapter, you will learn the Visual Basic techniques used to produce drop-down and pop-up menus.

3.1 USING THE MENU DESIGN WINDOW

Figure 3.1 shows the Menu Design window. To create a menu, you need to enter the definitions for each menu selection into this window. The Caption property defines the names of each menu control (as they will appear to the user). The Name property informs Visual Basic which event procedure to execute when a menu item is selected.

Properties of menu control definitions

Menu control list box

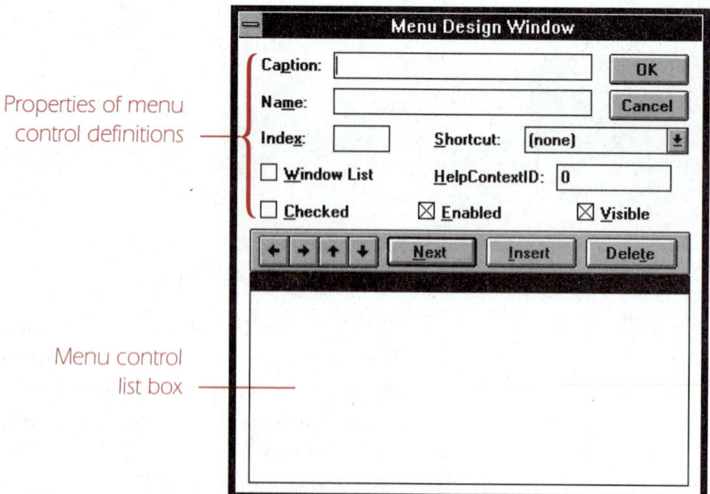

FIGURE 3.1 The Menu Design window

To Open the Menu Design Window

- Choose Menu Design from the Window menu (or click on the Menu Design button of the toolbar).

Figure 3.2 shows the definitions for a menu of a time and billing program (TIME.MAK). If you installed the example programs in the default directory, this project is located in C:\VB_LIB. Notice the items indented after the File and Report definitions. This shows that these items are subordinate to the File and Report menu titles—that is, they appear as choices within these menus.

To Indent a Menu Item

1. From the Menu Design window, select the item you wish to indent.
2. Click the right arrow button to indent the item.

EDITING KEYS

After defining a menu item, click on the menu control again to edit the definition. Table 3.1 shows a list of other editing options available.

Edit Option	Function
Left arrow button	Reverses indent by 1 level
Right arrow button	Indents menu item by 1 level
Up arrow button	Moves menu items up
Down arrow	Moves menu items down
Next	Creates a new menu item
Insert	Inserts a menu item
Delete	Removes a menu item
OK button	Saves changes
Cancel	Cancels changes

TABLE 3-1 EDIT FUNCTIONS OF THE MENU DESIGN WINDOW

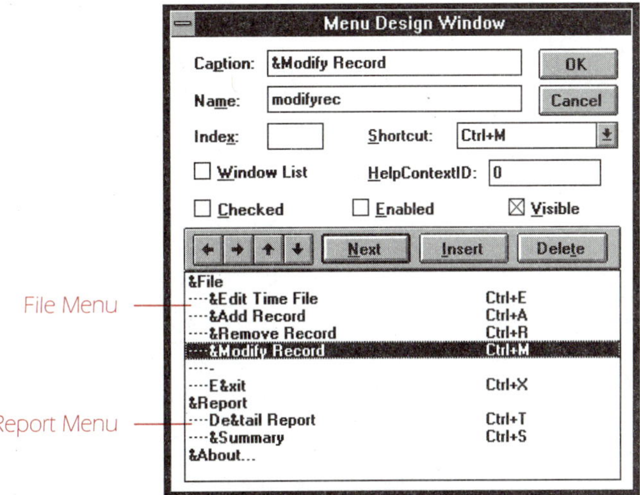

FIGURE 3.2 Menu controls for TIME.MAK

CREATING ACCESS KEYS

Access keys provide a quick way to open a menu. When an access key is assigned to a first level or *root menu* item, it is used to open the menu. For example, in Visual Basic, Alt+F opens the File menu. Once a menu is open, the letter of the access key alone is used to select items from the menu. The Edit menu of TEXT.MAK, for example, uses access keys to Cut, Copy and Paste text to and from the Clipboard. Figure 3.3 shows how the menu appears.

To Assign an Access Key

- In the Caption box, precede the menu item with an ampersand (&). The key immediately after the ampersand is the access key.

ASSIGNING SHORTCUT KEYS

Shortcut keys, like access keys, access menu items directly. In addition, shortcut keys provide a way to perform an operation without having to open a menu. To declare a shortcut key, select the name of the key from the Shortcut drop-down list. After you define a shortcut key, the key appears in the menu next to its associated menu control. The Options menu of TEXT.MAK, for example, uses the Ctrl+D shortcut key to insert the date into a file. Figure 3.4 shows how the menu appears.

SEPARATOR BARS

Separator bars organize menu controls. The File menu of TEXT.MAK uses one separator bar to separate the File Exit command from the other menu items (see Figure 3.5). You can also use a separator bar to improve the appearance of an application. For example, if a menu has only 3 items, the menu may seem incomplete unless a separator bar is used.

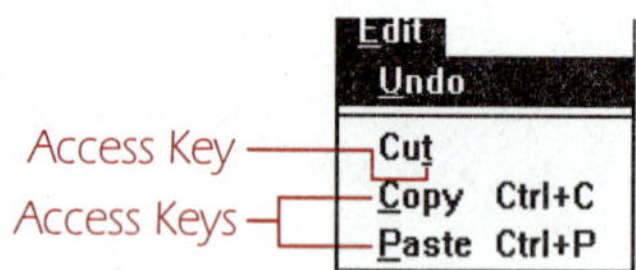

FIGURE 3.3 The Edit menu of TEXT.MAK

FIGURE 3.4 The Options menu of TEXT.MAK

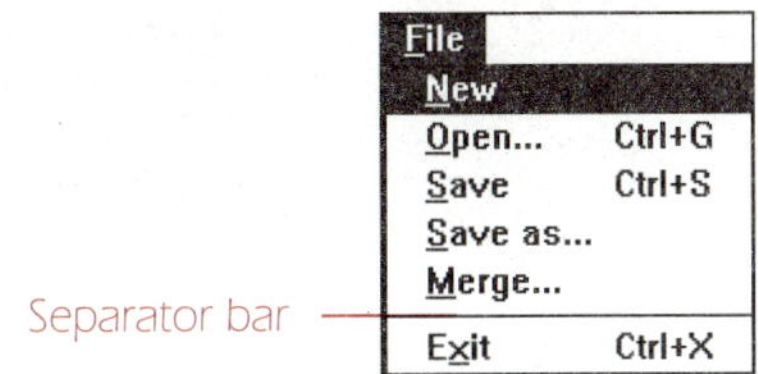

FIGURE 3.5 The File menu of TEXT.MAK

CASCADING MENUS

A particularly elegant feature of the Visual Basic menu designer is its ability to create submenus. Menus can be nested up to 4 levels deep. In practice, however, too many levels of menus can be awkward and confusing to use. In general, it is better to use a dialog box when nesting occurs beyond 1 level. Figure 3.6 shows an example of a submenu.

To Create a Submenu

- Use the right arrow button to indent each submenu item.

3.2 CONTROLLING MENUS AT RUN TIME

Some menu operations are available at both design time and at run time. For example, you can enable or disable a menu control or display a check mark by a menu item at either design time or at run time. Other menu operations are available only at run time. The following section discusses how to control menus during a run.

ENABLING/DISABLING MENU ITEMS

The Enabled property of a menu control makes a menu item selectable. When a menu control is disabled, it is not available for selection and appears grayed-out. You use this technique to restrict users from performing invalid operations. For example, in TIME.MAK, the record editing commands are not available until the Edit Time File option is selected. Figure 3.7 shows how the menu appears initially.

To Enable or Disable a Menu Item

- From the Menu Design window, click on the Enabled check box. Each time you select this box, the menu control's Enabled property is toggled on or off.

Or

- Make the same assignment in the program:

```
mnuOpenFile.Enabled = True
```

Corporate Databases
Database
New Database
Open Database
Close Database Ctrl+S
End Session Ctrl+X
Employee List
Sales List
Vendor List
Submenu

FIGURE 3.6 Cascading menus

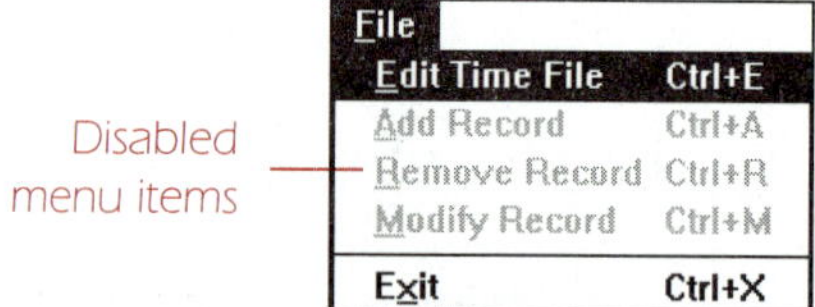

FIGURE 3.7 The File menu of TIME.MAK

DISPLAYING CHECK MARKS

Another way to restrict users from selecting invalid menu items is to use check marks. When a menu selection's Checked property is set to **True**, a check mark appears next to the item. At run time, clicking on the item toggles on or off the display of the check mark. In code, you can test if a menu item is selected the following way:

```
Sub PrtStdv (Sample_arr() As Single)

 ' Print standard deviation

 std = ArrStdv(Sample_arr())

 If CompStdv.Checked = True Then
   picture1.Print "  Stdv.: "; std
 End If

End Sub
```

FIGURE 3.8 The Statistics menu of STAT.MAK

The Statistics menu of STAT.MAK uses check marks to set defaults at run time. Figure 3.8 shows how the menu appears. When the File Compute option is selected, the program calculates statistics for each menu item that has a check mark.

USING MENU CONTROL ARRAYS

The Edit menu of TEXT.MAK uses a *menu control array* to implement the Cut, Copy and Paste commands. At run time, the program uses the index of the control array to determine which operation must be performed.

To Create a Menu Control Array

1. Set the Index property of each menu item.
2. The Index of the first control should be set to 0.
3. Assign the same name to each control in the array.

Example

```
Const CUT_TEXT = 0: Const COPY_TEXT = 1
Const PASTE_TEXT = 2

Select Case index

  Case CUT_TEXT

    Clipboard.Clear
    Clipboard.SetText text1.SelText

    ' Erase text from document after copying
    ' it to Clipboard

    text1.SelText = ""

  Case COPY_TEXT

    Clipboard.Clear
    Clipboard.SetText text1.SelText

  Case PASTE_TEXT

    text1.SelText = Clipboard.GetText()

End Select
```

ADDING MENU ITEMS AT RUN TIME

A program also can add items to a menu at run time. To accomplish this, you use the Menu Design window to create a menu control array.

To Add Menu Items at Run time

1. Use a control array to store the names of the menu items.
2. Set the Visible property of the menu controls that will be added to **False**.
3. At run time, set the Visible property of each new menu item to **True**.

After defining the menu control array, you add items to the menu by testing the Index property. For example:

```
Sub Option_List_Click (index As Integer)

 ' Display full menu

 If index = 2 Then
   Option_List(3).Visible = True
   Option_List(4).Visible = True
 End If

End Sub
```

CREATING POP-UP MENUS

Drop-down menus are elegant providing that the application has enough menu choices to justify their use. In some instances, it is easier to select a menu control from a pop-up menu since the menu does not have to be opened to make a selection.

To create a pop-up menu, each menu definition is entered into the Menu Design window. Several guidelines must be observed when created pop-up menus:

- The Caption property of the first menu item is left blank.
- Subsequent menu definitions are indented one level.
- The **PopupMenu** method is used to display the menu.

The **PopupMenu** method invokes a pop-up menu. Typically, the call to **PopupMenu** is placed in a form's MouseDown procedure. Since the MouseDown procedure returns the status of the mouse, you use this procedure to display the menu when a particular mouse event occurs. The following code, for example, shows how to invoke a pop-up menu when the right mouse button is pressed:

```
Sub Form_MouseDown (button As Integer, Shift As
                      ⇨ Integer, x As Single, y As Single)

 ' Show pop-up menu using definitions from menu design
 ' window

 Const RBUTTON = 2

 x = 2050: y = 1400
```

```
  If button = RBUTTON Then
    PopupMenu popup1, 0, x, y
  End If

End Sub
```

In the preceding example, <popup1> is a reference to a menu control defined in the Menu Design window. This menu item must have at least one submenu.

Alternatively, you can display a pop-up menu when a program starts. By including the call to **PopupMenu** in the Form_Load procedure, the menu is automatically available when you run the program.

Exercise: Creating a Drop-down Menu

1. Create a new project by selecting the New Project command from the File menu.
2. Click on the Menu Design icon (or select the Menu Design command from the Window menu)
3. In the Caption input box of the Menu Design window, type **&File**.
4. In the Name input box, type **mnuFileMenu**.
5. Click on Next.
6. Click the right arrow button to indent the next menu definition.
7. In the Caption input box, type **Compute &Loan**.
8. In the Name input box, type **mnuLoan**.
9. From the Shortcut drop-down list, assign the Ctrl+L shortcut key to this menu item.
10. Click on Next.
11. Finish entering the definitions listed below.

Caption	**Name**	**Indented**	**Shortcut Key**
&Print Loan	mnuPrint	1 level	Ctrl+P
-	mnuSeparator	1 level	
E&xit	mnuExit	1 level	Ctrl+X
&About	mnuAbout	No Indent	

NOTE: To remove the indentation from the last menu item, use the left arrow button.

12. When you are done, click on OK to save the menu.

If you receive an error at this point, it is probably because you entered a definition wrong. Figure 3.9 shows how the Menu Design window should appear when you are finished. Notice that even the definition for the separator bar must be indented.

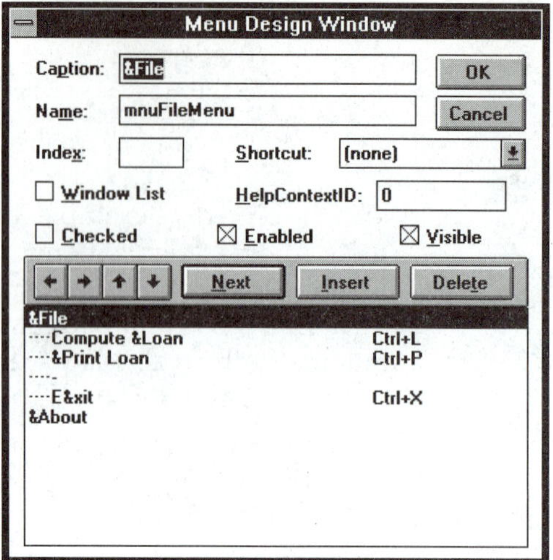

FIGURE 3.9 Controls for the drop-down menu Exercise

In order to use the menu, each control must be linked to an event procedure. The following steps outline how this is done:

1. Select File Compute Loan from the menu you just created.
2. In the mnuLoan_Click procedure, enter the following code:

```
' Read principal, interest and term of loan

principal = loanprinc.Text
periods = loanper.Text
interest = loaninter.Text

' Compute loan payments

interest = interest / 12
temp = (1 + interest) ^ (periods * -1)
payments = principal * interest / (1 - temp)

loanpmt.Caption = Format(payments, "$#####0.0#")
```

3. From the Visual Basic Window menu, choose Project.
4. In the Project Window, click on the View Form button.
5. Select File Print Loan from the user-defined menu.
6. Enter the following code:

```
Form1.PrintForm
```

7. Select Project from the Visual Basic Window menu.
8. In the Project Window, click on the View Form button.
9. Select File Exit from the user-defined menu (not from Visual Basic!).
10. Put an **End** statement in this procedure.

11. Using the steps previously outlined, enter the following code in the mnuAbout procedure:

```
' Show program credits dialog

newline = Chr(13) + Chr(10)

line1 = newline
line2 = Space(1) + "Sample Menu" + newline + newline
line3 = Space(5) + "Program" + newline

message = line1 + line2 + line3

MsgBox message, 0, "ABOUT"
```

The menu is now complete. Since it references objects that have not been created yet, these controls must be drawn on the form before the program will run. To do this:

1. Draw the following controls on the form. Figure 3.10 shows where each object should be placed.

Control Name	Property	Value
label1	Caption	Principal:
label2	Caption	Periods:
label3	Caption	Interest:
label4	Caption	Payments:
label5	BorderStyle	1 - Fixed Single
text1	Text	null string
text2	Text	null string
text3	Text	null string

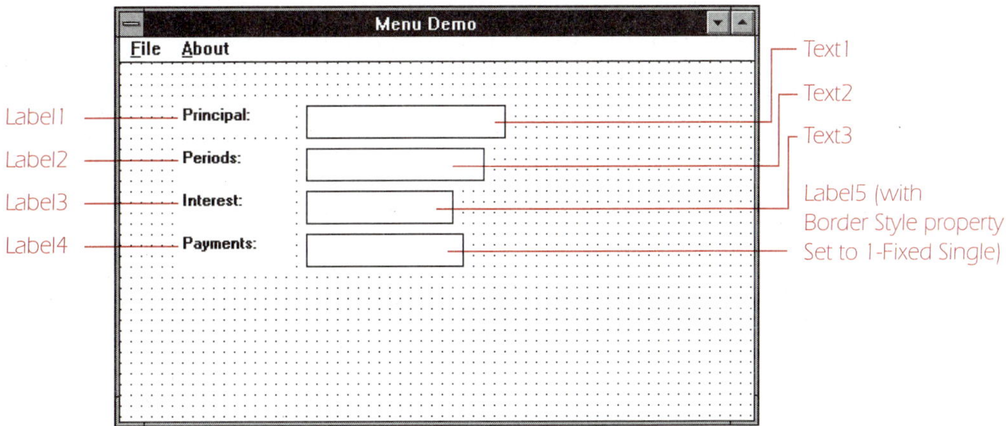

FIGURE 3.10 Other controls for the menu exercise

2. Change the default settings of the following objects:

text1	Name	loanprinc
text2	Name	loanper
text3	Name	loaninter
label5	Name	loanpmt
label5	Caption	null string
Form1	Caption	Menu Demo

3. Save the project and run it.

Once the form is completed, you can test the menu by computing a loan. To do this:

1. In the loanprinc text box, type `10000`.
2. In the loanper text box, type `48`.
3. In the loanint text box, type `.07`.
4. Select File Compute Loan.
   The payments ($239.46) should appear in the loanpmt label control.
5. Print the loan by selecting File Print Loan.
   Since the program contains no error checking, be sure to check your printer connection first.
6. After printing the loan, click on About and Select OK to continue.
7. Choose File Exit from the menu to quit.

SUMMARY

The Menu Design window allows you to create enhanced menus in Visual Basic. You use the Menu Design window to create shortcut and access keys, separator bars, check marks, menu control arrays and submenus. At run time, you can also enable/disable menus items, add menu selections and display pop-up menus.

REVIEW QUESTIONS

1. What is the difference between a shortcut key and an access key?
2. How do you define a shortcut key and an access key?
3. To enable or disable a menu item, what property do you set?
4. How can you add items to a menu at run time?
5. To define a menu control array, what must you do?
6. How can you display a pop-up menu?
7. What would happen if you neglected to add a **Show** statement in the Form_Load procedure before the call to **PopupMenu**?
8. Code a procedure to display a floating pop-up menu. The menu should appear on the form only when a Click event occurs.

CLASS PROJECTS

1. Using the Menu Design window, create a drop-down menu called System with the following menu items:

   Display **S**ystem Information
   Change System **D**ate
   Change System **T**ime
   (menu separator)
   Exit

HINT: Chapters 17 and 18 (in Part III The Library) show how to get system information and change the date and time in an application.

   Use a standard naming process for each menu item to distinguish menu controls from other controls:

   e.g., `mnuSysInfo`

2. Add a first level menu item to the above menu called About. Call this menu control mnuAbout. Then use **MsgBox** in the mnuAbout_Click procedure to display a program credits dialog.

HINT: Use Chr$(13) + Chr$(10) to define a new line character.

4 USING DIALOG BOXES

A *custom control* is a Visual Basic extension file that has an associated icon in the Toolbox. These files have a .VBX file extension. The *common dialog* control, shown in Figure 4.1, is a custom control that displays one of five common dialogs: Open, Save As, Color, Font and Print. In Chapter 1, you learned how to create simple dialogs using text boxes, labels and other similar controls. In this chapter, you will learn how to display common dialogs and how to create more sophisticated interfaces using Visual Basic's file controls.

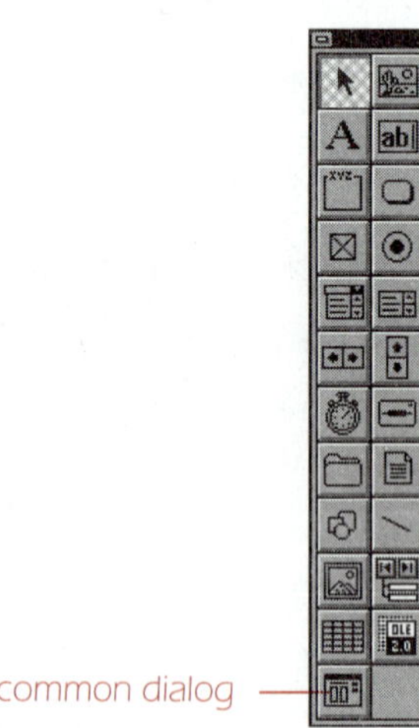

FIGURE 4.1 The common dialog custom control

4.1 DISPLAYING COMMON DIALOGS

Common dialogs are easy to display and customize. By setting a few simple properties, you tap into the power of these professionally designed dialogs. In some cases, you must write code to complete an operation. For example, the Print dialog does not actually print a document. It merely returns the print options you select.

When the Action property of the common dialog control is set to 1, Visual Basic displays the Open dialog box (see Figure 4.2). This dialog searches directories, changes paths and reads files into memory.

The Filter property of the common dialog control determines which files appear in the file list. To set the Filter property, you use the following syntax:

```
[formname.]commdialog.Filter[=description|filter1|...]
```

Example

```
Sub cmdOpen_Click ()

 ' Show Open dialog box

 Const OPENFILE = 1

 On Error GoTo open_err

 CMDialog1.DialogTitle = "Open File"

 description1 = "All Files(*.*)"
 filter1 = "*.*"
 description2 = "Text Files(*.txt)"
 filter2 = "*.txt"

 CMDialog1.Filter = description1 + "|" + filter1 +
             ⇨ "|" + description2 + "|" + filter2
 CMDialog1.Action = OPENFILE
 label1.Caption = CMDialog1.Filename

open_err:

 ' Exit sub if user selected Cancel button

 Exit Sub

End Sub
```

NOTE: When you distribute an application that uses the common dialog control, you must install the CMDIALOG.VBX file in the WINDOWS\SYSTEM directory of the target drive.

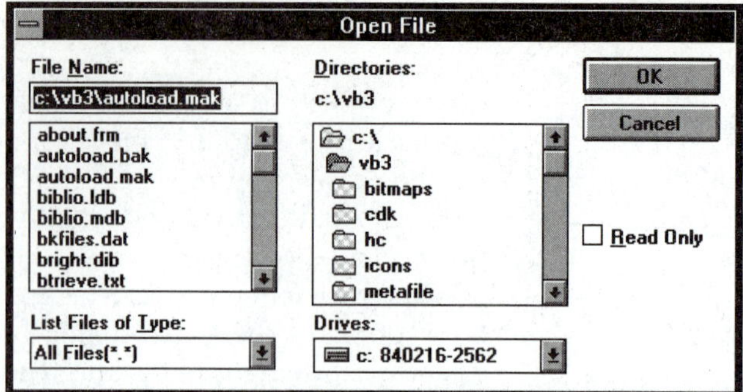

FIGURE 4.2 The Open common dialog

DISPLAYING A FILE SAVE AS DIALOG BOX

When the common dialog Action property is set to 2, Visual Basic shows the Save As dialog box. The following procedure demonstrates how it can be applied:

```
Sub cmdSave_Click ()

 ' Show Save As dialog box

 Const SAVE_AS = 2

 On Error GoTo save_err

 CMDialog1.DialogTitle = "Save As"

 description1 = "All Files(*.*)"
 filter1 = "*.*"
 description2 = "Text Files(*.txt)"
 filter2 = "*.txt"
```

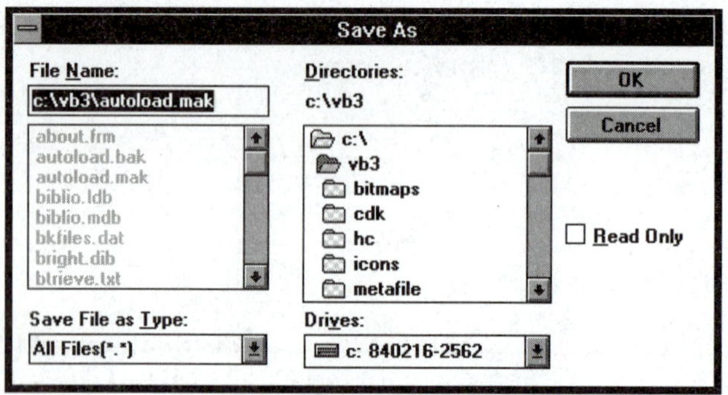

FIGURE 4.3 The Save As common dialog

```
 CMDialog1.Filter = description1 + "|" + filter1 +
              ⇨ "|" + description2 + "|" + filter2
 CMDialog1.Action = SAVE_AS
 label1.Caption = CMDialog1.Filename

save_err:

 ' Exit procedure if user selects Cancel button

 Exit Sub

End Sub
```

Notice that the code used to display this dialog is virtually the same as the code needed to display the Open dialog. Figure 4.3 shows how the Save As dialog appears at run time.

DISPLAYING A COLOR PALETTE

When the Action property of the common dialog is set to 3, Visual Basic displays the Color dialog that sets program colors at run time. When the Flags property is set to 3, Visual Basic displays the full dialog box (which allows you to define your own custom colors). By default, this option is disabled until you choose the Define Custom Colors... button from the Color dialog.

The following code shows how to initialize the Color dialog box. Notice that error checking is included so the form will not be set to black if the Cancel button is selected:

```
Sub cmdColor_Click ()

 ' Show Color dialog box

 On Error GoTo setcolor_err

 Const COLOR_DIALOG = 3
 Const SHOW_CUSTCOLOR = 3

 CMDialog1.CancelError = True
 CMDialog1.Flags = SHOW_CUSTCOLOR
 CMDialog1.Action = COLOR_DIALOG

 ' Set new background color

 Form1.BackColor = CMDialog1.Color
 label1.BackColor = CMDialog1.Color
```

```
setcolor_err:

 ' User selected Cancel - exit sub to prevent
 ' background from being set to black

 Exit Sub

End Sub
```

DISPLAYING A FONTS DIALOG BOX

When the common dialog Action property is set to 4, the Font dialog appears (see Figure 4.4). The CF_BOTH constant causes Visual Basic to display both the printer and screen fonts.

The following example shows how to display the Font dialog:

```
Sub cmdFont_Click ()

 ' Show Font dialog box

 On Error GoTo fontset_err:

 Const FONTS_DIALOG = 4
 Const CF_BOTH = &H3&

 CMDialog1.CancelError = True
 CMDialog1.Flags = CF_BOTH
 CMDialog1.Action = FONTS_DIALOG

 label1.FontName = CMDialog1.FontName
 label1.Caption = CMDialog1.FontName

fontset_err:
```

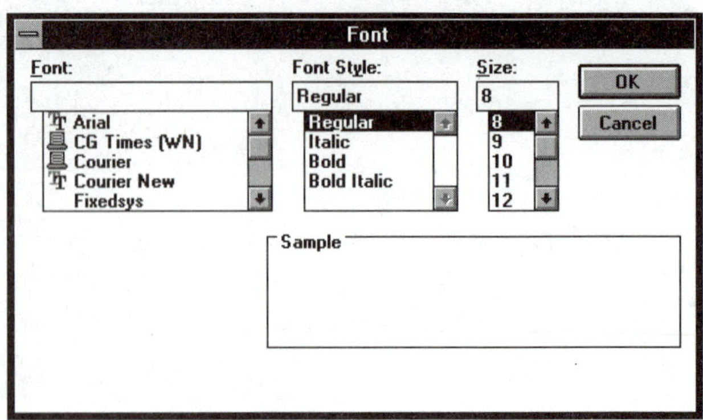

FIGURE 4.4 The Font common dialog

```
  ' Exit procedure if user selects Cancel button

  Exit Sub

End Sub
```

In the preceding example, the CF_BOTH constant is set to the hexadecimal code &H3&. By using constants this way, your applications will be easier to read and maintain.

NOTE: CONSTANT.TXT contains a list of constant definitions you can use in a program. Since this file is big, you will probably want to copy blocks from it rather than including the entire file in a project.

DISPLAYING A PRINT DIALOG BOX

When the common dialog Action property is set to 4, Visual Basic displays the Print dialog box. Notice that the Min and Max properties are used to control the print range. Figure 4.5 shows how the dialog appears at run time.

The following example shows how to use the Print dialog box.

```
Sub cmdPrint_Click ()

  ' Show Print dialog box

  On Error GoTo print_err:

  CMDialog1.Min = 0          ' Minimum pages
  CMDialog1.Max = 100        ' Maximum pages

  Const PRINT_DIALOG = 5
```

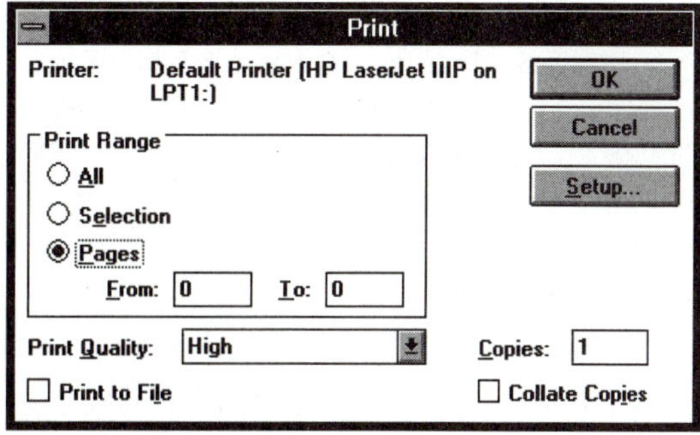

FIGURE 4.5 The Print common dialog

```
    CMDialog1.CancelError = True
    Copies = CMDialog1.Copies
    CMDialog1.Action = PRINT_DIALOG

    If CMDialog1.FromPage > CMDialog1.ToPage Then
     MsgBox "Invalid print range", 0, "Print Error"
     Exit Sub
    End If

    label1.Caption = "Print pages: " +
                   ⇨ Str(CMDialog1.FromPage) + " to " +
                   ⇨ Str(CMDialog1.ToPage)

print_err:

    ' Exit procedure if user selects Cancel button

    Exit Sub

End Sub
```

4.2 USING FILE CONTROLS

The *file controls* of Visual Basic create custom dialog boxes that interact with DOS. Figure 4.6 shows what these controls look like in the Toolbox. In many cases, the Open and File Save common dialogs can be used to perform the same operations easier. When a particular operation is beyond the capabilities of the common dialog control, however, you can create your own custom dialogs.

THE FILE LIST BOX CONTROL

The *file list box* control shows a list of files in the current directory (or the directory indicated by the last **ChDir** statement). The Pattern property of the file list box control determines which files appear in the list. By default, all files in the current directory appear. For example, if the Pattern property is set to *.MAK, Visual Basic displays all files in the current directory ending with .MAK.

To Specify a File Pattern

- Assign the file specification to the Pattern property of the file list box control:

```
file1.Pattern = "*.MAK"
```

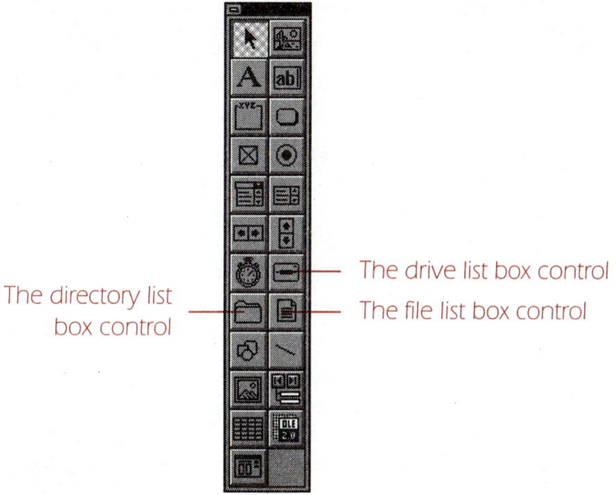

FIGURE 4.6 File controls in Visual Basic

THE DIRECTORY LIST BOX CONTROL

The *directory list box* control displays a list of files on the current drive (see Figure 4.7). Although you can select a directory from the list at run time, no path change occurs at the DOS level unless a **ChDir** statement appears in code like this:

```
Sub Dir1_Change ()

 ChDir dir1.Path

End Sub
```

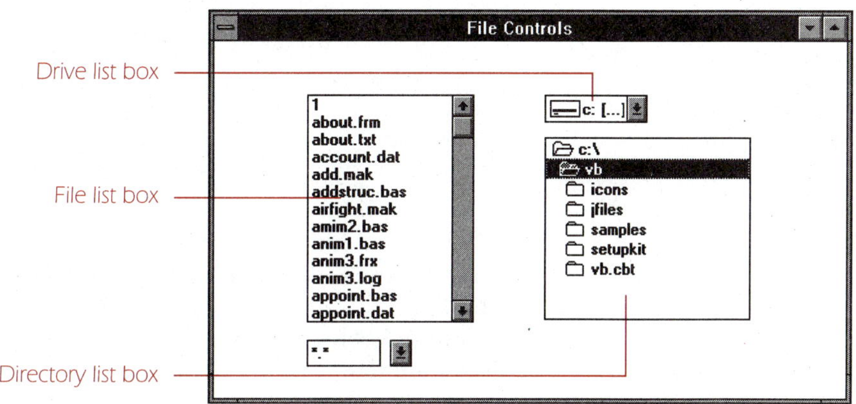

FIGURE 4.7 File controls on a form

You can also synchronize file controls so they work together. The following example shows how to display a list of files from the directory indicated by a directory list box control:

```
Sub Dir1_Change ()

 ' Display files on current drive

 file1.Path = dir1.Path
 ChDir dir1.Path

End Sub
```

CHANGING THE CURRENT DRIVE

The *drive list box* control sets the current drive at run time. When an item is selected from a drive list box, a Change event occurs. In code, you can switch the current drive the following way:

```
Sub Drive1_Change ()

 ' Set new path

 ChDrive drive1.Drive
 dir1.Path = drive1.Drive

End Sub
```

In the preceding example, the Path property of dir1 is set to the Drive property of drive1. This assignment causes Visual Basic to update the directory list so that it reflects the drive change.

Visual Basic automatically reads all the valid drives on a system into the drive list box control. You can also indicate which drive appears at the top of the list by making this assignment:

```
drive1.Drive = "C:\"
```

4.3 A SAMPLE FILE CONTROLS APPLICATION

The BKFILES.MAK application, shown in Figure 4.8, demonstrates how to use file controls. The source code for this example is contained on the program disk.

BKFILES.MAK is a backup utility program. It copies a list of files from one drive to another. To accomplish this, the program uses the following library routines:

Fileschanged	Returns a list of files recently updated in a directory.
Copylist	Copies a list of files and uses bar graph to shows progress of operation.

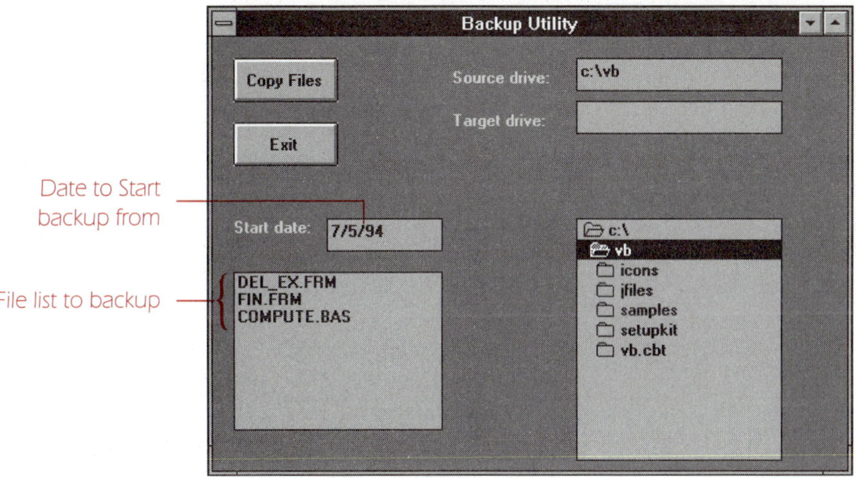

FIGURE 4.8 The backup utility (BKFILES.MAK)

The Form_Load procedure sets the default drive and calls Show_files to display a list of files recently updated in the current directory. <Startdate> indicates when the files should be copied from. By default, the program displays files modified on the current date. At run time, you can specify a different date by entering it in the Start date box.

```
Dim path As String
Dim filespec As String
Dim target As String
Dim startdate As String
Dim bdate As String


Sub Form_Load ()

 ' Backup Utility

 sourcedrive.Text = dir1.Path
 begindate.Text = Date
 startdate = Date

 Call Show_files

End Sub
```

```
Sub Show_files ()

 ' Show files recently updated

 filespec = "*.*"

 startdate = begindate.Text

 Call Fileschanged(path, filespec, list1, bdate)

End Sub
```

The directory list box control (dir1) indicates the source directory to use for the file transfer. When the program loads, dir1 displays a list of files that have changed since <startdate>. You can override this default by choosing another directory in the directory list box. To change directories, the program calls Dir1_Change:

```
Sub Dir1_Change ()

 ' Change directory

 ChDir (dir1.Path)
 path = dir1.Path
 sourcedrive.Text = dir1.Path

 filespec = "*.*"

 bdate = begindate.Text

 Call Fileschanged(path, filespec, list1, bdate)

End Sub
```

At run time, when you select the Copy button, the cmdCopy_Click procedure executes. Before copying files, the program prompts you to insert a disk. If no target path is specified, files are automatically copied to the A:\ drive:

```
Sub cmdCopy_Click ()

 ' Copy recently updated files

 Dim filespec As String, fileno As Integer
 Dim filename As String, total_files As Integer
 Dim source As String

 fileno = 1
 filename = "BKFiles.Dat"
```

```
total_files = list1.ListCount
sourcedrive.Text = dir1.Path

response = MsgBox("Is disk drive ready", 33, "Backup
            ⇨ Utility")

source = sourcedrive.Text
target = targetdrive.Text

If target = "" Then
 target = "A:\"
End If

If response = 1 Then
 If CVDate(begindate.Text) <> Date Then
   startdate = begindate.Text
   Call Fileschanged(path, filespec, list1, bdate)
   total_files = list1.ListCount
 End If
  retval = Copylist(Form1, fileno, filename, source,
            ⇨ target, total_files)
End If

End Sub
```

To copy the files, BKFILES.MAK calls the library function Copylist. This function copies the files and uses a bar graph to show progress of the operation. Figure 4.9 shows how the bar graph looks during a copy.

Percentage of files copied

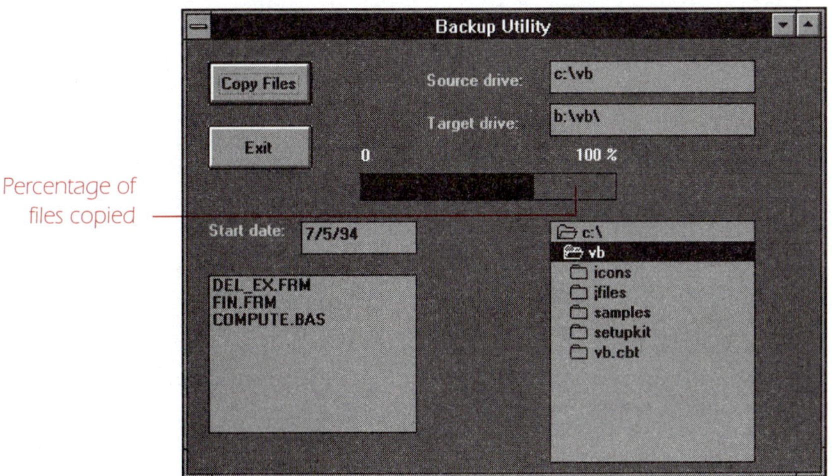

FIGURE 4.9 The backup utility during a copy

Exercise: Displaying a Color Dialog

1. From the File menu, choose New Project.
2. Using the Toolbox, draw a command button and the common dialog control on a form. Set their properties as follows:

Control	Property	Value
common dialog	CancelError	True
command1	Caption	Color
command1	Name	cmdColor

3. Insert the following code in the cmdColor procedure:

```
Const COLOR_DIALOG = 3

On Error GoTo setcolor_err

' Show Color dialog box

CMDialog1.Action = COLOR_DIALOG

' Set new background color

Form1.BackColor = CMDialog1.Color

setcolor_err:

' Error routine

Exit Sub
```

4. Save the program and run it.
5. Click on the Color button.
6. From the Color dialog, select a color.
7. Click on OK. The background color of the form should change to the color you specified.
8. Select the Color button again.
9. Click on Define Custom Colors... An expanded dialog will appear. Click inside the custom colors box (see Figure 4.10). Notice Visual Basic shows the mixture of **RGB** colors required to produce the color.
10. Choose the Cancel button.

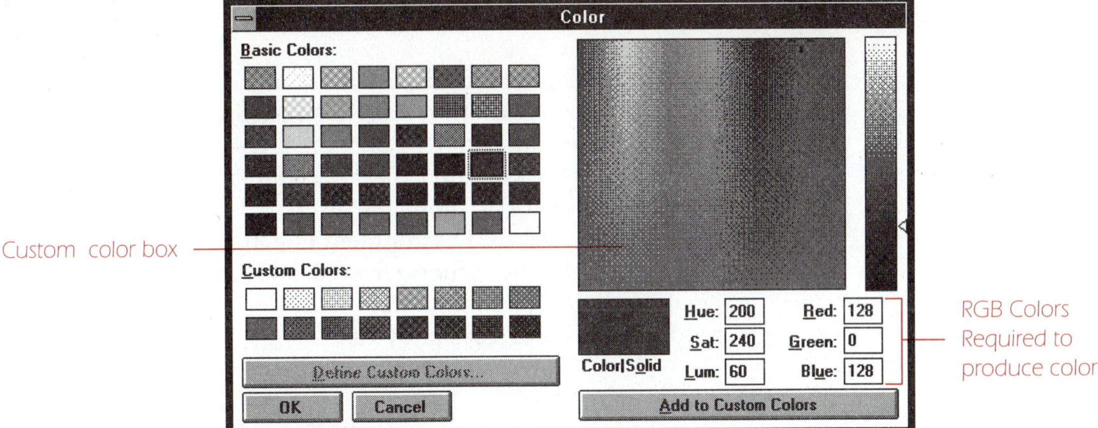

FIGURE 4.10 The expanded Color dialog

SUMMARY

In this chapter, you learned how to display the Open, Save As, Color, Font and Print common dialogs. You have also learned how to use file controls and how to apply library functions to create your own custom dialogs.

REVIEW QUESTIONS

1. What is a custom control?
2. What kinds of dialogs can you display with the common dialog custom control?
3. What property do you set to display a common dialog? Give some examples.
4. Code a routine to display an Open dialog.
5. What property activates/deactivates error checking in common dialogs?
6. How can you display an expanded color dialog?
7. What are file controls? Give some examples.
8. What file control allows you to display a list of files in a directory?
9. Code a routine to display a list of files that end with a .FRM file extension.
10. How can you change the current directory?
11. What library routines allow you to copy files and display a list of recently updated files in a directory? To use these procedures, what modules must you include in a project?

NOTE: Part III, The Library, contains the necessary module listings for each function of the library.

CLASS PROJECTS

1. Create a dialog box to display a list of fonts available for the currently installed screen and printer devices (use the library routine Fontlist—see Part III, Screen and Printer Functions).
2. Using the Open common dialog, create a pick list of .EXE files in the Windows directory. Allow the user to launch each application using Runapp (see Part III, Environment Functions).
3. Using the Filelist function covered in Part III, Environment Functions, create a dialog to show a list of files in a directory, their dates of last modifications and sizes in bytes.

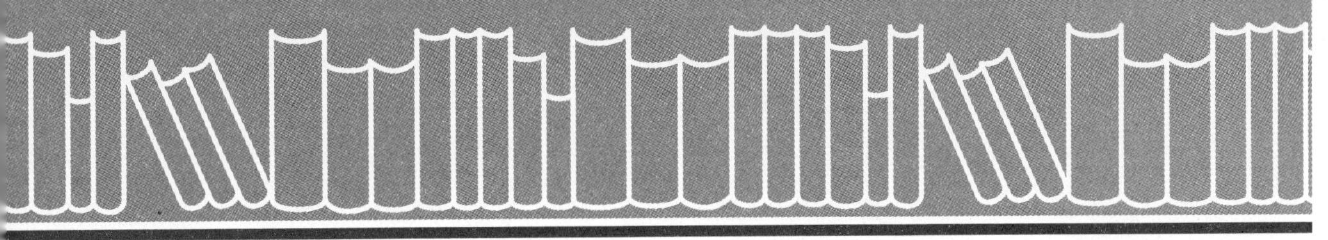

PART II

POWER PROGRAMMING

In this section, you will learn how to generate even more powerful applications using the power features of Visual Basic. After reading this section, you should be able to manage databases, save and restore grids, incorporate memos in applications, use DDE and OLE, produce charts and graphs, design reports, handle errors, perform animation, make use of custom controls and third party extensions, call dynamic link libraries (DLLs), and install programs.

5 ERROR HANDLING AND DEBUGGING

In Visual Basic, there are two ways you can deal with errors in an application. You can debug a program by monitoring its source code or you can write error handlers to trap bugs. A skillful programmer must be knowledgeable of both methods. In this chapter, you will learn how to effectively deal with errors, both before and after they occur.

5.1 DEBUGGING APPLICATIONS

Visual Basic provides several tools that debug applications. These tools include breakpoints, watch expressions, single stepping, procedure stepping, monitoring the values of variables and properties and test executing code blocks.

In most cases, to use the debugger, you must first be in break mode. To do this, select Break from the Debug menu or use the toolbar. Alternatively, you can press Control Break, setup a watch expression, or define a breakpoint to activate the debugger.

USING THE TOOLBAR TO ACCESS THE DEBUGGER

The toolbar in Visual Basic provides quick access to the debugger's tools. Figure 5.1 shows what these tools are. Most of the debugging options are available only after a program is in break mode. To enter break mode from the toolbar, select the Break button.

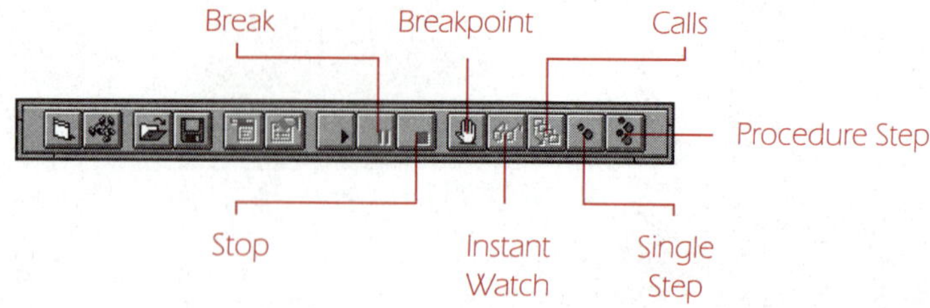

FIGURE 5.1 Debugging options on the toolbar

ERRORS THE DEBUGGER CAN TRAP

Once an application is compiled, Visual Basic traps *syntax errors*. Some errors, however, cannot be detected until a program is run (*run time errors*). This situation occurs when code is correct in terms of syntax, but causes an invalid operation at run time. For example, if you inadvertently assign the contents of a text box to an integer variable, the error will not be apparent until run time.

Logic errors are produced from code that executes without causing a compilation or run time error, but still yields invalid results. These types of errors or *bugs* can occur for any number of reasons, including forgetting to initialize a variable, using an incorrect formula, or failing to observe the correct order of mathematical precedence.

Logic errors usually are isolated and corrected using the debugger. However, since only the programmer knows the internal logic of an application, the debugger merely points out possible sources of errors. Ultimately, it is up to you to interpret what it finds and determine how to resolve problems.

THE DEBUG WINDOW

The *Debug window* is a multipurpose tool for evaluating and testing source code. It appears in the lower right corner of the screen when a program enters break mode.

Figure 5.2 shows what it looks like before a watch expression is entered. Inside the window, you type code in the *Immediate pane*. Valid expressions include assignments, procedure calls and **Print** methods.

Once a watch expression has been defined, the Debug window divides into two parts, adding the *Watch pane* on top that displays the results of expressions being monitored.

To setup a watch expression, either at design time or while a program is in debug mode, select the Add Watch option from the Debug menu. A dialog box will appear. Inside it, enter the expression you wish to evaluate and then the scope of the expression.

The scope can be local to a procedure, available throughout a form, or global throughout an application. The debugger can also be activated conditionally. The following options are available:

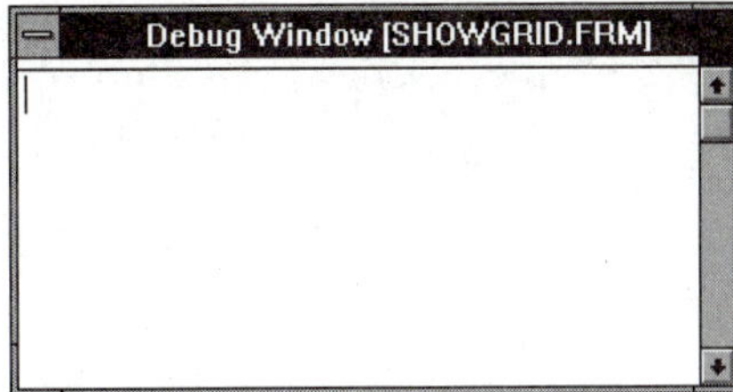

FIGURE 5.2 The Debug window (with no watch expression set)

- Watch Expressions—default (manually enter break mode)
- Break when Expression is **True**
- Break when Expression has Changed

SAVING DEBUGGING CODE

Visual Basic also permits you to save the debugging information in a program. To do this, precede each **Print** method you wish to monitor with the **Debug** object. The following procedure shows how this can be done:

```
Sub AddRec_Click

 ' Add new record to file

 Put #fileno, cur_rec, recvar
 Debug.Print "One record added."

End Sub
```

Once the **Debug** object is used, the output appears in the Instant pane. Although the debugging information has no effect on the .EXE file, it is considered good practice to remove this code before building the executable program.

SETTING BREAKPOINTS

Breakpoints set at design time to enter Break mode are particularly useful when you need to analyze a set of code but don't want to trace an entire application. When Visual Basic encounters a breakpoint, execution stops at the line immediately preceding it. From there, other debugging tools can be used to evaluate a specific part of the program.

To set a breakpoint, move the cursor to the statement following the one where the program should pause and press the F9 key. You can also set a breakpoint using the toolbar or Debug menu's Breakpoint command. Using either method, Visual Basic highlights the line of code at the breakpoint. Pressing F9 again while on the same line removes the breakpoint.

Another way to pause execution is to use the **Stop** statement. Unlike breakpoints, however, **Stop** statements are not cleared at the end of the session.

SINGLE STEPPING & PROCEDURE STEPPING

The Single Step command from the Debug menu lets you trace the flow of logic throughout a program. This feature allows you to observe the behavior of a program and actually step inside it to see how it works. *Single stepping* comes in handy when evaluating conditional expressions. It lets you see in slow motion whether certain statements are executing and when they are being performed.

To Single Step

- In break mode, select the Single Step command from the Debug menu or Press F8. Alternately, you can select the same option from the toolbar

Procedure stepping is similar to single stepping except that it continues to evaluate the current routine when a call is made rather than transferring control to other procedures. Technically speaking, a procedure step does not actually skip over another procedure. It simply executes it faster so the programmer is not burdened with the details of the operation. This technique is useful in many cases since a transfer of control to any other routine could mean a long delay before control passes back to the original **Sub** or **Function**.

To Procedure Step

- In break mode, select the Procedure Step command from the Debug menu or Press Shift-F8. Alternatively, choose the same option from the toolbar.

SETTING THE NEXT STATEMENT TO BE EXECUTED

Sometimes a problem is related to other problems and cannot be fixed until the programmer knows all the causes. In this case, you can step over the lines of code that may be causing the error by setting the next statement to be executed. To do this:

1. Move the cursor to the line of code where the program will resume (assuming the application is already in Break mode).
2. Select Set Next Statement from the Debug menu.
3. Choose one of the following commands:

    Run/Continue
    Single Step
    Procedure Step

THE CALLS DIALOG BOX

This option lets you see what procedures are executing and when they are being performed. Figure 5.3 shows the Calls dialog box.

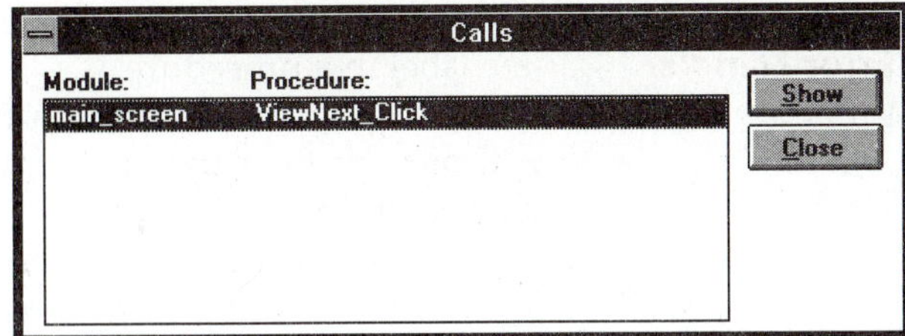

FIGURE 5.3 The Calls dialog box

The left side of the window shows the names of the files (or modules) that contain each procedure. The Calls dialog box lists the procedures with the most current one on top.

To Display the Calls Dialog Box

1. Select the Break option from the toolbar to activate the debugger.
2. Click on the Calls button on the toolbar or select the Calls command from the Debug menu or press Ctrl-L.

This Calls dialog is particularly useful when testing a program's code while subroutines are being performed. If you have ever forgotten to change the name of a procedure after renaming its associated control on a form, you know Visual Basic shows no mercy to these kinds of careless mistakes. If an object created with the Toolbox references an empty procedure at run time, no error will result and the wrong function will be called. In this case, the Calls dialog box can save hours of debugging time.

THE RIGHT APPROACH

No one debugging tool by itself holds the answer. In any given situation, the ideal approach will depend on the specifics of the problem. Moreover, different techniques are often combined to achieve a greater understanding of the application.

Tips

- Instead of using the Print method to display output in the Instant pane, use a question mark for shorthand.
- The Debug window retains a list of commands in the order in which they were typed. By clicking on one and pressing Enter, you can repeat the same assignment, query or procedure call without having to retype the expression.

5.2 ERROR TRAPPING

Instead of handling errors after they have occurred, you can design a program to test for errors before they happen by setting error checks. An *error handler* is a special part of a program that reports the status of an application and enables it to recover from a run time error.

To Write an Error Handler

1. Use the **On Error Goto** statements to branch control to a line number or line label in a procedure.
2. Precede the line label with an **Exit Sub** or **Exit Function** statement. This will prevent the program from executing the error routine when a run time error does not occur.
3. In the error handler, place the statements that will report the problem (optional) and the code that will inform the program how to respond if an error occurs:

Example

```
Sub FindRec ()

  On Error Goto Err_Handler
    .            .            .
    .            .            .

  Exit Sub

Err_Handler:

  ' Error routine

  If Err = 52 Then
     MsgBox "File not open", 0, "Run Time Error"
  Else
     MsgBox Error, 0, "Run Time Error"
  End If

  Resume Next

End Sub
```

NOTE: Although not usually recommended for general purposes, the Goto statement must be used here to transfer control to the error routine. However, a line label can be used instead of a line number and this will make your programs easier to read.

In the preceding example, the **MsgBox** function reports the problem and the **Error** statement returns the error message. The **Resume Next** statement then informs the program which line of code to execute. When Visual Basic encounters this statement, control passes back to the line following the error. Other possibilities include:

Resume	Control passes back to the statement that caused the error (use this option only if the error routine takes corrective action—e.g., open a file that is not already open).
Exit Function **Exit Sub**	Terminates the current procedure and returns control to the calling routine.

Error Err Generates a run time error (used to simulate errors for debugging purposes).

It is also possible to prevent a program from crashing when a run time error occurs without writing an error handler. By using **On Error Resume Next**, an application can regain control after the statement that caused the error. Through the use of the **Err** statement, the value of the most recently occurring error can be tested. However, if you do this, assign the value of **Err** to a variable or it may be lost when another **Resume Next** is executed.

REDEFINING ERROR MESSAGES

Sometimes an error message can be obscure and hard to understand. This is because Visual Basic uses the same messages for different errors. An invalid division operation, for example, can produce a Division by zero, Overflow or an Illegal function call message.

The **Err** statement returns the error number of an error. The Visual Basic language reference contains a listing of each possible error that can occur. You can use the **Err** statement to create your own custom error messages:

```
Endmonth_err:

 ' Error routine

 If Err = 13 Then
   MsgBox "Unable to convert date...", 0,"Run Time
        ⇨ Error"
 ElseIf Err = 461 Then
   MsgBox "Invalid date format...", 0, "Run Time
        ⇨ Error"
 Else
   MsgBox Error, 0, "Run Time Error"
 End If

 Endmonth_err = Err

 Exit Function

End Function
```

Notice that the error routine returns an error number or value that the program can use later to determine what action it should take next. If no error occurs, the function returns 0.

Another point of interest in the previous example is that if an unanticipated error occurs, the **Else** path traps it using the general message returned from Visual Basic. This ensures that the program will always have a fail-safe way of handling each problem.

DETERMINING WHERE AN ERROR OCCURRED

The easiest way to determine which procedure caused an error is to include the name of the procedure in the error message. The following code fragment demonstrates how this can be done:

```
MsgBox Error, 0, "Savefile"
```

Caution must be taken, however, since Visual Basic automatically transfers control to other procedures in the call list if the current routine does not contain an error handler or if an active error routine causes another run time error. To prevent this from happening, write a procedure that handles all error checking in one part of the program.

CENTRALIZING ERROR CHECKING

Creating a centralized error handler eliminates repetitive code and simplifies tracing a program's execution. One procedure in a centralized error handle is inherently more efficient than of repeating the same error traps in different parts of an application.

To create a centralized error handler, place the error checks in a code module. These files have a .BAS file extension. Once the routine is created, the code module is accessible from any part of the program and can be included in other projects.

FILECHK.BAS provides centralized error checking for file I/O operations. To include it in an application, simply add it to the current project. Subsequently, the error handler can be activated by placing a call to the Validate function.

```
Function Validate (operation As Integer, file_no As
      ⇨ Integer, filename As String, drive As String)

 ' Validate file operation - return 0 if successful,
 ' error number if not
 '
 ' FILE OPERATIONS:
 '
 ' OPEN_ERR - checks if file is open
 ' EXIST_ERR - checks if file exists
 ' ACCESS_ERR - checks if file is locked
 ' DRIVE_ERR - attempts to change drives (report
 ' error if unsuccessful)

 Const OPEN_ERR = 1
 Const EXIST_ERR = 2
 Const ACCESS_ERR = 3
 Const DRIVE_ERR = 4
```

```
On Error GoTo report_err

retval = 0

' Test if the current operation is valid - If run
' time error occurs, operation is not valid
' so branch to error routine

Select Case operation

   Case OPEN_ERR
       filelength = LOF(fileno)
   Case EXIST_ERR
       filecreated = FileDateTime(filename)
   Case ACCESS_ERR
       Unlock file_no
       Lock file_no
   Case DRIVE_ERR
       ChDir drive

End Select

Validate = retval

Exit Function

report_err:

' Report error message and return error number

Select Case Err

 Case 52
   MsgBox "File not open", 0, "Run Time Error"
 Case 53
   MsgBox "File not available", 0, "Run Time Error"
 Case 76
   MsgBox "Path or drive unavailable", 0, "Run Time
        ⇨ Error"
 Case Else
   MsgBox Error, 0, "Run Time Error"
End Select

Validate = Err

Exit Function

End Function
```

DEACTIVATING ERROR HANDLING

Visual Basic automatically turns off error checking for a procedure when control is returned to the calling procedure. However, you can also deactivate it in a procedure by using On Error Goto 0. The error handler (if present) is never executed.

Exercise: Writing an Error Handler

1. From the File menu, choose New Project.
2. Draw a command button on the form.
3. In the Command1_Click procedure, type:

```
On Error GoTo Err_handler

' Compute current value of investment

interest = interest / 12
temp = (1 + interest) ^ (term * -1)
currentval = payments * (1 - temp) / interest

Exit Sub

Err_handler:

' Error routine

Select Case Err
  Case 6
   MsgBox "Variable not initialized or beyond
        ⇨ maximum value", 0, "Run Time Error"
  Case 11
   MsgBox "Division by zero error", 0, "Run Time
        ⇨ Error"
  Case Else
   MsgBox Error, 0, "Run Time Error"
End Select

Resume Next
```

4. Run the program.
5. Click on the command button. This should produce an error since the program contains no initialization code for the test expression.
6. Click on OK to close the message box.

SUMMARY

In this chapter, you learned how to debug applications and set error traps. You have also learned how to take preventative steps to avoid run time errors and how to create centralized error handlers.

REVIEW QUESTIONS

1. How can you activate the debugger?
2. What are the 3 types of errors that can occur in a program?
3. What is the purpose of the Immediate pane?
4. Which is better, single stepping or procedure stepping? When would you use each?
5. How can you save debugging code in an application?
6. What is the purpose of the Calls dialog box?
7. Create a new form and enter the following code in the Form_Load procedure:

   ```
   x = 2 * 2
   Form1.Print x
   ```

   Why doesn't this output appear on the form? What debugging tools can be used to locate the problem?
8. The following code fragment creates a run time error when <filename> does not exist:

   ```
   filedat = FileDateTime(filename)
   ```

   How can this be used to your advantage?
9. Write an error routine to prevent the preceding example from causing a run time error.
10. What would happen if you neglected to add an **Exit Function** statement before the error handler?
11. How can you test for the existence of a directory?
12. What statements are used to report an error message, return an error number, transfer control to an error handler, exit a procedure, simulate a run time error and deactivate error checking?

6 DATABASE ACCESS

Visual Basic offers a variety of ways to manage file information. It supports both traditional methods of file access and the database engine supplied with versions 3.0 and 4.0. Appendix D covers sequential access, random access and binary access. In this chapter, you will learn how to work with the database engine and how to incorporate database objects into applications. You will also learn how to perform queries and work with the database features of the Professional Edition of Visual Basic.

6.1 THE DATABASE ENGINE

The DATAMGR.EXE program, supplied with versions 3.0 and 4.0, lets you create tables like the ones used by Microsoft Access. To invoke it, you select the Data Manager command from the Window menu. In the sample exercises, you will learn how to create and use these tables.

THE DATA CONTROL

The *data control*, shown in Figure 6.1, is a tool that provides an interface between Visual Basic and its database engine. To use the data control, you select its associated button from the Toolbox.

After the data control is placed on a form, other controls can be bound to the data control to create *data aware* controls. A data aware control is a control that automatically responds to a database event. For example, you can bind a text box to the data control to make it automatically read and update a particular field from a table. You can also make other controls data aware. Figure 6.2 shows a summary of objects that apply.

To Create a Data Aware Application

1. For databases created in Microsoft Access format, set the DatabaseName property of the data control to the name of the database. To do this, double click on the DatabaseName property in the Properties window. Visual Basic will display a list of files in the current directory.
   or
   For Btrieve, dBase, Microsoft FoxPro and Paradox databases, set the DatabaseName and the Connect properties. Table 6-1 shows a list of valid settings.
2. Set the RecordSource property of the data control to the name of the database table.
3. Set the DataSource property of each data aware control to the name of the data control (Data1, Data2, etc.).
4. Set the DataField property of each data aware control to the name of the field that it will draw information from.

TIP: You can get a list of all the fields in the table by double clicking on the DataField property. Each time you double click on this property, a different field is displayed.

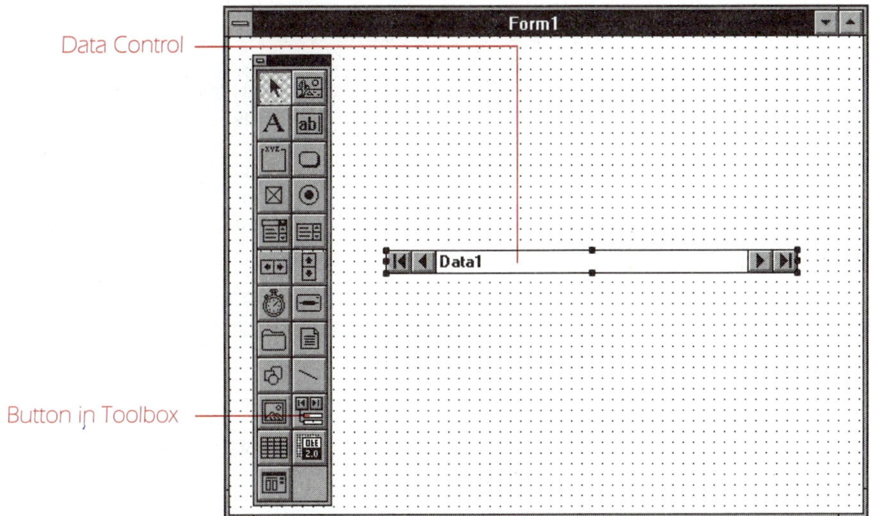

FIGURE 6.1 The data control

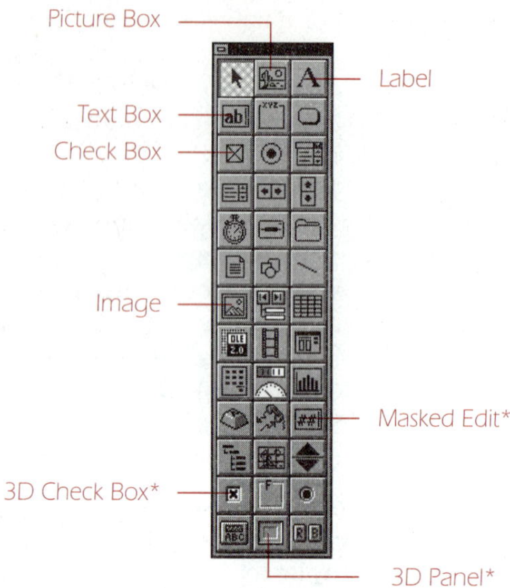

FIGURE 6.2 Data aware controls (* = Professional Edition)

Database Type	Connect Property
Btrieve	btrieve;
dBase	dBase III; or dBase IV;
FoxPro	FoxPro 2.0; or FoxPro 2.5;
Paradox	paradox; pwd=password;
ODBC*	odbc; dsn=server; uid=user; pwd=password

TABLE 6-1 DATABASE CONNECT PROPERTIES (* = FEATURE AVAILABLE ONLY IN PROFESSIONAL EDITION)

Exercise: Creating an Inventory Program

1. Create a new project with the following controls (place each object on the form as it appears in Figure 6.3).

Control	Property	Value
label1	Caption	Part Name:
label2	Caption	Part Number:
label3	Caption	Description:
label4	Caption	In Stock:
text1	Text	null string
text2	Text	null string

continued

text3	Text	null string
command1	Caption	Add
command2	Caption	Subtract
Form1	Caption	Inventory Program
label5	Name	totstock

2. Click on the totstock label control. Set its Caption property to a null string.
3. Set the BorderStyle property of the totstock label control to 1 - Fixed Single.
4. Select the data control button from the Toolbox. Place the object on the form between the command buttons and other controls.
5. Click on the data control. Using the size handles, stretch the control so that it appears like Figure 6.4.
6. Set the data control's properties as follows:

Property	**Value**
Exclusive	True
Caption	null string

7. In the Properties window, set the DatabaseName property of the data control to C:\VB_LIB\INVEN.MDB. If you installed the example files in another directory, switch to the appropriate path. Note that you can get a list of all the available databases on a drive by double clicking on the DatabaseName property.
8. Indicate the name of the table that contains the records by double clicking on the RecordSource property. Since the database contains only 1 table, Visual Basic automatically lists its name (Inven) when this property is selected.

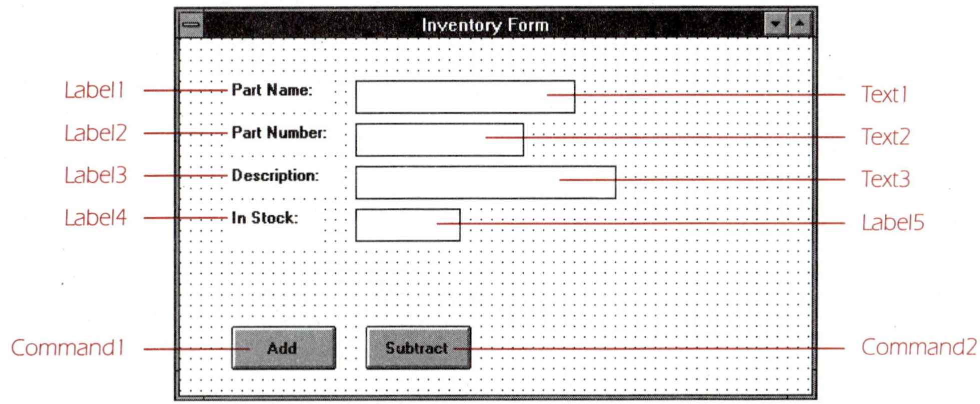

FIGURE 6.3 Controls for the inventory program

FIGURE 6.4 Sizing the data control

9. Click on the text box adjacent to the label with the Part Name Caption.
10. Using the Properties window, set the DataSource property of the text box to Data1. Visual Basic automatically returns this name if you double click on the DataSource property.
11. Set the DataField property of the text box to the part_name field. To accomplish this, double click on the property to choose the first field in the table.
12. Set the other data aware controls' properties as follows:

Control	Property	Value
text2	DataSource	Data1
text2	DataField	part_num
text3	DataSource	Data1
text3	DataField	part_descrip
totstock	DataSource	Data1
totstock	DataField	in_stock

13. In the Command1_Click procedure, type:

```
amount = InputBox("Quantity to Add: ")
totstock = Val(totstock.Caption) + Val(amount)
```

14. In the Command2_Click procedure type:

```
amount = InputBox("Quantity Used: ")
totstock = Val(totstock.Caption) - Val(amount)
```

15. Save the program and run it.

If you receive an error at this point, it is probably because you forgot to set a property value (or set one incorrectly). Figure 6.5 shows how the form should look when you are done. Once you have the program running, you

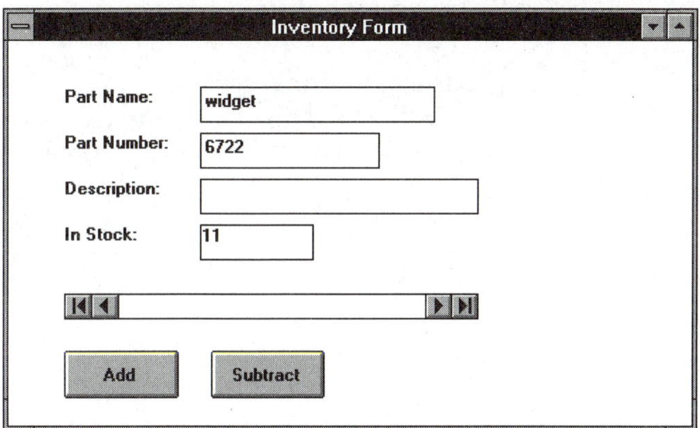

FIGURE 6.5 The completed inventory program

can test it by editing a field, choosing the Add or Subtract (inventory) buttons or using the data control to browse through the table. Notice that Visual Basic automatically updates the table when you browse from record to record.

6.2 BINDING OTHER DATA AWARE CONTROLS

As mentioned before, you can also bind the data control to a check box, label, picture box or image control. The following section will demonstrate how this is done. In Chapter 14, you will learn how to work with other data aware controls provided in the Professional Edition of Visual Basic.

BINDING LABELS

The procedures for binding labels are basically the same as text boxes. Since labels are read-only, however, you use them only when you wish to provide restrictive access to a table's fields. It is also possible to create a view-only interface by setting the ReadOnly property of the data control to **True**. The advantage of using labels instead is that you can provide restrictive access to some fields while permitting users to edit other bound fields in text boxes. The following example shows how to bind a label to the data control. Although you can write code to bind the label, you will find that it is much faster to set these properties at design time.

Control	Property	Setting
Data1	DatabaseName	C:\VB_LIB\CUST.MDB
Data1	RecordSource	Cust
label1	DataSource	Data1
label1	DataField	Amount

BINDING CHECK BOXES, PICTURE BOXES AND IMAGE CONTROLS

The procedures needed to bind other controls to a table are similar to those used to bind text boxes and label controls. The only difference is that a check box can only be bound to a Boolean type field and a picture box or image control must be bound to a Binary field. To add graphics to a table, you can use the Visual Basic **LoadPicture** function. The following example shows how to load an image created in Paintbrush:

```
Sub cmdLoad_Click ()

 ' Prompt for a file name

 fieldpic = InputBox("Picture to load - including full
      ⇨ path : ")

 ' Assign picture image to bound picture box

 picture1.Picture = LoadPicture(fieldpic)

End Sub
```

Once you have assigned a graphic to a bound picture box, the image is automatically saved when you move to the next record in the table. The ability of Visual Basic to display graphic images stored this way makes it possible to show visual representations of table information. For example, you can show what an item in inventory looks like to an employee before pulling stock. To create the graphics, you can use either Microsoft Paintbrush (supplied with Windows) or ICONWRKS.MAK (provided with Visual Basic).

TIP: By hiding other controls on the form, you can use the PrintForm **method to print bound picture boxes or image controls.**

6.3 WRITING CODE TO ACCESS THE DATABASE ENGINE

Although you can use the data control to handle some editing operations automatically, other editing procedures require writing code. To facilitate database handling, Visual Basic includes the *database manipulation language* to manage data. For example, to remove a record from a table, you can write code like this:

```
Data1.Recordset.Delete
Data1.Recordset.MoveNext
```

The Recordset property of the data control determines the operations that it can perform. In the preceding example, it is used to remove a record. To accomplish this, the **Delete** method is applied. After removing the record, the file pointer is repositioned at the next record in the file using **MoveNext**.

Using similar logic, you can add records to the file using the **AddNew** method. The following example shows how this is done:

```
Data1.Recordset.AddNew
```

The data control automatically updates a table when focus is moved to another record—that is, when one of its buttons is selected. In code, you can also save a file using the **Update** method.

Example

```
Data1.Recordset.Update
```

MOVING THE RECORD POINTER

There are several techniques you can use to move the record pointer around the recordset. Table 6-2 shows a summary of methods that apply.

Alternatively, you can move to the beginning of the file using the **Refresh** method. When a **Refresh** is executed, Visual Basic closes the file, reopens it and then positions the record pointer at the first record.

Example

```
Data1.Refresh
```

USING BOOKMARKS

Another useful technique is to use *bookmarks* to move around the recordset. A bookmark is a placeholder that records the last record position in a file. For example, you can use a bookmark to return to a record after moving to another record or after refreshing the table.

Example

```
lastpos = Data1.Recordset.Bookmark
Data1.Recordset.MoveLast
MsgBox ("Press Enter to return to bookmark")

Data1.Recordset.Bookmark = lastpos
```

Method	Function	Example
MoveNext	Move to Next record	Data1.Recordset.MoveNext
MovePrevious	Move to Previous record	Data1.Recordset.MovePrevious
MoveFirst	Move to first record	Data1.Recordset.MoveFirst
MoveLast	Move to last record	Data1.Recordset.MoveLast

TABLE 6-2 RECORDSET MOVEMENT METHODS

EDITING RECORDS

Once a record becomes current, you can read any field of that record. The following example shows how to display the value of a field called <balance>:

```
MsgBox(Data1.Recordset("balance"))
```

It is also possible to reference a field by reading or assigning a value to the bound control. For example, this simple assignment updates the value of the <balance> field:

```
balance.Text = "100.00"
Data1.RecordSet.Update
```

Several other techniques can also be used to reference the values of fields. The following procedure demonstrates these methods:

```
Sub cmd_OK_Click ()

 'Display value of cust field
 MsgBox (Data1.Recordset.Fields("cust"))
 'Shortcut method 1
 MsgBox (Data1.Recordset("cust"))
 'Shortcut method 2
 MsgBox (cust.Text)
 'Reference field by number
 MsgBox (Data1.Recordset.Fields(0).Value)
 'Shortcut method
 MsgBox (Data1.Recordset(0))

 'Use Edit method to edit field
 Data1.Recordset.Edit

 'Change field value
 Data1.Recordset.Fields("cust") = "Al Smith"
 'Shortcut method 1
 Data1.Recordset("cust") = "Al Smith"
 'Shortcut method 2
 cust.Text = "Al Smith"
 'Use field index to update
 Data1.Recordset.Fields(0).Value = "Al Smith"
 'Shortcut method
 Data1.Recordset(0) = "Al Smith"

 'Save changes
 Data1.Recordset.Update

End Sub
```

TRANSACTION PROCESSING

By default, Visual Basic automatically saves changes to a database when the record pointer is moved to another record. In many applications, however, this feature would not be advantageous. Since changes to a table made in auto-commit mode cannot be undone, you may wish to deactivate this feature.

By setting the Transactions property of a database to **True** and using the **BeginTrans** statement in a program, you can rollback changes to a database. Once a **BeginTrans** statement is issued, all pending transactions are volatile until either a **CommitTrans** or **Rollback** statement is executed. **Rollback** reverses a transaction and **CommitTrans** saves and ends transactions.

When using **BeginTrans**, you must be sure to end each transaction using **CommitTrans** or the changes will automatically roll back at the end of each session. It is also important to realize that **BeginTrans** affects all open databases in an application (regardless of when they were opened). Therefore, you must be sure you fully understand all the possible side effects of **BeginTrans** before using it in a program. The following example demonstrates how **BeginTrans** can be incorporated in an application:

```
Sub cmd_OK_Click ()

 Const ICON_QUESTION = 33
 Const OK_UPDATE = 1

 ' Move to beginning of file

 Data1.Refresh

 BeginTrans

 ' Increase unit price by .10 for each item

 While Data1.Recordset.EOF <> True
  itemcost.Text = itemcost.Text + (itemcost.Text * .1)
  Data1.Recordset.MoveNext
 Wend

 retval = MsgBox("OK to update prices", ICON_QUESTION,
      ⇨  "Price List")

 If retval = OK_UPDATE Then
  CommitTrans
 Else
  Rollback
 End If

 Data1.Refresh

End Sub
```

TIP: Although the data control provides an interface between Visual Basic and its database engine, the control itself does not actually have to appear on a form. Once the data control is bound to other controls, you can hide it by setting its Visible property to False. **Then, in code, you can simulate the effects of the arrow buttons on the data control using the following methods:**

MoveNext
MovePrevious
MoveFirst
MoveLast

CREATING MULTI-USER APPLICATIONS

The Exclusive property of the data control determines whether access to a table is single-user or multi-user. By default, this property is set to **False**. Thus two or more work stations can access the same information simultaneously. If this property setting is changed at run time, the data control's **Refresh** method must be applied before it will take effect.

Once a database table is opened for multi-user access, the Options property controls what operations are valid within the recordset. You can use this property to restrict users from performing certain operations. Table 6-3 shows a list of valid property settings. Combine these property settings by adding the Option values to achieve more than one form of access.

NOTE: When the Exclusive property is set to False, **you must run SHARE.EXE from DOS. This program should not be loaded, however, if you are using Windows for Workgroups.**

Constant Name	Purpose	Option Setting
DB_DENYWRITE	Denies write access to other users	1
DB_DENYREAD	Denies read access to other users	2
DB_READONLY	Denies write access to all users	4
DB_APPENDONLY	Permits record appending access only	8

TABLE 6-3 OPTION PROPERTY SETTINGS

PERFORMING QUERIES

A *query* is an instruction that causes a database to either return a subset of records or perform an operation on a part of the recordset. At design time or at run time, you can use the DatabaseName property or Connect property to set the name of a database or query file. You can also accomplish the same thing by setting the RecordSource property to a Microsoft Access SQL (Structured Query Language) query. In the latter case, you do not have to purchase any special add-on products to initiate a query. The only restriction is that you must enclose the SQL query in parentheses like this:

```
Data1.RecordSource = "SELECT * FROM Employees WHERE
      ⇨ salary > 20000"
Data1.Refresh
```

This example returns a list of employees making over $20,000 salary from the Employees table. Before the query can take effect, the **Refresh** method must be applied.

Visual Basic also supports the **FindFirst**, **FindNext**, **FindPrevious** and **FindLast** methods that allow you to seek the first, next, previous and last occurrences of a search criteria. For example, you can find the first customer in the <custname> field of a table using code like this:

```
Data1.Recordset.FindFirst "custname = 'Jane Smith'"
```

6.4 DATABASE FEATURES OF THE PROFESSIONAL EDITION

The Professional Edition of Visual Basic contains many additional tools you can use to control databases. With the Professional Edition, you can declare data access objects, use "shorthand" syntax and even perform interactive queries. This section introduces the database features of the Professional Edition.

CREATING DATA ACCESS OBJECTS

Using the Professional Edition, you can define variable names to use instead of properties. These names can be used as "shorthand" notation and to make your code easier to understand. For example, in the Standard Edition, to reference a table, you must enter the full syntax like this:

```
' Standard Edition example

Data1.DatabaseName = "C:\VB\EMPLOY.MDB"
Data1.RecordSource = "Employ"
Data1.Refresh

' Change first record

Data1.Recordset.Edit
Data1.Recordset("Employee Name") = "Laura Adams"
Data1.Recordset("Amount") = Val("638.985")
Data1.Recordset.Update

Data1.Recordset.Close
```

Assuming the **Employee Name** field is not bound to any control on the form, to reference this field, you must type:

```
Data1.Recordset("Employee Name")
```

With the Professional Edition, the same operation can be performed this way:

```
tbl("Employee Name")
```

To access a table like this, <tbl> must be declared using **Dim** and assigned to the table using **Set**. Before you can make this assignment, you must also define and **Set** a database object variable.

Syntax:

```
Dim DB_object As Database
.     .     .
.     .     .
Set DB_object = OpenDatabase("PATH_OF_DATABASE"
                           ⇨ [,fileaccess])
```

The <fileaccess> argument lets you specify the database access that other users will have. Note that this parameter is the functional equivalent of the Options property of the data control.

This next example shows how to declare the database and table objects. This code also demonstrates how to open a table for DB_DENYWRITE access:

```
Const DB_DENYWRITE = 1

' Declare database and table objects

Dim DB As Database, tbl As Table

Set DB = OpenDatabase("C:\VB\EMPLOY.MDB")

' Open table and lock records so other users
' cannot write to table

Set tbl = DB.OpenTable("Employ", DB_DENYWRITE)
```

Notice that <DB> is declared as type **Database**. Afterwards, **Set** is used with **OpenDatabase** to open EMPLOY.MDB and assign the data to the <DB> object variable. Once this is done, the table is opened for DB_DENYWRITE access (deny write access to other users) and the contents of the table are assigned to <tbl>.

Using this technique, you can now easily add a record to the table:

```
' Add new record

tbl.AddNew
tbl("Employee Name") = "Gina Palomino"
tbl("Amount") = Val("400.50")
tbl.Update
```

```
tbl.Close
DB.Close
```

Although Visual Basic automatically closes database and table objects declared local within the procedure, it is generally considered good practice to always close the database and table yourself. To close a database or table, you use the **Close** method:

Example

```
cust_table.Close

custDB.Close
```

CREATING QUERYDEFS WITH ACCESS SQL

With the Professional Edition of Visual Basic, you can also declare QueryDefs to use on Access tables. A QueryDef allows you to manipulate table information using SQL commands. By declaring a variable as type **QueryDef**, you can **Set** the variable to the database using **CreateQueryDef**. For example:

```
Dim DB As Database, tbl As Table, my_query As QueryDef
.      .      .
.      .      .
Set my_query = DB.CreateQueryDef("Test Query")
```

"Test Query" is the name of the query Visual Basic uses to identify the object. <my_query> is an object variable of type **QueryDef**. Once you have declared this object, you then assign the **SQL** property to the object variable:

```
my_query.SQL = "SELECT * FROM Employ WHERE Amount < 500"
```

The **SQL** property can be any valid SQL string that Access supports. In this case, the query will return all employee records where the **Amount** field is greater than $500.00 dollars.

After setting the **SQL** property, you need to create one more object to perform the query. By declaring an object of type **Dynaset**, you can use **CreateDynaset** to **Set** the new object to the results of the query:

```
Dim dynaset_obj As Dynaset
.      .      .
.      .      .
Set dynaset_obj = my_query.CreateDynaset()
```

Once this is done, you can run a test query using a **Do..Loop** like this:

```
Do While Not dynaset_obj.EOF
 MsgBox (dynaset_obj("Employee Name"))
 dynaset_obj.MoveNext
Loop
```

The following procedure shows the complete steps for defining and performing a QueryDef:

```
' Declare database, table, query and dynaset objects

Dim DB As Database, tbl As Table, my_query As QueryDef
Dim dynaset_obj As Dynaset

Set DB = OpenDatabase("C:\VB\EMPLOY.MDB")
Set tbl = DB.OpenTable("Employ")

' Create query

Set my_query = DB.CreateQueryDef("Test Query")
my_query.SQL = "SELECT * FROM Employ WHERE Amount < 500"
Set dynaset_obj = my_query.CreateDynaset()

Do While Not dynaset_obj.EOF
 MsgBox (dynaset_obj("Employee Name"))
 dynaset_obj.MoveNext
Loop

tbl.Close
my_query.Close
```

CREATING INTERACTIVE QUERIES

One of the advantages of using QueryDefs is that you can perform queries that interact with users at run time. The following code fragment shows how you can modify the preceding example to interact with users during a run:

```
Dim search_amount As String
.     .     .
.     .     .
search_amount = InputBox("Find all employees who sold
                  ⇨ less than? ")
my_query.SQL = "SELECT * FROM Employ WHERE amount < "
             ⇨ & search_amount
```

When this code executes, the program will prompt the user to enter the search criteria during the run. Notice that the **&** operator is used to concatenate <search_amount> with the SQL query string.

SORTING A DATABASE

With the Sort property of a Dynaset, you can reorder database records in a table. Although you cannot directly sort the records of a dynaset, you can create a **Snapshot** of the table and then use the Sort property to rearrange the records:

```
Dim DB As Database, dynaset_obj  As Dynaset
Dim sortinfo As Dynaset, snap_dat As Snapshot

Set DB = OpenDatabase("C:\VB\EMPLOY.MDB")
Set snap_dat = DB.CreateSnapshot("Employ")

snap_dat.Sort = "[Employee Name] Desc"

Set snap_dat = snap_dat.CreateSnapshot()

Do While Not snap_dat.EOF
 MsgBox (snap_dat("Employee Name"))
 snap_dat.MoveNext
Loop
```

Notice that you must use the **CreateSnapshot** method twice to reorder the records: first to **Set** the **Snapshot** object to the table and then to capture the new order. The preceding example sorts the records by descending order using the **Desc** option. If you do not specify a sort order, ascending order or **Asc** is assumed.

NOTE: You can also reorder a table by setting the Table.Index property to the name of an index you create with the Data Manager utility. The Data Manager, however, automatically reorders the records by the primary index you select.

Exercise: Creating a Table

1. From the File menu, choose New Project.
2. From the Window menu, choose Data Manager.
3. When the Data Manager loads, from the File menu, choose New Database.
4. A pop-up menu will appear showing the two types of databases you can create (Access 1.0 and Access 1.1). Choose Access 1.1.
5. In the File Name box, type Maillist.
6. Click on OK to create the database.
7. From the Database dialog, choose New.
8. In the Table Name box, type Maillist.
9. Click on OK to create the table.
10. In the Table dialog, choose the Fields Add button (see Figure 6.6).
11. In the Add Field dialog, enter the following field definitions:

    Field Name: Name
    Field Type: Text
    Field Size: 20

12. Click on OK to save the field.

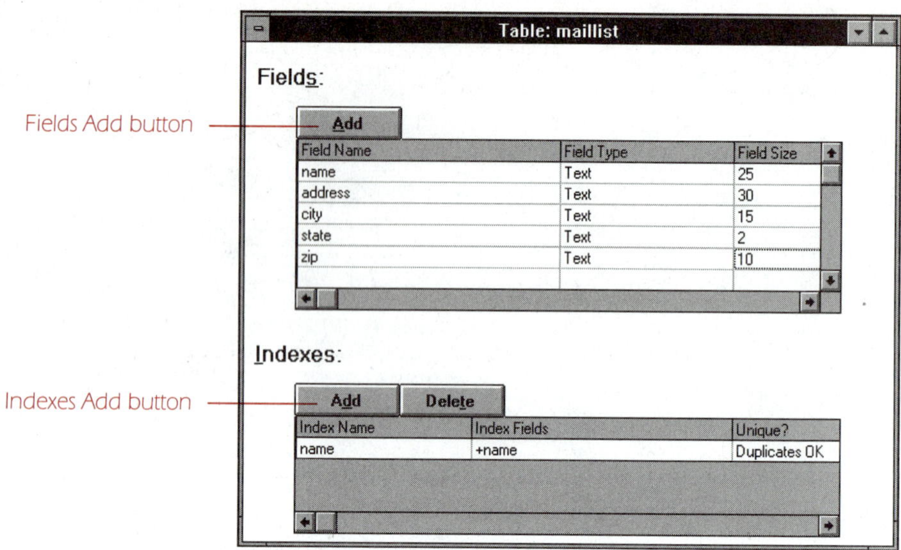

FIGURE 6.6 The Table dialog

13. Using the method previously described in steps 10 and 11, define the other fields in the table:

Field Name	Field Type	Field Size
Address	Text	30
City	Text	15
State	Text	2
Zip	Text	10

14. From the Table dialog, choose the Indexes Add button. Do not confuse this button with the Fields Add button.
15. In the Index Name box, type Name.
16. From the Table list box, double click on Name.
17. Choose Done.
18. Close the Table dialog by pressing Ctrl+F4.
19. From the Database dialog, choose Open. This will open the table so it can be edited.
20. In the window that appears showing the table structure, click on Add.
21. Enter the following test records:

Name	Address	City	State
Jones Bob	somewhere	NY	NY
Smith Sally	down there	Dallas	TX

22. From the Data Manager File menu, choose Close Database. This will save and close the table.
23. Choose File Exit to return to Visual Basic.

SUMMARY

In this chapter, you learned how to use the database features of the Standard and Professional Editions of Visual Basic. You also learned how to perform queries, roll back transactions, sort and index tables, and create multi-user applications.

REVIEW QUESTIONS

1. How can you bind a text box to the data control?
2. Give three examples of data aware controls.
3. The database engine creates files in what format?
4. How can you perform a query in Visual Basic?
5. How can you deactivate auto-commit mode?
6. What statement allows you to undo transactions?
7. How can you move the record pointer around the recordset?
8. What methods allow you to add, remove and change records in a table? Give examples of each.
9. What is the Options property of the data control used for?
10. Before you can run a data aware application across a network, what program must you execute from DOS?

CLASS PROJECTS

1. Write a program to keep track of patient appointments for a doctor's office. Using the PATI.MDF (included on the program disk), bind each field in the Pati table to a text box. The user should be able to schedule new appointments, edit existing ones and cancel appointments.

HINT: By default, Microsoft Access tables created in Visual Basic are multi-user. Therefore, you must run SHARE.EXE (from DOS) or set the Exclusive property of the data control to False.

2. Create a mailing list program using the MAILLIST.MDF database you created earlier. Include three buttons on the form to add, update and delete records.

7 DYNAMIC GRIDS

The *grid control* is a spreadsheet-like matrix of rows and columns that displays various forms of information. Each intersection of a row and column marks a different cell. This chapter shows how to initialize a grid, select its rows and columns, display text and graphics and how to change the size of a grid at run time.

Although you can display information on a grid, you cannot directly edit its cells. However, you can assign the contents of a grid to text boxes, make the necessary changes, and then reassign the contents of the text boxes back to the grid. This technique is demonstrated in section 7.2, Working With Grids.

NOTE: When you distribute an application that uses the grid control, you must install the GRID.VBX file in the WINDOWS\SYSTEM directory of the target drive.

7.1 INITIALIZING A GRID

Figure 7.1 shows what a sample grid might look like. The gray cells on the left and at the top of the grid are *fixed rows and fixed columns.* At run time, when the horizontal or vertical scroll bars are selected, these cells do not scroll. You use the fixed rows and fixed columns of a grid to display heading and other labels.

To Set the Number of Fixed Rows and Columns

- At design time or at run time, set the FixedRows and FixedCols properties of the grid control to the number of fixed rows or fixed columns (default 1)—e.g., Grid1.FixedRows = 2.

NOTE: If a grid is sized too small to fit all the rows and columns it contains, Visual Basic will automatically add scroll bars.

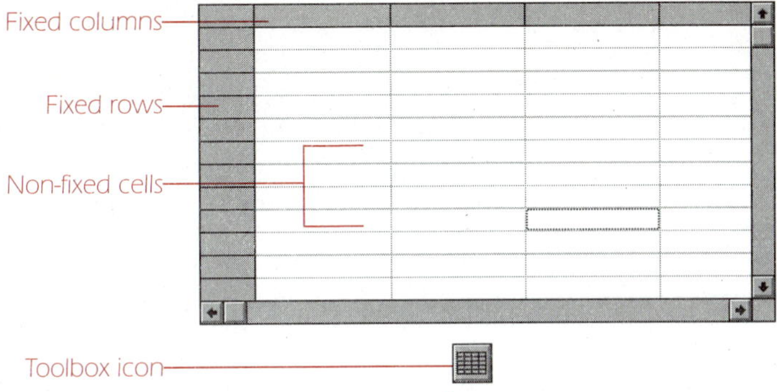

FIGURE 7.1 The grid control

In the *non-fixed rows and columns*, you display records from tables, the results of calculations, messages, and graphics. These rows and columns scroll when the horizontal or vertical scroll bars are selected.

To Set the Number of Non-Fixed Rows and Columns

- At design time or at run time, set the Rows and Cols properties of the grid control to the number of non-fixed rows or non-fixed columns—e.g., Grid1.Cols = 10.

SETTING THE ROW AND COLUMN SIZES

The ColWidth and RowHeight properties are available only at run time. Use ColWidth to set the width of a column and RowHeight to specify the height of a row. The following example shows how to initialize the column width of a grid:

```
Sub Form_Load ()

 ' Load and initialize grid

 Const MAXCOL = 15
 Const MAXROW = 10

 Grid1.Rows = MAXROW
 Grid1.Cols = MAXCOL

 For i = 1 To MAXCOL - 1
   Grid1.Col = i
   Grid1.ColWidth(i) = 1400 ' twips
 Next

End Sub
```

7.2 WORKING WITH GRIDS

This section discusses how to work with grids after they have been initialized. In the following pages, you will learn how to display information on a grid, change the text alignment of cells, how to display graphics and how to change the size of a grid at run time.

DISPLAYING TEXT ON A GRID

While a program is running, you display information on a grid using the Text property. The Row and Col properties determine the position of the *active cell*. These properties are not the same as the Rows and Cols properties which set the number of non-fixed rows and columns in a grid.

Example

```
Sub Form_Load ()

 ' Set active cell

 Grid1.Row = 0
 Grid1.Col = 0

 Grid1.Text = "test"

End Sub
```

In the preceding example, a string is displayed in the first row and column of the grid (in the fixed rows and columns—position 0,0). You can also display text in the non-fixed rows and columns:

```
Grid1.Row = 2
Grid1.Col = 3
Grid1.Text = "Hello"
```

NOTE: This example assumes that the Rows and Cols properties have been set at design time.

ALIGNING TEXT IN CELLS

Two properties control the text alignment of cells; ColAlignment and FixedAlignment. ColAlignment sets the column alignment of non-fixed cells. FixedAlignment sets the alignment of fixed cells.

To Set The Column Alignment

- Set the ColAlignment or FixedAlignment properties to one of the following:

```
0 = Align text left (default)
1 = Align text right
2 = Align text centered
```

Example

```
Const CENTER = 2
Const MAXCOL = 5

For column% = 1 to MAXCOL - 1
  Grid1.FixedAlignment(column%) = CENTER
  Grid1.ColAlignment(column%) = CENTER
Next
```

SELECTING CELLS AT RUN TIME

APPOINT.MAK, shown in Figure 7.2, demonstrates how to select cells in a grid. The source code for this example is included on the program disk.

APPOINT.MAK is an appointment scheduler application. At run time, when you click on a cell, a Click event occurs. The Grid1_Click procedure intercepts this event and calls the Add Appointments screen:

```
' Add new record

Add_Screen.Show
Add_Screen.lastname.SetFocus
```

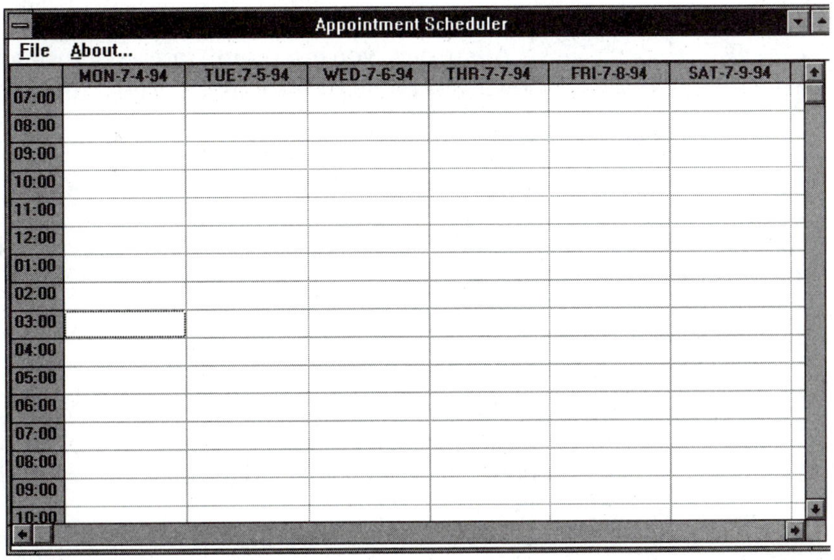

FIGURE 7.2 The appointment scheduler application, APPOINT.MAK

The Add Appointments screen contains 3 text boxes: *lastname*, *firstname* and *note*. After entering the appointment information, clicking on OK saves the appointment. The program then displays the last name of the appointment contact in the active cell:

```
' Print name on grid

Main_Screen.Grid1.Text = lastname.Text.
```

When a cell is selected at run time before scheduling a new appointment, the program tests if the active cell contains any information. If the cell length is greater than zero, APPOINT.MAK assumes you want to delete the appointment:

```
If Len(Grid1.Text) <> 0 Then
.      .      .
.      .      .
```

To remove an appointment, the program sets the active cell to a null string:

```
' Delete record from grid

Main_Screen.Grid1.Text = ""
```

CHANGING THE SIZE OF A GRID AT RUN TIME

At run time, you add rows to a grid by setting the Rows property. Since large grids take longer to load, you use this method to *dynamically* size the grid at run time:

```
MainScr.Grid1.Rows = MainScr.Grid1.Rows + 1
```

Alternately, you insert rows into a grid using the **AddItem** method. The following example shows how to insert a row and initialize it at the same time:

```
Dim rowno As Integer

rowno = 3

' Insert row into grid

Grid1.AddItem Chr(9) + "486" + Chr(9) + "66 Megahertz",
       ⇨ rowno
```

This example inserts a row at the forth row position of the grid (or if you prefer, the third non-fixed row position). If the row number argument is omitted, the end of the grid is assumed. Notice that character code 09 is used to separate the cell items.

The **RemoveItem** method removes a row from a grid. The following example shows how to apply it:

```
Sub RemoveRec_Click ()

 ' Delete record routine

 Const ICON_QUESTION = 33
 Const HOURGLASS = 11
 Const ARROW = 0

 Dim rec_no As Long

 rec_no = Grid1.Row
 response = 1

 response = MsgBox("Delete this record?",
              ⇨  ICON_QUESTION, "")

 If response = 1 Then

   Grid1.RemoveItem rec_no

   ' Turn mouse pointer into hour glass while
   ' deleting record

   Screen.MousePointer = HOURGLASS

   retval = Deleterec(fileno, filename, rec_no,
                ⇨ timerec)

   Call Delnull(fileno, filename, timerec)
   Call ShowGrid

   ' Reset normal pointer

   Screen.MousePointer = ARROW

   ' Update grid row counter

   nextrec = nextrec - 1

 End If

End Sub
```

DISPLAYING GRAPHICS ON A GRID

The grid control displays graphic images in .BMP (bitmap) and .ICO (icon) formats. To create the graphics, use either Microsoft Paintbrush provided with Windows or ICONWRKS.MAK supplied with Visual Basic. The following code shows how to display an icon using **LoadPicture**. Figure 7.3 shows what the graphics look like.

```
Sub Form_Load ()

 ' Initialize new grid

 Dim rows As Integer, cols As Integer
 Dim twips As Integer

 rows = 10: cols = 5: twips = 1400

 Call Initgrid(Grid1, rows, cols, twips)

 Grid1.Row = 3: Grid1.Col = 2
 Grid1.RowHeight(3) = 500 ' twips

 Grid1.Picture =
        ⇨  LoadPicture("C:\vb\icons\industry\cars.ico")

End Sub
```

REMOVING GRAPHICS FROM A GRID

To remove a graphic image from a grid, use the **LoadPicture** function with no argument. The following example shows how to do this:

```
Grid1.Picture = LoadPicture()
```

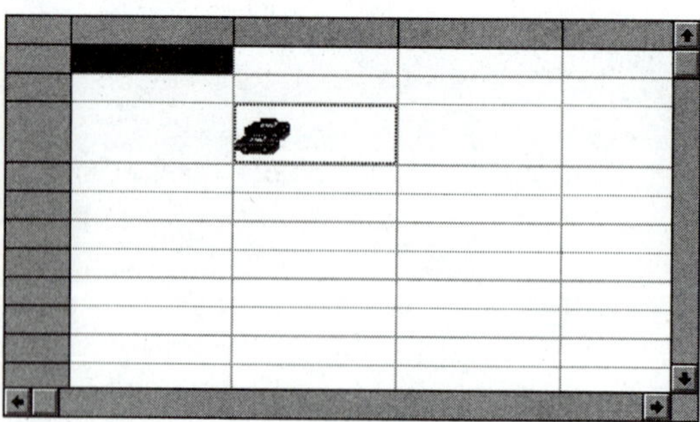

FIGURE 7.3 Displaying an icon on a grid

COMBINING TEXT AND GRAPHICS

In Visual Basic, you can even combine text and graphics in a single cell. Figure 7.4 shows an example (taken from GRIDIMG.MAK). Notice that the text automatically wraps around the graphics in the cell. To accomplish this, the following code is needed:

```
Sub Form_Load ()

 ' Initialize new grid
 Dim rows As Integer, cols As Integer
 Dim twips As Integer

 rows = 10: cols = 5: twips = 1400

 Call Initgrid(Grid1, rows, cols, twips)

 Grid1.Row = 3: Grid1.Col = 2
 Grid1.RowHeight(3) = 600 ' twips

 ' Load graphics from disk

 Grid1.Picture =
        ⇨  LoadPicture("C:\vb\icons\industry\cars.ico")

 ' Add text

 Grid1.Text = "Annual Car Auction"

End Sub
```

ADDING MULTIPLE GRAPHICS

By setting the FillStyle property to 1, Visual Basic assigns the Picture property to all the selected cells of a grid. You use this technique to create wallpaper and other background displays (see Figure 7.5).

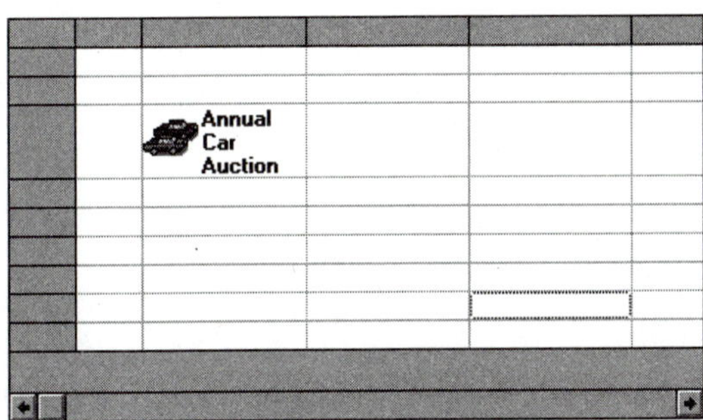

FIGURE 7.4 Combining text and graphics

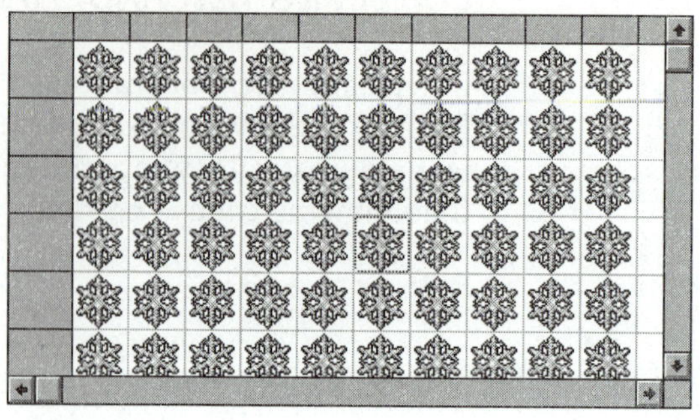

FIGURE 7.5 Displaying multiple graphics on a grid

The following property settings are used to select a range:

```
SelStartRow   (first selected row)
SelStartCol   (first selected column)
SelEndRow     (last selected row)
SelEndCol     (last selected column)
```

Example

```
Sub Form_Load ()

 Grid1.Cols = 12
 Grid1.Rows = 12

 For i = 1 To 10
   Grid1.ColWidth(i) = 1200 ' Twips
 Next

 Grid1.FillStyle = 1

 ' Select first 10 rows

 Grid1.SelStartRow = 1
 Grid1.SelStartCol = 1
 Grid1.SelEndRow = 10
 Grid1.SelEndCol = 10

 ' Set column width

 For i = 1 To 10
   Grid1.ColWidth(i) = image1.Width
 Next

 ' Set row height
```

```
  For i = 1 To 10
    Grid1.RowHeight(i) = image1.Height
  Next

  ' Assign picture to all cells

  Grid1.Picture = image1.Picture

End Sub
```

USING GRID FUNCTIONS FROM THE LIBRARY

The library includes several functions that improve your control over grids. Table 7-1 summarizes the purposes of each. To use these routines, you add the GRIDFUNC.BAS module to a project. For more information on using the grid functions of the library, refer to Part III, Grid Functions.

Function	Description
Cleargrid	Clears a grid.
Gridfill	Restores contents of a grid saved using Gridsave
Gridsave	Saves a grid to a file.
Initgrid	Sets the column width and number of rows and columns in a grid.
Timesched	Prints a 60 minute time schedule on a grid.

TABLE 7-1 GRID LIBRARY ROUTINES

LIMITATIONS OF THE GRID CONTROL

The grid control is elegant, but it has two limitations. In both the Standard and Professional Editions, the maximum number of rows that you can define is 16099. The grid control also does not support in-place editing. With the DataGrid custom control by Sheridan Software Systems, you can create tables similar to the ones used by Microsoft Access. Since it works directly with the data control, most editing operations are handled automatically. For more information about the DataGrid custom control, contact Sheridan Software Systems.

Exercise: Creating a Sample Grid

1. From the File menu, choose New Project.
2. From the Toolbox, select the grid custom control.
3. Size the grid and place it on the form as it appears in Figure 7.6.

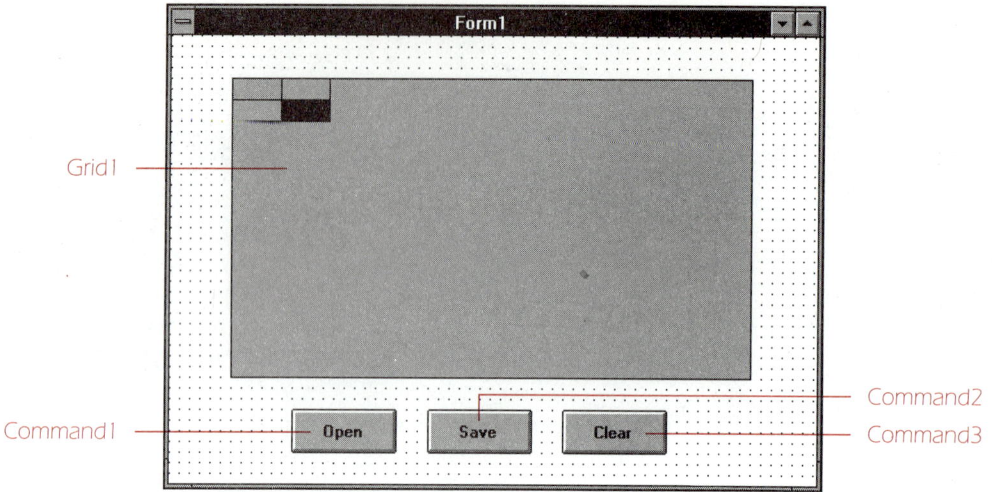

FIGURE 7.6 Controls for the custom grid

4. Add the following controls to the form, placing the objects as they appear in Figure 7.6:

Control	Property	Value
command1	Caption	Open
command2	Caption	Save
command3	Caption	Clear

5. Rename each control as:

command1	Name	cmdOpen
command2	Name	cmdSave
command3	Name	cmdClear

6. In the cmdOpen procedure, type:

```
totrows = 10: totcols = 5: start = 1
fileno = FreeFile

' Restore grid from file

filename$ = InputBox("File Name:")
```

```
retval = Gridfill(fileno, filename$, Grid1,
              ⇨ totrows, totcols, start)
```

7. In the cmdSave procedure, type:

```
totrows = 10: totcols = 5: start = 1
fileno = FreeFile

' Save grid to file

filename$ = InputBox("Save As:")

retval = Gridsave(fileno, filename$, Grid1,
              ⇨ totrows, totcols, start)
```

8. In the cmdClear procedure, type:

```
Call Cleargrid(Grid1)
```

9. In the Form_Load procedure, type:

```
Const MAXCOL = 5, MAXROW = 100, TWIPS_PER_COLUMN
        ⇨ = 1400

' Set number of rows, columns and column widths

Call Initgrid(Grid1, MAXROW, MAXCOL,
          ⇨ TWIPS_PER_COLUMN)

Grid1.Row = 0   ' Fixed row

Grid1.Col = 1: Grid1.Text = "Name"
Grid1.Col = 2: Grid1.Text = "Age"
Grid1.Col = 3: Grid1.Text = "Sex"

Grid1.Row = 1

Grid1.Col = 1: Grid1.Text = "Sally"
Grid1.Col = 2: Grid1.Text = "27"
Grid1.Col = 3: Grid1.Text = "F"

Grid1.Row = 2

Grid1.Col = 1: Grid1.Text = "Bob"
Grid1.Col = 2: Grid1.Text = "30"
Grid1.Col = 3: Grid1.Text = "M"
```

10. In the Declaration section of the form, type:

```
' Set integer default

DefInt A-Z
```

11. From the File menu, choose Add File...
12. Type C:\VB_LIB\GRIDFUNC.BAS. Note this step assumes you installed the library modules in the default C:\VB_LIB directory.
13. Save the project and run it.
14. When the form loads, the grid should appear with the test data. Save the grid by clicking on Save. Call this file GRID.DAT.
15. Click on Clear (this will erase the two test records).
16. Now restore the grid by choosing the Open button. When the program prompts for a file name, enter GRID.DAT.

SUMMARY

In this chapter, you learned how to use the grid custom control. You have also learned how to set the row and column sizes, display text and graphics, change the alignment of cell contents, save and restore grids and size grids at run time.

REVIEW QUESTIONS

1. What is the grid control?
2. What is the difference between the Row and Rows properties and the Col and Cols properties?
3. What is the difference between the fixed and non-fixed rows and columns of a grid?
4. How can you display text on a grid?
5. What properties control the alignment of grid text?
6. How can you erase a value in a cell?
7. What properties or methods allow you to add and remove rows from a grid?
8. Create the following grid:

   5 rows
   50 columns

9. Write a loop to set the column width of a range of cells.
10. How can you display graphics on a grid?
11. At run time, when you select a cell, what grid event occurs?
12. What is the maximum number of rows you can display on a grid?
13. In order to use the grid functions of the library, what module must you include in a project?
14. Create a routine to display test data on a grid. Use the library to save and restore the contents of each cell.

CLASS PROJECTS

1. Write a program to display a 60 minute time schedule on a grid using the library function Timesched (see Part III, Grid Functions).
2. Generate an application to calculate and display a depreciation schedule on a grid using the straight line method.

HINT: The sample FINPROJ.MAK applications shows how to calculate depreciation schedules. The Show_Strline procedure of DEPREC.FRM demonstrates how this can be done. Use the Strline function of COMPUTE.BAS to compute the schedule.

3. Modify the above program to allow the user to save/restore depreciation schedules from a file. Be sure to clear the grid each time (using the library function Cleargrid) before displaying a new schedule.

8 MEMO HANDLING

Visual Basic provides a rich assortment of tools to create memo handlers. These tools include text boxes, scroll bars, the **Clipboard** object and the ability to create multiple document interfaces. This chapter shows how to create memo handlers using these objects.

Many of the memo handling techniques and functions described in this chapter use the developer's library included with this book. Table 8.1 shows a summary of these functions. To include these routines in an application, you add the TEXTOPER.BAS module to a project.

8.1 CREATING MEMO HANDLERS

When the MultiLine property of a text box control is set to **True**, text automatically wraps around in the text box. You use this technique to create memo handlers. READMEMO.MAK demonstrates how this is done. By setting the ScrollBars property to 3—Both, scroll bars appear in the text box (see Figure 8.1). Although scroll bars are not required to move around in a multiline text box, they add an elegant touch to a memo handler.

Function	Description
Edittext	Handles cut, copy and paste operations.
Findtext	Finds string patterns in a text box.
Memowrite	Saves contents of a text box to a file.
Mergetext	Merges two text files.
Readmemo	Retrieves a text file from disk.
Undolast	Reverses last edit operation in a text box.

TABLE 8.1 MEMO HANDLING FUNCTIONS OF THE LIBRARY

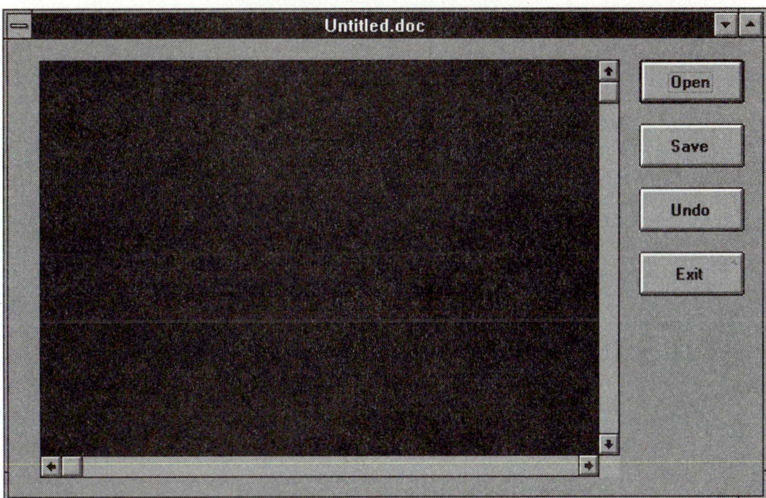

FIGURE 8.1 Multiline text box with scroll bars

SAVING A TEXT BOX TO A FILE

The code in the cmdWrite procedure of READMEMO.MAK demonstrates how to save a text box to a file. To do this, the program assigns the contents of the control to a variable. It then calls the library function Memowrite to save the memo under the name the user specifies. If the file does not exist, it is created. If the file does exist, it is replaced:

```
Sub cmdWrite_Click ()

 fileno = 1: filevar = text1.Text
 err_switch = False

 ' Check if file exists before saving it

 Do While Form1.Caption = "Untitled.doc" = True

  filename = InputBox("Save file as: ")
  If Fileexists(filename, err_switch) = False Then
     Form1.Caption = filename
  Else
    If filename <> "Untitled.doc" Then
       retval = MsgBox("File exists, overwrite", 33,
                   ⇨ "Warning")
       If retval = 1 Then
          Form1.Caption = filename
       End If
    End If
  End If
```

```
 Loop
  retval = Memowrite(fileno, filename, filevar)
  Form1.Caption = filename

End Sub
```

READING FILES INTO TEXT BOXES

Using similar logic, cmdRead_Click reads a memo file into a text box. To do this, the program calls the library function Readmemo:

```
Sub cmdRead_Click ()

 ' Open text file for editing

 fileno = 1

 file_OK = False

 Do While file_OK = False
  filename = InputBox("Enter file name:", "File Open")
  file_OK = Valfile(filename)
  If filename = "" Then
   Exit Sub
  End If
 Loop

 ' Read file into text box

 text1.Text = Readmemo(fileno, filename)
 Form1.Caption = filename

End Sub
```

USING THE CLIPBOARD OBJECT

The sample text editor application (TEXT.MAK), shown in Figure 8.2, demonstrates how to cut, copy and paste text in a memo handler. The Edit menu uses a menu control array to implement these operations. The Index property of each menu control is set as follows:

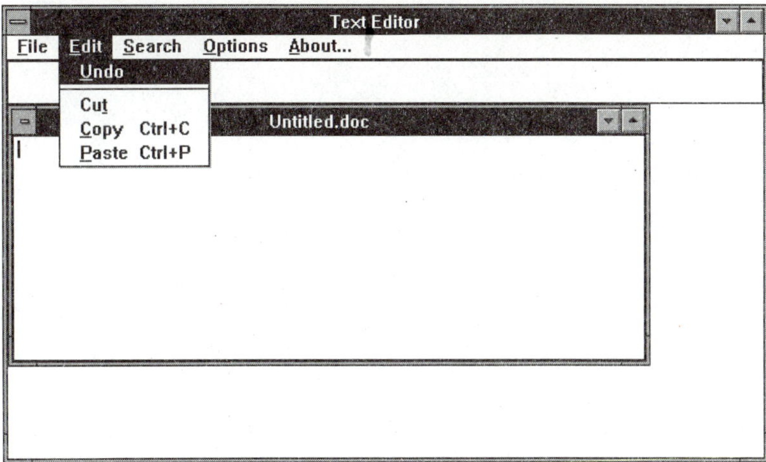

FIGURE 8.2 The text editor program, TEXT.MAK

Menu Control	**Index**
Cut	0
Copy	1
Paste	2

In the CtrlArr_Click procedure, a call is made to the library function Edittext. Edittext accepts as an argument the index of the menu control array. It then uses the index to determine which operation must be performed. To accomplish this, the following code is needed:

```
Const CUT_TEXT = 0
Const COPY_TEXT = 1
Const PASTE_TEXT = 2

Select Case index

 Case CUT_TEXT

    Clipboard.Clear
    Clipboard.SetText text1.SelText

    ' Erase text from document after copying
    ' it to Clipboard

    text1.SelText = ""

 Case COPY_TEXT
```

```
        Clipboard.Clear
        Clipboard.SetText text1.SelText

    Case PASTE_TEXT

        text1.SelText = Clipboard.GetText()

End Select
```

Edittext uses the **Clipboard** object and the **Clear**, **SetText** and **GetText** methods to cut, copy and paste text to and from the Clipboard. One function call in the program serves this purpose:

```
Sub CtrlArr_Click (index As Integer)

 ' Call text handler routine

 Call Edittext(index, text1)

End Sub
```

REVERSING EDIT OPERATIONS IN A TEXT BOX

The Undo command of the Edit menu in TEXT.MAK allows you to reverse changes to the text box. To accomplish this, the Undolast function of the library calls the Windows API (Application Programming Interface) function Sendmessage. The advantages of using Undolast over Sendmessage are that it is easier to implement, safer to use and requires no special knowledge of the Windows API. The following code shows how to call Undolast in a program:

```
Sub Undotext_Click ()

 ' Undo last edit

 Call Undolast(text1)

End Sub
```

SEARCHING FOR STRINGS

The Find command of the Search menu locates a string in the text box. To accomplish this, the OK_Search_Click procedure of the Find dialog calls the library function Findtext:

```
Sub OK_Search_Click ()

  ' Find dialog (SearchForm)

  target_str = search.Text

  ' Make search case sensitive if option is selected

  If option1.Value = True Then
    uppercase = False
  Else
    uppercase = True
  End If

  start_search = Findtext(Form1, text1, target_str,
               ⇨ start_search, seekfirst, uppercase)

  Unload SearchForm

End Sub
```

To indicate the search pattern, you can either mark the range with a mouse or type the string in the Find dialog box. Figure 8.3 shows what this dialog looks like.

To find the next match, the program sets the <seekfirst> flag to **False** and passes the position of the last match to Findtext:

```
Sub FindNext_Click ()

 ' Search for next match

 seekfirst = False

 start_search = Findtext(Form1, text1, target_str,
              ⇨ start_search, seekfirst, uppercase)
```

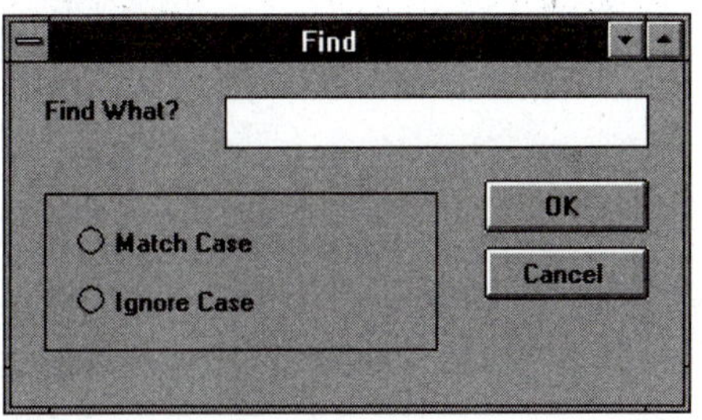

FIGURE 8.3 The Find dialog

```
    If start_search = 0 Then
        MsgBox "Pattern not found", 0, "SEARCH"
    End If

End Sub
```

<Start_search> is a global variable defined in TEXTOPER.BAS. The definition for this variable must be global to retain the value of the last position after each search. For more information on using Findtext, refer to String and Memo Handling Functions in Part III of this book.

USING OPEN DIALOGS

The easiest way to retrieve a file is to use **InputBox**. Alternatively, you can use the Open common dialog or create your own file opener form using Visual Basic's standard file controls.

The Filelist function of the library retrieves memos. TEXT.MAK uses this function to fill a list box with various file information. These parameters include:

- File names
- File sizes
- Dates of last modifications

Figure 8.4 shows what the file opener form (FOPEN.FRM) looks like. The following code shows how the program initializes the list:

```
Sub Form_Load ()

  ' Fill list box with file information in the
  ' current directory
```

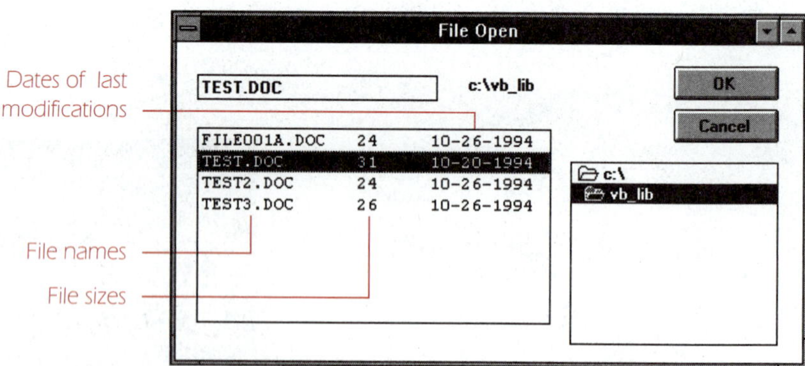

FIGURE 8.4 The file opener dialog

```
 path = dir1.Path
 filespec = "*.doc"
 retval = Filelist(path, filespec, list1)

 label2.Caption = dir1.Path

End Sub
```

To fill the list box, Filelist accepts three arguments. <Path> is the current path indicated by the directory list box control (dir1). <Filespec> is the file specification type (*.doc). <List1> is the name of the list box control to use.

At run time, you can search other directories using the directory list box control. When this happens, a Change event occurs:

```
Sub Dir1_Change ()

 ' Change directory

 ChDir (dir1.Path)
 path = dir1.Path

 list1.Clear
 retval = Filelist(path, filespec, list1)

 label2.Caption = dir1.Path

End Sub
```

When a file is chosen from the list, the program extracts the file size and date information from the string and assigns the result to the text1.text box of the file opener form. To accomplish this, the following code is needed:

```
Sub List1_Click ()

 ' Show file name in text box if user clicks
 ' on entry in list

 Const MAX_FILE_LENGTH = 12   ' Characters

 text1.Text = Left(list1.Text, MAX_FILE_LENGTH)

End Sub

Sub List1_DblClick ()

 ' Open file if user double clicks on its name
 ' in list

 Const MAX_FILE_LENGTH = 12   ' Characters
```

```
    text1.Text = Left(list1.Text, MAX_FILE_LENGTH)
    Call cmdOK_Click

End Sub
```

CREATING TOOLBARS

A *toolbar* is a collection of graphical controls that provides quick access to an application's commands. Toolbars are often implemented using picture boxes, image controls and 3D buttons (Professional Edition only). By setting the Picture property of each control to an icon or bitmap, you create toolbars for memo handlers or other types of applications. Figure 8.5 shows an example.

This toolbar uses four Visual Basic icons: FOLDER02.ICO, DISK02.ICO, ARW09LT.ICO and MAIL10.ICO. For a complete listing of icons available in Visual Basic, see Appendix B Icon Library of the *Visual Basic Programmer's Guide*.

8.2 MULTIPLE DOCUMENT INTERFACES

A *multiple-document interface* (MDI) is a document-centered application where multiple instances of forms are maintained by a single *parent window*. In Chapter 1, you learned that an instance is an occurrence of an object. In a MDI application, each open form is a separate instance. Figure 8.6 shows a sample MDI application.

To Create a Multiple-Document Interface

1. From the File menu, choose New MDI Form.
2. Create a new form (or switch to another form in the project—e.g., Form1).
3. Set the MDIChild property of the second form to **True**.

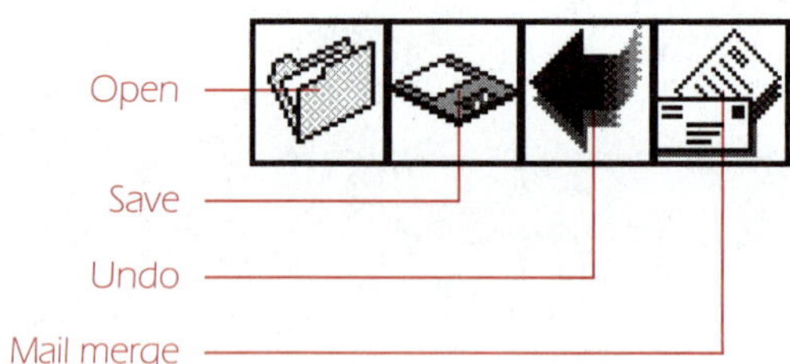

FIGURE 8.5 A sample toolbar

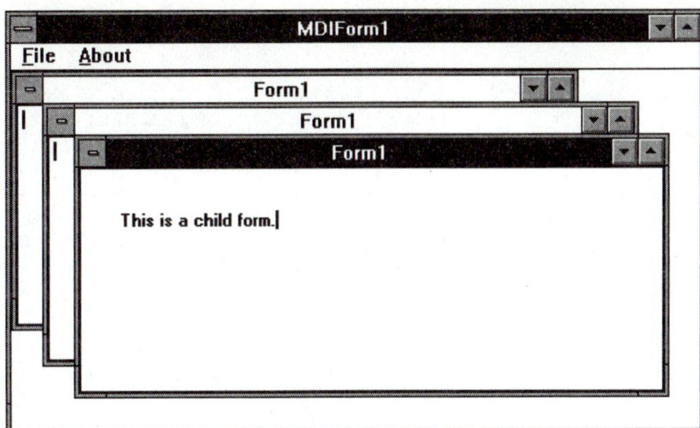

FIGURE 8.6 *A sample MDI application*

USING MDI'S AT RUN TIME

To create a new instance of a form, use the **New** reserved word. The following code shows how this is done:

```
Sub mnuNew_Click ()

 ' Create new instance of form

 Dim new_win As New Form1

 new_win.Show

End Sub
```

At run time, when you create a new instance of a form, the child form appears in the *internal area* of the parent window—that is, the area below the title bar and menu bar of the parent form. When a child form is minimized, it appears in the parent window not on the desktop.

As the name implies, the technology behind MDI's was originally designed for document-centered applications in which you can have several documents open at the same time in different windows. The **ME** reserved word references the current form. You also use **ME** to distinguish multiple instances of forms. The following example shows how to display the name of a file in the title bar of the active window:

```
Sub mnuSave_Click ()

 ' Save current memo

 fileno = 1
 filevar = text1.Text
```

```
 filename = InputBox("File Name:")

 retval = Memowrite(fileno, filename, filevar)
 Me.Caption = filename

End Sub
```

NOTE: In MDI applications, only controls that have an Align property can be used in a toolbar.

MAINTAINING MDI APPLICATIONS

Although you can use **ME** to reference the current instance of a MDI child, to determine if a document in a window is updated, it is necessary to use an array. The following code shows how to manage multiple forms in a MDI container:

```
Global FormArray() As New Form1  ' Declare dynamic form
                                 ' array
Global total_wins_open     ' Total MDI child forms open

Sub mnuNew_Click ()

 ' Increment MDI Child counter

 total_wins_open = total_wins_open + 1

 ' Store new form instance in dynamic array

 ReDim Preserve FormArray(total_wins_open)

 ' Set Caption property of form to uniquely identify
 ' document

 FormArray(total_wins_open).Caption = "Document" +
             ⇨ (RTrim(Str(total_wins_open)) + 1)

End Sub
```

FormArray is a global array of form instances. This definition must appear in the Declaration section of a module (.BAS file). At run time, when the user selects the File New option, the program creates a new form and stores it in the array. By setting the Caption property of a form to a unique value, you reference forms by name. In the preceding example, the mnuNew_Click procedure sets the Caption property each time a new form is created. Using this method, you determine if a file is updated:

```
Sub Text1_Change ()

 ' Report immediately if document has changed

 MsgBox (Me.Caption + " has updated ")

End Sub
```

For this example to work, the default form (or first form instance) must be given a unique name. The following code shows how this can be done:

```
Sub MDIForm_Load ()

 ' Set default form

 Form1.Caption = "Document1"

End Sub
```

TIP: Once you have determined that a document needs to be updated, store this information in the Tag property of the form or create a parallel array to hold this information.

Exercise: Creating a Multiple Document Interface Application

1. From the File menu, choose New Project.
2. Use the New MDI Form command of the File menu to create the MDI form (parent window).
3. From the Window menu, choose Project.
4. In the Project window, click on Form1.frm.
5. Choose the View Form button.
6. Set the MDIChild property of Form1 to True.
7. Add the following menu to the child form (Form1):

Caption	Name	Indent
&File	mnuFile	No
&New	mnuNew	Yes
&Open	mnuOpen	Yes
&Save	mnuSave	Yes
-	mnuSeparator	Yes
E&xit	mnuExit	Yes

8. Draw a text box on the child form. Set its Left and Top properties both to 0. This will align the text box in the upper left corner of the form.
9. Set the MultiLine property of the text box to **True**.

10. Set the Text property of the text box to a null string.
11. Double click on the form. This will put you in the Code window.
12. From the Procedures drop-down list, choose Resize.
13. Add the following code to the Form_Resize procedure:

```
' Size text box to fit interior of form

text1.Height = scaleheight
text1.Width = scalewidth
```

    At run time, when the File New command is selected, this code will size the text box to fit the interior of each form instance.
14. In the mnuNew_Click procedure of the child form, type:

```
' Create new instance of form

Dim new_win As New Form1

new_win.Show
```

15. In the mnuOpen_Click procedure, type:

```
' Open document in current window

fileno = FreeFile
filename = InputBox("Enter file name:", "File Open")
text1.Text = Readmemo(fileno, filename)

Me.Caption = filename

Close fileno
```

16. In the mnuSave_Click procedure, type:

```
' Save document

fileno = FreeFile
filevar = text1.Text

filename = InputBox("File Name:")

retval = Memowrite(fileno, filename, filevar)

Me.Caption = filename

Close fileno
```

    Caution: Since the file save routine contains no error checking, be careful not to overwrite any existing files.

17. In the mnuExit procedure, type:

```
End
```

18. From the File menu, choose Add File...
19. Add the TEXTOPER.BAS module to the project.
20. Save the project and run it.

To test the program, use the File New command to create new windows (child forms). Then enter some text in one of the windows and try saving a document. Afterwards, you can use the File Open command to retrieve the document.

LIMITATIONS OF THE TEXT BOX CONTROL

The maximum size text file you can edit in a text box is slightly under 32K. Therefore, it is unlikely that you will be able to develop a major word processor in Visual Basic. However, many applications rely on simple editors to perform routine tasks. The sample statistical application (STAT.MAK) discussed in Chapter 2 and in Part III, Statistical Functions, uses a simple editor to enter figures for a bar graph.

Many other applications use text editors to perform routine operations. For instance, you can use a text editor to send messages over a modem, import scanned text files, or edit work orders before printing them.

SUMMARY

In this chapter, you learned how to create memo handlers using Visual Basic's standard controls. You have also learned how to use the **Clipboard** object, incorporate library routines in a memo handler, create toolbars and develop multiple document interface applications.

REVIEW QUESTIONS

1. Before you can edit multiple lines in a text box, what property must you set?
2. What property allows you to add scroll bars to a textbox?
3. To undo changes in a text box, what library routine do you call?
4. What Visual Basic object allows you to cut, copy and paste text in a text box? Name 3 methods that apply to it.
5. How can you extract a file name from a long string?
6. Define the following terms:

   multiple document interface
   internal area
   child form

7. How can you save a memo to a file? Give an example.
8. Code a procedure using Readmemo to retrieve a text file for editing.
9. In a multiple document interface application, what Visual Basic menu command allows you to create the parent window?
10. To define a child form, what form property must be set?
11. True or False: In a multiple document interface application, only one parent window can be defined?
12. How can you create a child form at run time in a multiple document interface application?

CLASS PROJECTS

1. Create a toolbar for a memo handler with the following features:

   - Import text files
   - Update text files
   - Reverse edits

   Using the icons listed below, create the project. Be sure to set the MultiLine property of the text box to **True.** When you are done, the form should look like Figure 8.7.

Object	Property	Icon File
picture1	Picture	C:\VB\ICONS\OFFICE\FOLDER02.ICO
picture2	Picture	C:\VB\ICONS\COMPUTER\DISK02.ICO
picture3	Picture	C:\VB\ICONS\ARROWS\ARW09LT.ICO
Form1	Caption	UNTITLED.TXT

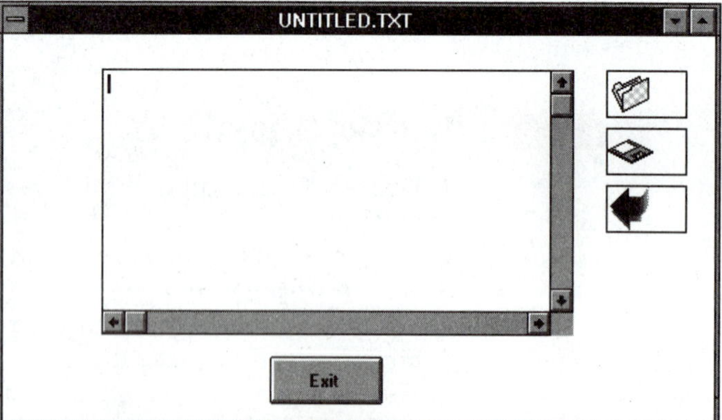

FIGURE 8.7 The project editor

9 DYNAMIC DATA EXCHANGE

Dynamic Data Exchange (DDE) is a technology for sharing information with other Windows-based applications. With DDE, you create data links to other programs that automatically update when new information is received. This chapter shows how to create DDE links at both design time and at run time, and how to handle DDE errors.

9.1 USING DDE

In DDE, the process in which two applications communicate is known as a *conversation*. The application that starts the communication is the *destination application* or *destination,* for short. The application that responds to the conversation is the *source application*. In Microsoft Visual Basic 1.0, the destination application used to be referred to as the *client* and the source application was known as the *server*. These terms are no longer used although you may run across older references when reviewing other code examples.

CREATING LINKS AT DESIGN TIME

At design time, you establish a DDE link by copying information to the Clipboard and then using the Paste Link command in another application to create the link. When you produce a link this way, Visual Basic automatically sets the correct properties needed to initiate the conversation.

To Create a Link at Design Time

1. In the source application, select the item you wish to link (text, numbers, bitmap, etc.).
2. From the Edit menu of the Source application, choose Copy.
3. In the destination application, choose the destination of the copy such as a text or picture box.

4. Choose the Paste Link command from the Edit menu of the destination application.

NOTE: If a Visual Basic form is the source of a conversation, you must set the LinkMode property of the form to 1 - Source.

Not all applications that support DDE allow you to setup links using Copy and Paste Link. If the Paste Link command does not appear in the Edit menu of the destination, check the program's documentation to see if it supports DDE. If the Paste Link command is available but is disabled, it means the destination cannot accept data in the format supplied by the source.

Once a link is established, the destination is automatically refreshed each time the source changes. For example, if you create a link between a Visual Basic text box and a Lotus 1-2-3 for Windows spreadsheet, every time you enter or edit keystrokes in the text box, the new value appears in the cell that contains the link. Figure 9.1 shows an example of a spreadsheet linked to a Visual Basic application. Although you can create links this way, Visual Basic will terminate the link at run time. Some applications refresh links automatically when the destination is executed. However, you may find that it is necessary to write code to re-establish the link.

NOTE: Applications that contain DDE links created at design time will be larger than DDE links created at run time since Visual Basic must include information about the links in the .EXE file.

CREATING LINKS AT RUN TIME

Although you can easily create DDE links at design time, there is always a sacrifice in terms of flexibility. For example, if you load a project that contains a link created at design time, Visual Basic automatically attempts to reestablish the link with the other application. This causes an error to occur if the source application is not currently running. In contrast, when you create a link at run time, you can monitor DDE events, trap errors and even launch other programs when they are not in memory.

To create a DDE link at run time, you must specify at least three items—the application name, the topic and the link mode. The *application name* is the name of the source application. You can get this name by consulting the program's documentation. The *topic* is the subject of a DDE conversation. Word for Windows, for example, recognizes .DOC and .DOT files as topics. Before the link can take effect, you must specify the LinkMode. Table 9.1 shows a list of options that are available. The following example shows how to create an automatic link between two Visual Basic applications:

```
Const AUTOMATIC_LINK = 1, NO_LINK = 0

retval = Shell("SOURCE", 1)     ' Run source application
```

```
text1.LinkMode = NO_LINK           ' Remove any
                                   ' existing links
text1.LinkTopic = "Source|Form1"   ' Set topic of
                                   ' conversation
text1.LinkItem = "Text1"           ' Set link item
text1.LinkMode = AUTOMATIC_LINK    ' Begin automatic link
```

In the preceding example, the source application, SOURCE.EXE, contains no code. For it to be recognized as a Source, the LinkMode property of the form must be set to 1 - Source. The form also contains a text box called text1, which will be the topic of the conversation. This program must be compiled to disk. The destination application contains one object—a text box (also called text1).

You can compile the destination to disk or run it from Visual Basic. Once you have created the link, you can swap between the two programs by pressing Alt+Tab. Alternately, you can make the swap by pressing Ctrl+Esc and choosing an application from the Task List. Any information you type in the text box of the source will automatically appear in the text box of the destination.

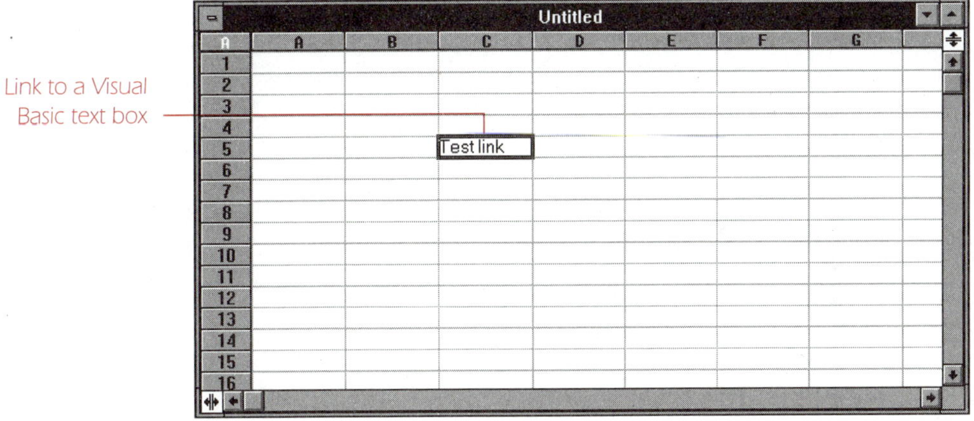

FIGURE 9.1 DDE link to a Lotus 1-2-3 spreadsheet

Setting	Description
0 - None	Removes any existing links.
1 - Automatic	Source automatically supplies data.
2 - Manual	Source supplies data only when requested.
3 - Notify	Inform destination when source has new data.

TABLE 9-1 LINKMODE PROPERTY SETTINGS

NOTE: In Microsoft Visual Basic 1.0, automatic links were referred to as "hot

links" and manual links were known as "cold links". The documentation has changed to conform to new standards in Windows terminology.

CREATING MANUAL LINKS

Sometimes it is better not to automatically update links in a DDE conversation. For example, if a large spreadsheet, word processing document or bitmap has changed, processing time may be significantly delayed during the update. In such cases, you may wish to refresh the link only when a certain button is selected. When the LinkMode property of a control is set to 2-Manual or 3-Notify, you must use the **LinkRequest** method to activate the link. This next example shows how to create a manual link and request information from a Visual Basic source:

```
Sub Form_Load ()

  Const MANUAL_LINK = 2, NO_LINK = 0

  retval = Shell("SOURCE", 1)       ' Run source
                                    ' application

  text1.LinkMode = NO_LINK          ' Remove any
                                    ' existing links
  text1.LinkTopic = "Source|Form1"  ' Set topic of
                                    ' conversation
  text1.LinkItem = "Text1"          ' Set link item
  text1.LinkMode = MANUAL_LINK      ' Begin manual link

End Sub


Sub cmdRequest_Click ()

  ' Request data from source

  text1.LinkRequest

End Sub
```

Basically, the coded to establish a manual link is the same as the code for an automatic link. The only difference is that you set LinkMode to 2-Manual instead of 1-Automatic and that you must use **LinkRequest** to update the link. In the preceding example, a command button called cmdRequest is used to execute the **LinkRequest**.

DDE WITH OTHER WINDOWS APPLICATIONS

You create links to other Windows applications using the same principles. Each application has its own conventions for establishing DDE links. To determine the topics that a program supports, check the program's documentation. The following code creates a link between a Visual Basic text box and a Word for Windows document. This example assumes that Word is loaded with the document already open. For this code to work, the file must contain a bookmark. In Word for Windows 6.0, you can define a bookmark by pressing Ctrl+Shift+F5.

```
Sub Form_Load ()

  Const MANUAL_LINK = 2, NO_LINK = 0, TIMEOUT_OFF = -1

  ' Remove any existing links
  text1.LinkMode = NO_LINK
  ' Turn off time out error
  text1.LinkTimeout = TIMEOUT_OFF
  ' Set topic of conversation
  text1.LinkTopic = "Winword|C:\WinWord\Temp.Doc"
  ' Set link item to Word bookmark
  text1.LinkItem = "\Doc"
  ' Begin manual link
  text1.LinkMode = MANUAL_LINK

End Sub


Sub cmdRequest_Click ()

  ' Request data from source - Winword

  text1.LinkRequest

End Sub
```

POKING INFORMATION INTO A SOURCE

Although the destination application normally receives information, it is also possible to poke data into the source. The **LinkPoke** method is used for this purpose.

Example

```
Sub Form_Load ()

  Const AUTOMATIC_LINK = 1, NO_LINK = 0
```

```
    ' Run source application
    retval = Shell("SOURCE", 1)
    ' Remove any existing links
    text1.LinkMode = NO_LINK
    ' Set topic of conversation
    text1.LinkTopic = "Source|Form1"
    ' Set link item
    text1.LinkItem = "Text1"
    ' Begin automatic link
    text1.LinkMode = AUTOMATIC_LINK

End Sub


Sub cmdPoke_Click ()

    ' Poke data into source

    text1.LinkPoke

End Sub
```

The **LinkPoke** method pokes or sends information to the source application. In the preceding example, a value is sent to the source by reversing the normal route of communication.

THE LINKEXECUTE METHOD

Another useful technique is to use the **LinkExecute** method to make the source perform an operation. The following example creates a link to WinWord (Word for Windows) and uses **LinkExecute** to save and close a document:

```
Sub cmdOK_Click ()

    Const TIMEOUT_OFF = -1
    Const NOLINK = 0
    Const MANUAL_LINK = 2
    Const NO_RESPONSE = 282
    Const MAXIMIZE = 3

    On Error GoTo link_err

    ' Create manual link to WinWord (Microsoft Word)

    text1.LinkTimeout = TIMEOUT_OFF
    text1.LinkMode = NOLINK
    text1.LinkTopic = "WinWord|System"
    text1.LinkMode = MANUAL_LINK
```

```
  ' Save and close current document

  text1.LinkExecute "[FileClose 1]"

  ' Move focus to Word

  AppActivate "Microsoft Word"

  Exit Sub

link_err:   ' Error handler

  If Err = NO_RESPONSE Then
    retval = Shell("C:\WINWORD\WINWORD.EXE", MAXIMIZE)
  Else
    MsgBox (Error)
  End If

  Resume

End Sub
```

This example uses **LinkExecute** to save and close a Microsoft Word document. Notice that the LinkTimeout property is turned off to prevent a time out error (since Word can take a considerable amount of time to load). Also note that if Word is not in memory, the program automatically runs it using the **Shell** command. The System topic returns information about the application. If a program supports the System topic, you can get a list of formats and other topics that the application supports this way.

9.2 MONITORING DDE EVENTS

To achieve greater control over DDE, you can monitor events as they occur. Table 9.2 shows a list of events that apply.

Event	Description
LinkOpen	Occurs when a conversation begins.
LinkClose	Occurs when a conversation ends.
LinkExecute	Occurs when a destination application sends a command string to be executed by a Visual Basic source.
LinkNotify	Occurs when the source in a notify link has new information.

TABLE 9-2 DDE EVENTS

THE LINKOPEN AND LINKCLOSE EVENTS

When a Visual Basic control begins a conversation, it causes a LinkOpen event to occur. You can write code to intercept this event:

```
Sub Text1_LinkOpen (Cancel As Integer)

  ' Show topic of conversation

  MsgBox ("Linked initiated with " & text1.LinkTopic)

End Sub
```

The preceding example displays a message to inform the user that a link has been established. This technique is particularly useful in debugging applications. You can also test how many links are currently active by writing code like this:

```
Dim total_links As Integer


Sub Text1_LinkOpen (Cancel As Integer)

  ' Count total number of links

  total_links = total_links + 1

End Sub


Sub Text1_LinkClose ()

  ' Link terminated, adjust counter

  total_links = total_links - 1

End Sub
```

For this example to work, <total_links> must be declared in the Declarations section of the form or as a global variable. By maintaining a count of how many conversations are currently active, you can restrict users from initiated more links after a certain point by setting the <Cancel> flag to **True** in the LinkOpen procedure.

THE LINKNOTIFY EVENT

When the LinkMode property of a control is set to 3-Notify, a LinkNotify event occurs whenever the source application has new information. You can use this event to debug applications and also to determine the status of a link.

THE LINKEXECUTE EVENT

The LinkExecute event procedure of a form is useful in applications where a Visual Basic form is the source of a conversation. This procedure accepts two arguments:

cmdStr A command string to be executed by the source.
Cancel Determines the status of the operation:

```
Cancel = 0  Source application agrees to
perform operation (cmdStr).
Cancel = 1  Source application returns negative
acknowledgment.
```

<cmdStr> is any command meaningful to the source application. This argument has no pre-defined format or meaning. You can use it to create macro languages of DDE operations your applications support.

Example

```
Sub Form_LinkExecute (Cmdstr As String, Cancel As
                    ⇨ Integer)

  ' Perform macro command

  If Cmdstr = "[OPEN]" Then
    Call Openfile
    Cancel = False
  ElseIf Cmdstr = "[UPDATE]" Then
    Call Updatefile
    Cancel = False
  ElseIf Cmdstr = "[BALANCE]" Then
    Call Showbalance
    Cancel = False
  Else
    Cancel = True
  End If

End Sub
```

9.3 HANDLING DDE ERRORS

In DDE, there are two types of errors that can occur in a conversation—run time errors and errors that occur while no code is executing. In Chapter 5, you learned how to trap standard run time errors. In DDE, however, it is possible that an error can occur while a program seems idle.

Technically, Visual Basic is never completely idle. The programs you write in Visual Basic must share the same system resources as other Windows applications. Thus Visual Basic must yield to other programs in order to work in a multitasking environment. This means that while a program may seem idle, events are really occurring behind the scene.

One of the routine operations that Visual Basic handles, is monitoring DDE events. If a source application attempts to supply information in an invalid format to a Visual Basic destination, a LinkError will occur. Similarly, if a source attempts to transmit data that is too large for a Visual Basic control to accept, a LinkError will also result. In any case, you can test for DDE errors by placing code in the LinkError procedure of a control. The following example demonstrates how this is done.

```
Sub Text1_LinkError (linkerr As Integer)

  Const MB_ICONEXCLAMATION = 48
  Const NO_LINK = 6, NO_UPDATE = 8, LOW_MEMORY = 11

  Select Case link_err
    Case NO_LINK
      errmsg = "Destination unable to connect"
    Case NO_UPDATE
      errmsg = "Destination unable to poke data"
    Case LOW_MEMORY
      errmsg = "Low memory - unable to perform DDE
              ⇨ operation"
    Case Else
      errmsg = Error
  End Select

  ' Show DDE error message

  MsgBox errmsg, MB_ICONEXCLAMATION, "DDE Error"

End Sub
```

Notice the use of the MB_ICONEXCLAMATION constant. If an error occurs, MB_ICONEXCLAMATION displays an exclamation mark icon in the message box along with the error message (see Figure 9.2).

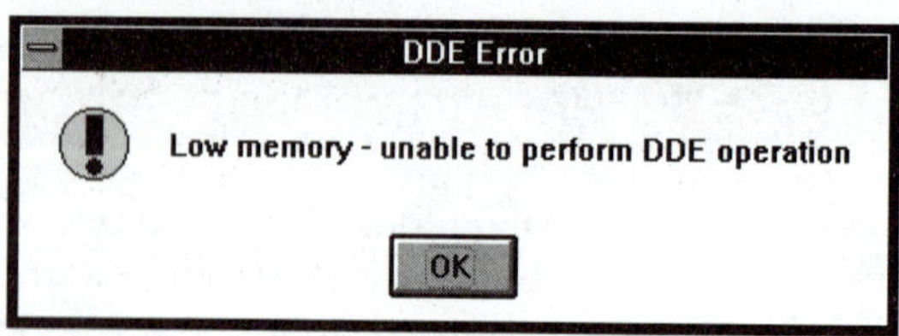

FIGURE 9.2 The DDE error handler dialog

When a Visual Basic application is the source of a conversation, you can test for DDE errors by placing code in the LinkError procedure of the form. If Windows is unable to respond to an event due to a time out error (error 282), you can use the **DoEvents** statement to force Visual Basic to temporarily yield to other Windows applications (so that pending updates can be performed).

Example

```
Sub Form_LinkError (LinkErr As Integer)

  Const NO_LINK = 6, NO_UPDATE = 8, LOW_MEMORY = 11
  Const TIME_OUT_ERR = 282, MB_ICONEXCLAMATION = 48

  Select Case link_err
    Case TIME_OUT_ERR
      DoEvents
    Case NO_LINK
      errmsg = "Destination unable to connect"
    Case NO_UPDATE
      errmsg = "Destination unable to poke data"
    Case LOW_MEMORY
      errmsg = "Low memory - unable to perform DDE
            ⇨ operation"
    Case Else
      errmsg = Error
  End Select

  ' Show DDE error message

  MsgBox errmsg, MB_ICONEXCLAMATION, "DDE Error"

End Sub
```

TESTING IF AN APPLICATION IS RUNNING

If an application attempts to initialize a DDE conversation with a source that is not already running, a run time error will occur. To prevent this error, you can use the **Shell** command to run the source application. The **Shell** command, however, does not check if a program is already in memory. Therefore, it is possible that two or more copies of the source may be running at the same time. Thus the destination must have a way of testing if a program is active. The following code shows how you can check the status of an application. The **AppActivate** statement gives focus to the source application. If the source is not in memory, the error handler traps the error and launches the source:

```
Sub Form_Load ()

  Const NO_LINK = 0, AUTOMATIC_LINK = 1, NOT_ACTIVE = 5

  On Error GoTo link_err

  ' Attempt to maximize source application

  AppActivate "SOURCE"

  ' Remove any existing links
  text1.LinkMode = NO_LINK
  ' Set topic of conversation
  text1.LinkTopic = "Source|Form1"
  text1.LinkItem = "Text1"          ' Set link item
  ' Begin automatic link
  text1.LinkMode = AUTOMATIC_LINK

  Exit Sub

link_err:

  ' Run source application if its not already in
  ' memory

  If Err = NOT_ACTIVE Then
    retval = Shell("SOURCE", 1)
  End If

  Resume Next

End Sub
```

NOTE: You could also use the library procedure Is_active to check if a program is in memory.

Exercise: Creating a Link Between Two Visual Basic Applications

1. From the File menu, select New Project.
2. Set the LinkMode property of the form to 1 - Source.
3. Set the Caption property of the form to Source Application.
4. Draw a text box on the form.
5. Save both the form and the project as SOURCE.
6. From the File menu, choose Make EXE File...

7. Click on OK to accept the default name SOURCE.EXE.
8. From the File menu, choose New Project.
9. Set the Caption property of the form to Destination Application.
10. Draw the following controls on the form:

    text box
    command button

11. Set the properties of each control as:

Control	Property	Value
text1	Text	null string
command1	Caption	Request
command1	Name	cmdOK

12. In the Form_Load procedure, type:

```
Const MANUAL_LINK = 2, NO_LINK = 0

' Run source application
retval = Shell("SOURCE", 1)

' Remove any existing links
text1.LinkMode = NO_LINK

' Set topic of conversation
text1.Linktopic = "Source|Form1"

' Set link item
text1.LinkItem = "Text1"

' Set default link mode (manual)
text1.LinkMode = MANUAL_LINK
```

13. In the cmdOK_Click procedure, type:

```
' Request data from source application

text1.LinkRequest
```

14. Save both the project and the form as DESTIN.
15. From the Run menu, choose Start. Visual Basic will execute both the source and the destination applications.
16. Switch to the Source by pressing Alt+Tab.
17. In the text1 text box, change the default text value *text1* to *link test.*
18. Switch back to the destination application by pressing Alt+Tab.
19. Click on Request to update the link. The text box of the destination should now display the same string that appears in the text box of the source.

SUMMARY

This chapter showed you how to create DDE links at both design time and at run time. You also learned how to check if an application is in memory, create links between two Visual Basic forms, display custom error dialogs and write DDE macro commands.

REVIEW QUESTIONS

1. What is DDE? Give three examples of when you might use it.
2. What are the disadvantages of creating links at design time?
3. How do you specify the topic of a conversation?
4. To establish a link, what properties must you set?
5. What are the three types of links you can create?
6. What property do you set to create a manual link?
7. To declare a Visual Basic form as a source, what property do you set?
8. To remove a DDE link from a control, what must LinkMode be set to?
9. How can you send a command to a source for it to execute?
10. What method do you use to request information from a source?
11. What method do you use to poke information into a source?
12. What is the purpose of the LinkExecute procedure?
13. Name three significant events that can occur during a DDE conversation.
14. How can you test if a link is successful?
15. Are there any special considerations for trapping DDE errors?
16. What error code does Visual Basic return during a time out error?
17. Code an error routine to trap/report DDE errors. Use the LinkError procedure of a control.

CLASS PROJECTS

1. Write a program to communicate with another Windows application. Use any software available on your system.
2. Modify the above program to include error checking and the ability to detect if a program is in memory.

CREATING LINKED AND EMBEDDED OBJECTS

Object linking and embedding (OLE) is a technology that allows you to share information with other Windows-based applications. It differs from *dynamic data exchange* in that your applications can control the views of other programs. This chapter examines the Visual Basic techniques used to produce linked and embedded objects.

10.1 USING THE OLE CONTROL

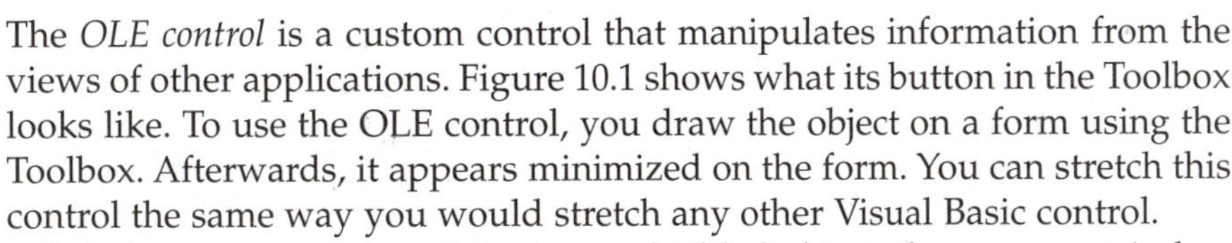

The *OLE control* is a custom control that manipulates information from the views of other applications. Figure 10.1 shows what its button in the Toolbox looks like. To use the OLE control, you draw the object on a form using the Toolbox. Afterwards, it appears minimized on the form. You can stretch this control the same way you would stretch any other Visual Basic control.

Before you can create a linked or embedded object, there are certain key terms you should be familiar with. Table 10.1 summarizes these terms.

NOTE: When you distribute an application that uses the OLE custom control, you must install the MSOLE2.VBX file in the WINDOWS\SYSTEM directory of the target drive.

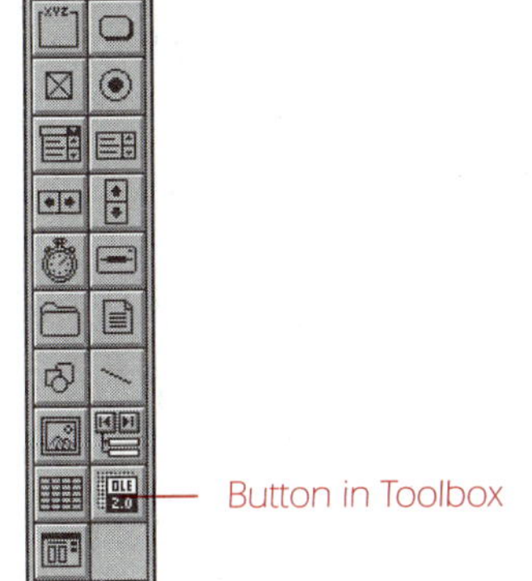

FIGURE 10.1 The OLE control

CREATING OLE OBJECTS AT DESIGN TIME

At design time, you create new OLE objects using the Insert Object dialog box. When the OLE control is drawn on a form, this window appears automatically. Figure 10.2 shows how it looks.

Key Term	Description
OLE object	A unit of data created by an OLE application.
Linked Object	A reference to an object stored and maintained by another Windows-based application.
Embedded Object	An OLE object that is maintained by a Visual Basic application.
Container application	A program that displays objects from other applications.
Class	Determines the source application for an OLE object and the type of data that it can contain.
Verb	An action that can be performed on an object.
In-place activation	The ability to edit an object within the boundaries of the OLE control.
OLE Automation	An industry standard for controlling OLE objects remotely from applications.

TABLE 10-1 KEY TERMS IN OLE

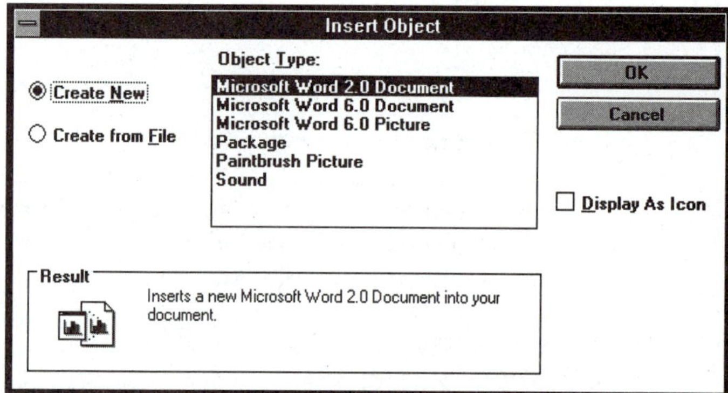

FIGURE 10.2 The Insert Object dialog

To Create an Embedded Object at Design Time

1. Using the Toolbox, draw the OLE control on a form.
2. From the Object Type list box of the Insert Object dialog, choose the object type you wish to create (such as a Microsoft Word 6.0 document).
3. Click on OK to create the object.
4. Using the source application's menus and built-in editing commands, create the object.
5. Save the object under a unique name.
6. Close the source application.

After leaving the application, the object will appear in the OLE control. Since this control will act as a working area for the object, size it appropriately. Once you have sized the control, run the program to test the embedded object. To do this:

1. From the Run menu, choose Start.
2. Double click on the OLE control to activate the object.

You edit the OLE object just as you would in the application that created the object. For example, you can use the menus of the source application that are now part of the OLE container to make the changes. Since each object supports its own set of editing capabilities, the type of changes you make will depend on the objects you create. For more information on editing objects, refer to the Maintaining Embedded Objects section later in this chapter.

CREATING OBJECTS FROM FILES AT DESIGN TIME

There are several other ways to create linked and embedded objects at design time. The preceding steps show how to create a new embedded object. You can also create an object from an existing file or template. To do this, use the following steps:

1. Draw the OLE control on a form. The Insert Object dialog box will appear.
2. From the Insert Object dialog, choose the Create From File option.
3. Use the Browse button to search the file list. You can also change paths by entering a new path in the File box.
4. Create a linked object by choosing the Link check box *or*
   Create an embedded object by leaving this option blank.

TIP: Since linked objects do not support in-place editing, you may wish to select the Display as Icon option whenever you create a linked object.

5. Click on OK to create the object.
6. If the object is embedded in the OLE control, size the control to create the working area size you need.
7. Run the program.
8. Double click on the OLE control to activate the linked or embedded object.

NOTE: Since Visual Basic saves embedded objects as part of an application, the resulting executable file will be considerably larger if you create objects at design time.

10.2 EDITING OBJECT DEFINITIONS

At design time, you can edit an object by selecting the OLE control with the right mouse button. When this happens, Visual Basic displays a pop-up menu that shows all the verbs that pertain to the object. Figure 10.3 shows how the menu looks for an embedded object.

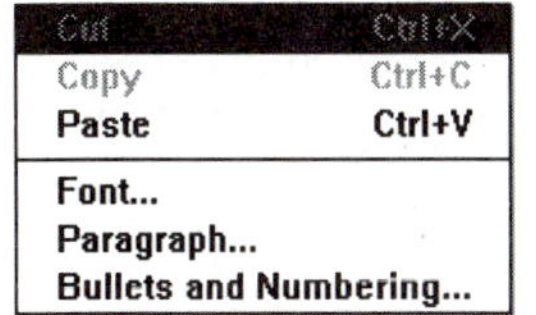

FIGURE 10.3 The OLE pop-up menu

The Insert Object command creates a new object by redefining the current object. Since the OLE control can contain only one object at a time, embedding a new object removes the old one. You can also delete an object by choosing the Delete Embedded Object command. The Paste Special option (which is covered in the next section) copies an object from another Windows application using the Clipboard. When the Clipboard is empty, this command is not available.

PASTING OBJECTS FROM THE CLIPBOARD

At design time, you can create linked or embedded objects by pasting objects from the Clipboard. To do this, you use the Paste Special command. Figure 10.4 shows how this dialog appears.

To Paste an Object From the Clipboard

1. From the source application, select the data or object you wish to copy by using the Copy command of the Edit menu.
2. In Visual Basic, click on the OLE control to display a pop-up menu of verbs supported.
3. Choose the Paste Special command.
4. Choose either the Paste option to create an embedded object or the Paste Link option to create a linked object.
5. Click on OK to create the object.

10.3 CREATING OBJECTS AT RUN TIME

At design time, when you create an object, you use the Paste Special or Insert Object dialogs. At run time, you set the properties of the OLE control in code. The following example shows how you can do this:

```
' Load a Lotus Write document

Const OLE_CREATE_LINK = 1

OLE1.Class = "LotusWriteDocument"
OLE1.SourceDoc = "C:\LWrite\Docs\Mydoc.sam"
OLE1.Action = OLE_CREATE_LINK
```

The preceding example creates a link to a Lotus Write document. To accomplish this, the Class property is set to the class name of the application (LotusWriteDocument). This name is not the same name that appears in the Object Type list box of the Insert Object dialog. To get the class name of an application, consult the program's documentation or use **MsgBox** to display the value of the Class property.

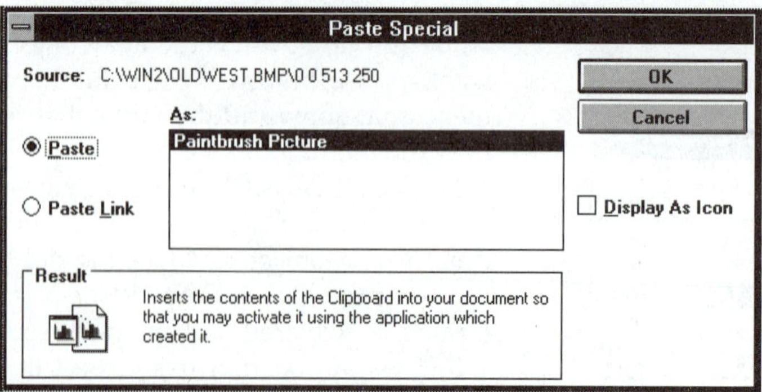

FIGURE 10.4 The Paste Special dialog

NOTE: If you use the later method, you must first create the object at design time in order to test its Class property. Once you have the correct name, you can delete the object and recreate it at run time.

The SourceDoc property of the OLE controls determines the source object (or file name). The Action property specifies the action to perform. When this property is set to 1, a link to the source application is created. When the Action property is set to 0, an embedded object is created.

If you set the Action property to 14, Visual Basic displays the Insert Object dialog. You can use this technique to allow users to create their own linked or embedded objects at run time.

CREATING LINKS WITHIN FILES

The LinkItem property of the OLE control allows you to specify part of a document as a link object. Each application has its own conventions that you use to specify this property. In Microsoft Excel, you set LinkItem to a cell address using R1C1 syntax. You can also indicate a cell range using code like this:

```
OLE1.LinkItem = "R1C1:R15C6"        ' A1..F15
```

10.4 MAINTAINING EMBEDDED OBJECTS

By definition, a linked object is a reference to an object maintained by another Windows-based application. To save a linked object, you use the Save or Update command from the application that created the object. In contrast, with embedded objects, your applications must have a way of maintaining OLE objects. The OLE_EX.MAK application included with this book demonstrates how you can do this. If you installed the example files in the default path, this program is located in the C:\VB_LIB directory. Figure 10.5 shows how the program looks with an embedded Microsoft Word 6.0 document.

The cmdRead_Click procedure retrieves an OLE object from disk by calling the library function OLERead. OLERead opens the file for binary access and reads its contents into the OLE2 control:

```
Sub cmdRead_Click ()

   ' Read data associated with object

   Dim fileno As Integer

   fileno = FreeFile
   filename = InputBox("File name?")

   retval = OLERead(fileno, filename, OLE2)

End Sub
```

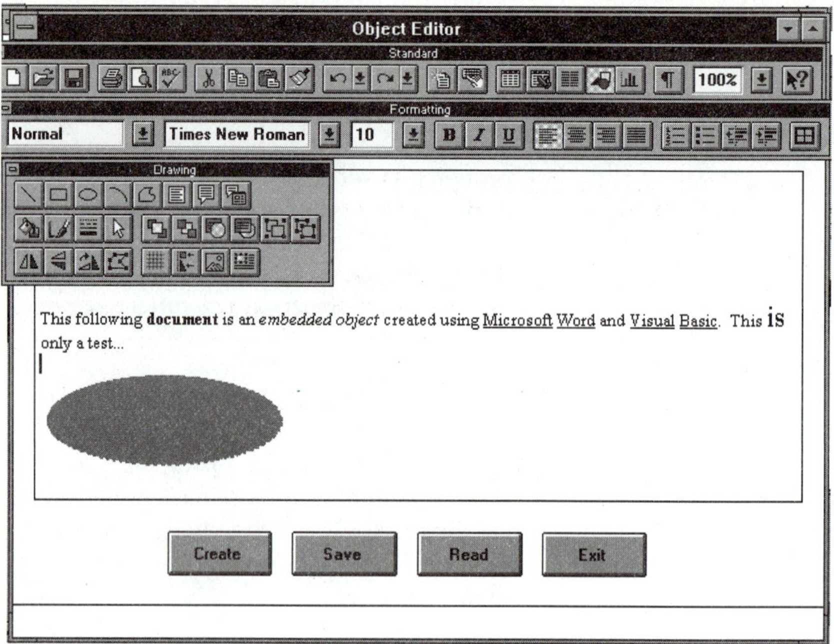

FIGURE 10.5 The Object Editor with an embedded Microsoft Word document

Once you retrieve an object, you can edit it the same way you would in the application that created the object. In this case, the toolbars in Microsoft Word are made available to the container application so you can edit the document, format text, check spelling and add graphics. In addition, you can move the toolbars and even stretch them vertically or horizontally. Since Visual Basic saves the position, size and appearance of each toolbar with the object, a single container application can have many views.

SAVING AN EMBEDDED OBJECT

After editing an object in OLE_EX.MAK, choosing the Save button updates it. To accomplish this, the cmdSave_Click event procedure calls the library function OLESave:

```
Sub cmdSave_Click ()

    ' Save data associated with object

    Dim fileno As Integer

    fileno = FreeFile
```

```
    If filename = "" Then
      filename = InputBox("Save file as?")
    End If

    retval = OLESave(fileno, filename, OLE2)

End Sub
```

The cmdCreate_Click procedure of OLE_EX.MAK creates a new object by displaying the Insert Object dialog. To do this, the program sets the OLE Action property to the value of the CREATE_OBJECT constant (14):

```
Sub cmdCreate_Click ()

  ' Create new linked or embedded object at run time

  Const CREATE_OBJECT = 14

  OLE2.Action = CREATE_OBJECT

End Sub
```

When reading OLE objects, keep in mind that you must supply the correct path in order to access the object. Otherwise, your container application may display an older version of the object or not be able to access the object at all. The OLERead and OLESave functions were written to make working with objects easier. To use these functions, you must include the ENGINE.BAS file in each project.

10.5 USING OLE AUTOMATION

With OLE Automation, you can expose the objects an application supports so that other applications can use them. Using this technique, you can write code to manipulate foreign objects as if they were part of Visual Basic. For example, a word processor might reveal a paragraph, bookmark or selection. To generate this kind of object, you use the **CreateObject** function.

Syntax

```
CreateObject (application.class)
```

The <class> of an OLE Automation object consists of two parts. The name of the application that is creating the object, followed by a separator (period) and then a class or topic the application supports. For example, a word processor might recognize a class called Document.

Not all Windows applications support OLE Automation. To determine if an application supports this feature, check the program's documentation. The following example shows how to create an object using OLE Automation:

```
Dim t_obj As Object ' Declare object variable

Set t_obj = CreateObject("TextEdit.Document")
```

By declaring <t_obj> as type **Object** and using the **CreateObject** function to generate the object, you can then assign the object to the object variable using **Set**. Once you have made this assignment, you inherit all the functionality of the object. For example, if the object supports the **Insert** and **Print** methods, you can manipulate the object like this:

```
t_obj.Insert "Test String"              ' Send message to
                                        ' foreign
                                        ' application
t_obj.Print                             ' Print object
t_obj.SaveAs "C:\TEXTEDIT\DOC1.TXT"     ' Save object
```

NOTE: Unlike object linking and embedding, objects created through OLE Automation do not appear in the OLE control, nor are they maintained by Visual Basic.

Exercise: Creating a Link to Paintbrush

1. From the Toolbox, select the OLE control. The Insert Object dialog will appear.
2. Instead of creating an object now, you are going to create a link at run time. To do this, select the Cancel button.
3. Set the SizeMode property of the OLE control to 2 (AutoSize).
4. Drag the OLE1 control to the upper left corner of the form. This will center the picture on the form when the program runs.
5. In the Form_Load procedure, type:

```
OLE1.Class = "PBrush"
OLE1.SourceDoc = "c:\vb_lib\oldwest.bmp"

' Create linked object

OLE1.Action = 1
```

NOTE: This code assumes that you have installed the sample programs in the C:\VB_LIB directory. If these files are installed in another path, substitute the correct drive and directory names.

6. Run the program.
7. The picture of an old west scene should appear in the OLE container (see Figure 10.6). Double click on the OLE control to start Paintbrush.

NOTE: If you receive an error at this point, it is probably because your system does not have enough memory to invoke Paintbrush. Try closing some applications by pressing Ctrl+Esc. If you still do not have enough memory, it may be because you have too many memory resident programs in your AUTOEXEC.BAT file.

FIGURE 10.6 Link to a Paintbrush file

8. When Paintbrush is invoked, scribble a few quick lines on the canvas.
9. To demonstrate the principles of linking, close Paintbrush by selecting File Exit. The program will prompt you to save the changes. Click on No.
10. In Visual Basic, notice the image of the painting has changed to reflect the edits. Don't worry, these changes are still only volatile. Since the container application has no save option, the painting will return to its original state when you close the form.

SUMMARY

In this chapter, you learned how to create linked and embedded objects at both design time and at run time. You have also learned how to maintain objects, link ranges of cells and how to use OLE Automation.

REVIEW QUESTIONS

1. What is OLE?
2. Name some examples in which OLE can be applied.
3. What is the difference between a linked and embedded object?
4. How can you create an object at design time?
5. How can you create an object at run time?
6. When might it be better to create an object at run time as opposed to design time?
7. How can you get the class name of an application?
8. What property is used to specify the location of a file at run time?
9. Code a procedure to create an object at run time. Use a valid class name.

10. How can you embed a range of cells from a Microsoft Excel spreadsheet in an OLE container?
11. Define the following terms:

    OLE object
    Linked object
    Embedded object
    Container application
    Class
    Verb
    In-place activation
    OLE Automation

12. What are the advantages and disadvantages of creating embedded objects as opposed to linking objects?

CLASS PROJECTS

1. Generate a program that interactively creates linked and embedded objects at run time.
2. Create a link to a Microsoft Word document. Then add an option to the program so that the user can edit an object in the container application. What seems more practical?
3. Using any software you have available on your system, write a program to maintain an embedded object. Use any library routines you find helpful.

11 PRODUCING CHARTS AND GRAPHS

The *graph control*, which comes with the Professional Edition of Visual Basic, provides an interface between a Visual Basic application and the *Graphics Server library*. Through this control, you can create graphs without having to write a single line of code. This chapter shows how to create graphs, change the graph style, add labels, legends, symbols, grid lines, tick marks and produce various other charting effects.

11.1 USING THE GRAPH CONTROL

By default, the graph control draws a two dimensional bar graph when you select it from the Toolbox. You can easily change the type of graph that appears by setting the GraphType and GraphStyle properties. The following code, for example, displays a two dimensional pie chart:

```
Sub cmdPieChart_Click ()

 ' Display pie chart using random data

 Const DRAW = 2
 Const PIECHART = 1
 Const COLOR_LABELS = 2
 Const CLEAR_GRAPH = 1

 Graph1.DrawMode = CLEAR_GRAPH

 Graph1.GraphType = PIECHART
 Graph1.GraphStyle = COLOR_LABELS
```

```
    Graph1.DrawMode = DRAW

End Sub
```

Figure 11.1 shows how the graph looks.

NOTE: When you distribute an application that uses the graph control, you must install the GRAPH.VBX, GSWDLL.DLL and GSW.EXE files in the WINDOWS\ SYSTEM subdirectory of your customer's machine (see Chapter 16, Writing Setup Programs).

When the GraphStyle property is set to 1, the graph control draws a pie chart. For the data source, the graph control automatically generates random data. You can override this default by setting the GraphData property. In order to do this, however, you must understand how graphs are organized.

With most graph types, a chart is composed of three basic components: the graph data, the number of *data sets* per graph and the number of *points* per data set. A *point* refers to a specific data element in a graph. A *data set* is a group of data points. You can set these attributes at design time or at run time using the following properties:

Property	Description	Example
NumSets	Sets the number of data sets to be graphed	Graph1.NumSets = 4
NumPoints	Sets the number of data points in each data set	Graph1.NumPoints = 3
ThisSet	Refers to the current group of data elements	Graph1.ThisSet = 3
ThisPoint	Refers to the current point in a data set	Graph1.ThisPoint = 2

In pie charts, there is only one data set even if multiple data sets are defined. Therefore, each data point refers specifically to the first set (ThisSet = 1).

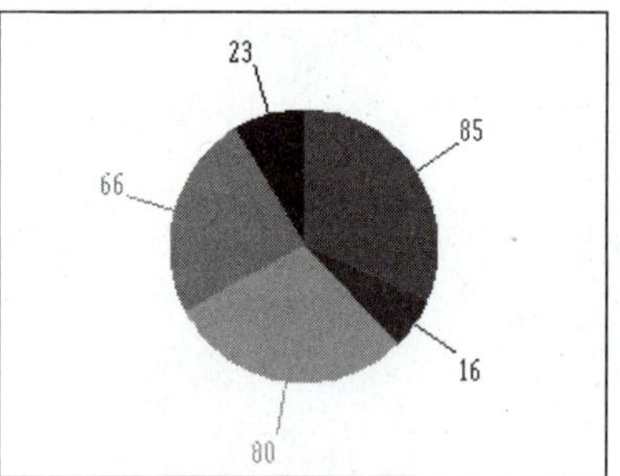

FIGURE 11.1 A two-dimensional pie chart

THE AUTOINC PROPERTY

The AutoInc property automatically increments the GraphData pointer. Thus it is possible to quickly initialize a graph by writing code like this:

```
Sub cmdGraph_Click ()

 Const DRAW = 2

 Graph1.AutoInc = 1
 Graph1.NumPoints = 3
 Graph1.NumSets = 4
 Graph1.GraphType = 3 ' Bar graph

 ' Fill each point within each set with test data

 For i = 1 To Graph1.NumPoints * Graph1.NumSets
   anyvalue = i * 20
   Graph1.GraphData = anyvalue
 Next

 Graph1.DrawMode = DRAW

End Sub
```

When AutoInc is set to 1, Visual Basic automatically increments the value of ThisPoint. If ThisPoint is at the end of a set, the next set in the graph is filled with data.

GRAPH TYPES

Figure 11.2 on page 170 summarizes the graph types available in Visual Basic. Each GraphType is further broken down into various graph styles. You can get a quick idea of how a graph will look in a particular style by setting the GraphStyle property. Section 11.2, Customizing Graphs, shows how this is done.

11.2 CUSTOMIZING GRAPHS

This next section shows how to customize graphs by applying various property settings. Except where noted, each property can be set at both design time and at run time.

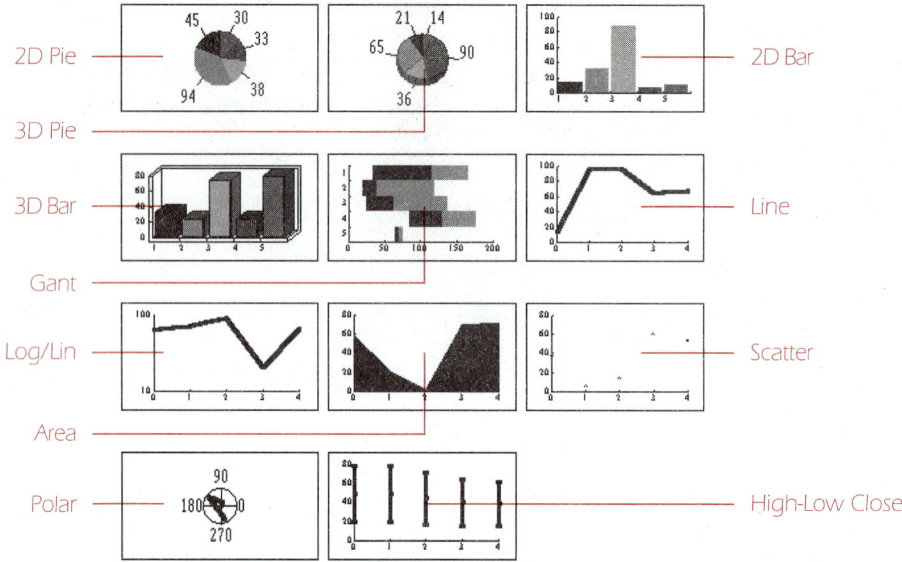

FIGURE 11.2 Graph types available in Visual Basic

THE GRAPHTITLE PROPERTY

The GraphTitle property displays a title over a graph. The string cannot be more than 80 characters. If the title does not fully appear, stretch the graph control so that it does.

Example

```
Sub cmdTitle_Click ()

 Const LINEGRAPH = 6
 Const DRAW = 2
 Const CLEAR_GRAPH = 1

 Graph1.DrawMode = CLEAR_GRAPH
 Graph1.GraphType = LINEGRAPH

 ' Display graph title

 Graph1.GraphTitle = "Pseudo Company"
 Graph1.DrawMode = DRAW

End Sub
```

When working with graphs, it is important to keep in mind that no graph will be drawn until DrawMode is set to 2 (DRAW). Thus you can set multiple graph properties before displaying a graph. Notice that you can also use this property to clear a graph. When DrawMode is set to 1, the previous graph image is erased before the next one appears.

LEGENDTEXT PROPERTY

When the LegendText property is set, a color coded index with labels appears to the right of the graph (see Figure 11.3). Each label marks a different data point in the graph.

Example

```
Sub cmdLegend_Click ()

 ' Display legend text for stacked bar graph

 Const DRAW = 2
 Const BAR2D = 3
 Const STACKED = 2
 Const CLEAR_GRAPH = 1

 Graph1.DrawMode = CLEAR_GRAPH

 Graph1.AutoInc = 1

 Graph1.GraphType = BAR2D
 Graph1.GraphStyle = STACKED
 Graph1.NumSets = 4
 Graph1.NumPoints = 4

 Graph1.LegendText = "NORTH"
 Graph1.LegendText = "SOUTH"
 Graph1.LegendText = "EAST"
 Graph1.LegendText = "WEST"

 Graph1.DrawMode = DRAW

End Sub
```

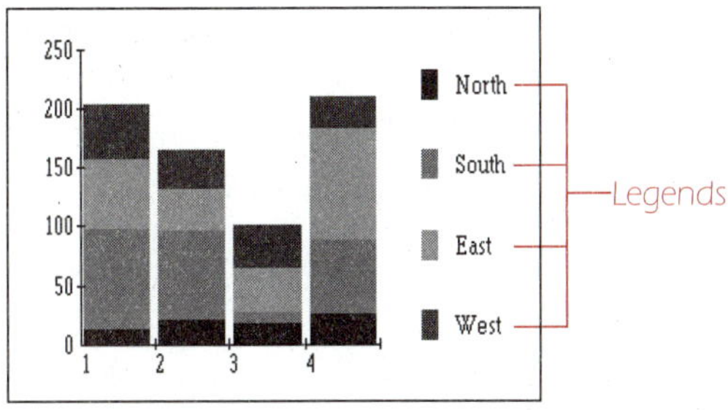

FIGURE 11.3 Displaying legends on graphs

THE LABELTEXT PROPERTY

By default, Visual Basic uses numeric labels to shows data points in a graph. The LabelText property replaces these numeric labels with the labels you define.

Example

```
Sub cmdLabel_Click ()

 Const DRAW = 2
 Const BAR3D = 4
 Const NOSTYLE = 0
 Const CLEAR_GRAPH = 1

 Graph1.AutoInc = 1

 Graph1.DrawMode = CLEAR_GRAPH
 Graph1.GraphType = BAR3D
 Graph1.GraphStyle = NOSTYLE

 Graph1.NumSets = 2
 Graph1.NumPoints = 4

 ' Display graph labels

 Graph1.LabelText = "Hardware"
 Graph1.LabelText = "Appliances"
 Graph1.LabelText = "TV/VCR"
 Graph1.LabelText = "Audio"

 Graph1.DrawMode = DRAW

End Sub
```

THE EXTRADATA PROPERTY

The ExtraData property creates exploding pie charts. You use this technique to draw attention to each slice or segment of the chart. Figure 11.4 shows such an example. To create this chart, the following code is needed:

```
Sub cmdExplode_Click ()

 ' Display 3D pie chart with exploding effect

 Const DRAW = 2
 Const PIECHART_3D = 2
```

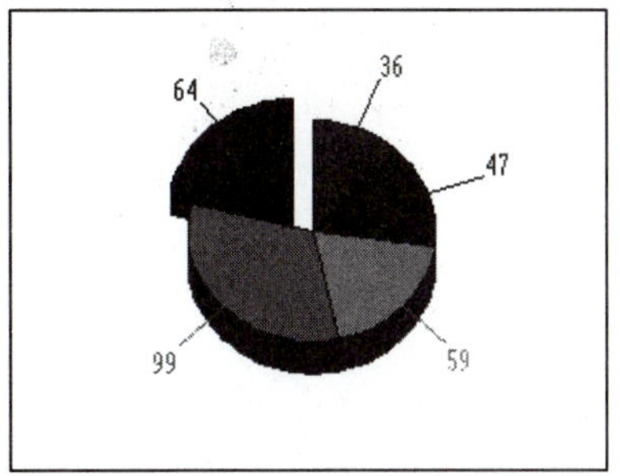

FIGURE 11.4 An exploding pie chart

```
 Const COLOR_LABELS = 2
 Const EXPLODE = 1
 Const CLEAR_GRAPH = 1

 Graph1.DrawMode = CLEAR_GRAPH
 Graph1.GraphType = PIECHART_3D
 Graph1.GraphStyle = COLOR_LABELS
 Graph1.ExtraData = EXPLODE

 Graph1.DrawMode = DRAW

End Sub
```

THE SYMBOLDATA PROPERTY

This property lets you specify the symbols that will be used in a line, scatter or polar graph. Figure 11.5 shows what each symbol looks like and how they apply.

THE GRIDSTYLE AND TICKS PROPERTIES

The GridStyle property displays grid lines on a graph. Figure 11.6 shows several examples. The following options are available:

GridStyle	Effect
0	No grid lines (default)
1	Horizontal grid lines
2	Vertical grid lines
3	Both horizontal & vertical grid lines

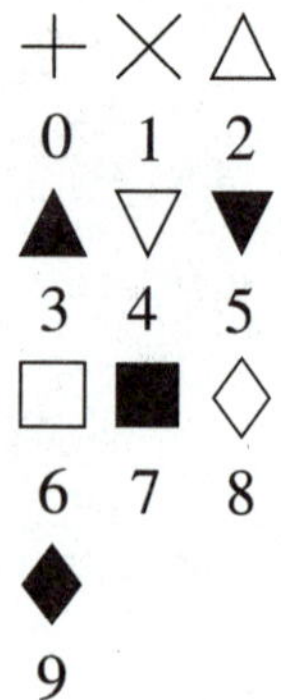

FIGURE 11.5 Graph SymbolData Settings

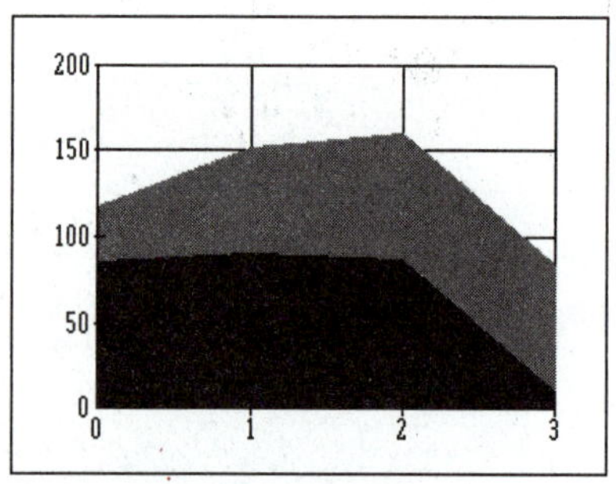

FIGURE 11.6 Displaying grid lines on a graph

Example

```
Sub cmdGridlines_Click ()

 Const DRAW = 2
 Const GRIDLINES_XY = 3
 Const AREAGRAPH = 8
 Const CLEAR_GRAPH = 1

 Graph1.AutoInc = 1
 Graph1.DrawMode = CLEAR_GRAPH
 Graph1.GraphType = AREAGRAPH
 Graph1.NumSets = 2
 Graph1.NumPoints = 4

 ' Show grid lines

 Graph1.GridStyle = GRIDLINES_XY
 Graph1.DrawMode = DRAW

End Sub
```

In many graphs, *ticks* are used to measure data points on the x and y axis's. When ticks are displayed on a graph, they appear as short horizontal or vertical lines (see Figure 11.7). The graph control normally suppresses tick marks. However, you can change this default by setting the Ticks property. Table 11.1 shows the property settings that apply.

Example

```
Sub cmdTicks_Click ()

 Const DRAW = 2
 Const SHOWTICKS = 1
 Const AREAGRAPH = 8
 Const CLEAR_GRAPH = 1

 Graph1.DrawMode = CLEAR_GRAPH

 Graph1.AutoInc = 1

 Graph1.GraphType = AREAGRAPH
 Graph1.NumSets = 2
 Graph1.NumPoints = 4

 ' Display tick marks on x axis

 Graph1.Ticks = SHOWTICKS
 Graph1.DrawMode = DRAW

End Sub
```

NOTE: The Ticks property has no effect on three-dimensional graphs.

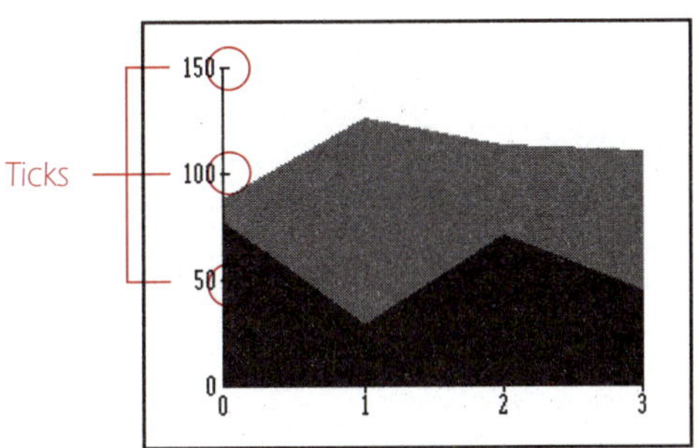

FIGURE 11.7 Displaying ticks on a graph

Setting	Effect
0	Ticks are not displayed (default)
1	Ticks are displayed on both the x and y axis
2	Ticks are displayed on the x axis
3	Ticks are displayed on the y axis

TABLE 11-1 TICKS OPTION SETTINGS

CREATING TRANSPARENT GRAPHS

The SeeThru property, allows you to create transparent graphs that can be displayed over bitmaps. This property is available only at run time. The following code shows how it can be applied:

```
Sub cmdTrans_Click ()

 ' Display transparent graph

 Const BAR3D = 4
 Const TRANSPARENT = 1
 Const GRIDLINES_XY = 3
 Const Z_CLUSTERED = 6
 Const CLEAR_GRAPH = 1
 Const DRAW = 2

 ' Hide graph while making transparent

 Graph1.Visible = False

 Graph1.DrawMode = CLEAR_GRAPH
 Graph1.GraphType = BAR3D
 Graph1.GraphStyle = Z_CLUSTERED
 Graph1.GridStyle = GRIDLINES_XY
 Graph1.GridStyle = 3
 Graph1.NumPoints = 3
 Graph1.NumSets = 7

 Graph1.SeeThru = TRANSPARENT

 ' Make graph visible

 Graph1.Visible = True

 Graph1.DrawMode = DRAW

End Sub
```

This example assumes that the Picture property of the form has been set to the name of a valid bitmap. You can use Microsoft Paintbrush supplied with Windows to create the graphics. To display a transparent graph, the Visible property of the graph control must be initially set to **False**. Then at run time, you set this property to **True** after setting the SeeThru property. Figure 11.8 shows an example of a graph displayed over a bitmap.

11.3 PRINTING A GRAPH

Although you can print a graph using the **PrintForm** method, this system fails to take advantage of high-resolution printers. A better way to print graphs is to use the DrawMode property. When DrawMode is set to 5, a high-resolution image of the graph is sent to the printer.

The PrintStyle property determines how colors are handled. Since the default color printing option may dither colors, you may wish to set the PrintStyle to 0 (monochrome).

Exercise: Displaying a Pie Chart

1. From the File menu, select New Project.
2. Set the Height property of the form to 6000 (twips).
3. From the Toolbox, select the graph control.
4. Using your mouse, size the graph control so that it appears approximately the same size as the graph in Figure 11.9.

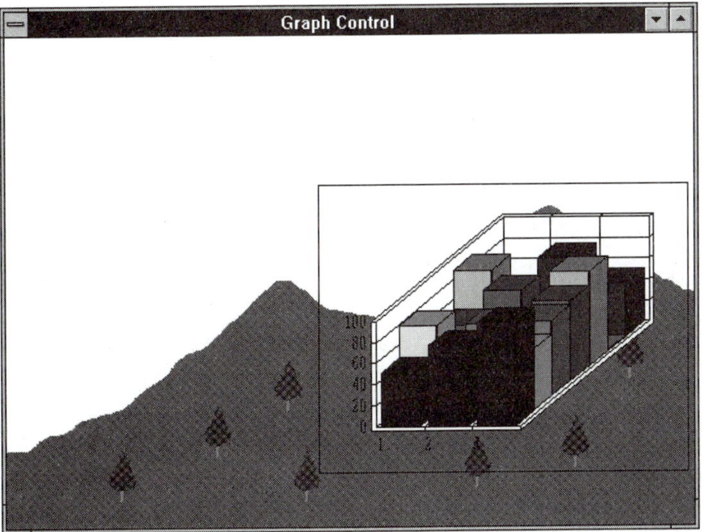

FIGURE 11.8 A transparent graph

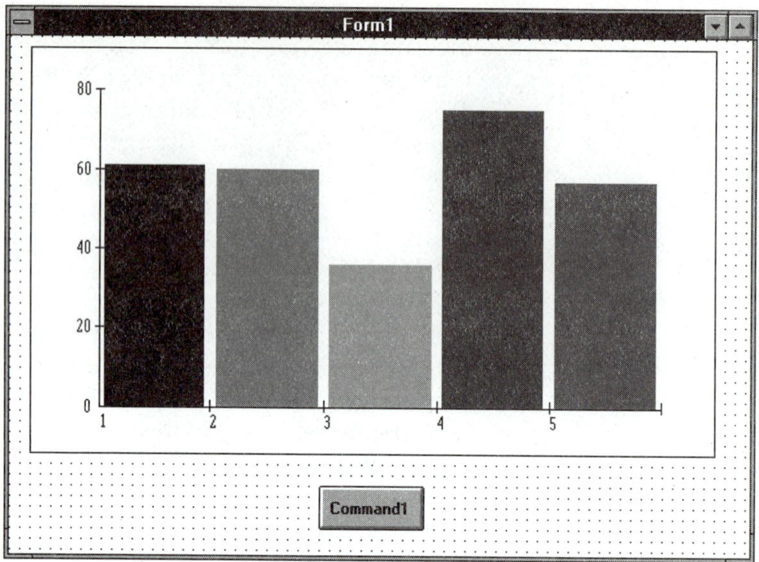

FIGURE 11.9 *Sizing the graph control*

5. Draw a command button on the form and set its properties as follows:

Property	**Value**
Name	cmdGraph
Caption	Graph

6. In the cmdGraph procedure, type:

```
Const PIE3D = 2
Const DRAW = 2

Graph1.GraphType = PIE3D

Graph1.GraphTitle = "Profits & Expenses"

' Fill graph with test data

Graph1.AutoInc = 1

For i = 1 To 5
 Graph1.GraphData = i * 5
Next

Graph1.LabelText = "Promotion"
Graph1.LabelText = "Net Profit"
```

```
Graph1.LabelText = "Marketing"
Graph1.LabelText = "Legal"
Graph1.LabelText = "Distribution"

Graph1.DrawMode = DRAW
```

7. Save the project and run it.
8. Click on the Graph button. Figure 11.10 shows how the graph should appear.
9. Try experimenting with the graph by applying different property settings. For example, change the GraphType or GraphStyle properties to display a different type of graph.

SUMMARY

In this chapter, you learned how to use the graph control. You have also learned how to print graphs, create exploding pie charts and how to display a transparent graph over a bitmap.

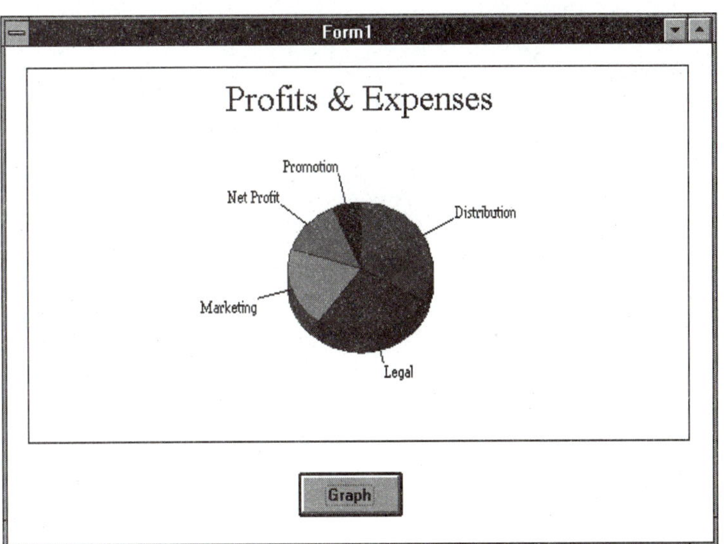

FIGURE 11.10 The completed graph

REVIEW QUESTIONS

1. What graph properties allow you to display legends, labels, ticks and grid lines on graphs? Show examples of how you would use each.
2. By default, when the graph control is drawn on a form, what type of chart appears?
3. How can you display a pie chart?
4. How can you display a three dimensional bar graph?
5. What is the purpose of the AutoInc property?
6. How many data sets does a pie chart have? How many data sets does a bar graph have?
7. To erase a graph, you set what property? Show an example of how you would use it.
8. Before the graphics server library actually draws a graph, what must DrawMode be set to?
9. When DrawMode is set to 5, what action does it perform?
10. How can you produce an exploding pie chart effect?
11. How can you display a transparent graph?

12 DESIGNING REPORTS

The Crystal Reports report designer, which comes with the Professional Edition of Visual Basic, creates custom reports quickly and easily. To print a report, you use the *Crystal custom control* to run the report from Visual Basic. This chapter shows how to access the report generator, design a report, link files, use formulas and print reports.

To Access Crystal Reports from Visual Basic

- From the Window menu, choose the Report Designer command.

NOTE: When you distribute an application that uses the Crystal custom control, you must install the CRYSTAL.VBX file in the WINDOWS\SYSTEM subdirectory of your customer's machine.

The first time the report designer is invoked, you will be asked to register the program. Since the Crystal custom control is an extension of Visual Basic, you must register this product with Crystal Services if you intend to develop new software using it. After filling out the Registration dialog, the main screen will appear. Figure 12.1 shows what it looks like.

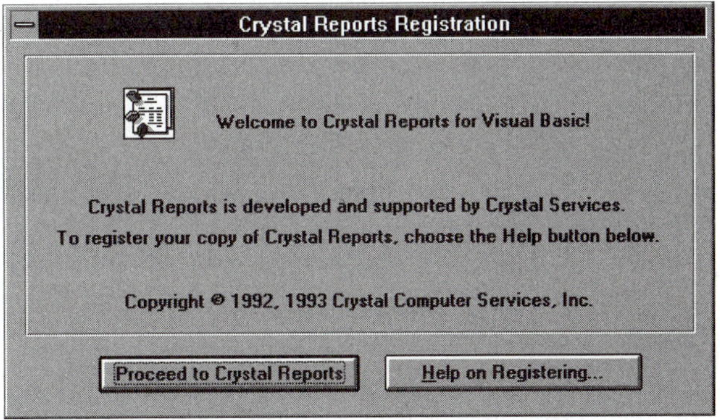

FIGURE 12.1 The Crystal Reports Registration dialog

12.1 USING CRYSTAL REPORTS

The Crystal Reports *button bar* provides quick access to many of the program's commands. You can review what each button does by moving the mouse pointer over the button bar. The description for each associated button appears in the status bar at the bottom of the screen.

CREATING A REPORT

To create a report, select the New Report command from the File menu or choose the same option from the button bar. Afterwards, enter the name of the database that the report will draw information from in the File Open dialog. If the data source is not a Microsoft Access database, you can specify a different file format by choosing the format from the file type drop-down list.

PLACING FIELDS

After opening a file, you create a report by placing fields from the table onto the report. The report designer automatically shows the Insert Database Fields dialog. This window contains all the field definitions in the table. For your convenience, the Insert Database Fields dialog remains open while you build the report.

To Insert a Database Field

1. Double click on the field in the Insert Database Fields dialog. Crystal Reports will show a field mask approximately the same size as the field.
2. Place the field on the report in the Details section of the report (see Figure 12.2).

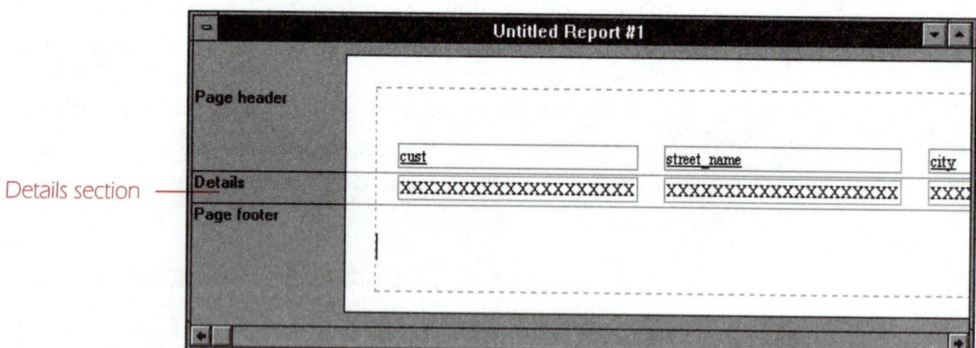

FIGURE 12.2 A report layout

The Details section contains the record information. When you place a field in this section, the report designer automatically adds the correct field heading above it in the Page header section.

USING THE INSERT MENU

The Insert menu allows you to define new report fields. Table 12.1 shows a summary of its commands.

ADDING DATABASE FIELDS

The Database Field... command from the Insert menu displays the Insert Database Fields dialog. Crystal Reports automatically displays this dialog when you create a report.

ADDING TEXT FIELDS

The Text field... command from the Insert menu creates new text fields. When you choose this option, Crystal Reports displays the Edit Text Field dialog (see Figure 12.3). In this window, you can define a multiple line heading or other label. For example, you can add a footnote to the report or enter the report title. After typing the field, clicking on Accept saves the field definition. Crystal Reports will then display a field mask that you can drag onto the report.

Menu Command	Description
Database Field...	Inserts a database field
Text Field...	Inserts a text field
Formula Field...	Inserts a formula field
Subtotal...	Inserts a subtotal field
Grand Total...	Inserts a grand total field
Summary...	Inserts a summary field
Group Section...	Inserts a new group section
Print Date Field	Inserts a date field
Page Number Field	Inserts a page number field
Group Number Field	Inserts a group number field
Graphic	Inserts a graphic image
Box	Inserts (draws) a box

TABLE 12-1 THE INSERT MENU

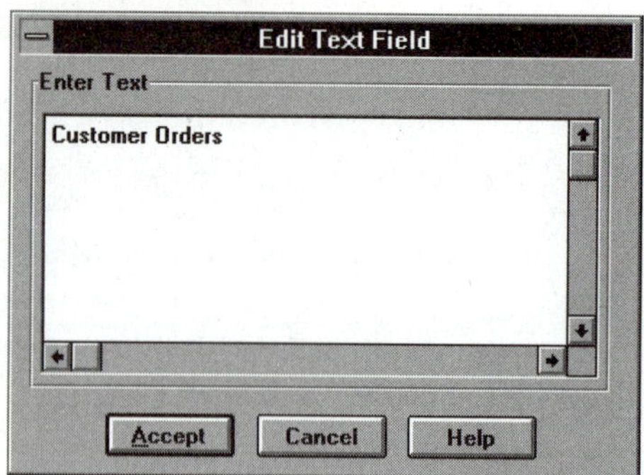

FIGURE 12.3 The Edit Text Field dialog

ADDING SUMMARY FIELDS

The Summary... command displays summary statistics for a field. This option is useful in billing applications where group totals must be printed. You can use the Summary command to print other statistics as well.

To Define a Summary Field

1. Click on the field you wish to summarize.
2. From the Insert menu, choose the Summary command or choose the Insert Summary Field button from the button bar. The Insert Summary dialog will appear.
3. From the summary type drop-down list, choose the summary type you wish to perform, such as sum, average, maximum, minimum, or standard deviation.
4. Click on OK.

FORMATTING A REPORT

The Format menu changes the formatting of a report. You can also add formatting to a report by selecting a field with the right mouse button. Crystal Reports displays a list of formatting options that apply to the current report element in a pop-up menu. For example, if you select a summary field, the menu in Figure 12.4 appears.

CREATING FILE LINKS

Sometimes a report must draw information from different databases. The File Links command from the Database menu establishes file links. Alternatively, you can use the Add File to Report command from the Database menu to create the link.

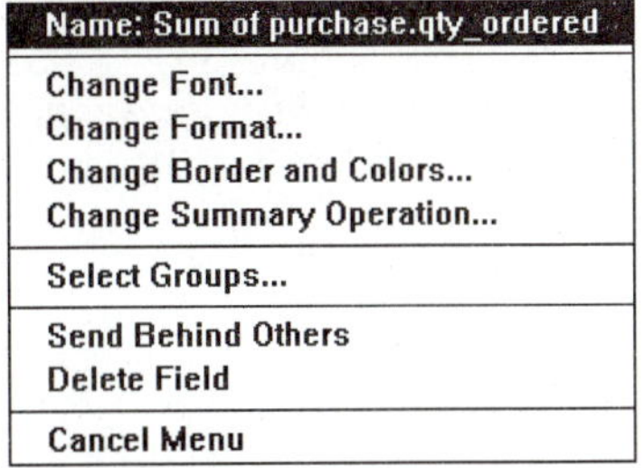

FIGURE 12.4 Using pop-up menus in Crystal Reports

To Create a File Link

1. From the Database menu, select Add File to Report.
2. From the Choose Database File window, enter the name of the file to be linked.
3. Click on OK to add the file to the report.
4. From the File Links dialog, choose the New button.
5. Choose the name of the link file from the Link From File drop-down list.
6. Click on OK to create the link.

These steps assume that both tables are indexed by a common field and that the key fields are identical in structure. Once you have defined a link, you can add any field from the link table onto the report using the Insert Database Fields dialog.

SETTING FILTERS

When you click on a field with the right mouse button, Crystal Reports shows a pop-up menu of field options that apply to the current report element. By choosing the Select Records command from this menu, you can set a *filter* that determines which records will appear in the report. For example, you can set a filter to show selected employee salaries or residents of a specified area.

The Select Records dialog, shown in Figure 12.5, lets you specify filters. Table 12.2 shows a summary of filter types that can be set.

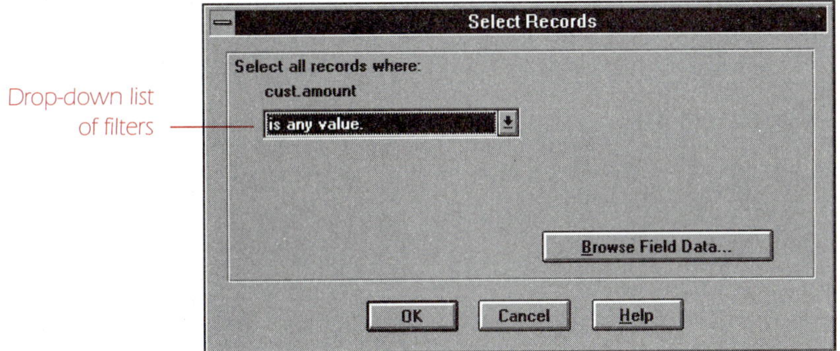

FIGURE 12.5 The Select Records dialog

Filter Type
is any value (default)
is equal to
is not equal to
is less than
is greater than
is less than or equal to
is greater than or equal to
is between
is one of
is not one of
satisfies the test below:

TABLE 12-2 CRYSTAL REPORTS FILTERS

To Set a Filter

1. From the scroll box of the Select Records dialog, choose the filter type you want to set. Optionally, select the Browse Field Data... button to preview the records before setting the filter.
2. Click on OK.

12.2 USING FORMULAS

A particularly useful feature of Crystal Reports is its ability to perform computations using the formula editor. This editor computes expressions based on the values of other report elements.

To Create a New Formula

1. From the button bar, select the Insert Formula Field button.
2. In the Formula name box of the Insert Formula dialog, type the name of the formula. Crystal Reports will display the Edit Formula dialog.
3. Click on OK.
4. In the Formula text window of the Edit Formula dialog, type the expression (see Rules for Defining Formulas later in this section).
5. Choose Accept to save the formula.
6. Place the formula field on the report where you want it to appear.

RULES FOR DEFINING FORMULAS

The Fields list of the Edit Formula window, shows a list of field names that can be used in a report. When you define a formula, however, you do not use the names as they appear in this window. Instead, you use the abbreviated syntax shown in Table 12.3.

Formula Example	Description
{mytable.employee}	References a database or report field
{@bonus}	References a formula field
Sum ({mytable.sales}, {mytable.employee})	References a summary field (e.g., sum of sales for each employee)
Sum ({mytable.sales})	References a grand total field

TABLE 12-3 CRYSTAL REPORTS FORMULAS

Crystal Reports automatically returns the correct field reference when you select an item from the Fields list. For example, if you choose a field derived from a database file, the name of the field appears in braces and is preceded by the source file name. You can choose an item from this list by either double clicking on the item or using the Select button.

USING MATHEMATICAL OPERATORS

Many of the functions and mathematical operators used to define formulas mimic Visual Basic commands. For example, you can use the +,–, * and / operators to perform addition, subtraction, multiplication and division. In addition, you can use the **AND**, **NOT** and **OR** logical operators as well.

MAKING ASSIGNMENTS

Crystal Reports automatically assigns the result of the expression to the formula field. It is not necessary and it would be invalid to make an assignment like this:

```
{testformula} = {myfile.discount} + 10
```

The following example shows how to correctly write the expression. This example adds $10.00 to {myfile.discount} and assigns the result to the formula field:

```
{myfile.discount} + 10
```

If you need to ask a question, use an **If Then Else** block. The following example computes bonuses for employees making over $500.00 in sales:

```
If {emplfile.sales} > 500 Then
  ({emplfile.sales} * .10) + {emplfile.sales}
Else 0
```

Although it may not seem necessary, the **Else** clause must be included in the decision structure in a Crystal Reports formula. In the preceding example, a zero is printed in the formula field if {Employ.Sales} is not greater than $500.00. To suppress the display of the zero, use the Select Records dialog to filter out non-zero values.

12.3 PRINTING REPORTS

After you have created a report, you can test print it by selecting the Print to Window button from the button bar. Crystal Reports will display the report in a minimized view (see Figure 12.6). You can expand this window by clicking on the Maximize button of the Print Window.

You can also write a procedure to print a report. The following example shows how this is done:

```
Sub Command1_Click ()

 On Error GoTo Print_err

 Const WINDOW = 0: Const PRINT_REPORT = 1

 Report1.Destination = WINDOW
 Report1.DataFiles(0) = "C:\VB\TEST.MDB"
 Report1.ReportFileName = "C:\VB\REPORT\TEST.RPT"
 Report1.Action = PRINT_REPORT

 Exit Sub

Print_err:

 MsgBox Error$
 Exit Sub

End Sub
```

When the Action property of the Crystal custom control is set to 1, Visual Basic prints the report indicated by the ReportFileName property to the destination specified by the Destination property. The following print options are available:

0 = Print to Window
1 = Print to Printer
2 = Print to File

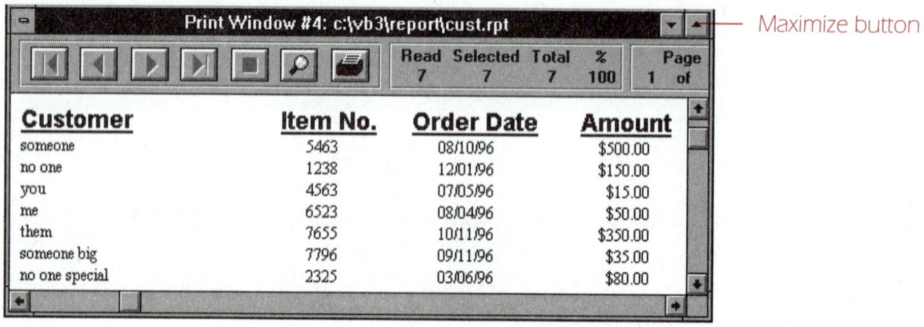

Print Window #4: c:\vb3\report\cust.rpt

Maximize button

Read 7 Selected 7 Total 7 % 100 Page 1 of

Customer	Item No.	Order Date	Amount
someone	5463	08/10/96	$500.00
no one	1238	12/01/96	$150.00
you	4563	07/05/96	$15.00
me	6523	08/04/96	$50.00
them	7655	10/11/96	$350.00
someone big	7796	09/11/96	$35.00
no one special	2325	03/06/96	$80.00

FIGURE 12.6 Printing a report

To print a report, the Crystal custom control must appear on a form. At run time, this control is invisible. Figure 12.7 shows what its button in the Toolbox looks like.

Exercise: Creating a Sample Report

1. From the File menu, select New Project.
2. Create a new report by selecting Report Designer from the Window menu.
3. If this is the first time you have used Crystal Reports, you will have to fill out the registration dialog. When you have finished, click on Done and then select Proceed to Crystal Reports.
4. From the Crystal Reports File menu, choose New Report or select the same option from the button bar.
5. In the File Open dialog, type C:\VB_LIB\EMPLOY.MDB.

NOTE: This step assumes that you installed the example files in the default path (i.e., C:\VB_LIB).

6. Click on OK.
7. In the Insert Database Field window, double click on the Employee field. A field mask will appear. Drag the mask into the Details section of the report. Place it on the report as it appears in Figure 12.8.
8. Using the method previously described in Step 7, place the Sales field on the report (next to the Employee field).

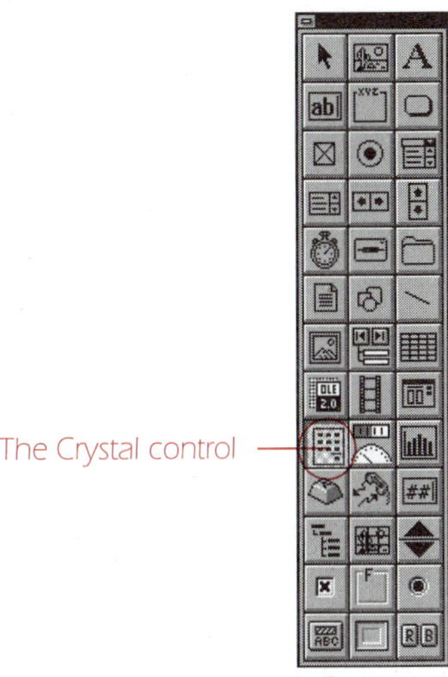

FIGURE 12.7 The Crystal Reports custom control

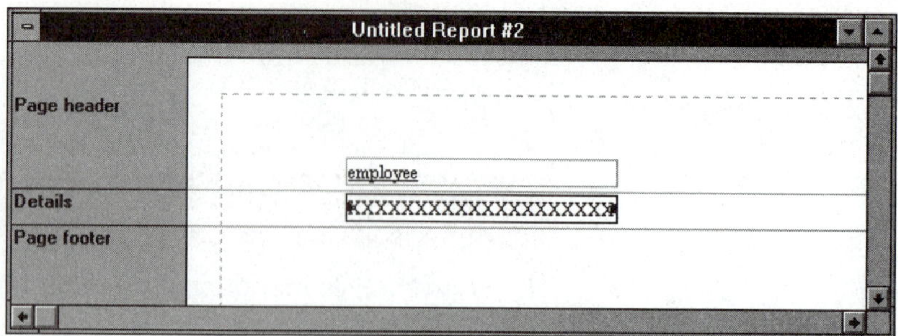

FIGURE 12.8 Placing the Employee field on the report

9. Click on the Sales field mask (not the Sales heading above it).
10. Choose the Insert Summary button from the button bar.
11. In the Insert Summary window, change the Maximum default to Sum. Afterwards, choose the OK button to clear the dialog.
12. From the Insert menu, select Text Field.
13. In the Edit Text Field window, type *Employee Report*.
14. Click on Accept.
15. Center the text field mask in the Page header section at the top of the page and then click the left mouse button to add the new heading field.
16. From the Print menu, select the Print to Window command or choose the same option from the button bar.
17. Click the maximize button to increase the size of the Print Window. Figure 12.9 shows how the report should look at this point.
18. Close the Print Window by pressing Ctrl+F4.

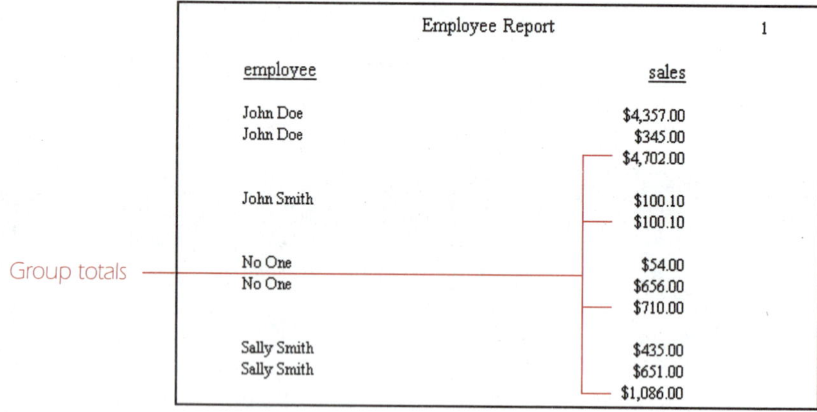

FIGURE 12.9 Viewing a report in the Print Window

The proceeding steps have demonstrated how to create a report. In this next section, you will learn how to insert page numbers, change heading styles and add drop-shadows to the report.

1. With the right mouse button, click on the Sales field heading. A pop-up menu will appear showing a list of format options available.
2. From the pop-up menu, choose Change Font...
3. Format each field heading as follows:

Heading	Font	Font Style	Size
Sales	CG Times (WN)	Bold	12
Employee	CG Times (WN)	Bold	12
Employee Report	CG Times (WN)	Bold	18

NOTE: After adding formatting to the report, you may have to realign the fields by dragging them back with your mouse.

4. With the right mouse button, click on the group summary field. From the format list, select Change Borders and Colors...
5. Click on the Drop Shadow check box.
6. Optionally, change the foreground and background color attributes.
7. Select OK to close the dialog.
8. From the Insert menu, select the Page Number Field option.
9. Place the field in the right margin of the Page header section.
10. Click on the Sales field (not on the heading above it).
11. From the Insert menu, choose Grand total...
12. Click on OK to insert the grand total field. Crystal Reports will automatically add the grand total into the Page footer section. Optionally, you can add a drop shadow to this field using the same techniques described in Steps 4–7.
13. With the right mouse button, click on the Employee field heading (not the field mask below it).
14. From the pop-up menu, choose Edit Text Field...
15. Using the Edit Text Field window, capitalize the "e" in employee.
16. Click on Accept to save the change.
17. Using the same technique, capitalize the "s" in the sales field heading. To do this, you may have to first trim the size of the employee heading that overlaps it.
18. From the File menu, choose File Save.
19. Type C:\VB_LIB\EMPLOY.RPT.
20. After saving the report, select File Exit to return to Visual Basic.
21. In Visual Basic, use the Toolbox to draw the following controls:

Control	Property	Value
Crystal	ReportFileName	C:\VB_LIB\EMPLOY.RPT
command1	Name	cmdPrint

22. In the cmdPrint procedure, type:

```
Const WINDOW = 0
Const PRINT_REPORT = 1

Report1.Destination = WINDOW
Report1.DataFiles(0) = "C:\VB_LIB\EMPLOY.MDB"
Report1.Action = PRINT_REPORT
```

23. Save the program and run it. Figure 12.10 shows what the finished report should look like.

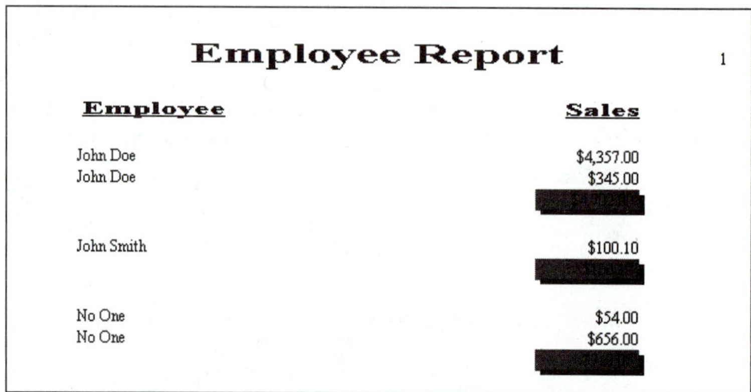

FIGURE 12.10 The finished report

SUMMARY

In this chapter, you learned how to create reports using the Crystal Reports report designer. In addition, you added summary fields, set file links, used formulas and wrote code to run reports.

REVIEW QUESTIONS

1. Where do you place database fields on a report?
2. How can you insert a summary field in a report?
3. How can you insert a grand total in a report?
4. In Crystal Reports formulas, what are the following symbols used for?

5. What dialog allows you to add fields from a database to a report?
6. How can you create a file link?
7. In order for a file link to be successful, are there any assumptions for the key fields?
8. Write a formula to compute sales tax for an item. Assume the name of the table is Sales and that the report contains the following fields:

```
itemcost
salestax
```

9. What Crystal Reports menu commands allow you to insert the date, page number and report title?
10. Before you can print a report in Visual Basic, are there any preparations that must be made?
11. Code a routine to print a report to a window.
12. What adjustment must be made in the program to send output to a printer or file?

13 GAME PROGRAMMING IN VISUAL BASIC

Visual Basic offers a rich array of objects used to develop game applications. With the Windows API, you can achieve even greater control over graphics and animation. This chapter discusses several techniques for developing entertainment software. You will also learn how to develop game strategies by studying the source code of the sample game AIRRAID.MAK.

13.1 ANIMATION TECHNIQUES

Although the art of game programming can take time to master, creating a simple animation routine in Visual Basic requires little effort. To perform animation, you can swap bitmaps in a picture box, move an image on a form, combine moving and swapping techniques or use graphics methods.

SWAPPING BITMAPS

The easiest way to achieve animation in Visual Basic is to swap bitmaps in a picture box or image control. FIRE.MAK demonstrates this technique. To simulate the effect of a house on fire, the program swaps two pictures created in Microsoft Paintbrush (see Figure 13.1).

The Form_Load procedure sets the timer interval (to 100 milliseconds). Upon each call to the Timer1_Timer procedure, the program shows a different bitmap. When <swapimage> is **True**, the Timer1_Timer procedure sets the current_house image control to the Picture property of house1. When <swapimage> is **False**, current_house is set to the picture of the second house (house2). This simple technique produces the illusion of a house burning:

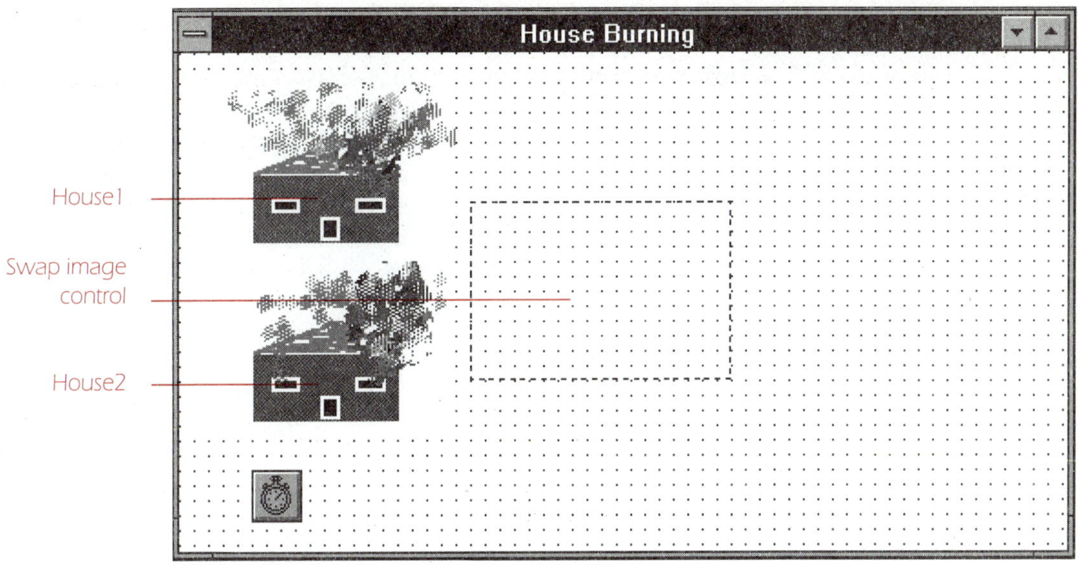

FIGURE 13.1 The FIRE.MAK demonstration program

```
Sub Form_Load ()

  ' Initialize image controls and timer

  house1.Visible = False: house2.Visible = False

  timer1.Interval = 100
  timer1.Enabled = True

End Sub


Sub Timer1_Timer ()

  Static swapimage As Integer

  ' Swap pictures of house

  If swapimage Then
    current_house = house1.Picture
  Else
    current_house = house2.Picture
  End If

  swapimage = Not swapimage

End Sub
```

MOVING IMAGES ON FORMS

Another way to achieve animation is to move an image control on a form. Although you can use a picture box to achieve the same effect, image controls are faster and thus better suited for animation. With the **Move** method, you can reposition an image control on a form. LAUNCH.MAK demonstrates how this can be done. When the form loads, a picture of a rocket moves upward on the form. Upon each call to the Timer1_Timer procedure, the value of the y coordinate is adjusted to reflect the rocket's new position:

```
Const TOP_OFFSET = -2200
Const DISTANCE_PER_MOVE = 75

Dim x As Integer, y As Integer


Sub Form_Load ()

 ' Get current rocket position

 y = rocket.Top: x = rocket.Left

 ' Set timer interval to 100 milliseconds

 timer1.Interval = 100

End Sub


Sub Timer1_Timer ()

 ' Check rocket position

 If y > TOP_OFFSET Then
    y = y - DISTANCE_PER_MOVE
 Else
   End
 End If

 ' Move rocket

 rocket.Move x, y

End Sub
```

The DISTANCE_PER_MOVE and TOP_OFFSET constants and x, y variables are defined in the Declaration section of the form. Their values are retained between procedure calls. DISTANCE_PER_MOVE determines how far the rocket moves on each timer event. TOP_OFFSET is the difference between the top of the form and how much the rocket can move off the screen before the demo ends (measured in twips).

By decreasing the value of the y coordinate, the **Move** method repositions the rocket higher on the form each time the Timer1_Timer procedure executes.

Note that when the program runs, the x and y coordinates are initialized to the Left and Top properties of the rocket image control. Using this technique, it is not necessary to know the actual coordinates involved in an animation sequence since the Left and Top properties return the initial position of the image control. Only the relative coordinates apply.

To activate the timer, the Interval property is set to 100 milliseconds (approximately 1/10th of a second). Since the default setting of the Timer's Enabled property is **True**, it is not necessary to set this property.

NOTE: In the Professional Edition of Visual Basic, you can use the Animate button to display simple animation effects. This control, however, offers little in terms of game programming and is primarily used as an alternative to command buttons and option buttons.

COMBINING ANIMATION TECHNIQUES

It is also possible to combine moving and swapping techniques to produce more realistic effects. TRAIN.MAK, for example, swaps bitmaps while moving an image control across a form.

GRAPHICS FOR THE TRAIN.MAK DEMO

The graphics for this example were created in Microsoft Paintbrush. The Image Attributes... command of the Options menu in Paintbrush changes the size of the drawing area. By setting Image Attributes to a 1" by 1" area, you produce a small bitmap that can be assigned to the Picture property of an image control. Then to edit the graphics, you can use the View Zoom In command to blow up the screen (see Figure 13.2).

Generally, it is better to keep graphics small in animation, although backgrounds are sometimes more effective in a larger format. Setting the Picture property of the form to a bitmap often creates more interesting contrasts in animation scenes.

SOURCE LISTING

Though its graphics are more elaborate, the source listing of TRAIN.MAK is fairly simple. When <swapimage> is **True**, Timer1_Timer sets the Picture property of the current_image image control to the picture of the first train (train1). When <swapimage> is **False**, current_image is set to the picture of the second train. Together these graphics create the illusion of smoke rising from the train's engine. Figure 13.3 shows how the form appears when the demo runs.

FIGURE 13.2 Using the Paintbrush View Zoom In command

FIGURE 13.3 The Train demonstration program

```
Dim x As Integer
Dim y As Integer


Sub Timer1_Timer ()

 Static swapimage As Integer

 ' Swap train pictures

 swapimage = Not swapimage
```

```
 If swapimage Then
   current_image.Picture = train1.Picture
 Else
   current_image.Picture = train2.Picture
 End If

 Call MoveImage(current_image, timer1, x, y)

End Sub


Sub MoveImage (current_image As Image, timerctrl As
          ⇨ Timer, x As Integer, y As Integer)

 Const MAXMOVES = 900
 Const DISTANCE_PER_MOVE = 10

 Static countmoves As Integer

 x = x - DISTANCE_PER_MOVE

 ' Move train

 current_image.Move x, y

 countmoves = countmoves + 1

 If countmoves > MAXMOVES Then
   timerctrl.Enabled = False
 End If

End Sub
```

To start the demo, the Form_Load procedure sets the timer and initializes the train position. Although it is possible to animate an image control by changing its Left and Top properties, this technique produces an unsteady animation effect since the image would have to move horizontally first and then vertically. Therefore, the Left and Top properties are used only to record the initial position of the train:

```
Sub Form_Load ()

 ' Record train position

 x = current_image.Left
 y = current_image.Top

 timer1.Interval = 50

End Sub
```

NOTE: On some monitors, you will see the outline of a picture box or image control during Move **operations if the background is brown. To avoid this, use an alternate color scheme.**

13.2 MORE ADVANCED ANIMATION TECHNIQUES

Visual Basic also supports animation using graphics methods. This next section discusses the various techniques you use to draw objects using these methods. In addition, you will also see how to detect keystrokes and restore background graphics.

CREATING A GUN FIRING EFFECT

The AIRPLANE.MAK example demonstrates how to create a gun firing effect. To accomplish this, the program using the **Line** method to draw a red line across the form. By setting DrawStyle to 2, the line is drawn as a series of dots. At high speeds, this produces the illusion of a gun firing:

```
        .       .       .       .
        .       .       .       .
Formctrl.Line (image5.Left + COL_OFFSET, image5.Top +
            ⇨ ROW_OFFSET)-(ENDTARGET_ROW,
            ⇨ ENDTARGET_COL), QBColor(FIRE_COLOR)
```

AIRPLANE.MAK also demonstrates how to swap multiple bitmaps. By maintaining a global, form-level or static variable, you can keep track of the current bitmap using a counter. When the counter reaches a certain number, you can then display a different bitmap. This technique is useful in slide animation but also works well for special effects. AIRPLANE.MAK uses the Angleattack procedure to animate a series of bitmaps. Together, these images produce the illusion of a plane diving. Figure 13.4 shows how the form appears.

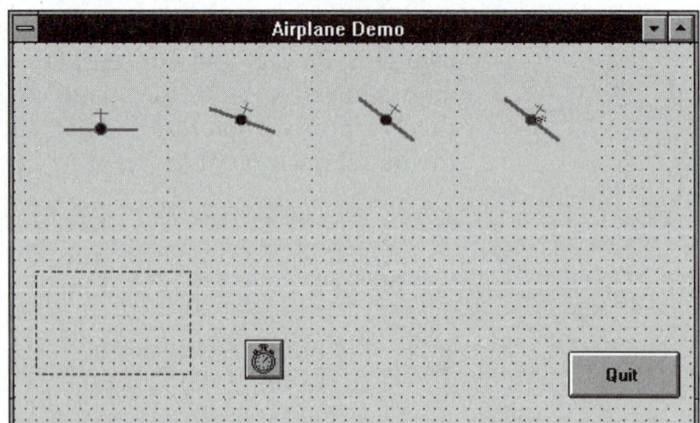

FIGURE 13.4 AIRPLANE.MAK

```
Sub Angleattack (Formctrl As Form, timer1 As Timer,
            ⇨ image1 As Image, image2 As Image,
            ⇨ image3 As Image, image4 As Image,
            ⇨ image5 As Image)

 ' Simulates an air-raid by firing at 90 degree angle

 Const ROW_OFFSET = 720: Const COL_OFFSET = 700
 Const ENDTARGET_ROW = 3500: Const ENDTARGET_COL = 3500
 Const FIRE_COLOR = 4: Const DOUBLE_LINE = 2
 Const TOTAL_MOVES = 50: Const XMOVES = 50
 Const YMOVES = 20

 Static x As Integer, y As Integer
 Static countmoves As Integer

 x = x + XMOVES: y = y + YMOVES

 countmoves = countmoves + 1

 ' Choose image to display

 If countmoves <= 3 Then
   image5.Picture = image1.Picture
   image5.Move x, y
   image5.Visible = True
 ElseIf (countmoves > 3) And (countmoves <= 7) Then
   image5.Picture = image2.Picture
   image5.Move x, y
 ElseIf (countmoves > 7) And (countmoves <= 12) Then
   image5.Picture = image3.Picture
   image5.Move x, y
 ElseIf (countmoves > 12) And (countmoves <=
      ⇨ TOTAL_MOVES) Then

   ' Clear screen after each gun fire

   Formctrl.Cls
   image5.Picture = image4.Picture
   image5.Move x, y

   ' Fire gun

   Formctrl.Line (image5.Left + COL_OFFSET, image5.Top
            ⇨ + ROW_OFFSET)-(ENDTARGET_ROW,
            ⇨ ENDTARGET_COL), QBColor(FIRE_COLOR)
```

```
 End If

 DrawStyle = DOUBLE_LINE

 If countmoves >= TOTAL_MOVES Then ' Quit
   Formctrl.Cls
   image5.Picture = image3.Picture
   timer1.Enabled = False
 End If

End Sub
```

USING COMPLEX BACKGROUNDS IN ANIMATION

Unlike its DOS counterparts, Visual Basic for Windows provides little support for restoring background graphics during animation. Although you can move an image control over a simple background scene with no problem, with complex background displays that use multiple colors, you will see an outline of the image control (or picture box) moving across the form. The TRAIN.MAK demo and sample game AIRRAID.MAK (covered later in this chapter), demonstrate how to perform animation with elaborate background displays. To accomplish this, the train moves over the railroad bridge (above the complex background scene). Similarly, in AIRRAID.MAK, the jet and helicopter fly above the mountains over a simple white background and the tank moves below the mountains across the sand.

With the Windows API BitBlit function, you can restore background images during animation. However, the technique to accomplish this is complex. It takes six calls to BitBlit to restore the background for any single object. Although it really only takes four calls to BitBlit to restore pixels on a form, you need to call BitBlit two more times to prevent the flickering that appears during screen captures.

In addition, you must also create two *masks* to define the area of the bitmap that will be transparent and the part of the bitmap that will blend in with the background. Because of the awkwardness of this function, a discussion of BitBlit is not covered here. Chapter 14 shows a better way to perform animation using two special add-on products, 3D Graphic Tools and Motion Works MediaShop. If you are serious about game programming, you will find these packages well worth the investment.

CREATING A BOMB DROPPING EFFECT

Visual Basic actually does provide some degree of screen restoration capabilities made possible through light pen technology. However, this technique is limited to graphics methods. For example, you can use the **Circle** method to draw a bomb on a form and then restore the background afterwards with 7 - Xor Pen. The Timer1_Timer procedure of BOMB.MAK demonstrates how this can be done. Upon each call to the timer, the circle is plotted lower and lower on the form to produce the illusion of the bomb dropping. After each move, the background is restored by Xoring the pixels:

```
Sub Timer1_Timer ()

 ' Show bomb dropping and restore background
 ' after each move

 Const WHITE = 15
 Const MAXMOVE = 10

 Static current_x
 Static current_y
 Static i

 Form1.DrawMode = 7   ' XorPen
 radius = 10

 Circle (current_x, current_y), radius, QBColor(WHITE)
 current_x = 3500
 current_y = current_y + 350
 Circle (current_x, current_y), radius, QBColor(WHITE)

 i = i + 1

 If i >= MAXMOVE Then
   explos.Visible = True
   bomb_x = 3000: bomb_y = 3500
   explos.Move bomb_x, bomb_y
   timer1.Enabled = False
 End If

End Sub
```

GRAPHICS METHODS VRS. PAINTED IMAGES

While it is undoubtedly easier to create game characters using a paint program, graphics methods posses some advantages. For example, it takes less memory to code a simple procedure to draw an image on a form than it does to store a painted image. In large game applications, you can reduce memory requirements significantly by applying graphics methods. Another advantage of using graphics methods is that you can quickly change colors, sizes and patterns of objects with minimal coding effort. Consider the following program which draws a rainbow on a form:

```
Sub cmdRainbow_Click ()

 Const MAXCOLORS = 5, HIGH_INTENSITY = 8
```

```
  Dim x As Integer, y As Integer

  ' Declare array to hold rainbow colors
  Static Colorset(MAXCOLORS) As Integer

  ' Starting coordinates of rainbow
  x = 1500: y = 1500

  ' Initialize rainbow colors
  For i = 1 To MAXCOLORS
     Colorset(i) = i + HIGH_INTENSITY
  Next

  Call Rainbow(Form1, x, y, Colorset()) ' Draw rainbow

End Sub


Sub Rainbow (Formctrl As Form, x As Integer, y As
         ⇨ Integer, Colorset() As Integer)

  ' Draw rainbow using colors in array

  Const RADIUS_INCREMENT = 150, STARTANGLE = 0,
         ⇨ ENDANGLE = 3.2

  Dim radius As Integer

  Formctrl.DrawWidth = 5

  radius = 300

  For i = 1 To UBound(Colorset)
    radius = radius + RADIUS_INCREMENT
    Formctrl.Circle (x, y), radius,
    QBColor(Colorset(i)), STARTANGLE, ENDANGLE
  Next

End Sub
```

The Rainbow procedure accepts an array of colors. By modifying the MAXCOLORS constant, you can change the number of arks that appear in the rainbow. Similarly, you can change the rainbow's colors by assigning new color codes to the <Colorset> array. Figure 13.5 shows other examples of game objects you can create using graphics methods. The source code for these examples is included on disk in the GRPHDEM.MAK project. You can study these examples to learn how to apply graphics methods and even reuse certain routines by adding the UTIL.BAS module to your projects.

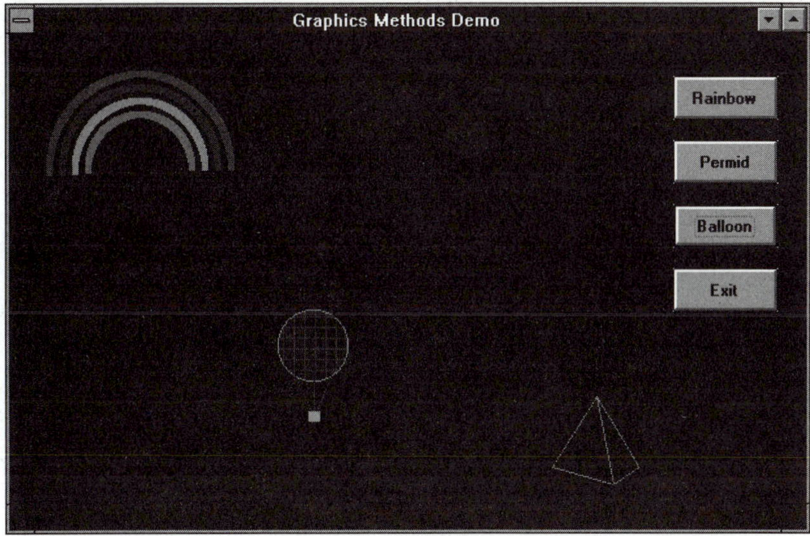

FIGURE 13.5 Using memory-saving graphics methods

DETECTING KEYSTROKES

So far you have learned how to perform animation using the **Move** method and Visual Basic's standard graphics methods. You can also write code to detect keyboard activity in a game. Two procedures, Form_KeyPress and Form_KeyDown are used for this purpose. Form_KeyPress monitors most keyboard events. Form_KeyDown detects low level keyboard activity. You use this procedure to monitor cursor events and to reassign key values.

The Form_KeyPress procedure of the sample game AIRRAID.MAK monitors keyboard events and uses them to set flags (see Figure 13.6). When the user presses the space bar, for example, the program sets the <fire_gun> flag to **True**. Later, this flag is tested and used to determine when the jet should fire its gun. To read the key pressed, the following code is used:

```
Sub Form_KeyPress (keyascii As Integer)

 Const SPACEBAR = 32: Const LESS_THAN = 44
 Const GREATER_THAN = 46: Const Ctrl_Q = 17
 Const UPPERCASE_B = 66: Const LOWERCASE_B = 98
 Const DISTANCE_PERMOVE = 100

 ' Get key pressed

 Select Case keyascii

   Case SPACEBAR
     fire_gun = True
```

FIGURE 13.6 The sample game, AIRRAID.MAK

```
    Case LESS_THAN
      jet_y = jet_y + DISTANCE_PERMOVE
    Case GREATER_THAN
      jet_y = jet_y - DISTANCE_PERMOVE
    Case UPPERCASE_B, LOWERCASE_B
      If dropbomb = False Then
        bomb_x = jet_x + 300
        bomb_y = jet_y + 500
        dropbomb = True
      End If
    Case Ctrl_Q
      End

  End Select

End Sub
```

When the player presses the > key, the jet flies up on the form. To accomplish this, the jet_y coordinate is adjusted to reflect the jet's new position:

```
jet_y = jet_y - DISTANCE_PERMOVE
```

Using similar logic, the jet flies down on the form when the < key is pressed:

```
jet_y = jet_y + DISTANCE_PERMOVE
```

When the B key is detected, the jet bombs the tank. If the jet's bomb or gun fire hits the tank or helicopter, the Picture property of the target is set to the Picture of the explosion bitmap:

```
.              .              .
.              .              .
helicopimage.Picture = explos.Picture
```

SPECIAL CONSIDERATIONS FOR DETECTING KEYSTROKES

In order to detect keystrokes on a form, the form must have focus. By default, a form with no controls on it automatically has focus. You can use a drop-down menu to start a game without interference from other controls. Alternately, you can place the controls to play the game on a separate form or use the same form but disable the start-up controls after the game begins.

13.3 ADVANCED ANIMATION

AIRRAID.MAK demonstrates several advanced animation techniques. This section shows how to test for hits and collisions, keep an animation sequence going, change game levels and detect the system hardware. In addition, you will learn how to apply the same low level routines that were used to develop Visual Basic's standard controls.

AIRRAID.MAK uses two techniques to test for hits and collisions. The program checks boundaries by testing the ranges of game objects and it checks the background color of pixels on the form. To test if the jet's gun fire hit the helicopter, the program checks the position of the helicopter. To do this, the following constants are used:

```
JET_GUN_OFFSET = 350: HELICOPTER_TOP_OFFSET = 100
JET_WIDTH_OFFSET = 800
```

JET_GUN_OFFSET is the distance in twips between the top of the jetimage image control and where the jet's gun is within the bitmap of the image control (see Figure 13.7). HELICOP_TOP_OFFSET is the distance between the top of the helicopimage image control and the top of the helicopter. JET_WIDTH_OFFSET is the width of the actual jet bitmap within the image control it is contained in. By adding these constants to the Left and Top properties of the jetimage and helicopimage image controls, you can determine the relative positions of the jet and helicopter:

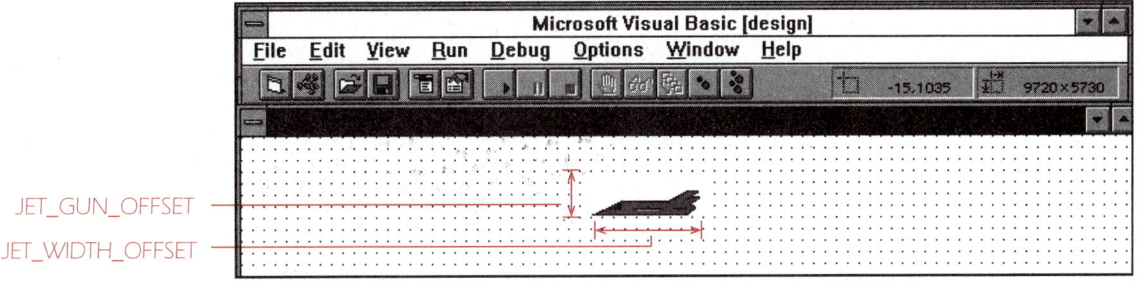

FIGURE 13.7 Coordinates of the Jet bitmap

```
Sub Check_hit ()

 ' Test if jet's gun fire hit helicopter - if so
 ' show explosion

 JET_GUN_OFFSET = 350: HELICOP_TOP_OFFSET = 100
 JET_WIDTH_OFFSET = 800

 If jetimage.Top + JET_GUN_OFFSET >= helicopimage.Top +
       ⇨ HELICOP_TOP_OFFSET Then

   If jetimage.Top + jetimage.Height <=
       ⇨ helicopimage.Top + helicopimage.Height Then

     If jet_x + JET_WIDTH_OFFSET >= helicop_x Then

       helicopimage.Picture = explos.Picture
       total_hits = total_hits + 1
       score = score + 100
       hit = True

     End If

   End If

 End If

End Sub
```

In terms of strategy, the jet flies from right to left on the form. The helicopter flies from left to right. Both the jet and helicopter can initiate an attack. The jet must either shoot the helicopter down or fly around it to avoid a collision. For a hit to occur, the jet's gun must not be above or below the top or bottom of the helicopter. The jet_x + JET_WIDTH_OFFSET >= helicop_x test is used to determine if the jet already passed the helicopter (in which case, a hit could not possibly occur).

Admittedly, this is no easy task to program. However, with any two objects on a form, you can calculate the relative distance between each game piece by displaying their Left and Top properties. Alternately, you can use the **Line** control to display various coordinates on a form and subtract the relative distance between the objects (see Figure 13.8).

AIRRAID also checks boundaries by testing the pixel colors of background graphics on the form. This technique is particularly useful in determining if the jetimage image control flies out of bounds. For example, if the jet crashes into a mountain, you test for this by checking if the pixel color of a point on the form directly below the jet matches the color of the mountains (dark gray). To accomplish this, the following code is used:

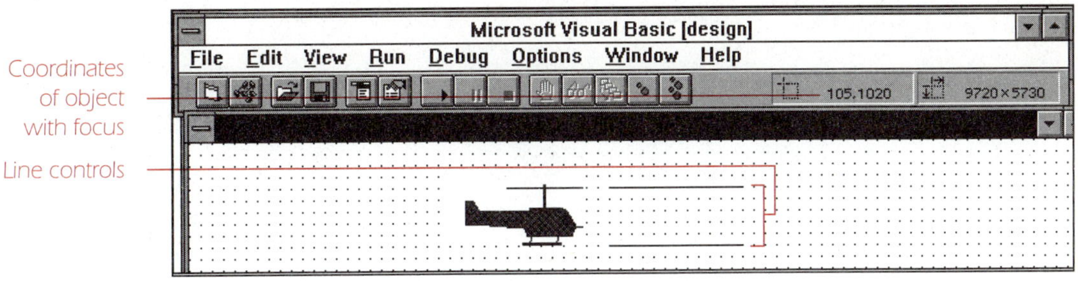

Coordinates of object with focus

Line controls

FIGURE 13.8 Using the line control to measure distance between objects

```
Function ImageRange (Formctrl As Form, x As Integer, y
            ⇨ As Integer, Boundaries() As Long)

 ' Test pixel color of background

 Dim inrange As Integer

 For i = 1 To UBound(Boundaries)
   If Formctrl.Point(x, y) = Boundaries(i) Then
     inrange = False
     Exit Function
   Else
     inrange = True
   End If
 Next

 ImageRange = inrange

End Function
```

The ImageRange function of UTIL.BAS, accepts an array of **RGB** colors to compare with a point on the form. If any color in the array matches the color returned by **Point**, the function returns **True**, indicating a collision. In which case, the picture of the jet is hidden and the explosion bitmap is shown.

AIRRAID.MAK uses the following color definitions to compare against the background:

```
Const BRIGHT_YELLOW = 65535
Const DARK_GRAY = 8421504
Const LIGHT_BLUE = 16711680
Const WHITE = 16777215
```

To get the **RGB** color of a screen area on a form, you can use the **Point** function to determine the color value. In AIRRAID.MAK, the sky is WHITE, the mountains are DARK_GRAY, the desert is BRIGHT YELLOW and the water is LIGHT_BLUE. You can get these values with a simple test like this:

```
Sub Form_MouseDown (Button As Integer, Shift As
                ⇨ Integer, x As Single, y As Single)

 ' Display pixel color of a point on form

 MsgBox (Point(x, y))

End Sub
```

By placing the call to **Point** in the Form_MouseDown procedure, you can determine a color value of an area on the form by clicking on the area. Some **RGB** colors return two color values. For this reason, it is important to test more than one pixel.

KEEPING AN ANIMATION SEQUENCE GOING

One of the easiest effects to achieve in Visual Basic is keeping an animation sequence going. To do this, you move each game piece back to its starting coordinates using the **Move** method. For example, when the tank moves to its maximum position on the form, AIRRAID.MAK resets its x and y coordinates back to its starting position in the lower left corner of the form:

```
If (tankimage.Left >= MAXPOS) Or (tank_hit = True) Then
    tank_x = 0
    tankimage.Move tank_x, tank_y
    If tank_hit Then
        tankimage.Picture = LoadPicture("tank.bmp")
        score = score + 100
        tank_hit = False
    End If
End If
```

TIP: If you set the timer interval too fast for Visual Basic to process events, the timer may become inactive, causing the game to freeze. Although it is possible to use DoEvents **to free the system resources, the game will still be temporarily inactive. If you need to make a game execute faster, increase the distance per move for each game character rather than changing the timer Interval property.**

SCORES AND STRATEGIES

In AIRRAID.MAK, bombing the tank is worth 100 points. Shooting down the helicopter also earns 100 points. As mentioned before, the helicopter can fire back against its enemy (the jet). To accomplish this, the program checks the range of the jet. If the jet is within firing range, the helicopter fires its gun (by drawing a line on the form). At higher levels, the helicopter's firing range becomes greater, making it almost impossible to dodge the helicopter. To accomplish this, the following code is used:

```
Function Get_firerange ()

 ' Set fire range for helicopter based on game level

 Const SHORT_FIRERANGE = 4000
 Const MEDIUM_FIRERANGE = 6500
 Const LONG_FIRERANGE = 9000

 Select Case gamelevel

   Case 1
    Get_firerange = SHORT_FIRERANGE
   Case 2
    Get_firerange = MEDIUM_FIRERANGE
   Case 3
    Get_firerange = LONG_FIRERANGE

 End Select

End Function


Sub Helicop_attack ()

 ' Test if helicopter's gun fire hit jet - if so
 ' show explosion

 HELICOP_FIREOFFSET = 350: JET_IMAGE_OFFSET = 100

 If helicopimage.Top + HELICOP_FIREOFFSET <=
          ⇨ jetimage.Top + JET_IMAGE_OFFSET Then
  If helicopimage.Top + helicopimage.Height >=
          ⇨ jetimage.Top + jetimage.Height Then
     jetimage.Picture = explos.Picture
     jethit = True
  End If
 End If

End Sub
```

CHANGING GAME LEVELS

After every 10 hits or 1000 points earned, AIRRAID switches levels. To make the game more interesting, a different background is shown after each successive level by setting the Picture property of the form:

```
Select Case total_hits
   Case 10
     newlevel = True
     Form1.Picture = LoadPicture("desert2.bmp")
     gamelevel = 2
     Scoreform.level.Caption = gamelevel
     tank_speed = MEDIUM_SPEED
   Case 20
     newlevel = True
     Form1.Picture = LoadPicture("desert3.bmp")
     gamelevel = 3
     Scoreform.level.Caption = gamelevel
     tank_speed = HIGH_SPEED
End Select
```

DETERMINING THE TYPE OF CPU

Although the technique is not demonstrated in AIRRAID.MAK, you can also write code to detect the hardware configuration for a game. The Sysconfig function of the library returns information about the system by calling the Windows API. You can also rewrite this **Sub** procedure as a function. If your game depends on system specific information, you can query the Windows API to set parameters for the game. The GetCPU function, for example, returns the active CPU to set the speed of an animation demo. To use it, you must include the UTIL.BAS module in a project. Afterwards, you can call GetCPU the following way:

```
Sub Form_Load ()

  ' Set game speed

 CPU = getCPU()

 If CPU = "486" Then
   timer1.Interval = 200
 ElseIf CPU = "386" Then
   timer1.Interval = 175
 ElseIf CPU = "286" Then
   timer1.Interval = 150
 Else
   timer1.Interval = 250
 End If

 Show

 MsgBox ("CPU Type: " & CPU)

End Sub
```

VISUAL BASIC PROFESSIONAL EDITION .DLL FUNCTIONS

With the Professional Edition of Visual Basic, you can access many of the same functions that were used to develop Visual Basic's standard controls. Table 13.1 shows a list of Visual Basic API functions that apply to graphics and animation. Although the documentation for these functions appears in Visual C++ syntax, you can also access these routines directly from Visual Basic. Chapter 15 discusses the Windows API and how to call DLLs from Visual Basic. For more information on this subject, refer to Chapter 15 or the Visual Basic professional features manuals.

13.4 ACCESSING WINDOWS API SOUND FUNCTIONS

Because Visual Basic works in a multi-tasking environment, it must share the same system resources as other Windows applications. For this reason, you must specifically request access to the PC speaker in order to use sound in a program. The SOUNDDEM.MAK application, shows how this is done:

```
Sub Form_Load ()

 ' Request access to speaker

 retval = OpenSound()

End Sub
```

The Form_Load procedure of SOUNDDEM.MAK calls the Windows API function OpenSound. The definition for this function is contained in SOUNDDEM.BAS. When the user selects one of the sound buttons, the program calls the library procedure SoundEffects to play one of seven predefined sound effects: jingle, falling, squashing, siren, sequence, laser gun or bird chirping. The following example shows how to simulate the sound of a laser gun:

Function	Description
VBM_Hittest	Checks if the mouse pointer enters the boundaries of a graphics container (such as an image control or picture box). Use this procedure to test the hit status of game objects.
VBInvalidateRect	Defines an area of a window to be refreshed by adding the rectangular coordinates of a control to the client area of the object to be refreshed.
VBSetControlFlags	Returns or sets a control's characteristics. With graphics controls, you can use this function to generate translucent images.
VBGetRectInContainer	Copies the contents of a control to another window.

TABLE 13-1 VISUAL BASIC API FUNCTIONS

```
Sub Lasergun_Click ()

 ' Simulate laser gun sound

 Const LASER = 6

 Call SoundEffects(LASER)

End Sub
```

After calling SoundEffects, you must call the Windows API function CloseSound so that other Windows applications can use the PC Speaker. The declaration for this routine is contained in SOUNDDEM.BAS.

Example:

```
Sub cmdExit_Click ()

 ' Free speaker so other programs can access it

 retval = CloseSound()

 End

End Sub
```

Although this technique will work, the speed of the microprocessor, amount of memory available and Windows version may influence the way sound is handled in a program. To complicate matters more, if your games involve animation, you will have to coordinate sound and graphics routines. With a sound card, you can better control sound activity. The multimedia MCI control provided in the Professional Edition allows you to record and play multimedia files using MDI (Media Control Interface) devices.

There are also a number of third party custom controls that can help simplify sound operations. The SoundBytes custom control package by the Waite group, for example, lets you record voices and other sound sources and play them back with minimal coding effort. The *Custom Controls and Other Companion Products and Services for Visual Basic for Windows* directory contains a listing of all third party vendors. You can also use this directory to find other custom controls that can simplify Windows GUI operations.

Exercise: Creating an Animation Demo

1. From the File menu, choose New Project.
2. From the Toolbox, choose the timer control.
3. From the Toolbox, choose the image control (see Figure 13.9).
4. Set the Interval property of the timer to 200 (milliseconds).

FIGURE 13.9 The image control

5. Set the background color of the form to bright yellow. If the Color Palette is unavailable, you can display it by selecting the Color Palette command from the Window menu.
6. Set the Name property of the image control to Jeep.
7. In the Properties window, double click on the Picture property.
8. In the File Name list box, type C:\VB_LIB\JEEP.BMP.

NOTE: This step assumes you installed the sample files in the default C:\VB_LIB directory.

9. Double click on the timer control. Then type the following code in the Timer1_Timer procedure:

```
Const MAXPOS = 6700

Static moveup As Integer
Static x As Integer

x = x + 125

If moveup Then
   y = 1500
Else
   y = 1510
End If
```

```
' Move jeep

jeep.Move x, y

moveup = Not moveup

If jeep.Left > MAXPOS Then
    End ' Quit
End If
```

10. Save the project and run it.

SUMMARY

In this chapter, you learned several techniques for performing computer animation in Visual Basic. These techniques include swapping bitmaps, moving images on a form, using graphics methods, detecting keystrokes, checking pixel colors and calling procedures in dynamic link libraries.

REVIEW QUESTIONS

1. To reposition a picture box or image control on a form, what method do you use?
2. Why is it better to use an image control instead of a picture box in computer animation?
3. What is wrong with changing the Left and Top properties of an image control to perform animation?
4. How can you get the initial position of an image control on a form?
5. To activate a timer, what property do you set?
6. Approximately, how long is 200 milliseconds?
7. Why is it important not to set a timer control too fast?
8. What property allows you to restore the background when you use graphics methods? What must this property be set to?
9. What Visual Basic function returns the background color of a pixel on a form? When could you use this?
10. To use sound in a program, what Windows API function must you call first? To free the PC Speaker after a sound routine, what Windows API function do you use?

CLASS PROJECTS

1. Create a program to swap two bitmaps or icons in a image control. Use any pre-defined icons that come with Visual Basic or bitmap included with the project examples. Alternately, you can create the graphics in Paintbrush or ICONWRKS.MAK.
2. Create an animation demo to move an image control on a form. Reset the image control each time it reaches the end of the form back to its original starting coordinates.
3. Using the Swapimages function of the library, write a program to swap two bitmaps (or icons) in an image control.

14 PROFESSIONAL FEATURES AND THIRD PARTY EXTENSIONS

The Professional Edition of Visual Basic includes many custom controls to improve applications. These tools allow you to control multimedia devices, communicate through the serial port, mask input, incorporate 3D controls in an interface, create status indicators, display outlines and more. Table 14-1 shows a summary of custom controls provided in the Professional Edition.

Control Name	Description
Animated button	When selected, swaps bitmaps to create a slide show or animation effect.
Communications	Permits serial communications in an applications.
Gauge	Displays a linear or needle type gauge over a user-defined graphic.
Graph	Displays a graph in one of several different styles.
Key Status	Sets or reports the status of the NUM LOCK, CAPS LOCK, INS or SCROLL LOCK keys.
MAPI Controls	Allows a Visual Basic application to interface with Microsoft Mail.
Masked Edit	Validates input using standard or user-defined data entry templates (masks)—also used to format output.
Multimedia MCI	Records and plays multimedia files on Media Control Devices.
Outline	A list that can contain subgroups of items which can be open for display or not.
Pen Controls	Allows for the creation of Pen Computing applications.
Picture Clip	Shows part of a bitmap on a form or picture box.
Spin button	Displays and increments/decrements values in a text box or similar control.
3D controls: 3D command button 3D group push button 3D frame 3D panel 3D check box 3D option button	3D objects that can emulate standard Visual Basic objects like a command button, check box, option button or frame. They also provide additional capabilities not available in standard controls. For example, with a 3D panel, you can display a status indicator to show progress of lengthy operations.

TABLE 14-1 CUSTOM CONTROLS PROVIDED IN THE PROFESSIONAL EDITION OF VISUAL BASIC

In previous chapters, you have learned how to use the Crystal custom control and the graph control. In this chapter, you will learn how to use other custom controls and how to extend Visual Basic with third party solutions.

14.1 DEVELOPING COMMUNICATIONS APPLICATIONS

With the communications control, you create applications that send and receive information through the serial port. At run time, this control is invisible on a form. Figure 14.1 shows how the communications control appears in the Toolbox.

Despite all its power and versatility, the communications control is easy to incorporate in an application. To get started, you need only be familiar with a few of its properties. Table 14-2 shows a list of communications control properties that control basic serial input and output communications.

PREPARING FOR A COMMUNICATION

Before you can send or receive information, the communications control must know what serial port to use. To indicate this parameter, you set the CommPort property. The following example shows how to set the communications control to COM1:

```
Comm1.CommPort = 1   ' Use COM1 for data transfer
```

FIGURE 14.1 The communications control

Properties	Description
CommPort	Determines the serial port the communications control uses.
Settings	Sets or returns communication parameters—baud rate, parity, data bits and stop bits.
PortOpen	Prepares and determines the state of a port before and after a communication.
Input	Gets and removes input from the receive buffer.
Output	Writes characters to the transmit buffer.

TABLE 14-2 KEY PROPERTIES IN THE COMMUNICATIONS CONTROL

If an application uses more than one communications control, each one must be assigned to a specific port. In addition to setting the CommPort property, you set the baud rate, parity, number of data bits and number of stop bits. The baud rate determines the speed of the data transfer. Parity specifies additional information such as how error checking will be handled. Table 14-3 shows a summary of its settings. The data bits and stop bits arguments determine how data is addressed. To indicate these parameters, the following conventions are used:

BBBB,P,D,S

BBBB = Baud rate
P = Parity
D = Data bits
S = Stop bits

Example

```
Comm1.Settings = "2400,N,8,1"   ' Set baud rate, parity,
                                ' data bits & stop bits
```

After setting the CommPort and Settings properties, you prepare the communications control for a transmission by opening the serial port. When PortOpen is set to **True**, the communications control opens the port. Setting PortOpen to **False** closes the port and clears the transmit and receive buffers.

Setting	Result
E	Even
M	Mark
N	No parity (default)
O	Odd
S	Space

TABLE 14-3 PARITY OPTIONS FOR SETTINGS PROPERTY

Example

```
Comm1.CommPort = 1                ' Use COM1 for data
                                  ' transfer
Comm1.Settings = "2400,N,8,1"    ' Set baud rate, parity,
                                  ' data bits & stop bits
Comm1.PortOpen = True             ' Open communications
                                  ' port
```

NOTE: The communications control generates a Device unavailable error (error code 68) if you forget to specify the CommPort property or if you indicate an invalid parameter in the Settings property.

SENDING AND RECEIVING INFORMATION

Once you have prepared the communications control for a transmission, you are ready to perform basic serial communications. The following simple example shows how this is done:

```
Sub cmdSend_Click ()

 Comm1.CommPort = 1                ' Use COM1 for data
                                   ' transfer
 Comm1.Settings = "2400,N,8,1"    ' Set baud rate,
                                   ' parity, data bits &
                                   ' stop bits
 Comm1.InputLen = 0                ' Read entire buffer

 Comm1.PortOpen = True             ' Open communication
                                   ' port
 Comm1.Output = "AT" + Chr(13)    ' Send Attention
                                   ' command to modem

End Sub

Sub cmdReceive_Click ()

 inbufferdata = Comm1.Input        ' Read contents of
                                   ' receive buffer
 Comm1.PortOpen = False            ' Close communication
                                   ' port

 MsgBox (inbufferdata)             ' Show contents of
                                   ' receive buffer

End Sub
```

The Input property reads characters from the receive buffer. The InputLen property determines the number of characters read. By setting InputLen to 0, the communications control reads all the characters in the receive buffer.

The Output property sends characters to the transmit buffer. In the preceding example, the Attention Command (AT) is sent to the modem. Afterwards, the Input property reads back the Attention Command and the OK response from the modem.

HANDLING COMMUNICATION ERRORS

The OnComm procedure of the communications control returns the most recent communications event. You use this procedure to trap errors and to monitor the status of a communication. For example:

```
Sub Comm1_OnComm ()

 ' Report most recent communications event

 Const BUFFER_FULL = 1010

 If Comm1.CommEvent <> 0 Then

   If Comm1.CommEvent = BUFFER_FULL Then
      MsgBox ("Transmission buffer full - try
          ⇨ increasing buffer size")
      commerr = True
   Else
     MsgBox (Comm1.CommEvent)
     commerr = True
    End If
  End If

End Sub
```

If the communications control generates a *buffer overrun error* (error 1010), the Comm1_OnComm procedure reports the error using **MsgBox**. To avoid this, try increasing the transmit buffer size by setting the OutBufferSize property. The default value for the transmit buffer is 512 bytes and 1024 bytes for the receive buffer. However, information can arrive very quickly and often faster than it can be processed. To reduce the possibility of data loss, use handshaking protocols. With handshaking, data is read in segments one small block at a time. The HandShaking property determines whether handshaking protocols are used. The following options are available:

Setting	Description
0	No handshaking - default
1	XON/XOFF handshaking
2	Request to Send (RTS) and Clear to Send (CTS) handshaking
3	RTS and XON/XOFF handshaking

DISTRIBUTING COMMUNICATION APPLICATIONS

When you distribute an application that uses the communications control, you must install the MSCOMM.VBX file in the \SYSTEM subdirectory of the Windows program files directory. Table 14-4 shows a list of other .VBX files required when distributing applications that use custom controls. The Setup Wizard determines which files are necessary to include in a project. For more information on distributing and installing applications, refer to Chapter 16, Writing Setup Programs.

ADDITIONAL INFORMATION ABOUT THE COMMUNICATIONS CONTROL

The communications control was developed by Crescent Software, Inc. For more information, see the *Visual Basic Professional Features Book I* or search Help under custom controls. You can also write directly to Crescent Software, Inc. for additional information. Since Crescent Software receives many queries, however, you must register this product to receive technical support.

Control	File Name
3D check box	THREED.VBX
3D command button	THREED.VBX
3D frame	THREED.VBX
3D group push button	THREED.VBX
3D option button	THREED.VBX
3D panel	THREED.VBX
Animated button	ANIBUTON.VBX
Communications	MSCOMM.VBX
Gauge	GAUGE.VBX
Graph	GRAPH.VBX, GSW.EXE, GSWDLL.DLL
Key status	KEYSTAT.VBX
MAPI	MSMAPI.VBX
Masked Edit	MSMASKED.VBX
Multimedia MDI	MCI.VBX
Outline	MSOUTLIN.VBX
Pen edit	PENCNTRL.VBX
Pen ink-on-bitmap	PENCNTRL.VBX
Pen on-screen keyboard	PENCNTRL.VBX
Picture clip	PICCLIP.VBX
Spin button	SPIN.VBX

TABLE 14-4 .VBX FILES FOR CUSTOM CONTROLS IN PROFESSIONAL EDITION

14.2 USING THE OUTLINE CONTROL

The Professional Edition of Visual Basic also offers another powerful tool called the outline control. Through this control, you create enhanced file lists or display program information for your users. Figure 14.2 shows what the outline control looks like in the Toolbox.

Like the directory tree in the File Manager, the outline control displays items hierarchically in a list. When you click on the plus button, the current item expands to reveal sub-items contained within the group. Clicking on the minus button collapses the item (see Figure 14.3).

To create a list such as this, you use the **AddItem** method or List property to define each item. After initializing the outline, you set the Indent property to display the items. The following example shows how to create and initialize a list:

```
' Add new items to list

Outline1.List(0) = "Product Information"
Outline1.List(1) = "Registration"
Outline1.List(2) = "Technical support"
Outline1.List(3) = "Upgrade notification"

' Set index level for each item
```

FIGURE 14.2 The outline control

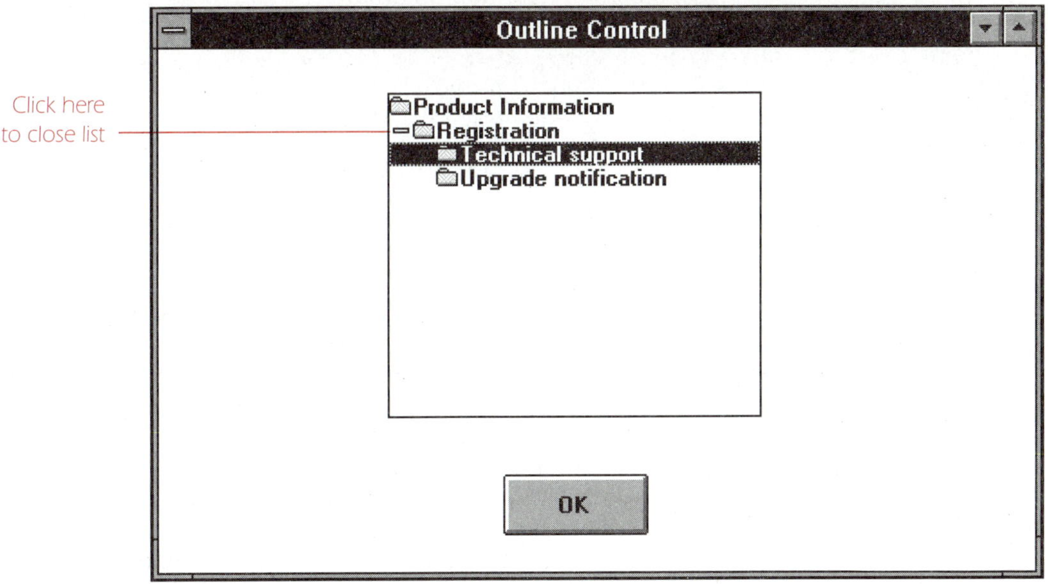

FIGURE 14.3 Expanding and collapsing an outline

```
Outline1.Indent(0) = 0: Outline1.Indent(1) = 1
Outline1.Indent(2) = 2: Outline1.Indent(3) = 2
```

The preceding code shows an outline using the default style (2 - Plus/minus & text). Table 14-5 shows a list of additional styles you can use.

READING LIST ELEMENTS

At run time, you can monitor list events. This next example shows how to read the path returned when a list element is selected:

```
Sub Outline1_Click ()

 ' Show complete path

 fpath = Outline1.FullPath(Outline1.ListIndex)
 MsgBox (fpath)

End Sub
```

When the user clicks on an item, the FullPath property returns the current entry and all the items before it. Each entry is separated by a delimiter (by default, the \ symbol is used). You use this technique to read and set the current directory. For example, if the second item in the list shown in Figure 14.4 on page 227 is selected, the FullPath property returns C:\MyApp\Data\Graphs.

Style Option	Description
0	Text only
1	Text and graphics
2	Plus/minus & text (default)
3	Text with pictures & plus/minus visual aids
4	Tree lines & text
5	Combines tree lines, text & pictures

TABLE 14-5 OUTLINE STYLE PROPERTY SETTINGS

NOTE: You can also redefine the delimiter the outline control uses by setting the PathSeparator property to the specified character.

USING GRAPHICS WITH THE OUTLINE CONTROL

By default, the outline control uses visual aids like the plus and minus buttons to show the status of list items. You can also define your own visual aids by setting the PictureOpen, PictureClosed and PictureLeaf properties.

Then to set the active picture, you specify the PictureType property. The following options are available:

Value	Description
0	Show PictureClosed bitmap/icon
1	Show PictureOpen bitmap/icon
2	Show PictureLeaf bitmap/icon

For example, when an item is expanded, you can show an icon of an open file cabinet. Then when the item is closed, you can show an icon of a closed file cabinet. This next example shows how this is done:

```
Const PICTCLOSED = 0
Const PICTOPEN = 1

Sub Outline1_Expand (ListIndex As Integer)

 ' Change default picture open style

 Outline1.PictureOpen = LoadPicture("C:\VB\ICONS\
                  ⇨ WRITING\BOOK01B.ICO")
 Outline1.PictureType(0) = PICTOPEN
End Sub

Sub Outline1_Collapse (ListIndex As Integer)

 ' Change default picture closed style
```

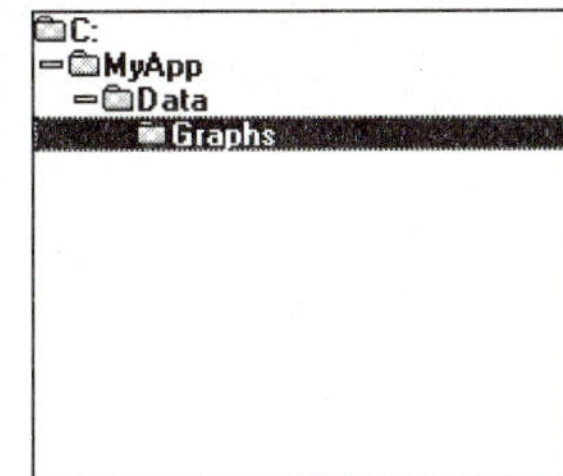

FIGURE 14.4 Reading paths from an outline

```
 Outline1.PictureOpen = LoadPicture("C:\VB\ICONS\
                    ⇨ WRITING\BOOK01A.ICO")
 Outline1.PictureType(1) = PICTCLOSED

End Sub
```

When an Expand event occurs, the Outline1_Expand procedure executes causing the picture of the BOOK01B.ICO icon from the Visual Basic Icon Library to appear next to the expanded item. This icon shows the picture of an open book. When a Collapse event occurs, a picture of a closed book appears in its place.

14.3 THE MASKED EDIT CONTROL

Another useful custom control supplied with the Professional Edition of Visual Basic is the masked edit control. With masked edit, you can create user-defined masks for getting input. Alternately, you can use one of the pre-defined masks to perform many common input operations. In the following section, you will learn how to create and apply both custom and standard masks.

CREATING A MASK

The Mask property allows you to specify a user-defined mask that you can use for validating input. A mask can contain any of the following special characters:

 # = Digit place holder
. = Decimal place holder
, = Thousands separator
: = Time separator
/ = Date separator
\ = Set next character to a literal—used to over-ride the default meaning of special mask characters (#.,:/&A?)
& = Place holder for character (ANSI characters between the ranges 32-126 and 128-255)
? = Place holder for letter—a-z or A-Z

NOTE: The actual characters used for time, date and currency place holders and separators is determined by Windows in the international settings configuration.

When you enter keystrokes into a mask, the keys you type appear at the next valid insertion point. For example, suppose you defined the following mask to read a zip code:

#####-####

At run time, when a zip code is specified, the masked edit control automatically knows to skip over the hyphen. If you type an invalid character, the control simply ignores the instruction.

The masked edit control also supports several pre-defined masks. The following options are pre-set for your convenience:

Standard Mask	Description
(###)###-####	phone number (Standard North American)
(###)###-#### Ext (#####)	phone number with extension
###-##-####	Social Security Number
##-???-##	Medium date - e.g., Jan-05-96
##-##-##	Short date - e.g., 01-05-96
##:## ??	Medium time - e.g., 02:30 PM
##:##	Short time - e.g., 21:15

To Use a Pre-defined Mask

1. In the Properties window, click on the Mask property.
2. Open the property options drop-down list by clicking on the third downward pointing arrow in the Properties window (see Figure 14.5).
3. From the list, choose the mask option you wish to use.

READING A MASK

There are two ways you can read the masked edit control. You can read the entire string by assigning the Text property of the control to a variable or you can use the ClipText property to get only the significant characters and disregard the mask.

Example

```
Sub cmdOK_Click ()

 ' Read masked edit control

 str1 = MaskedEdit1.ClipText
 str2 = MaskedEdit1.Text

 MsgBox ("Clipped: " & str1 & " Not Clipped: " & str2)

End Sub
```

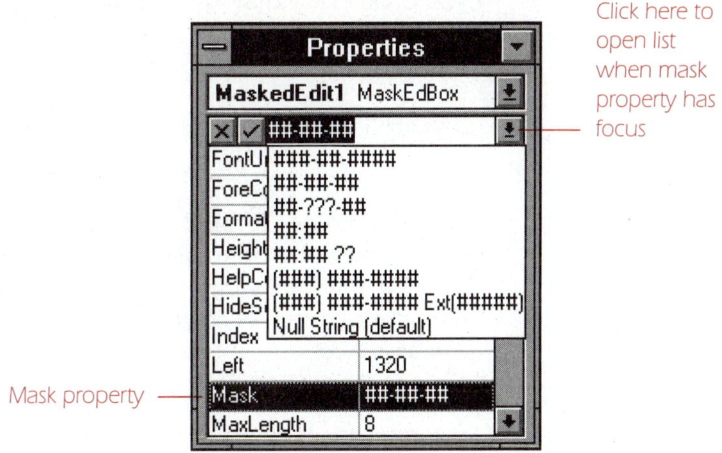

FIGURE 14.5 Using pre-defined masks

Both the Text and ClipText properties have their advantages and disadvantages. By using ClipText, you can save space on disk providing the contents of the mask are saved to a file. The Text property, however, is easier to read and can save you the trouble of having to format the output when you print it (though it may be necessary to remove these characters to process the data).

WRITING CUSTOM DATA ENTRY ROUTINES

The masked edit control also supports other properties that validate input and make data entry easier. The MaxLength property specifies the number of characters the user can enter into the control. When AutoTab is set to **True**, entering more characters than the MaxLength property permits will automatically move focus to the next control in the tab order. Leaving AutoTab set to its default value (**False**), causes a ValidationError event to occur when the user types more characters than the specified limit. By inserting a **Beep** statement in the ValidationError procedure, you can alert the user when too many characters have been typed:

```
Sub MaskedEdit1_ValidationError (InvalidText As String,
                          ⇨ StartPosition As Integer)

 ' Sound beep to alert user of data entry error

 Beep

End Sub
```

NOTE: This same code can also be used to sound a beep every time the user types an invalid character.

BINDING MASKS TO THE DATA CONTROL

Just as with a text box, you can bind a mask to the data control to display and edit table fields. To bind this control, set the DataSource property to the name of the data control and the DataField property to the name of the table field. This assumes that the data control is bound to a record source. For more information on creating "data aware" applications, refer to Chapter 6, Database Access.

14.4 USING 3D CUSTOM CONTROLS

In the Professional Edition of Visual Basic, you give your programs a 3D look by using the 3D check box, 3D command button, 3D group push button, 3D panel and 3D frame controls. Figure 14.6 shows the Toolbox icons you use to draw 3D controls on forms.

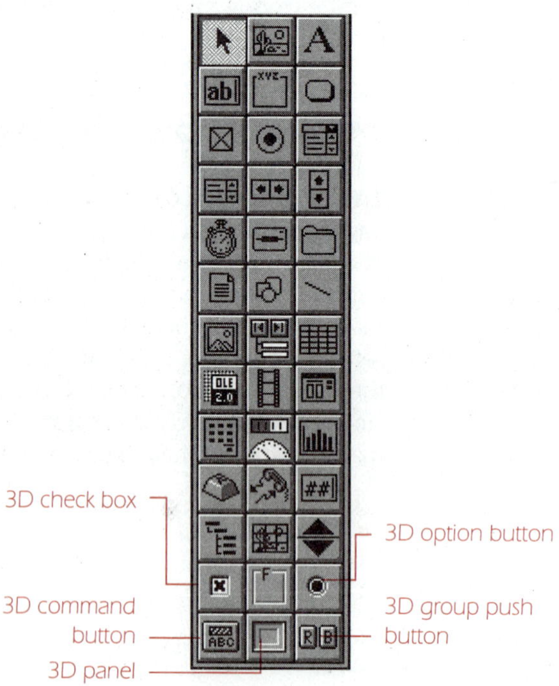

FIGURE 14.6 3D controls in the textbox

3D COMMAND BUTTONS

The 3D command button custom control works like a standard command button but has several additional features. With a 3D command button, you can display a bitmap or icon on a button and even add a 3D caption. This control also has a variable BevelWidth property that changes the 3D scale of the control. Figure 14.7 shows some examples of 3D command buttons.

Each button on the form has the following property attributes:

Property	Setting
BevelWidth	2 (default)
Font3D	2 - Raised w/ heavy shading
Picture	Bitmaps

When you draw a 3D command button on a form, the settings are retained for the next 3D command button drawn. Because the 3D caption requires a gray scale background, the BackColor property is not available for this control. The following example shows how to display a modal dialog box when the user clicks on a 3D command button. Notice that the code is entered into the Command3D1_Click procedure (the default event procedure created for this control):

```
Sub Command3D1_Click()

 ' Display message when user clicks 3D button

 MsgBox ("3D command button selected")

End Sub
```

3D GROUP PUSH BUTTONS

3D group push buttons, like 3D command buttons, display bitmaps (.BMP files). By default, only one button can be selected from a group at a time. You use this technique to provide restrictive access to certain commands in an application. Although the same operation can be performed with an option button, 3D group push buttons are flexible and visually appealing as well.

FIGURE 14.7 3D command buttons

Another advantage of 3D group push buttons is that you can use them to display different graphics when the button is in the up/down positions and when it is disabled. To accomplish this, you set the PictureUp, PictureDn and PictureDisabled properties. If the PictureDn or PictureDisabled properties are left unspecified, the 3D group push button control uses the PictureUp property when the button is selected or disabled (see Figure 14.8). Setting other combination of these properties may produce an inverted or dithered image of the picture the button displays.

THE 3D PANEL CONTROL

The 3D panel control, like the standard Visual Basic frame control and its 3D equivalent, can act as a container for other objects. With a 3D panel, however, you can create status indicators to measure time consuming events, display 3D captions with variable background and shadow colors and even bind the panel to the data control. By setting the BevelInner, BevelOuter, BevelWidth and BorderWidth options, you can produce many interesting effects. Figure 14.9 shows some possible combinations that can be achieved.

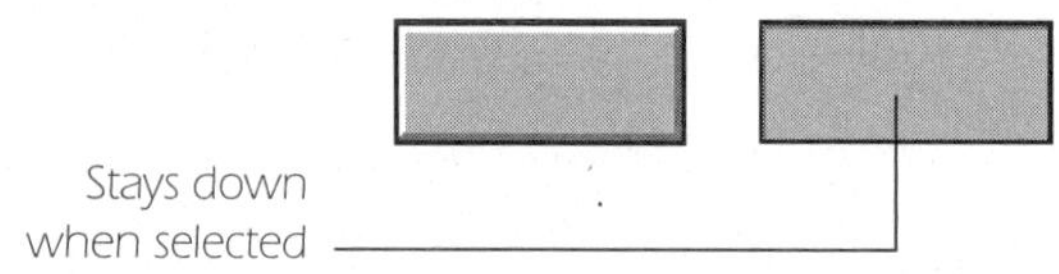

FIGURE 14.8 3D group push buttons

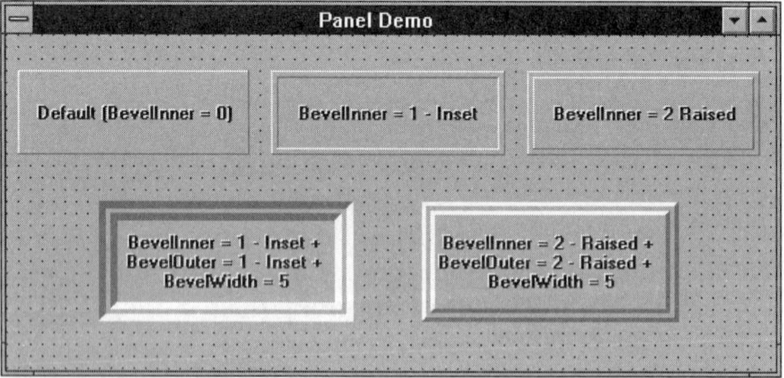

FIGURE 14.9 3D panel control

DISPLAYING 3D CAPTIONS

The 3D panel control also displays three dimensional text. To produce the illusion of a 3D caption, you set the Font3D and ShadowColor properties. The following example displays a 3D message on a panel in the default colors of black foreground and a dark gray shadow:

```
Sub Form_Load ()

 ' Display 3D caption on panel

 Panel3D1.FontSize = 17
 Panel3D1.Caption = "3D Caption"

End Sub
```

CREATING A STATUS INDICATOR

With the 3D panel control, you can create status indicators to report the progress of lengthy operations. For example, you can use a 3D panel to show how many files have been copied during a backup or searched while performing a query.

The FloodType property determines the type of status indicator the 3D panel displays. Table 14-6 shows a summary of options available. The painted area within the panel, appears in the color specified by the FloodColor property (the default is bright blue). To display a status indicator, you set the FloodPercent property to the percent of the area to fill. The following example shows how to set a 3D panel status indicator to the value returned by a horizontal scroll bar:

```
Sub Form_Load ()

 ' Initialize status indicator

 Panel3D1.FloodType = 1
 hscroll1.Min = 1: hscroll1.Max = 100

End Sub

Sub HScroll1_Change ()

 ' Flood panel area according to scroll bar's value

 Panel3D1.FloodPercent = hscroll1.Value

End Sub
```

USING OTHER 3D CONTROLS

Visual Basic also supports 3D check boxes, 3D option buttons and 3D frames. These controls are the functional equivalents of standard check boxes, option buttons and frames. Figure 14.10 shows how these controls look.

Like standard check boxes, 3D check boxes can be bound to the data control. Since this object returns only logical values (-1 or 0), you can only bind a 3D check box to a Boolean type fields. This technique can be used to add a professional touch to any program. For more information on using 3D controls and creating "data aware" applications, refer to Chapter 6 File Handling & Database Access or consult the *Visual Basic Professional Features Book I.*

FloodType	Description
0	No flooding (default).
1	Flood panel from left to right.
2	Flood panel from right to left.
3	Flood panel from top to bottom.
4	Flood panel from bottom to top.
5	Flood panel in widening circle.

TABLE 14-6 FLOODTYPE OPTIONS FOR THE 3D PANEL CONTROL

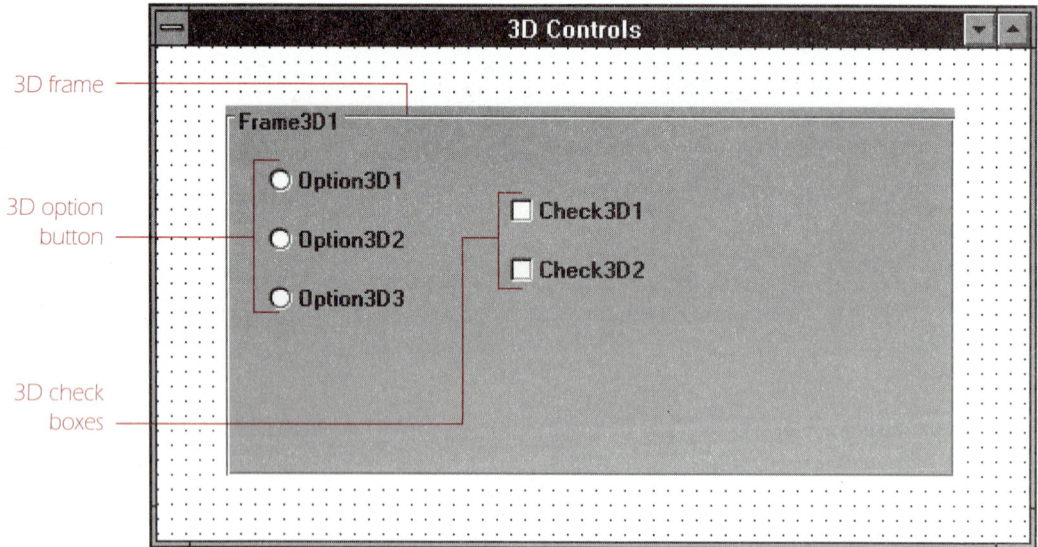

FIGURE 14.10 Other 3D controls

14.5 THE GAUGE CUSTOM CONTROL

With the Professional Edition of Visual Basic, you can also create a status indicator using the gauge control. This control displays a gauge over a user-defined bitmap (see Figure 14.11).

CREATING A GAUGE STATUS INDICATOR

By default, the image contained in the gauge control appears behind the gauge. You can also adjust the position of the gauge by setting the InnerTop, InnerBottom, InnerLeft and InnerRight properties.

Example

```
Sub Form_Load ()

 ' Set coordinates of gauge needle

 Gauge1.InnerTop = 10
 Gauge1.InnerBottom = 50
 Gauge1.InnerLeft = 10
 Gauge1.InnerRight = 10

End Sub
```

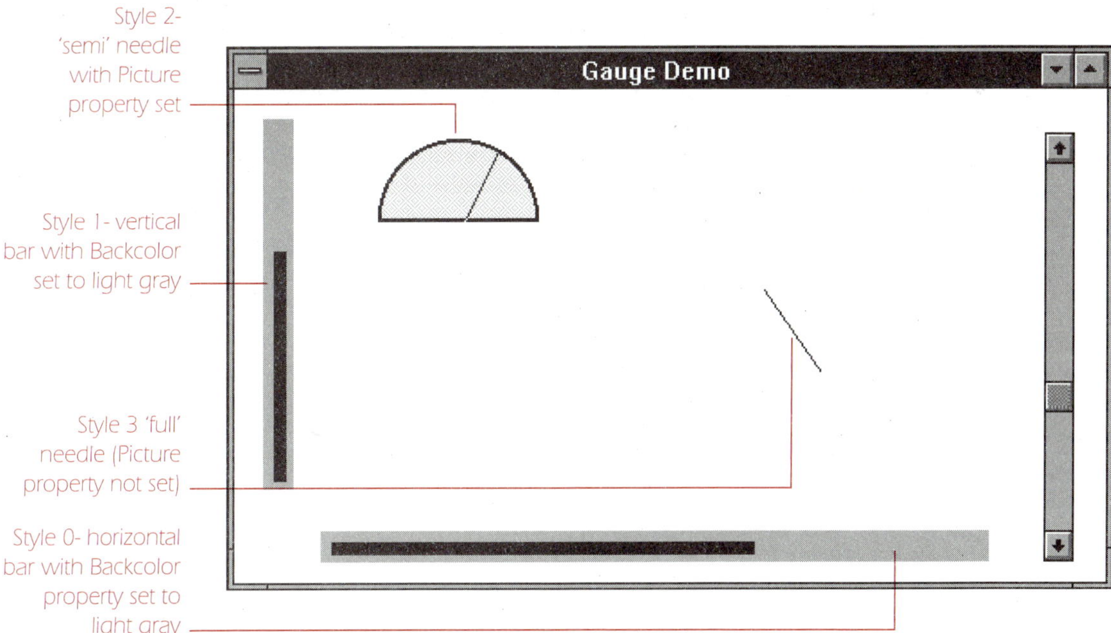

FIGURE 14.11 The guage control

To initialize the gauge control, you set the Min and Max properties to determine the range of values the control uses. For example, if you set Min to 1 and Max to 54, you can use the gauge control to display progress while shuffling a card deck. The Value property determines the current position of the gauge pointer. The following example shows how to set a gauge to the value returned by a scroll bar:

```
Sub VScroll1_Change ()

 ' Set gauge to value returned from scroll bar

 Gauge1.Value = vscroll1.Value

End Sub
```

CHANGING THE GAUGE STYLE

By default, the gauge control draws a linear gauge horizontally. The Style property determines the type of gauge that the control shows. The following options are available:

Style	Description
0	Draws a horizontal gauge
1	Draws a vertical gauge
2	Draws a 180 degree gauge
3	Draws a 360 degree gauge

Style 0 shows a linear gauge moving from left to right. Style 1 shows a linear gauge moving vertically upward. Style 2 shows a needle gauge that moves 180 degrees from the 9:00 O'Clock to 3:00 O'Clock positions. Style 3 shows a needle gauge moving 360 degrees (i.e., in a complete circle). By setting the Value property of each gauge to the value returned by a scroll bar, you can see how these movement patterns work:

```
Sub Form_Load ()

 ' Set style of each gauge control on form

 Gauge1.Style = 0: Gauge2.Style = 1
 Gauge3.Style = 2: Gauge4.Style = 3

End Sub

Sub VScroll1_Change ()

 ' Set each gauge to value returned from scroll bar
```

```
 Gauge1.Value = vscroll1.Value
 Gauge2.Value = vscroll1.Value
 Gauge3.Value = vscroll1.Value
 Gauge4.Value = vscroll1.Value

End Sub
```

NOTE: The Gauge subdirectory of the \VB\BITMAPS directory contains a list of bitmaps used for gauges.

14.6 USING THE MULTIMEDIA MCI CONTROL

The multimedia MCI control is one of the most powerful and versatile tools included in the Professional Edition of Visual Basic. With multimedia MCI, you can control audio boards, CD-ROM drives, MIDI sequencers, video disk players and more. Its device-independent operation means that a single set of commands can control any of these devices. Figure 14.12 shows what the multimedia MCI control looks like and what each of its buttons does.

NOTE: You can also customize the multimedia MCI control to show/hide specific buttons or rearrange them vertically.

In order to use the multimedia MCI control, your system must be preconfigured to work with Media Control Interface devices. There are several hardware/software configurations that can be achieved. In Windows version 3.1, for example, you can use the wave audio driver with an audio board. Table 14-7 shows some other possible configurations.

INITIALIZING THE MULTIMEDIA MCI CONTROL

Before you can use multimedia MCI, you must initialize the control. Initializing involves:

1. Indicating the device type.
2. Specifying the multimedia file name.
3. Opening the file.

The following procedure shows how to initialize the multimedia MCI control:

```
Sub Form_Load ()

 ' Set device and file name

 MMControl1.DeviceType = "WaveAudio"
 MMControl1.FileName = "C:\TEST.WAV"
 MMControl1.Command = "Open"

End Sub
```

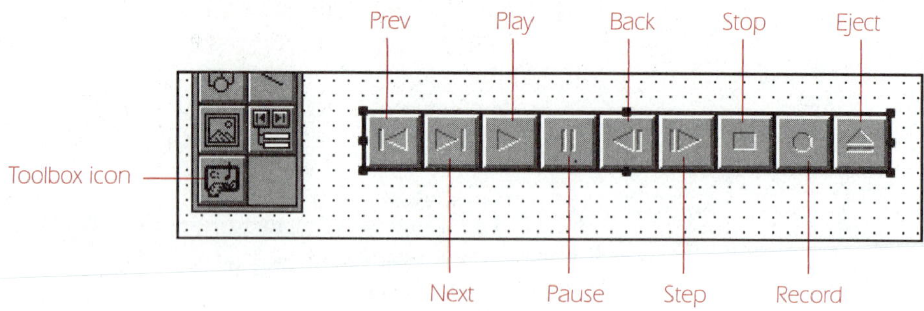

FIGURE 14.12 Multimedia MCI control

Configuration	MCI Device	MCI Driver
Audio Card Upgrade	Audio Card	CD Audio, Wave Audio & Sequencer
CD-ROM Upgrade	CD-ROM & Audio Card	CD Audio, Wave Audio & Sequencer
Video Player	N/A	Multimedia Movie

TABLE 14-7 HARDWARE AND SOFTWARE CONFIGURATIONS

Before using multimedia MCI, you must also indicate the type of device you are working with. The DeviceType property lets you specify this parameter. A device can be any of the following:

> **AVIVideo, CDAudio, DAT, DigitalVideo, MMMovie, Overlay, Scanner, Sequencer, VCR, Videodisc, WaveAudio and Other.**

Once you have initialized the multimedia MCI control, you can click on any button to test the way it works. For example, you can record a melody using a MIDI or other sound source, play music with an audio card or even show a video on your PC. Provided you have the right hardware and software driver to support it, there is really no end to what you can achieve with this control (except maybe become the master of all time, space and matter).

14.7 USING THIRD PARTY CUSTOM CONTROLS

The *Component Objects* and *Companion Products* for *Visual Basic* directory contains a listing of custom controls, dynamic link libraries and utility programs that extend Visual Basic. When you add a .VBX file for a custom control to a project, the icon for the control appears in the Toolbox. This system provides an easy way of incorporating third party solutions into applications. In the following section, you will see how four custom controls, Motion Works MediaShop, 3D Graphic Tools, MicroHelp HighEdit and the Windows Help Magician, can improve your programs and make developing easier.

MOTION WORKS MEDIASHOP AND 3D GRAPHIC TOOLS

If you are interested in doing multimedia presentations, Motion Works provides an ideal solution to GUI enhancement. With MediaShop, you can create "actors" for animation demos using its built-in graphics editor. This special product allows you to create translucent objects, edit graphic and video images and even change wave files.

MediaShop is a stand alone tool that you use to create presentations and other multimedia applications. The extended package includes a custom control for developing in Visual Basic. You can use this control to access objects created in MediaShop.

With little more effort, you can create even more stunning animation effects using 3D Graphic Tools by Micro System Options. This product lets you generate sophisticated 3D effects using state-of-the-art imaging techniques. With 3D Graphic Tools, you can add lighting and shading, picture and texture mapping, wireframes, anti-aliasing, contour drawing, translucent objects and more.

For more information on either of these products, contact:

For 3D Graphic Tools:

Micro System Options
P.O. Box 95167
Seattle, WA 98145-2167

For MediaShop:

Motion Works
524 Second Street
San Francisco CA 94107

NOTE: The *Component Objects* and *Companion Products* for *Visual Basic* directory is available to developers for a small handling and service charge. To receive the latest catalog, write to:

Fawcette Technical Publications
280 Second Street, Suite 200
Los Altos, CA 94022-3603

MICROHELP HIGHEDIT

With MicroHelp HighEdit, you can increase your control over memo handling in Visual Basic. This remarkable custom control allows you to create a fully functional word processor that supports extended fonts, printing, use of color and many other capabilities.

Although the developer's library included with this book provides many useful functions for producing memo handlers, with MicroHelp HighEdit, you can extend Visual Basic even further. For example, HighEdit includes a standard toolbar with line spacing, text justification and other formatting options already preset for your convenience. You can even add custom buttons to the toolbar and display status information during operations.

HighEdit also has a Professional Edition with extended capabilities for developing in Visual Basic and other languages. The *Component Object* and *Companion Products* directory contains a listing of the HighEdit custom control and other MicroHelp products. For more information, you can write to MicroHelp at:

MicroHelp Inc.
4359 Shallowford. Pkwy.
Marietta, GA 30066

THE HELP MAGICIAN

With the Help Magician, you can develop context sensitive help for your applications. This program dramatically simplifies the amount of effort required to produce help systems. It supports all the latest enhancements of the Help compiler including macros, secondary windows and non-scrolling regions. You can also add pop-ups, jumps, bitmaps, multiple fonts, bulleted lists, hotspots and more.

To develop a help system, you must have the Help Compiler which comes with the Professional Edition of Visual Basic. With the Help Magician, you can write help macros and test them right from its environment. The Help Magician automatically runs the compiler and can create or import .RTF files from Microsoft Word or Lotus Ami Pro. Since the Help Magician tests help macros without compiling, you can produce a help system with minimal effort and developing time.

The Help Magician also supports special formats that allow you to create jumps, pop-ups and hot spots by applying Rich Text Formats to text with a mouse. In version 2.5, you can even incorporate wave files into help systems. This product was developed by Software Interface Incorporated. For more information on the Help Magician, you can contact them at:

Software Interface Inc.
82 Cucumber Hill Rd, Suite 104D
Foster, RI 02825-1212

USING OTHER THIRD PARTY CUSTOM CONTROLS

The *Component Objects* and *Companion Products* for *Visual Basic* directory, contains a listing of over 120 tools available to developers. Visual Basic extension products span virtually every realm of development possible. These tools include support for converting icons to mouse pointers, interfacing with scanners, file compression, creating spreadsheets, connecting to mainframes, FAX send/receive transmissions, security enhancement and more. In short, if there is a feature missing from Visual Basic that you have not been able to get around, chances are there is a custom control already designed to meet your needs. Altogether considered, Visual Basic provides an ideal platform for developing powerful GUI applications without having to sacrifice accessibility, customization or ease of use.

Exercise: Creating a 3D Font Viewer

1. From the File menu, choose New Project.
2. Draw four 3D option buttons on the form.
3. Click on the first 3D option button.
4. Create a control array by naming each 3D option button as FontTst.
5. Set the Caption property of each control to:

Old Caption	New Caption
3DOption1	Raised w/ light
3DOption2	Raised w/ heavy shading
3DOption3	Inset w/ light shading
3DOption4	Inset w/ heavy shading

6. Using the Color Palette, set the background color of the form to light gray.
7. Set the Caption property of the form to 3D Font Viewer.
8. In the FontTst procedure, type:

```
Sub FontTst_Click (index As Integer, Value As
            ⇨ Integer)

 ' Set 3D font style for each control

      Select Case index
       Case 0
        font3dstyle = 1   ' Raised with light
       Case 1
        font3dstyle = 2   ' Raised with heavy
                          ' shading
       Case 2
        font3dstyle = 3   ' Inset with light
                          ' shading
       Case 3
        font3dstyle = 4   ' Inset with heavy
                          ' shading
     End Select

     For i = 0 To 3
       FontTst(i).Font3D = font3dstyle
     Next

End Sub
```

9. Save the project and run it.

SUMMARY

In this chapter, you learned how to use several custom controls provided in the Professional Edition of Visual Basic. You have also learned how to incorporate third party custom controls in applications to obtain greater control over program development.

REVIEW QUESTIONS

1. To prepare the communications control for a transmission, what properties must you set? Show an example.
2. What is the purpose of the outline control?
3. Code a routine to display a list using the outline control.
4. Write a procedure to read the value returned by a mask.
5. What symbols are used to specify numeric place holders, alphanumeric characters and special characters in a mask?
6. What is the difference between a 3D command button and a regular command button?
7. When might it be better to use a 3D group push button instead of a 3D command button?
8. Are there any advantages of using a 3D panel over a 3D frame?
9. Code a routine to show a status indicator on a panel.
10. Code a routine to show a status indicator on a gauge.
11. What are the benefits of using Motion Works MediaShop for multimedia presentations?
12. What third party extensions can be used to create a word processor or a help routine?

15 EXPOSING THE POWER OF THE WINDOWS API

The Windows API is a powerful collection of dynamic link libraries (DLLs) that manage memory, control windows and handle graphic and font operations. Linked to a program while the application is running, DLLs are maintained independent of applications and can be shared easily among various projects. This chapter shows how to work with DLLs and how to effectively manage Window's resources.

15.1 OVERVIEW OF DLLS

Before any DLL can be used in an application, you must explicitly declare it in the program or include its definition from another project. The DLLs used in animation projects in Chapter 13 were declared in the UTIL.BAS and SOUNDMOD.BAS code modules.

The developers library included with this book incorporates many procedures from DLLs to accomplish different tasks. By adding these modules to your projects, you gain access to both the developer's library and the DLLs on which they are based. In cases where no library routine exists for a particular need, you can draw upon an even greater resource of procedures through DLLs.

To Use a DLL Procedure in an Application

1. Use the **Declare** statement to define the DLL procedure in the Declaration section of a form or module. If this definition appears in a form, it is local to the form. If the definition appears in a module, it can be called from any file in the project (and can be included in other projects).
2. State whether the procedure is a **Sub** or **Function**.

3. Indicate the name of the DLL procedure, the library it is contained in and any arguments it will use.
4. Call the procedure.

For example, suppose you have declared the following DLL routine for use in a project:

```
Declare Sub ShowCursor Lib "User" (ByVal bShow%)
```

The Lib argument specifies the library (DLL) containing the ShowCursor procedure. Note that this argument is not case sensitive.

Once you have declared a DLL procedure in an application, you can call the procedure just as you would any other procedure. The following code fragment is taken from SCR.MAK. When the screen blanker form loads, the cursor is hidden using the ShowCursor function:

```
' Display screen saver form

Show

Call ShowCursor(False)
```

SPECIAL CONSIDERATIONS FOR DECLARING AND USING DLLS

You must be especially careful when using DLLs since Visual Basic has no way of verifying that you are passing the correct values. An incorrect argument may cause the program to crash and the possible loss of any work that has not been saved. Always exercise precaution and frequently backup your projects when experimenting with DLLs.

PROFESSIONAL EDITION EXTENSIONS

The Professional Edition of Visual Basic includes several files that make working with DLLs easier. These files are located in the \WINAPI subdirectory of your main Visual Basic program files directory. These files include:

- WIN31API.HLP Help file containing indexed list of Visual Basic DLL procedures and related structures.
- WINAPI.TXT Text file containing list of Visual Basic DLL procedures and related structures.
- WIN31WH.HLP Help file containing indexed and cross referenced list of DLL procedures and related structures for the entire Windows API.

Use the WIN31API.HLP file to find the declaration for each DLL. Alternatively, load WINAPI.TXT from disk into Microsoft Write and copy and paste routines directly from the file. Since this document is large, you will not be able to load the file into NotePad.

NOTE: Do not add WINAPI.TXT to your projects. This file is considerably large and will consume memory available to your programs.

PASSING ARGUMENTS BY VALUE

Since many DLLs are written in C, the method for communicating with DLL procedures must follow C syntax. By default, C uses *call by value* — that is, the value of a parameter, not its actual address, is passed to the function. With the exception of arrays, DLL's written in C assume all parameters are passed by *value*. Visual Basic, however, uses *call by reference*. Thus, a Visual Basic procedure by default is given access to the address of the variable (without using pointers). To pass a parameter in Visual Basic by *value*, you must use the **ByVal** reserved word in the DLL procedure declaration:

```
Declare Function RoundRect% Lib "GDI" (ByVal hDC%,
            ⇨ ByVal x1%, ByVal y1%, ByVal
            ⇨ x2%, ByVal y2%, ByVal x3%, ByVal y3%)
```

In the preceding example, the values of the x1, y1, x2, y2, x3 and y3 parameters are passed to the RoundRect procedure of the DLL. Notice the % (percent) symbol in the parameter list. As with QuickBASIC, you can use this mark as shorthand for the **Integer** data type. For more information on using type suffices, refer to Chapter 2, Programming in Visual Basic.

15.2 WORKING WITH DATA TYPES

Dynamic link libraries are extremely powerful and versatile. Entire books have been dedicated to covering them as the Windows API alone includes over 700 procedures. Knowledge Base, a Visual Basic supplement, contains additional techniques on using DLLs and other important topics. In the following section, you will see additional techniques that will improve your control over DLLs.

PASSING NON-EXPLICIT DATA TYPES

In some cases, DLLs are written to accept more than one data type for a particular argument. The following example demonstrates this technique:

```
.                        .                 .
.                        .                 .
Declare Function SystemParametersInfo Lib "User" (ByVal
         ⇨ uAction As Integer, ByVal uParam As
         ⇨ Integer,lpvParam As Any, ByVal fuWinIni
         ⇨ As Integer) As Integer
```

When you declare an argument **As Any**, all type restrictions are removed for the parameter. Visual Basic assumes that any parameters passed this way are called by reference. To pass the argument by value, you must precede the parameter with **ByVal** in the actual procedure call.

USING ALIASES IN DECLARATIONS

Sometimes it becomes necessary to use an alias in a DLL procedure declaration when the DLL uses identifiers that are invalid in Visual Basic. For instance, a Visual Basic identifier cannot be the same name as a reserved word. Nor can a Visual Basic identifier contain a hyphen or a leading underscore. These naming conventions may be perfectly valid in the DLL itself but otherwise conflict with Visual Basic's naming rules. In such cases, you can use an alias to refer to an invalid identifier in Visual Basic. Another advantage of using aliases is that you can assign a short name to an identifier to refer to a longer name, as the following procedure demonstrates:

```
Declare Function FindWindowByString% Lib "User" Alias
            ⇨ "FindWindow" (ByVal lpClassName$ ByVal
            ⇨ lpWindowName$)
```

By assigning an alias this way, the FindWindowByString procedure can now be referred to simply as FindWindow.

PASSING STRINGS TO DLLS

Because DLLs are often written in C, the rules for working with strings must obey C syntax. Unlike Visual Basic, C requires that all strings be terminated by a "null character" (i.e., binary zero). To pass a variable length Visual Basic string to a DLL, you must use the **ByVal** reserved word in the procedure declaration:

```
Declare Function GetWindowText Lib "User" (ByVal hWnd
            ⇨ As Integer, ByVal lpString As String,
            ⇨ ByVal aInt As Integer) As Integer
```

The one exception to the null-terminated string rule is when a DLL is written specifically for Visual Basic. In this case, you can pass a string to a DLL procedure without using **ByVal.** For a list of common DLL procedures written for Visual Basic, see the Control Development Kit in *Microsoft Visual Basic Professional Features Book I.*

It is also important to keep in mind that a DLL cannot modify the length of a string. When a C function in a DLL attempts to modify a string, no range tests are performed. If the string is too short, the DLL procedure will write beyond the end of the string corrupting memory.

There are two ways to safeguard against invalid string operations. The first is to use the **String** function to create a blank padded string 255 characters in length.

Example

```
mystr = String(255, 0)
```

Another way is to declare the string fixed in length.

Example

```
Dim mystr As String * 255
```

Since few DLL procedures modify strings beyond 255 characters, the preceding techniques will work in most cases. Before experimenting with any DLL procedure, always check the documentation for it.

WORKING WITH HANDLES

Many DLLs expect a numeric designator that identifies a control known as a *handle*. Among common handles are the *handles to Device Contexts* (hDC) and *handles to Windows* (hWnd) handles. Typically, the documentation for the DLL procedure will identify and describe each handle. In Visual Basic, you declare all handles as **ByVal Integer**. Since handles are numeric identifiers of objects, you cannot use them in mathematical operations. The following declaration uses the hDC handle to specify an area to paint within a graphics control:

```
Declare Function FloodFill% Lib "GDI" (ByVal hDC%,
            ⇨ ByVal X%, ByVal Y%, ByVal crColor&)
```

USING TYPES WITH DLLS

Some DLLs use **Type** definitions to maintain complex data structures. In this next example, a **Type** definition (or what is called a structure in C and C++) is used to hold the button status and position of a joystick:

```
Type JOYINFO
     wXpos As Integer
     wYpos As Integer
     wZpos As Integer
     wButtons As Integer
End Type
```

Assuming the necessary hardware and driver are installed, once you have declared the above structure in the project, you can get information about the joystick using the joyGetPos procedure:

```
Declare Function joyGetPos Lib "MMSYSTEM" (ByVal uJoyID
            ⇨ As Integer, lpCaps As JOYINFO) As Integer
```

The structure and declaration for this procedure is contained in WINMMSYS.TXT. If you are interested in adding joystick support to your game projects, you will want to copy the constants, global definitions, structures and procedure declarations from this file.

USING TYPES WITH STRING IDENTIFIERS

As you might expect, the rules for passing strings in **Type** definitions are basically the same as the rules for using regular strings. Unless the DLL is specifically written for Visual Basic, all string identifiers must be fixed in length.

PASSING ARRAYS TO DLL PROCEDURES

DLL procedures written for Visual Basic can often accept entire arrays using standard Visual Basic conventions. To pass an array in Visual Basic, you include the name of the array as an argument followed by empty parentheses:

```
Call TestDLLproc (MyArr())
```

In order to pass an entire array to a DLL procedure that is not written exclusively for Visual Basic, you pass the first element of the array to the DLL procedure. This works with numeric arrays because of the way numeric array elements are stored in memory (sequentially). However, with string arrays, this will cause a corruption of memory with DLLs not written for Visual Basic. Before experimenting with any DLL, always be sure to read the accompanying documentation.

Exercise: Making a Title Bar Blink

1. Create a new project.
2. In the Declaration section of the form, add the following procedure definitions:

```
Declare Function GetFocus Lib "User" () As Integer
Declare Function FlashWindow Lib "User" (ByVal hWnd
        ⇨ As Integer, ByVal bInvert%) As Integer
```

3. Set the properties of the form as follows:

Property	Value
Caption	Downloading Files
Height	3990
Width	4860
Picture	C:\WINDOWS\PARTY.BMP

NOTE: To set the Picture property, double click on the name of the property in the Properties window.

4. From the Toolbox, choose the timer control.
5. Set the timer Interval property to 350 milliseconds.
6. Double click on the timer control.

7. In the Timer1_Timer procedure, add the following code:

```
Sub Timer1_Timer ()
    Static counter As Integer
    window_status = Not window_status
    ' Get handle of form
    form_handle = GetFocus()
    ' Make title bar blink
    retval = FlashWindow(form_handle, window_status)
    counter = counter + 1
    If counter > 10 Then
        End
    End If
End Sub
```

8. Save the project and run it.

NOTE: Since the project calls two DLL procedures, be sure to save your work before running the program.

SUMMARY

In this chapter, you learned how to call and use dynamic link libraries. You have also learned how to work with aliases, disable type checking, the difference between *call by reference* and *call by value* and how to invoke DLLs with complex data structures.

REVIEW QUESTIONS

1. Why is it important to pass only fixed size strings to DLLs?
2. What is a handle? Are there any operations that are invalid to perform on them?
3. What is the difference between *call by reference* and *call by value*? Which does Visual Basic use?
4. Why is it important to save your work before experimenting with any dynamic link library?

5. Assuming the following Declaration is already coded in the program, how would you call the GetActiveWindow procedure?

```
Declare Function GetActiveWindow Lib "User" () As
            ⇨ Integer
```

6. Where must the declaration for this procedure be listed in the program?
7. How do you pass arrays to DLLs?
8. How can you get the handle of a control?

CLASS PROJECTS

1. Using the Windows API GetKeyboardType function and the following declaration, show the keyboard type:

```
Function GetKeyboardType Lib "Keyboard" (ByVal
            ⇨ kboption)
```

Set the *kboption* argument to 0 (return keyboard type). Then report the status of the keyboard as follows:

Return Value	Meaning
1	83-key PC or Compatible
2	102-key Olivetti
3	84-key AT or Compatible
4	101 or 102 Enhanced
5	1050 Nokia
6	9140
7	Japanese

16 WRITING SETUP PROGRAMS

One of the advantages of using Visual Basic for developing applications is that it comes with a setup utility that you can use to install the programs you create. The SetupWizard will automatically create the project's executable file, copy the correct files to the installation disk and even compress the files onto the disk. After running the SetupWizard, you simply execute the setup program that it creates from the Program Manager to install your program. This chapter provides a quick start to the SetupWizard and will also show you how to create your own custom setup programs.

16.1 USING THE SETUPWIZARD

In most cases, the SetupWizard can be used to install applications. Microsoft also provides the source code for a custom setup program. This project (SETUP1.MAK) is located in the \SETUPKIT\SETUP1 subdirectory of your Visual Basic program files directory. You can modify this program for your own purposes. Custom installations are necessary when you need to:

- Provide partial installations of applications. This is useful in large programs where not all the files are required to use the main components of a program.
- Call routines in DLLs or VBX files in your setup program.
- Use your own compression utility in the installation.

With hard drives becoming increasingly larger, you may wish to use the SetupWizard for all your applications. If you create programs that are very large, five megabytes or more, you can create your own custom setup utility for your customers.

In the following exercise, you will create a distribution disk for the sample application BKFILES.MAK. If you installed this project in the default directory, the source code is located in C:\VB_LIB. For this exercise, you will need two things:

- A blank formatted disk.
- A boot disk to start your computer from a floppy - necessary only if you automatically load SHARE.EXE in your AUTOEXEC.BAT file.

NOTE: To successfully create the distribution disk(s), you must either start your computer from a blank formatted disk or temporarily insert a REM statement before SHARE.EXE in your AUTOEXEC.BAT file. If you use the latter approach, remove the REM statement afterwards since the database engine uses this DOS program for the data control when the Exclusive property is set to False - **default.**

Exercise: Running the SetupWizard—Quick Start

1. From the Visual Basic program group, double click on the Application Setup Wizard icon to start the program. Note that you may have to use the vertical scroll bar to see this program item.
2. Once the SetupWizard is loaded, in the Project File box, type C:\VB_LIB\BKFILES.MAK. If you enter this path incorrectly, the Next button will appear disabled. Note that you can also browse through the file list to see the names of your projects by choosing the Select MAK File button.
3. Click on the *Rebuild the project's EXE file* check box. This will create an executable version of the program that will run without Visual Basic.
4. Afterwards, choose Next to continue.
5. Visual Basic will inform you that it cannot search the program for files needed by the installation since you did not provide the SetupWizard with a file format that it can read. If you created a copy of the program and saved it in text format using Visual Basic's File, Save Text... command, the SetupWizard could scan your program for necessary objects needed to complete the installation. Since this is a small project, you can ignore this extra step by clicking on No to abort the search but continue the installation.

   Another dialog will appear (see Figure 16.1). From this window, you can select any special options that your program uses so the SetupWizard will know what files to copy. Since the BKFILES.MAK project uses no data access, OLE automation, DDE, Crystal Reports or financial functions, you can also ignore this step by clicking on Next.

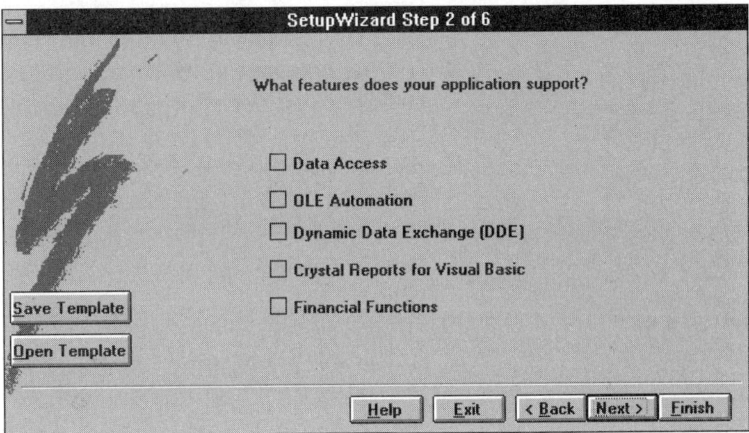

FIGURE 16.1 The file options setup dialog

6. The SetupWizard will prompt you for the name of the drive that will be used for creating the distribution disk (A: or B:) and the capacity of the drive (1.2 M. Disk, 1.44 M. Disk, etc.). If you do not know the capacity, check your computer's user guide or choose the one you think is correct from the drop-down list. The SetupWizard will not proceed until the correct drive information is entered. In all, there are 8 possible configurations (2 drives times 4 drive capacities). When you are done, click on Next to continue.
7. After specifying the disk drive configuration, the SetupWizard will prompt you for any additional files you would like to add or remove from the installation. The SetupWizard does not include the name of the setup program or the VBRUN300.DLL in this list (since these files are included in every installation). Click on Next to continue without changing the default file installation.
8. After completed these preliminary steps, the SetupWizard will automatically compress the distribution files and temporarily store them on your hard drive. Once the SetupWizard is done compressing the files, it will prompt you to insert the blank formatted disk. Do not confuse this disk with the boot disk you created earlier. If the setup program detects any files on the disk, it will reject the disk and prompt you again to reenter a new disk.
9. The SetupWizard will now automatically copy all the files needed to install the BKFILES.MAK project. Once it is done, it will show the message *Master distribution disks are finished.* You have now successfully created the distribution disk for this project. To quit the SetupWizard, choose Exit.
10. From the Program Manager, select File and then Run...Type either A:\SETUP or B:\SETUP (depending on which drive you previously specified).
11. The setup program (SETUP. EXE) will inform you that it is preparing for the installation. Afterwards, the main setup screen will appear (see

Figure 16.2). By default, the setup program will copy the distribution files to a directory by the same name as the project. If you change this name, be sure to include the drive specification (e.g., C:\TESTDIR). Note that it is not necessary (and it would be invalid) to include the name of the project's .EXE file after the directory.

12. When you are done, click on Continue... The setup program will copy the files to your hard drive and quickly flash a status indicator showing the progress of the operation. When it is done, the setup program will show the message *BKFILES Installation is Complete!* Click on OK to end the setup.
13. To test the installation, double click on the BKFILES icon in the BKFILES program group (or whatever program group you installed it in). The icon that the Program Manager shows is the same icon that is assigned to the Icon property of the Startup form of the project. You can use the ICONWRKS.MAK application (included with Visual Basic) to change the default icon to a custom user-defined icon. Optionally, you can select any of the pre-defined icons shipped with Visual Basic for your program as well. If you installed these files in the default directory, you will find them located in C:\VB\ICONS\.

NOTE: The entire Icon Library is shown in Appendix B of the *Visual Basic Programmer's Guide.*

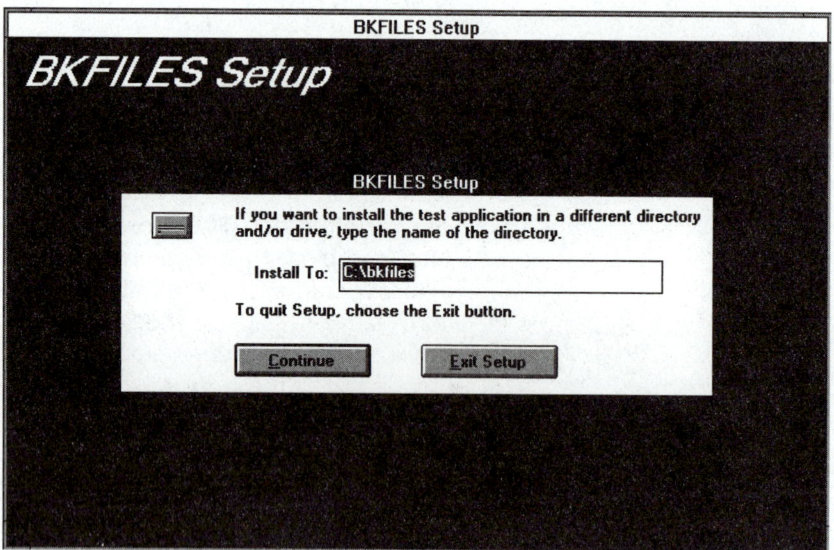

FIGURE 16.2 The main setup screen

16.2 WRITING CUSTOM SETUP PROGRAMS

Although the SetupWizard will work for many installations, for larger and more specialized applications, you may wish to write your own setup program. The Setup Toolkit (not to be confused with the SetupWizard) is a collection of programs and utilities you can use to develop custom setup programs. These files are located in the \SETUPKIT\ subdirectory of your Visual Basic program files directory. The Setup Toolkit consists of the following files:

SETUP.EXE	Copies any files necessary to run your custom setup program to your customer's machine and then executes the setup program.
SETUP1.EXE	A sample setup program that uses DLLs to perform a custom installation.
SETUP.LST	Text file containing the list of file names necessary to pre-install your application (see Planning a Setup).
SETUP1.BAS	Visual Basic code module containing procedures used by the sample setup program (SETUP1.EXE).
SETUPKIT.DLL	Dynamic link library used to perform installation.
VER.DLL	Decompresses and copies files—also tests the version stamp or time and date of installed files on the hard drive.

PLANNING A SETUP

With the SetupWizard, you do not have to worry about all the details of the installation such as how to determine the names of paths and how to create program items because the SetupWizard handles these operations for you. With the Setup Toolkit, however, you must create a list of *pre-installation* files (i.e., any special files needed by your setup program to make the installation), manually compress the files yourself and code the logic of the setup program. In the following sections, you will learn how to perform each of these operations.

DETERMINING WHICH FILES ARE NEEDED BY THE SETUP PROGRAM

When you create the distribution disks for a custom installation, at minimum, you need the following files:

SETUP.EXE	(runs your custom setup program)
SETUP1.EXE	(or whatever you have named your setup program)
SETUP.LST	(lists pre-installation files).
VER.DLL	(copies files)
VBRUN300.DLL	(DLL for running applications)

In addition to these files, your application may require additional ones. For example, your program may call routines in other dynamic link libraries or use custom controls to perform the installation. As a rule, any files that the setup program itself needs to install a project must be listed in the

SETUP.LST file. These special files are necessary for the *pre-installation* of your application.

SETUP.LST is a text file located in the C:\VB\SETUPKIT\KITFILES\ subdirectory of your Visual Basic program directory. The first line of this file must list the name of the setup program. For instance, suppose SETUPAPP.EXE is the name of the executable file you created for the installation. SETUP.EXE reads SETUP.LST and uses it to determine the name of your custom setup program (SETUPAPP.EXE). SETUP.EXE then executes SETUPAPP.EXE on your customer's machine. Prior to executing SETUPAPP.EXE, SETUP.EXE installs any necessary files required for running your custom installation program. The names of these special files (usually .VBX or .DLL) must appear one per line after the name of the custom setup program.

SETUP1.MAK is a sample program you can use as a template for your custom setup. SETUP.LST lists the names of the programs SETUP1.MAK uses to install the LOAN.EXE application (located in the C:\VB\SAMPLES\GRID\ subdirectory of your Visual Basic program directory). To perform the installation, the following files are listed in SETUP.LST:

- SETUP1.EXE
- VBRUN300.DLL
- SETUPKIT.DLL

Normally, you would change the first line of this file to the name of the executable version of your program. To create the .EXE file, you can use the File, Make EXE File... command of Visual Basic to compile your source code into a .EXE file (see Appendix B). VBRUN300.DLL (or whatever the most current version of this file is) must be included in SETUP.LST as well as SETUPKIT.DLL. Each of these files is necessary in order to install your application on your customer's machine. In addition, if your setup program calls any other DLL (or VBX) files, you must also list these names here as well. The Distribution Notes in the *Visual Basic Programmer's Guide*, on-line Help and professional features manuals lists the names of any special files you must include with your projects.

NOTE: SETUP.LST lists only the names of the files necessary for the pre-installation of your applications. The actual working files of your projects (data files, text files, bitmaps, VBX and DLL files not required for pre-installation) are copied by your custom setup program.

COMPRESSING FILES

If you are like most programmers, you will probably want to compress your files to conserve disk space. Microsoft provides a compression utility which works from DOS called COMPRESS.EXE. This program is located in the \SETUPKIT\KITFILES subdirectory of your Visual Basic program files directory. To use the compression utility, at the DOS prompt, type:

```
compress -r filename
```

Filename is the name of any program you wish to compress. The -r switch will replace the last character of the file with an underscore in its compressed version. This switch is necessary to compress and decompress files using the Setup Toolkit. With the exception of SETUP.EXE, SETUP.LST and VER.DLL, you can compress any file on the distribution disks. Whether the files are compressed or not, VER.DLL will correctly copy the files to the destination drive. In any case, the files will be automatically decompressed and restored to their original names during the installation (provided you use the same version of the compression utility). For more information on using COMPRESS.EXE, refer to the COMPRESS.TXT file located in the \SETUPKIT\KITFILES subdirectory of your Visual Basic program files directory.

PLANNING THE LAYOUT OF THE FILES

In order to create a setup program, you must know which files will be located on which disks. The first distribution disk should always contain at least the following:

- SETUP.EXE
- SETUP.LST
- .EXE name of your setup program (can be any name except the reserved name SETUP.EXE)
- SETUPKIT.DLL
- VBRUN300.DLL
- VER.DL_

The layout of the other disks will depend on what type of files your application contains and the sizes of the files. While there is no correct single approach, in general, it is best to organize files by file classes and label each disk indicating what it contains and with instructions on how to install the program.

CREATING DISTRIBUTION DISKS FOR THE PROGRAM

There are a few special considerations that must be made when creating the distribution disks. Unlike the SetupWizard, you must copy the files to the distribution disks using the DOS COPY command or a software utility. In addition, you must rename the VER.DLL to VER.DL_ when you make the copy to prevent Windows from using it when you insert the setup disk. To do this, at the DOS prompt type:

```
COPY ver.dll A:\ver.dl_
```

This will copy and rename the file at the same time. Afterwards, the following files must also be copied:

- SETUP.EXE
- SETUP.LST
- .EXE name of your setup program (can be any name except the reserved name SETUP.EXE)
- SETUPKIT.DLL
- VBRUN300.DLL

NOTE: If you compress any of these files, be sure to replace the last character of the file with an underscore when you make the copy.

Once you have copied the main setup files to the first distribution disk, copy the remaining files required by your application to the other distribution disks.

COPYING FILES TO THE DESTINATION DRIVE

Another issue to keep in mind is that in order to write an installation program, you must know exactly where each file must be installed. Fundamentally, the project and its related files can be divided into the following classes:

File Class	Extension
Program files	.EXE
Initialization files	.INI
Custom controls	.VBX
Operating system files	.DLL

Some of these files must be installed in specific directories. A typical installation for example would copy the program files into the main application's directory, the .INI files (initialization files used to control configuration options in some Windows applications) should be copied into the Windows program directory and operating system files and custom controls should go into the \SYSTEM subdirectory of the main Windows program directory. Since you cannot assume that Windows is installed on every machine in its default directory configuration, you must call the Windows API functions GetWindowsDirectory() and GetSystemDirectory() to determine where each file group must be installed. You can find examples of these procedures in the source code of SETUP1.MAK.

MODIFYING THE SETUP1.MAK PROJECT

The easiest way to create a custom setup program is to modify the code in the SETUP1.MAK project. This project is located in the SETUP1 subdirectory of the \VB\TOOLKIT\. directory. To edit the source code, you use the following steps:

1. Modify the APPNAME, APPDIR, WINSYSNEEDED and OTHERNEEDED constants in the Declaration section of SETUP1.FRM to suite your custom setup needs. These constants are explained later in this section.
2. Change the arguments in the PromptForNextDisk procedure to the names of your custom setup's applications parameters (see comments in SETUP1.BAS).
3. Use the CopyFile procedure to copy all the files on the current distribution disk.
4. Repeat steps 2 and 3 for each distribution disk.
5. Use the CreateProgManGroup and CreateProgManItem procedures (defined in SETUP1.BAS) to generate a new program group and install the icon for the application.

The APPNAME constant is the name of the project. APPDIR is the default directory in which the project should be installed. WINSYSNEEDED is the total number of bytes (uncompressed) of the files that must be installed into the Windows program files directory and \SYSTEM subdirectory of Windows. OTHERNEEDED is the total file size in bytes of the application files of your project.

Example

```
Const APPNAME = "NIGHT FLIGHT"
Const APPDIR = "C:\NFLIGHT"
Const WINSYSNEEDED = 53451
Const OTHERNEEDED = 43272
```

TESTING THE INSTALLATION

Once you have created the setup program and distribution disks, you are ready to test the installation. To run the setup program, from the Program Manager in Windows, select File and then Run... Afterwards, proceed by inserting the disk in the appropriate drive and then execute the program by typing:

```
A:\SETUP
```

NOTE: Regardless of what you called your custom setup program, you must type SETUP here since SETUP.EXE always executes the actual setup program.

If you experience any problem testing the installation, first check the distribution disks to make sure they contain all the required files. Afterwards, if necessary, you can use the debugger to trace through your logic in the program.

SUMMARY

In this chapter, you learned how to use the SetupWizard and how to write a custom setup program. You have also learned how to create distribution disks, compress files and test installations.

REVIEW QUESTIONS

1. What is the difference between the pre-installation and the actual installation of a program?
2. Which of the following operations can you perform with the Setup-Wizard?
   - compress files on the distribution disk
   - copy files to a hard drive
   - install custom controls
   - install DLLs
3. Why is it necessary to sometimes write a custom setup program?
4. To test for the directories that Window's program files and system files are installed in, what Windows API functions do you call?
5. How can you determine the version stamp or time and date of a program on the hard drive? Why is this necessary?

CLASS PROJECTS

1. Using the SetupWizard, install AIRRAID.MAK in the Games program group. Be sure to use the *Rebuild the project's EXE file* option to create the executable version of the program. For this exercise, you will need to copy the following bitmaps to the distribution disk:

   TANK.BMP
   JET.BMP
   DESERT2.BMP
   DESERT3.BMP

   Use the SetupWizard to copy and install the files.

Afterwards, test the installation by running the project. You should see an icon of a jet appear in the Games program group.

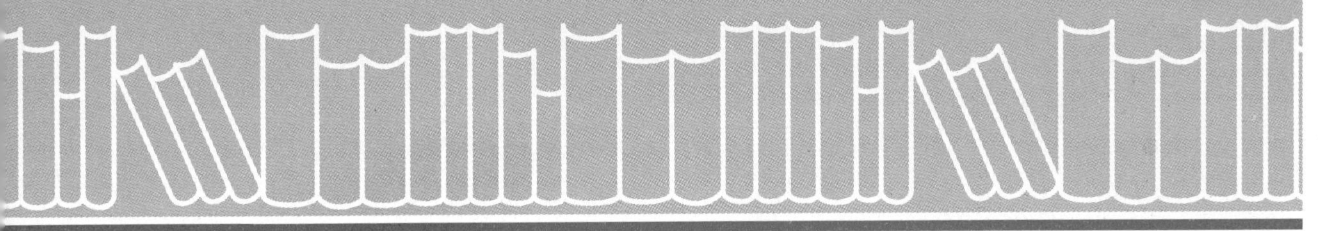

PART III

THE LIBRARY

In Parts I and II of this book, you learned how to program in Visual Basic. The following section discusses how to use the library. These procedures are listed categorically by the purposes they serve.

The documentation for each routine includes the necessary modules you must include in a project to call procedures. Each function is listed in a standard format that includes the function names, syntax, return values, defaults, remarks, related functions and coding examples.

The source code for the library and the examples are included on disk. You can modify any of these procedures and customize them to your own needs for your own programs. You cannot, however, use the source code to market a competing version of the library.

17 DATABASE AND FILE HANDLING FUNCTIONS

The database routines of the library, provide quick access to file information. Prior to version 3.0, developers had to rely on ODBC (Open Database Connectivity), random access and binary access to achieve database support in Visual Basic. With the coming of the Jet database engine, it is no longer necessary to use ODBC or master Visual Basic files to maintain databases (though ODBC is still used to access Microsoft SQL and ORACLE).

Many of the library procedures for file I/O were written for random access. These functions are supplied for compatibility with previous versions of Visual Basic. To use these routines, you must declare a user **Type** that defines the structure of each record. This definition must appear in the Declaration section of a module (.BAS file). Once you have declared the definition, you can add a record to a random access file like this:

```
Sub cmdSave_Click ()
 ' Save record to disk

 client.valid_add = True
 client.last_name = lastname.Text
 client.first_name = firstname.Text
 client.phone_no = phone.Text

 Call Saverec(fileno, filename, client)

End Sub
```

This example assumes that <filename> has been opened for random access and that the project contains a module with a valid user type.

Example

```
Type Struct1
  valid_add As Integer
  last_name As String * 18
  first_name As String * 18
  phone_no As String * 13
End Type

Global client As Struct1
```

Function	Description
DBEngine	Adds, updates and removes records using the database engine
Deleterec	Removes a record from a random access file
Delnull	Removes inaccessible records at the end of a random access file
Initscroll	Initializes a scroll bar for browsing records in a random access file
Lastrec	Calculates the total number of records in a random access file
OLERead	Reads an OLE object from a file
OLESave	Saves an OLE object to a file
Replacerec	Updates a record in a random access file
Saverec	Appends a record to a random access file
Scrollupdate	Reads a record into memory each time the scroll bar is clicked

DBENGINE

Adds, updates or removes records using the database engine

Syntax

```
Function DBEngine (<data control> As Data, <edit
              ⇨ option> As Integer)
```

Returns

–1 if successful, 0 if not

Arguments

data control—name of data control to use
edit option:

1 = add record
2 = update record
3 = remove record

Module

ENGINE.BAS

Remarks

DBEngine adds, changes or deletes records from a file using the database engine supplied with Microsoft Visual Basic 3.0. It works with most popular file formats including Microsoft Access, FoxPro, Paradox, Btrieve, etc.

See Also

Deleterec, Replacerec, Saverec

Example

ORDERS.MAK, shown in Figure 17-1, demonstrates the use of DBEngine. The Edit menu contains the following options:

Add record
Delete record

To update a record, click the Save button. The engine automatically handles this operation, however, if you move to another record after making an edit.

```
Sub Addrec_Click ()

 ' Add record procedure

 Const ADDREC = 1

 Dim edit_option As Integer

 edit_option = ADDREC
```

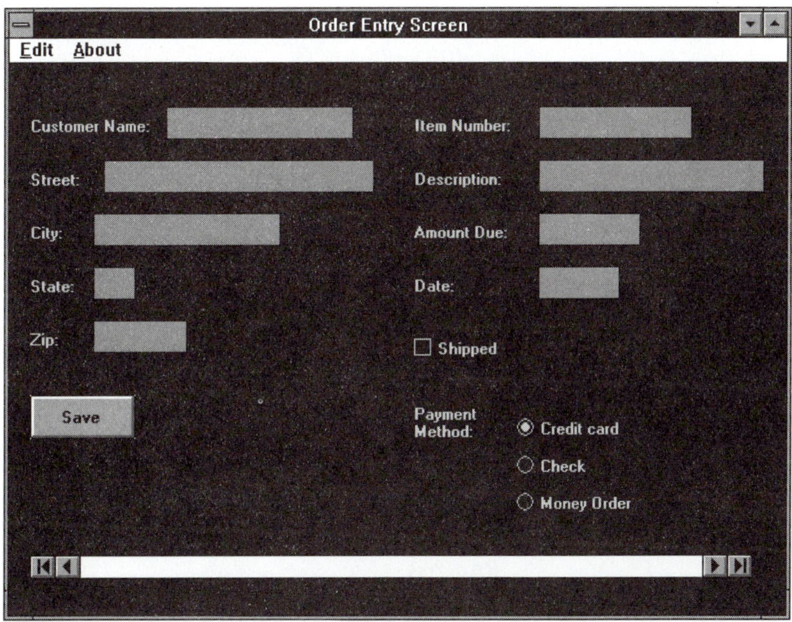

FIGURE 17.1 The ORDERS.MAK application

```
  retval = DBEngine(data1, edit_option)
End Sub

Sub cmd_Save_Click ()
  ' Update record procedure
  Const SAVEREC = 2
  Dim edit_option As Integer
  edit_option = SAVEREC
  retval = DBEngine(data1, edit_option)
End Sub

Sub Delrec_Click ()
  ' Delete record procedure
  Const DELREC = 3
  Dim edit_option As Integer
  edit_option = DELREC
  retval = DBEngine(data1, edit_option)
End Sub
```

DELETEREC

Removes a record from a random access file

Syntax

```
Function Deleterec (<file number> As Integer,
              ⇨ <file name> As String, <record number>
              ⇨ As Long, <record name> As Struct1)
```

Returns

–1 if successful, 0 if not

Arguments

file number	- file number of active work area
file name	- file name of active work area
record number	- record to be deleted
record name	- name of user-defined type containing record information

Module

DBMOD.BAS

Remarks

Deleterec removes a record from a random access file. Each record following the one removed is copied down one position in the file. This system has one problem. After calling Deleterec, a blank record is left at the bottom of the file. To remove the record, use Delnull.

See Also

Delnull

Example

The following procedure shows how to delete a record from a file. The horizontal scroll bar records the current record's position (see Figure 17-2). When the user clicks the Delete button in DB_DEL.MAK, the program removes the record using the value indicated by the scroll bar.

FIGURE 17.2 The DB_DEL.MAK demonstration

```
Dim filepath As String

Sub Form_Load ()

 ' Uses definitions from DB_DEF.BAS file

 fileno = 1
 filepath = "c:\vb_lib\cust.dat"

 ' Initialize horizontal scroll bar

 retval = Initscroll(Form1, hscroll1, fileno, filepath,
                 ⇨ client)

 ' Show first record

 Call Showrecs

End Sub


Sub Delrec_Click ()

 ' Delete record from file

 Dim filepath As String

 filepath = "c:\vb_lib\cust.dat"

 rec = hscroll1.Value

 res = MsgBox("Delete this record? ", 33)

 If res = 1 Then

   If Emptyfile(filepath) <> True Then

      retval = Deleterec(fileno, filepath, rec,
                   ⇨ client)

      ' Update horizontal scroll bar after delete

      Call Hscroll1_change

   End If

 End If

End Sub
```

```
Sub Hscroll1_change ()

 Dim client As Struct1

 retval = Scrollupdate(hscroll1, fileno, filepath,
                   ⇨ client)

 ' Read field values into label controls if
 ' return value is set to True

 If retval = True Then

   last_namelabel.Caption = client.last_name
   first_namelabel.Caption = client.first_name
   phone_numlabel.Caption = client.phone_no

 End If

End Sub


Sub Showrecs ()

 ' Show record on form

 last_namelabel.Caption = client.last_name
 first_namelabel.Caption = client.first_name
 phone_numlabel.Caption = client.phone_no

End Sub


Sub Exit_Click ()

 ' Remove blank records at end of file

 Call Delnull(fileno, filepath, client)

 ' Quit

 End

End Sub
```

DELNULL

Removes blank records from the end of a random access file

Syntax

```
Function Delnull (<file number> As Integer, <file name>
              ⇨ As String, <record name> As Struct1)
```

Returns

Nothing

Arguments

file number - Number of file to clean
file name - Name of file to clean
record name - Name of user-defined type containing record information

Module

DBMOD.BAS

Caution

To check for invalid records, Delnull tests the value of a field called <valid_add>. If <valid_add> is set to either a 1 or -1, it is assumed to be valid. To safely remove blank records, the following definition must be added to the record structure:

```
valid_add As Integer
```

Each time a record is added to the file, the program must set <valid_add> to either 1 or -1. You can also use the Visual Basic constant (and reserved word) **True** for this purpose:

```
client.valid_add = True
```

Remarks

Delnull purges blank records in random access files, thus freeing disk space. Use it anytime you delete a record (or before terminating a program).

See Also

Deleterec

Example

The following code fragment taken from DB_DEL.MAK, demonstrates the use of Delnull. The horizontal scroll bar keeps track of the record to delete. At the end of the session, a call is made to Delnull to remove blank records from the bottom of the file. For a complete listing of this example, refer to the discussion of Deleterec.

```
Sub Exit_Click ()

 ' Remove blank records at end of file

 Call Delnull(fileno, filename, client)

 ' Quit

 End

End Sub
```

INITSCROLL

Initializes a scroll bar for browsing records in a file

Syntax

```
Function Initscroll (<form name> As Form, <scroll bar>
       ⇨ As Control, <file number> As Integer,
       ⇨ <file name>  As String, <record> As Struct1)
```

Returns

–1 if successful, 0 if not

Module

DBMOD.BAS

Arguments

form name - form containing scroll bar
scroll bar - name of scroll bar
file number - number of file to read records from
file name - file to read records from
record - name of user-defined type containing record information

Remarks

Initscroll initializes a scroll bar for browsing records in a file. Specifically, it performs the following operations:

- Opens the file for random access.
- Sets the lower and upper bounds of the scroll bar (according to how many records are in the file).
- Reads the first record into memory.

See Also

Scrollupdate

Example

DB_DEL.MAK shows how to use Initscroll. When the program runs, Initscroll opens the CUST.DAT file and displays the first record on the form. Afterwards, it calls Scrollupdate to show other records in the file. For more information on this example, see the discussion of Deleterec.

```
Sub Form_Load ()

 ' Uses definitions from DB_DEF.BAS

 fileno = 1
 filename = "cust.dat"

 ' Initialize horizontal scroll bar

 retval = Initscroll(Form1, hscroll1, fileno, filename,
                  ⇨ client)

 ' Show first record

 Call Showrecs

End Sub
```

LASTREC

Calculates total records in a random access file

Syntax

```
Function Lastrec (<file number> As Integer, <file name>
               ⇨ As String, <record name> As Struct1
               ⇨ <file option> As Integer)
```

Returns

Number of the last record

Arguments

file number - number of file
file name - name of file
record name - name of user-defined type containing record information
file option:

1 = **bases calculation on open file**
2 = **bases calculation on closed file**

Module

DBMOD.BAS

Defaults

Computes total records based on the current status of the file (as it exists in memory)

Remarks

Lastrec calculates the total number of records in a random access file by dividing the total number of bytes by the size of a fixed length record. It is useful in record append and browse routines. By default, Lastrec bases its calculation on open files. This ensures that the total number of records returned will always reflect the file's current status.

See Also

DBEngine, Saverec

Example

MERGE.MAK demonstrates the use of Lastrec. When the user selects the Copy button, the program appends the records from the source file (CUST.DAT) to the target file (MERGE.DAT). The results appear in the Target picture box.

```
Sub Copy_Click ()

 If Filestatus(source_fileno, 0) = 0 Then
    Call Openfile(source_fileno, source_filename,
             ⇨ client, file_access)
 End If

 ' Copy records from source file to target file
```

```
  retval = Addrecs(source_fileno, target_fileno,
           ⇨ source_filename, target_filename, client)

  ' Calculate total number of records in target file

  lastrecord = Lastrec(target_fileno, target_filename,
                 ⇨ client, file_option)

  ' Display results of copy

  For i = 1 To lastrecord
    Get #target_fileno, i, client
    target.Print client.last_name
  Next

End Sub
```

OLEREAD

Reads an OLE object from a file

Syntax

```
Function OLERead(<fileno> As Integer, <filename> As
           ⇨ String, <OLEctrl> As Control)
```

Returns

–1 if successful, 0 if not

Module

ENGINE.BAS

Arguments

fileno - number of file
filename - name of file
OLEctrl - OLE control

Remarks

OLERead reads an object from a file created using OLESave. To accomplish this, OLERead opens the file for binary access. Afterwards, you can edit the object in the container application (provided the object supports in-place editing).

See Also

OLESave

Example

The cmdRead_Click procedure of OLE_EX.MAK retrieves an OLE object from disk by calling OLERead. Afterwards, the object appears in the container application. At run time, the user can create and maintain objects using the Create, Save and Read buttons.

```
Sub cmdRead_Click ()

 ' Read data associated with object

 Dim fileno As Integer

 fileno = FreeFile
 filename = InputBox("File name?")

 retval = OLERead(fileno, filename, OLE2)

End Sub
```

OLESAVE

Saves an OLE object to a file

Syntax

```
Function OLESave(<fileno> As Integer, <filename> As
             ⇨ String, <OLE> As Control)
```

Returns

–1 if successful, 0 if not

Module

ENGINE.BAS

Arguments

fileno - number of file
filename - name of file
OLE - OLE control

Remarks

OLESave stores an OLE object to a file. After saving the object, you can restore it with OLERead.

See Also

OLESave

Example

OLE_EX.MAK demonstrates how to maintain OLE objects. At run time, when the user clicks on Save, the program prompts for a file name and uses it to save an object.

```
Sub cmdSave_Click ()

 ' Save data associated with object

 Dim fileno As Integer

 fileno = FreeFile

 If filename = "" Then
    filename = InputBox("Save file as?")
 End If

 retval = OLESave(fileno, filename, OLE2)

End Sub
```

REPLACEREC

Updates a record in a random access file

Syntax

```
Function Replacerec (<file number> As Integer, <record
         ⇨ number> As Long, <record name> As Struct1)
```

Returns

–1 if successful, 0 if not

Arguments

file number - number of file
record number - number of record to update
record name - name of user-defined type containing record information

Module

DBMOD.BAS

Remarks

Replacerec updates records in files opened for random access. It overwrites the contents of a record with the updated information.

See Also

DBEngine, Saverec

Example

UPDATE.MAK uses Replacerec to modify a record each time the user clicks the Save button. To determine where the next write should occur, the global variable <rec> records the position of the record pointer. At run time, when the user clicks on Next, the program adds 1 to <rec>. Similarly, when the user selects the Previous button, the program subtracts 1 from <rec>.

```
Dim filechanged As Integer

Sub Form_Load ()

  ' Uses definitions from DB_DEF.BAS

  ' Load and display form

  Show

  ' Single user access

  file_access = 1

  fileno = 1: filename = "cust.dat": rec = 1

  Call Openfile(fileno, filename, client, file_access)

  ' Get first record and display it

  Call Showrec

End Sub
```

```
Sub cmdUpdate_Click ()

 ' Update record routine

 client.last_name = text1.Text
 client.first_name = text2.Text
 client.phone_no = text3.Text

 retval = Replacerec(fileno, rec, client)

 filechanged = False

End Sub


Sub cmdNext_Rec_Click ()

 ' Show next record

 last = Lastrec(fileno, filename, client, 1)

 Call Check_Update

 If rec < last Then
    rec = rec + 1
    Call Showrec
 End If

End Sub


Sub cmdPrev_Rec_Click ()

 ' Show previous record

 Call Check_Update

 If rec > 1 Then
    rec = rec - 1
    Call Showrec
 End If

End Sub
```

```
Sub Check_Update ()

 Const ICON_QUEST = 33

 If filechanged = True Then
   retval = MsgBox("Record has changed - Update",
             ⇨ ICON_QUEST)
 End If

 If retval = 1 Then
   Call cmdUpdate_Click      ' Save record
 End If

End Sub


Sub Showrec ()

 ' Show current record

 Get fileno, rec, client

 text1.Text = client.last_name
 text2.Text = client.first_name
 text3.Text = client.phone_no

 filechanged = False

End Sub


Sub Text1_KeyPress (keyascii As Integer)

 ' Set fileupdated flag to True if user edits record

 If keyascii <> 0 Then
    filechanged = True
 End If

End Sub


Sub Text2_KeyPress (keyascii As Integer)

 ' Set fileupdated flag to True if user edits record

 If keyascii <> 0 Then
    filechanged = True
 End If
```

```
End Sub


Sub Text3_KeyPress (keyascii As Integer)

 ' Set fileupdated flag to True if user edits record

 If keyascii <> 0 Then
    filechanged = True
 End If
End Sub
```

SAVEREC

Appends a record to a random access file

Syntax

```
Sub Saverec (<file number> As Integer, <file name> As
         ⇨ String, <record name> As Struct1)
```

Returns

Nothing

Arguments

file number - number of file to append record to
file name - name of file to append record to
record name - name of user-defined type containing record information

Module

DBMOD.BAS

Remarks

Saverec appends records to a random access file by calculating the total number of records and adding the new one at the bottom. Thus it hides the details of the operation and provides a convenient way of adding records.

See Also

DBEngine, Replacerec

Example

ADD.MAK uses Saverec to enter new customers into a file. After saving the records, the List button displays the file's contents in a picture box.

```
Sub Form_Load ()

 ' Uses definitions from DB_DEFIN.BAS

 fileno = 1
 filename = "cust.dat"

 ' Single user access

 file_access = 1

 ' Calculate EOF based on open file

 file_option = 1

 Call Openfile(fileno, filename, client, file_access)

End Sub


Sub cmdSave_Click ()

 ' Save record to disk

 client.valid_add = True
 client.last_name = last_nametext
 client.first_name = first_nametext
 client.phone_no = phonetext

 Call Saverec(fileno, filename, client)

 ' Clear text boxes

 last_nametext = ""
 first_nametext = ""
 phonetext = ""

End Sub


Sub cmdList_Click ()

 Dim i As Long

 ' Hide data entry form

 Form1.Hide
```

```
 ' Show record viewer form

 Form2.Show

 lastrecord = Lastrec(fileno, filename, client,
                  ⇨ file_option)

 ' Print records to a picture box

 For i = 1 To lastrecord
   retval = Getrec(fileno, i, client)
   Form2.Picture1.Print Tab(9); client.last_name,
          ⇨ client.first_name, client.phone_no
 Next

End Sub


Sub cmdOK_Click ()

 ' Hide record viewer form

 Unload Form2

 ' Show data entry form

 Form1.Show

End Sub


Sub cmdExit_Click ()

 ' Remove blank records and exit

 On Error GoTo exiterr

 Call Delnull(fileno, filename, client)
 End

exiterr:

 ' Error routine

 MsgBox Error, 0, "Runtime Error"
 Resume Next

End Sub
```

SCROLLUPDATE

Reads a record into memory each time the user clicks the scroll bar

Syntax

```
Function Scrollupdate (<scroll bar> As Control,
      ⇨ <file number> As Integer, <file name>
      ⇨ As String, <record> As Struct1)
```

Returns

–1 if successful, 0 if not

Arguments

scroll bar - name of horizontal or vertical scroll bar
file number - file handle
file name - file to read records from
record - name of user-defined type containing record information

Module

DBMOD.BAS

Remarks

Scrollupdate reads a record into memory each time the user clicks the scroll bar. It conveniently handles one of the most tedious routines in Visual Basic—record browsing. Clicking on the ends of the bar returns the next or previous record. Clicking on the middle of the bar and dragging the scroll box, permits random access.

See Also

Initscroll

Example

DB_DEL.MAK demonstrates the use of Scrollupdate. The horizontal scroll bar keeps track of the record pointer. Each time the user clicks on the bar, Scrollupdate shows a different record in the file.

```
Sub Hscroll1_change ()

 Dim client As Struct1

 retval = Scrollupdate(hscroll1, fileno, filename,
                ⇨ client)
```

```
  ' Read field values into label controls if
  ' return value is set to True

  If retval = True Then

    last_namelabel.Caption = client.last_name
    first_namelabel.Caption = client.first_name
    phone_numlabel.Caption = client.phone_no

  End If

End Sub
```

18 DATE AND TIME FUNCTIONS

The library includes several routines that facilitate date and time handling. You can use these procedures to develop appointment schedulers, time clocks, calendars, financial and accounting applications, system utilities, etc.

Many of the date functions have date format switches in the parameter lists. Where a date format option is not provided, you can use Dateformat to choose among several international formats.

Date Function	Description
Begmonth	Returns first day of month formatted as a string
Begweek	Returns beginning of work week formatted as a string
Dateformat	Changes the date format
Endmonth	Returns last day of month formatted as a string
Setdate	Sets the system date
Showday	Returns the day of the week for any date

Time Function	Description
Settime	Sets the system time
Timediff	Returns the difference between two time arguments

BEGMONTH

Calculates first day of month

Syntax

```
Function Begmonth (<date> As String, <date switch> As
                ⇨ Integer, <dformat> As Integer)
```

Returns

First day of the month

Arguments

date - date to base answer from
date switch:

1 = long (includes day of week)
2 = short (excludes day of week)

dformat - date format to use (for a complete list of available formats, refer to the discussion of Dateformat)

Module

DATEFUNC.BAS

Defaults

Short date format (does not include day of week)

Remarks

Begmonth calculates the first day of a month by extracting the month from a date argument and using it to build the answer. It is useful in appointment scheduling and billing applications where a perpetual calendar must be maintained.

See Also

Endmonth, Showcalend

Example

DATEDEMO.MAK demonstrates the use of Begmonth and Endmonth. When the user selects the Monthly Report option from the File menu, the account balance for the month appears in the Picture1 picture box.

```
Sub Monthly_Rep_Click ()

 ' Demonstrate Begmonth and Endmonth

 Dim date1 As String, date_switch As Integer
 Dim dformat As Integer

 date_switch = 2

 date1 = Now

 bdate = Begmonth(date1, date_switch, dformat)
 edate = Endmonth(date1, date_switch, dformat)
```

```
picture1.FontName = "Courier"
picture1.Cls

picture1.Print " BEGINNING PERIOD: " + bdate
picture1.Print " ENDING PERIOD: " + edate
picture1.Print
picture1.Print " CURRENT TRANSACTIONS: "
picture1.Print
picture1.Print " 04/18/94 Payment";
picture1.Print space(18) + "250"
picture1.Print " 05/05/94 Sam's Scuba Gear";
picture1.Print space(18) + "NY, NY 398"
picture1.Print " 05/08/94 North Central";
picture1.Print "Dallas Texas 575"
picture1.Print " 05/14/94 Midnight Express ";
picture1.Print "ShopShort Hills NJ 64"
picture1.Print
picture1.Print " PAYMENTS: 250"
picture1.Print " BALANCE: 1037"

End Sub
```

BEGWEEK

Returns beginning of work week

Syntax

```
Function Begweek (<days-to-add> As Integer)
```

Returns

Beginning of work week

Arguments

days-to-add - number of days to add to answer—use this argument to return subsequent week dates.

Module

DATEFUNC.BAS

Defaults

Assumes work week begins on Monday

Remarks

Begweek returns the first day of the week formatted as mm/dd/yy. Use Dateformat to change the way the date appears.

See Also

Begmonth, Endmonth, Showcalend

Example

APPOINT.MAK demonstrates the use of Begweek. When the form loads, the program prints the date heading for Monday at the top of the grid. It then calculates and prints the other date headings by adding to the date Begweek returns.

```
Sub Show_week ()

 ' Print date headings at top of grid

 Dim total_weeks As Integer, days As Integer
 Dim Monday As String

 total_weeks = extra_days

 Grid1.Row = 0: Grid1.Col = 1
 Grid1.FixedAlignment(1) = 2

 ' Calculate beginning of week

 Monday = Begweek(total_weeks)
 Grid1.Text = "MON-" + Dateformat(Monday, 1)

 Grid1.Col = 2
 Grid1.FixedAlignment(2) = 2
 Grid1.Text = "TUE-" + Dateformat(Str(CVDate(Monday)
                                     ⇨ + 1), 1)
 Grid1.Col = 3
 Grid1.FixedAlignment(3) = 2
 Grid1.Text = "WED-" + Dateformat(Str(CVDate(Monday)
                                     ⇨ + 2), 1)
 Grid1.Col = 4
 Grid1.FixedAlignment(4) = 2
 Grid1.Text = "THR-" + Dateformat(Str(CVDate(Monday)
                                     ⇨ + 3), 1)
 Grid1.Col = 5
 Grid1.FixedAlignment(5) = 2
 Grid1.Text = "FRI-" + Dateformat(Str(CVDate(Monday)
                                     ⇨ + 4), 1)
 Grid1.Col = 6
```

```
    Grid1.FixedAlignment(6) = 2
    Grid1.Text = "SAT-" + Dateformat(Str(CVDate(Monday)
                              ⇨ + 5), 1)
    Grid1.Col = 7
    Grid1.FixedAlignment(7) = 2
    Grid1.Text = "SUN-" + Dateformat(Str(CVDate(Monday)
                              ⇨ + 6), 1)

End Sub
```

DATEFORMAT

Changes the date format

Syntax

```
Function Dateformat (<date> As String, <format> As
              ⇨ Integer)
```

Returns

Formatted date

Module

DATEFUNC.BAS

Arguments

date - date to format
format:

1 = mm-dd-yy (American)
2 = month name dd, yyyy (American)
3 = dd-month name-yyyy (European)
4 = mm/dd/yyyy (American)
5 = dd.mm.yy (European)
6 = dd/mm/yy (European)
7 = yy-mm-dd (Japanese)

Defaults

Format option 1 (mm-dd-yy)

Remarks

Dateformat switches the date format among several international options. However, it does not change the setting in the Windows Control Panel. This approach has its advantages and disadvantages. Its main benefit is that the user can switch the date format for one application without affecting others. Its prime disadvantage is that you must use Windows to change the default setting.

See Also

Setdate, Showcalend

Example

DATEDEMO.MAK uses the library routine to change the date setting in a program at run time. When the user selects the Change Date Format option from the Options menu, a pick list appears with all the available formats. After a selection is made, the program saves the setting on disk for the next run.

```
' Define Type to store date format

Type Datetype
 date_format As Integer
End Type

Global daterec As Datetype


Sub DateForm_Click ()

 ' Create list of available date formats

 Form2.List1.AddItem "mm-dd-yy"
 Form2.List1.AddItem "month name dd, yyyy"
 Form2.List1.AddItem "dd-month name-yyyy"
 Form2.List1.AddItem "mm/dd/yyyy"
 Form2.List1.AddItem "dd.mm.yy"
 Form2.List1.AddItem "dd/mm/yy"
 Form2.List1.AddItem "yy-mm-dd"

 ' Switch to Form2 and show list of date
 ' format options

 Form2.Show

End Sub
```

```
Sub NewDateformat_Click ()

 ' Get date format user picked, switch to it
 ' and save it on disk

 Dim filename As String, fileno As Integer
 Dim rec1 As Integer, listno As Integer

 fileno = FreeFile
 filename = "newdt.dat"
 rec1 = 1

 listno = List1.ListIndex

 datestr = Dateformat(listno + 1)
 Form1.datelabel = datestr
 daterec.date_format = List1.ListIndex

 Open filename For Random As #fileno
 Put fileno, rec1, daterec

 Close #fileno
 Unload Form2

End Sub


Sub Cancel_Opt_Click ()

 Unload Form2

End Sub
```

ENDMONTH

Returns the last day of a month

Syntax

```
Function Endmonth (<date> As String, <date switch> As
              ⇨ Integer, <date format> As Integer)
```

Returns

Last day of the month

Module

DATEFUNC.BAS

Arguments

date - date to base answer from
date switch:

1 = long (includes day of week)
2 = short (does not include day of week)

date format - format of date (for a complete list of available date formats, see the discussion of Dateformat)

Defaults

Short date format

Remarks

Endmonth computes the last day of a specified month. On leap year, it adds one day to the month if it is February.

See Also

Begmonth, Begweek, Showcalend

Example

DATEDEMO.MAK uses Begmonth and Endmonth to show the period for a monthly payroll schedule. When the user selects the Monthly Payroll option from the File menu, the program displays the dates for the current period.

```
Sub Monthpay_Click ()

 Dim newline As String, doublespace As String
 Dim date_format As Integer, month_no As Integer
 Dim year_no As Integer, date_switch As Integer
 Dim date1 As String, dformat As Integer

 ' Exclude day of week from date displays

 date_switch = 0

 newline = Chr(13) + Chr(10)
 doublespace = newline + newline

 date1 = Now
 bdate = Begmonth(date1, date_switch, dformat)
 month_no = Month(Now)
 year_no = Year(Now)
```

```
  edate = Endmonth(date1, date_switch, dformat)

  message = "Pay period from: "

  MsgBox (message + doublespace + bdate + newline +
       ⇨ edate)

End Sub
```

SETDATE

Sets system date

Syntax

```
Sub Setdate
```

Returns

Nothing

Module

DATEFUNC.BAS

Arguments

None

Remarks

Setdate lets you change the system date conveniently from an application. It is easy to use and saves the trouble of switching to the Windows Control Panel.

See Also

Settime, Showcalend

Example

When the user selects Set Date from the Options menu in DATEDEMO.MAK, a message box appears that shows the current date and prompts the user for a new one. Selecting the OK button confirms the setting and Cancel aborts.

```
Sub DateSet_Click ()

  ' Change the system date

  Call Setdate
```

```
  ' Show date

  datelabel = Date

End Sub
```

SHOWDAY

Returns the day of the week for any date

Syntax

```
Function Showday (<date> As String, <date format> As
               ⇨ Integer)
```

Returns

Weekday the date falls on

Arguments

date - date to compute weekday from
date format:

1 = Short (omits day of week)
2 = Long (includes day of week)

Module

DATEFUNC.BAS

Defaults

To short date format and the current date if date parameter is a null value

Remarks

Showday returns the day of the week a date falls on. Use it to track appointments, determine when bills are due and log daily events.

See Also

Setdate, Showcalend

Example

DATETIME.MAK uses Showday to record when a company vehicle is returned along with the driver's name and the return time. When the user presses Enter, the program automatically enters the date into a text box. Optionally, the user can over-ride the function by typing another date.

```
Sub Form_Load ()

 ' Demonstrate Showday
 '
 ' Uses definitions in the VEH.BAS file
 '
 ' Load and display form

 Show

 Dim fileno As Integer, filename As String
 Dim check_in As Struct1, file_access As Integer

 fileno = 1
 filename = "vehicle.dat"

 ' Open file for single user access

 file_access = 1
 Call Openfile(fileno, filename, check_in, file_access)

End Sub


Sub Date_In_KeyPress (keyascii As Integer)

 ' Automatically enter date when user presses
 ' Enter in date field

 Const KEYENTER = 13

 If keyascii = KEYENTER Then
    date_in = Showday(Date, 2) + "-" + Str(Date)
    time_in.SetFocus
    keyascii = 0' Turn off beep
 End If

End Sub
```

SETTIME

Sets the system clock to the time the user specifies

Syntax

```
Sub Settime
```

Returns

Nothing

Arguments

None

Module

DATEFUNC.BAS

Remarks

Settime changes the system time conveniently from an application. This procedure is easy to use and saves the user the trouble of having to switch to the Windows Control Panel to change the system clock.

See Also

Setdate

Example

DATEDEMO.MAK demonstrates the use of Settime. When the user selects the Set time command from the Options menu, an input box appears. After entering the new time, clicking on OK saves the change and the Cancel button aborts.

```
Sub ChgTime_Click ()

 ' Change system time

 Call Settime

End Sub
```

TIMEDIFF

Finds the difference between two times

Syntax

```
Function Timediff (<starting time> As String, <ending
              ⇨ time> As String)
```

Returns

Difference in time in hours and minutes

Arguments

starting time - beginning of period (base time)
ending time - end of period

Module

DATEFUNC.BAS

Remarks

Timediff calculates the difference between two time strings. The times must be in 24 hour format (military or international time). All arguments must be in 4-digit form (for example, 0930 rather than 930). Separators such as colons, are optional.

See Also

Settime, Timesched

Example

DATEDEMO.MAK computes hours worked for a time clock procedure. When the user selects the Time Clock option from the File menu, the program prompts for the "time in" and "time out". It then shows the difference in hours and minutes.

```
Sub Timeclock_Click ()

 ' Time difference demonstration

 Dim time1 As String, time2 As String
 Dim diff As String, message1 As String
 Dim message2 As String, message3 As String

 ' Get starting and ending times
```

```
message1 = "Enter time in (in 24 hour format -
                        ⇨ hh:ss):"
message2 = "Enter time out (in 24 hour format -
                         ⇨ hh:ss):"
message3 = "Hours worked"

time1 = InputBox(message1, "Time Clock")
time2 = InputBox(message2, "Time Clock")

' Calculate time difference

diff = Timediff(time1, time2)

' Show difference

If diff <> "" Then
   MsgBox "Difference in times: " + diff, 0, message3
End If

End Sub
```

19 ENVIRONMENT FUNCTIONS

The library provides several functions that allow you to obtain information from DOS. You can use these functions to change drives, copy files, run other Windows applications, check for the existence of files and directories, display the hardware configuration and perform various other system operations. By studying these examples, you will learn how to incorporate these routines in your own applications.

Function	Description
Chgdrive	Attempts to change drive and returns error number if unsuccessful
Copylist	Copies a list of files and displays bar graph showing progress of operation
Direxists	Checks if a directory exists
Fileexists	Checks if a file exists
Filelist	Returns a list of files in a directory with their dates of last modifications and sizes in bytes
Fileschanged	Returns a list of files that have recently been modified in a directory
Filestatus	Checks if a file is open
Is_active	Checks if a program is in memory
Runapp	Runs a Windows application
Sysconfig	Returns the system configuration (CPU type, available memory and if a match coprocessor and network are installed)

CHGDRIVE

Changes current drive

Syntax

```
Function Chgdrive (<drive name> As String)
```

Returns

–1 if successful, error number if not

Arguments

drive name - drive to switch to

Module

ENVIR.BAS

Remarks

Chgdrive like the **Chdrive** command, changes the active work drive. Unlike **Chdrive**, the function returns an error number if it fails. Use Chgdrive to determine what action a program should take when a path change is unsuccessful.

See Also

Copylist, Direxists, Fileexists, Filelist, Sysconfig

Example

DIRDRV.MAK shows how to apply the Chgdrive function. When the user selects the Change Drive button, the program prompts for a drive specification and then makes the switch. Afterwards, the program resets the default drive for the next run.

```
Sub cmdChDrive_Click ()

 Const ICON_INFO = 64

 Dim drive As String, temp As String, message As String

 ' Record current drive before making switch

 temp = CurDir$

 drive = InputBox("Enter drive name to switch to : ")

 ' The Left function will remove any invalid characters
 ' from the string and return only the drive name.
```

```
' Later the program will add the correct drive suffice

drive = Left(drive, 1)

drive = drive + ":\"

message = "Insert disk and Enter new drive
       ⇨ specification"

MsgBox message, ICON_INFO, "Environment Functions"

' Try switching to drive - report error if
' unsuccessful

If Chgdrive(drive) <> True Then
   MsgBox "Drive change unsuccessful", ICON_INFO,
       ⇨ "Environment Functions"
Else
   MsgBox "Now reading drive " + drive, ICON_INFO,
       ⇨ "Environment Functions"
End If

' Reset original drive

retval = Chgdrive(temp)

End Sub
```

COPYLIST

Copies a list of files and uses bar graph to show progress of operation

Syntax

```
Function Copylist (<form name> As Form, <fileno> As
      ⇨ Integer, <file name> As String, <source> As
      ⇨ String, <target> As String, <total files> As
      ⇨ Integer)
```

Returns

–1 if successful, 0 if not

Arguments

form name - form on which to display graph
fileno - number of text file containing file list to copy
file name - name of text file containing list

source - source drive name
target - target drive and directory
total files - number of files to copy

Module

ENVIR.BAS

Remarks

Copylist reads a list of file names from a text file and copies them to the target drive. As it makes the copy, a bar graph shows the progress of the operation.

See Also

Chgdrive, Direxists, Fileexists, Runapp, Sysconfig

Example

BKFILES.MAK uses Fileschanged to create a list of files that have recently been updated in a directory. After creating the list, the program uses Copylist to back up the files.

```
Dim Path As String
Dim filespec As String
Dim target As String
Dim startdate As String
Dim bdate As String


Sub Form_Load ()

 ' Backup Utility

 sourcedrive.Text = dir1.Path
 begindate.Text = Date
 startdate = Date

 Call Show_files

End Sub


Sub Show_files ()

 ' Show files recently updated

 filespec = "*.*"
```

```
 startdate = begindate.Text

 Call Fileschanged(Path, filespec, list1, bdate)

End Sub


Sub cmdCopy_Click ()

 ' Copy recently updated files

 Dim filespec As String, fileno As Integer
 Dim filename As String, total_files As Integer
 Dim source As String

 fileno = 1
 filename = "BKFiles.Dat"
 total_files = list1.ListCount
 sourcedrive.Text = dir1.Path

 response = MsgBox("Is disk drive ready", 33, "Backup
               ⇨ Utility")

 source = sourcedrive.Text
 target = targetdrive.Text

 If target = "" Then
    target = "A:\"
 End If

 If response = 1 Then

  If CVDate(begindate.Text) <> Date Then
    startdate = begindate.Text
    Call Fileschanged(Path, filespec, list1, bdate)
    total_files = list1.ListCount
 End If

 retval = Copylist(Form1, fileno, filename, source,
               ⇨ target, total_files)

 End If

End Sub
```

DIREXISTS

Checks if a directory exists

Syntax

```
Function Direxists (<path> As String, <option switch>
                ⇨ As Integer)
```

Returns

–1 if **True**, 0 if not

Arguments

path - string containing drive and directory information
option switch:

1 = show error message
0 = suppress error message

Module

ENVIR.BAS

Remarks

Direxists checks for the existence of a directory by trying to switch to it. If an error occurs, it means the path is invalid. When <option switch> is set to 0, Direxists traps the error without alerting the user. If <option switch> is set to 1, Direxists shows the error in a modal dialog box.

See Also

Chgdrive, Copylist, Fileexists, Filelist, Runapp, Sysconfig

Example

This example, taken from DIRDRV.MAK, uses Direxists to check for the existence of a directory. If the path is not found, the program shows a message using **MsgBox**. Notice the use of the ICON_INFO constant. By including this parameter in the call to **MsgBox**, you can display a custom dialog with an information icon (see Figure 19.1).

```
Sub cmdChgDir_Click ()

 Const ICON_INFO = 64

 Dim path As String, show_errmessage As Integer
```

FIGURE 19.1 Displaying a message with the information icon

```
prompt = "Enter path to check - e.g., c:\vb_lib"
path = InputBox(prompt)

' Suppress error message

show_errmessage = 0

If Direxists(path, show_errmessage) = False Then
    MsgBox "Directory is invalid", ICON_INFO,
        ⇨ "Environment Functions"
Else
    MsgBox "Directory does exist", ICON_INFO,
        ⇨ "Environment Functions"
End If

End Sub
```

FILEEXISTS

Checks if a file exists

Syntax

```
Function Fileexists (<file name> As String, <error
                    ⇨ switch> As Integer)
```

Returns

–1 if file exists, 0 if not

Arguments

file name - file to check
error switch:

> **1 = show error message**
> **2 = suppress error message**

Module

ENVIR.BAS

Remarks

Fileexists checks for the existence of a file. Use it to prevent files from being accidentally overwritten.

See Also

Copylist, Direxists, Filelist, Memowrite, Readmemo, Sysconfig

Example

This example uses Fileexists to check for the existence of a file before saving it. READMEMO.MAK warns the user if a naming conflict arises. The program then gives the user another chance to name the file.

```
Sub cmdWrite_Click ()

 fileno = 1: filevar = text1.Text
 err_switch = False

 ' Check if file exists before saving

 Do While Form1.Caption = "Untitled.doc" = True

  filename = InputBox("Save file as: ")

  If Fileexists(filename, err_switch) = False Then
     Form1.Caption = filename
  Else
    If filename <> "Untitled.doc" Then
       retval = MsgBox("File exists, overwrite", 33,
                   ⇨ "Warning")
       If retval = 1 Then
          Form1.Caption = filename
       End If
    End If
  End If

 Loop

 retval = Memowrite(fileno, filename, filevar)
 Form1.Caption = filename

End Sub
```

FILELIST

Creates a list of files in a directory with their dates of last modifications and sizes in bytes

Syntax

```
Function Filelist (<path> As String, <filespec>
                ⇨ As String, <list name> As ListBox)
```

Returns

–1 if successful, 0 if not

Arguments

path - string containing drive and directory names
filespec - file specification (e.g., *.TXT shows all files with a .TXT extension)

NOTE: The <filespec> argument is case insensitive. Therefore, .TXT, and .txt are treated the same.

list name - list box control to show files in

Module

ENVIR.BAS

Remarks

Filelist returns a list of file information in the current directory. You can use this function to create a custom file opener dialog.

See Also

Chgdrive, Copylist, Direxists, Fileexists, Runapp, Sysconfig

Example

TEXT.MAK demonstrates the use of Filelist. When the user selects the Open or Save buttons, an enhanced file list appears.

```
Dim filespec As String, Path As String


Sub Form_Load ()

  ' Fill list box with file information in the
  ' current directory

 filespec = "*.doc"
```

```
 path = dir1.Path
 retval = Filelist(Path, filespec, list1)

 label2.Caption = dir1.Path

End Sub


Sub Dir1_Change ()

 ' Change directory

 ChDir (dir1.Path)
 path = dir1.Path

 list1.Clear
 retval = Filelist(Path, filespec, list1)

 label2.Caption = dir1.Path

End Sub
```

FILESCHANGED

Creates a list of files recently modified in a directory

Syntax

```
Sub Fileschanged (<Path> As String, <filespec> As
      ⇨ String, <listctrl> As ListBox, <bdate> As
      ⇨ Variant, <datapath> As String)
```

Returns

Nothing

Arguments

path - drive and directory name
filespec - file specification to use
listctrl - list box to show output in
bdate - date to back up files from
datapath - path where backup information will be saved - default is "C:\BKFILES.DAT"

Defaults

Copies all files modified on the current date if <bdate> is a null string

Module

ENVIR.BAS

Remarks

Fileschanged creates a list of files that have recently been modified. It searches the specified directory and reports any files that have changed since <bdate>. The file names appear in <listctrl>. The output is also saved in the file designated by the <datapath> argument.

See Also

Chgdrive, Copylist, Direxists, Fileexists, Filelist

Example

BKFILES.MAK uses Fileschanged to create a list of files that have recently been updated in a directory. After creating the list, the program uses Copylist to back up the files.

```
Sub Show_files ()

 ' Show files recently updated

 filespec = "*.*"

 startdate = begindate.Text

 Call Fileschanged(Path, filespec, list1, bdate)

End Sub
```

FILESTATUS

Checks if a file is open

Syntax

```
Function Filestatus (<file number> As Integer, <file
                  ⇨ option> As Integer)
```

Returns

–1 if **True**, 0 if not

Arguments

file number - handle of file
option switch:

> **0 = suppress error message**
> **1 = show error message**

Module

ENVIR.BAS

Remarks

Filestatus checks if a file is open. It is useful in database applications that periodically open and close files. The function provides an easy way of detecting if a file is open or not before problems can occur.

See Also

Fileexists, Filelist

Example

SECURE.MAK demonstrates the use of Filestatus. The program uses the library routine to check if the file must be opened before trying to encrypt it.

```
Sub Encode_Click ()

 ' Encrypt file

 retval = Encryptfile(fileno, file_name)

 ' Reopen file if necessary

 If Filestatus(fileno, 0) = 0 Then
    Open file_name For Binary As #fileno
 End If

 total_bytes = LOF(fileno)
 file_data = Input$(total_bytes, #fileno)
 text1.Text = file_data

 Close #fileno

End Sub
```

NOTE: This example assumes that <fileno> and <file_name> have been declared globally and are initialized in the Form_Load procedure.

IS_ACTIVE

Checks if a program is in memory

Syntax

```
Function Is_active (<application> As String)
```

Returns

–1 if successful, 0 if not

Arguments

application - name of program to check

Module

ENVIR.BAS

Remarks

With Is_active, you can test if a program is running before attempting to communicate with it. This function is particularly useful in DDE operations. For example, you can use Is_active to prevent multiple copies of a program from being started at the same time. For a complete discussion of DDE, refer to Chapter 9 Dynamic Data Exchange.

See Also

Runnapp

Example

The following code shows how to use Is_active. This example assumes that the source application has been compiled to disk and that the following objects have been created:

Program	Object	Property	Setting
Source	Form1	LinkMode	1 (Source)
Source	text1	Text	null value
Target	text1	Text	null value

```
Sub Form_Load ()

 Const NO_LINK = 0, AUTOMATIC_LINK = 1

 Dim app_name As String
```

```
   app_name = "Source"                        ' Source applica-
                                              ' tion name

   retval = Is_active(app_name)               ' Check if source
                                              ' is running

   If retval <> True Then                     ' Start program
                                              ' if error
      retval = Shell("Source", 1)             ' occurred
   End If

   text1.LinkMode = NO_LINK                   ' Remove any
                                              ' existing links
   text1.LinkTopic = "Source|Form1"           ' Set topic
                                              ' of conversation
   text1.LinkItem = "Text1"                   ' Set link item
   text1.LinkMode = AUTOMATIC_LINK            ' Begin automatic
                                              ' link

End Sub
```

RUNAPP

Runs a Windows application

Syntax

```
Function Runapp (<path> As String)
```

Returns

–1 if successful, 0 if not

Arguments

path - location of program to execute (drive, directory and file name)

Module

ENVIR.BAS

Remarks

Runapp runs an executable program. Use it to run Windows and DOS applications. If unsuccessful, Runapp, unlike **Shell**, traps the error and returns 0.

See Also

Filelist, Is_active, Sysconfig

Example

ENVIR.MAK demonstrates the use of Runapp. When the user clicks on Run, the program prompts for the name of a file to execute. Once the application is loaded into memory, it remains resident until you close it.

```
Sub Exec_Click ()

 ' Run a program in Windows

 Dim pathname As String

 pathname = InputBox("Enter name of Windows application
                 ⇨ to run:")

 retval = Runapp(Form1, pathname)

End Sub
```

SYSCONFIG

Shows the system configuration

Syntax

```
Sub Sysconfig
```

Returns

Nothing

Arguments

None

Module

ENVIR.BAS

Remarks

Sysconfig returns the system configuration by querying the Windows API. Specifically, it shows the amount of RAM available, whether a math coprocessor is present, if a network is installed and the CPU type. One function call makes it easy to perform.

See Also

Chgdrive, Copylist, Direxists, Fileexists, Filelist, Runapp

Example

Show the system configuration. When the user clicks on the Environment button in ENVIR.MAK, the program detects the hardware and the amount of memory available. Figure 19.2 shows how the dialog appears.

FIGURE19.2 The Sysconfig library routine

```
Sub GetEnvir_Click ()

  ' Show system configuration:
  '
  ' Math coprocessor installation
  ' Network installation
  ' CPU type: 286, 386, 486 or other
  ' Available memory

 Call Sysconfig

End Sub
```

20 GRAPHIC AND SOUND FUNCTIONS

The library includes four special procedures you can use to produce simple sound and animation effects. Chapter 13 covers game programming in Visual Basic. You can also use any of the third party custom controls discussed in Chapter 14 to increase your control over Visual Basic objects in GUI operations.

Function	Description
Drawcard	Generates a card deck
Mouseset	Sets the position of the mouse pointer
Soundeffects	Plays one of several pre-defined sound effects
Swapimages	Swaps graphics in a picture box or image control

DRAWCARD

Generates a card deck

Syntax

```
Sub Drawcard (<pictctrl> As PictureBox)
```

Returns

Nothing

Arguments

pictctrl - name of picture box to draw card in

Module

UTIL.BAS

Remarks

Drawcard creates a card deck one card at a time. The following conventions are used:

A = Ace
K = King
Q = Queen
J1 = Jack
J2 = Joker
2..9 Regular Cards

H = Heart
D = Diamond
C = Club
S = Spade

Once a card is drawn, its image can be saved and later read back with the Visual Basic **SavePicture** and **LoadPicture** functions. By specifying the Image property of the picture box, you can import the deck into PaintBrush and edit the cards.

TIP: Use the Paintbrush View Zoom In command to enlarge the card while editing it.

See Also

Mouseset, Soundeffects, Swapimages

Example

DRAWCARD.MAK shows how to use the library procedure. When the user chooses the Draw button, the program prompts for the necessary input and then draws the card in a picture box. Afterwards, choosing the Save As button writes the card image to disk.

```
Sub cmdDrawCard_Click ()

  ' Create new card

  Call Drawcard(picture1)

End Sub


Sub cmdSave_Click ()

  validname = False

  Do While validname = False
```

```
    ' Get card name

    cardname = InputBox("Save card as: ")
    If cardname = "" Then
       Exit Sub
    End If

    cardname = UCase(cardname)

    retval = InStr(1, cardname, ".BMP")

    If retval <> 0 Then
       validname = True
    ElseIf InStr(1, cardname, ".") = 0 Then
      cardname = "C:\VB_LIB\" + UCase(cardname) + ".BMP"
      validname = True
    End If

  Loop

  ' Save card image to a file

  SavePicture picture1.Image, cardname

End Sub
```

MOUSESET

Sets position of mouse pointer

Syntax

```
Sub Mouseset (x As Integer, y As Integer)
```

Returns

Nothing

Arguments

x - column position of mouse (in pixels)
y - row position of mouse (in pixels)

Module

UTIL.BAS

Remarks

Mouseset is particularly useful in animation since Visual Basic provides little control over the position of the mouse pointer. Use Mouseset to prevent the mouse cursor from interfering with graphics routines. Notice that the coordinates must be given in pixels (not twips).

See Also

Soundeffects, Swapimages

Example

The following procedure, taken from the sample game GATER.MAK, shows how to use Mouseset. When the form loads, the mouse pointer is positioned at the upper left hand corner of the form (away from the grid).

NOTE: The README.DOC file on the program disk contains additional information about this example.

```
Sub Form_Load ()

 ' GATER.MAK - Frank J. Engo

 Dim x As Integer, y As Integer

 x = 50: y = 50

 ' Set initial mouse position

 Call Mouseset(x, y)

 Grid1.Row = 5: Grid1.Col = 5

 Call Initgrid

 player_x = 5: player_y = 5

 ' Show alligators

 Call Show_enemies

 timer1.Enabled = True
 timer1.Interval = 500
 time_left = 30
 prev_time = Time
 gamelevel = 1
 players = 5

 ' Set initial strategy and initialize target array
```

```
    Call Targetscheme_1
    Call Init_targ_array
    Call Show_score

End Sub
```

SOUNDEFFECTS

Plays one of several pre-defined sound effects

Syntax

```
Sub Soundeffects (<soundoption> As Integer)
```

Returns

Nothing

Arguments

soundoption - sound effect to play:

1 = Jingle
2 = Falling
3 = Siren
4 = Squash
5 = Sequence
6 = Laser Gun
7 = Bird Chirp

Module

SOUNDMOD.BAS

Note

Because of the way sound is handled in Windows 3.0, this procedure may not perform adequately on versions of Windows prior to 3.1.

Remarks

Soundeffects plays one of several pre-defined sound effects. Before calling this procedure, you must call the Windows API function OpenSound to request permission to use the PC Speaker. Then, after calling Soundeffects, you call CloseSound to free the system resources. The declarations for both these modules are contained in SOUNDMOD.BAS.

See Also

Swapimages

Example

The following example shows how to call Soundeffects. The SOUNDDEM.MAK project plays a different sound effect each time you select a button on the form (see Figure 20.1).

```
Sub Form_Load ()

 ' Request access to speaker

 retval = OpenSound()

End Sub


Sub Jingle_Click ()

 ' Play short jingle

 Const JINGLE = 1

 Call Soundeffects(JINGLE)

End Sub


Sub Falling_Object_Click ()

 ' Simulate falling object sound

 Const FALLING = 2

 Call Soundeffects(FALLING)
```

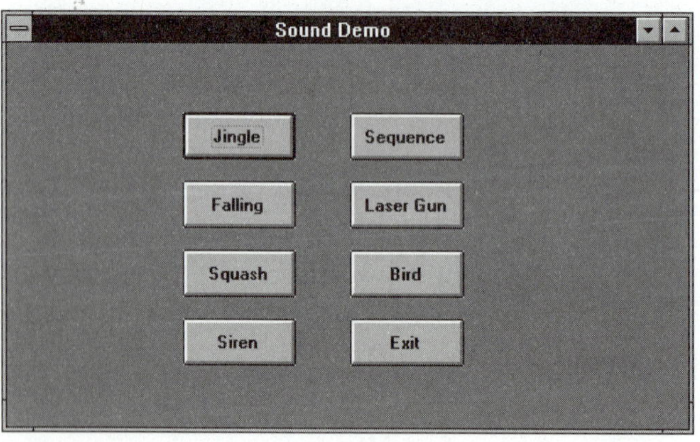

FIGURE 20.1 The Soundeffects procedure

```
End Sub

Sub Siren_Sounding_Click ()
 ' Simulate siren sounding
 Const SIREN = 3
 Call Soundeffects(SIREN)
End Sub

Sub Squashing_Click ()
 ' Simulate squashing sound
 Const SQUASH = 4
 Call Soundeffects(SQUASH)
End Sub

Sub Sequence_Click ()
 ' Play sequence sound effect
 Const SEQUENCE = 5
 Call Soundeffects(SEQUENCE)
End Sub

Sub Lasergun_Click ()
 ' Simulate laser gun sound
 Const LASER = 6
 Call Soundeffects(LASER)
End Sub
```

```
Sub Bird_Click ()

 ' Simulate bird sound

 Const BIRD = 7

 Call Soundeffects(BIRD)

End Sub


Sub cmdExit_Click ()

 ' Free speaker so other programs can access it

 retval = CloseSound()

 End

End Sub
```

SWAPIMAGES

Swaps graphics in a picture box or image control

Syntax

```
Sub Swapimages (<pic1> As Control, <pic2> As Control,
              ⇨ <swap_pic> As Control)
```

Returns

Nothing

Arguments

pic1 - name of first picture box or image control to swap
pic2 - name of second picture box or image control to swap
swap_pic - name of picture box or image control that will be used to make the swap

Module

UTIL.BAS

Remarks

Swapimages provides an easy way to perform animation. It swaps two pictures in a picture box or image control. You can create the graphics in either Microsoft Paintbrush supplied with Windows or ICONWRKS.MAK provided with Visual Basic.

See Also

Mouseset, Soundeffects

Example

ANIM.MAK demonstrates the use of Swapimages. When the form loads, the program animates a UFO by swapping two very similar pictures of the space ship. Together, the three image controls create the illusion of a spinning flying saucer. Figure 20.2 shows how the form appears.

```
Dim x, y As Integer


Sub Form_Load ()

 ' Hide pictures of space ships initially

 UFO1.Visible = False: UFO2.Visible = False

 ' Get starting position of image control used for swap

 x = current_ship.Left: y = current_ship.Top
```

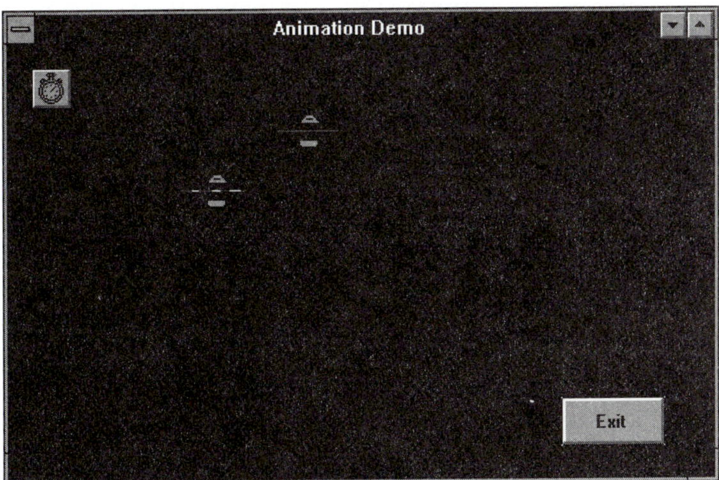

FIGURE 20.2 The Swapimages procedure

```
 ' Start UFO demo

 timer1.Interval = 120

End Sub


Sub Timer1_Timer ()

 ' Swap UFO pictures

 Call Swapimages(UFO1, UFO2, current_ship)

 x = x + 40: y = y - 40

 ' Move space ship

 current_ship.Move x, y

 ' Quit

 If y <= 0 Then
   timer1.Enabled = False
 End If

End Sub
```

21 GRID FUNCTIONS

The grid control of Visual Basic displays information in a spreadsheet format. Although you cannot edit cells directly, grids are very useful in some applications. The sample appointment scheduler program, for example, demonstrates the flexibility of this custom control. Each cell in the grid corresponds to an exact time slot throughout the day. Thus you can quickly schedule an appointment by clicking on a cell. The tabular format of the grid control also allows you to view an entire week's appointments in one glance.

Function	Description
Cleargrid	Clears a grid
Gridfill	Restores contents of a grid previously saved
Gridsave	Saves contents of a grid to a file
Initgrid	Sets the column width and number of rows and columns in a grid
Timesched	Prints a 60 minute schedule on a grid

CLEARGRID

Clears rows and columns in a grid

Syntax

```
Sub Cleargrid (<grid name> As Grid)
```

Returns

Nothing

Arguments

grid name - grid to clear

Module

GRIDFUNC.BAS

Remarks

Cleargrid clears a grid by assigning a null string to all its cells. Use it before displaying output.

See Also

Gridfill, Gridsave, Initgrid, Timesched

Example

READGRID.MAK shows how to apply Cleargrid. After reading a list of system components from a file, the cmdClear_Click procedure clears the grid.

```
Sub cmdClear_Click ()

 ' Clear grid cells

 Call Cleargrid(Grid1)

End Sub
```

GRIDFILL

Restores contents of a grid from a file

Syntax

```
Function Gridfill (<file number> As Integer,
     ⇨ <file name> As String,<grid name> As Grid,
     ⇨ <rows> As Integer, <columns> As Integer,
     ⇨ <start> As Integer)
```

Returns

–1 if successful, 0 if not

Arguments

file number - handle of file containing grid information
file name - file containing grid information
grid name - grid to restore
rows - number of rows to restore
columns - number of columns to restore
start - row to start at

Module

GRIDFUNC.BAS

Remarks

Gridfill restores the contents of a grid from a file. One function call makes it easy to perform. It assumes the grid has previously been saved using Gridsave.

See Also

Cleargrid, Initgrid, Savegrid, Timesched

Example

The following example demonstrates how to use Gridfill. When the user clicks on the Open button in READGRID.MAK, the program reads the information in the GRID.DAT file and uses it to restore the grid.

```
Dim fileno As Integer, filename As String
Dim rows As Integer, cols As Integer, total_twips As
         ⇨ Integer
Dim start As Integer


Sub Form_Load ()

 ' Load and initialize grid

 fileno = 1: filename = "c:\grid.dat"
 rows = 50: cols = 5: start = 1: total_twips = 1400

 ' Initialize new grid

 Call Initgrid(Grid1, rows, cols, total_twips)

 ' Display headings

 Call Prt_headings

End Sub
```

```
Sub cmdOpen_Click ()

 ' Restore grid from file

 retval = Gridfill(fileno, filename, Grid1, rows, cols,
               ⇨ start)

End Sub


Sub Prt_headings ()

 ' Set row and column alignment

 Grid1.FixedAlignment(1) = 2
 Grid1.ColAlignment(1) = 2

 Grid1.FixedAlignment(2) = 2
 Grid1.ColAlignment(2) = 2

 Grid1.FixedAlignment(3) = 2
 Grid1.ColAlignment(3) = 2

 ' Print grid headings

 Grid1.Row = 0: Grid1.Col = 1
 Grid1.Text = "Microprocessor"

 Grid1.Row = 0: Grid1.Col = 2
 Grid1.Text = "Megahertz"

 Grid1.Row = 0: Grid1.Col = 3
 Grid1.Text = "RAM"
End Sub
```

GRIDSAVE

Saves the contents of a grid to a file

Syntax

```
Function Gridsave (<file number> As Integer,
    ⇨ <file name> As String, <grid name> As
    ⇨ Grid, <rows> As Integer, <columns>
    ⇨ As Integer, <start> As Integer)
```

Returns

–1 if successful, 0 if not

Arguments

file number - file handle
file name - file to save grid to
grid name - grid to save
rows - number of rows to save
columns - number of columns to save
start - first row to save

Module

GRIDFUNC.BAS

Remarks

Savegrid saves the contents of a grid to a file. To do this, it records the position of each cell and its contents. After saving a grid, you can restore it later using Gridfill.

See Also

Cleargrid, Gridfill, Initgrid, Timesched

Example

Save a grid to a file. When the user clicks on the Save button in SAVEGRID.MAK, the program uses Gridsave to record the contents of each cell.

```
Dim fileno As Integer, filename As String, start As
                    ⇨ Integer
Dim totrows As Integer, totcols As Integer, nextrow As
                    ⇨ Integer


Sub Form_Load ()

 ' Initialize new grid

 fileno = 1: filename = "grid.dat"

 Dim rows As Integer, cols As Integer
 Dim twips As Integer, gridvar As GridStruc

 rows = 100: cols = 5: twips = 1400

 Call InitGrid(Grid1, rows, cols, twips)
```

```
 Call Prt_headings

End Sub


Sub cmdAddRecord_Click ()

 ' Add new row to grid

 Dim newline As String

 nextrow = nextrow + 1
 newline = Chr$(13) + Chr$(10)

 microproc = InputBox("Microprocessor type : " + new
      ⇨ line + newline + "286, 386, 486 or Pentium?")

 Grid1.Row = nextrow: Grid1.Col = 1
 Grid1.Text = microproc

 meghz = InputBox("How many megahertz?")

 Grid1.Row = nextrow: Grid1.Col = 2
 Grid1.Text = meghz

 Grid1.Row = nextrow: Grid1.Col = 3

 megbytes = InputBox("How much RAM?")
 Grid1.Text = megbytes

 ' Enable save command after at least 1 record is
 ' added to grid

 cmdSaveGrid.Enabled = True

End Sub


Sub cmdSaveGrid_Click ()

 totrows = 100: totcols = 5: start = 1
 fileno = 1
 filename = "grid.dat"

 ' Save grid to file
```

```
 retval = GridSave(fileno, filename, Grid1, totrows,
              ⇨ totcols, start)

End Sub


Sub Prt_headings ()

 ' Set row and column alignment

 Grid1.FixedAlignment(1) = 2
 Grid1.ColAlignment(1) = 2

 Grid1.FixedAlignment(2) = 2
 Grid1.ColAlignment(2) = 2

 Grid1.FixedAlignment(3) = 2
 Grid1.ColAlignment(3) = 2

 ' Print grid headings

 Grid1.Row = 0: Grid1.Col = 1
 Grid1.Text = "Microprocessor"

 Grid1.Row = 0: Grid1.Col = 2
 Grid1.Text = "Megahertz"

 Grid1.Row = 0: Grid1.Col = 3
 Grid1.Text = "RAM"

End Sub


Sub cmdExit_Click ()

 ' End session

 End

End Sub
```

INITGRID

Initializes a grid by setting the column width, total rows and total columns

Syntax

```
Sub Initgrid (<grid name> As Grid, <rows> As Integer,
        ⇨ <columns> As Integer, <twips> As Integer)
```

Returns

Nothing

Arguments

grid name - grid to initialize
rows - number of rows in grid
columns - number of columns in grid
twips - number of twips per column (approximately 1400 per inch)

Module

GRIDFUNC.BAS

Defaults

Sets column width to 1400 twips (about 1 inch)

Remarks

Initgrid is a useful procedure for anyone who uses the grid control. It gives the user a rough idea of how a grid should look quickly and easily.

See Also

Cleargrid, Gridfill, Gridsave, Timesched

Example

GRIDTIME.MAK demonstrates the use of Initgrid. The program uses Initgrid to set the size of each column. Afterwards, the program prints a 60 minute time schedule on the grid.

```
Sub Sched_Click ()

 Dim schedtype As Integer
 Dim rows As Integer, cols As Integer
 Dim twips As Integer

 rows = 100
```

```
    cols = 4
    twips = 1500

    Call Initgrid(Grid1, rows, cols, twips)
    Call Timesched(Grid1)

    cmdOK_bal.Enabled = False

End Sub
```

TIMESCHED

Displays a 60 minute time schedule on a grid

Syntax

```
Sub Timesched (<grid name> As Grid)
```

Returns

Nothing

Arguments

grid name - grid on which to show schedule

Module

GRIDFUNC.BAS

Remarks

Timesched prints a 60 minute schedule on a grid. It is useful in time management applications that track appointments.

See Also

Cleargrid, Gridfill, Gridsave, Initgrid

Example

GRIDTIME.MAK uses Timesched to display a 60 minute schedule on a grid (see Figure 21.1). Notice how it hides the details that would otherwise clutter up the program.

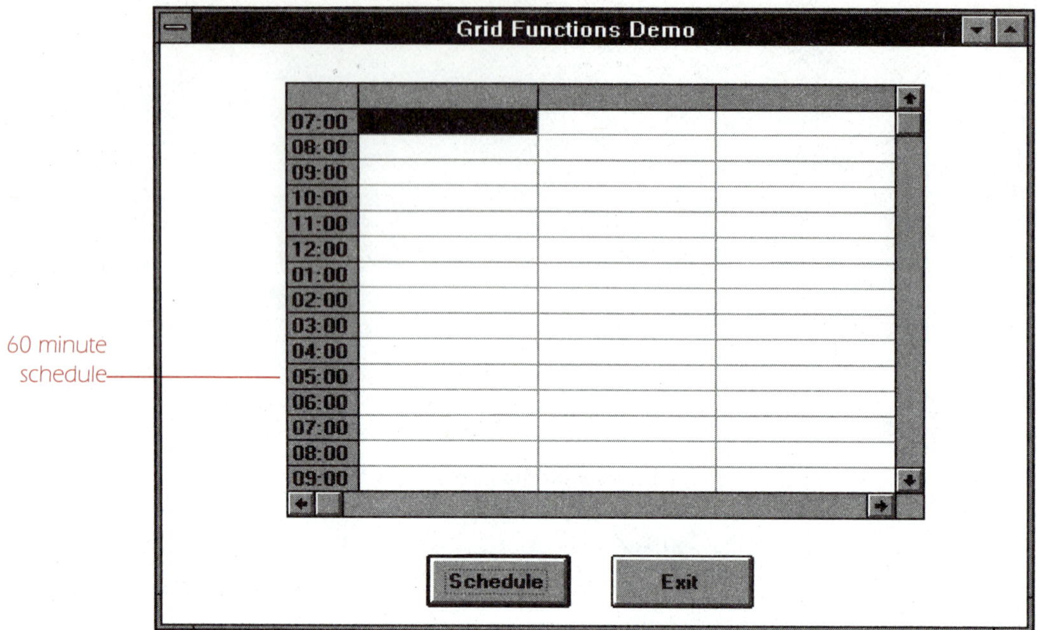

FIGURE 21.1 Displaying a 60 minute time schedule on a grid

```
Sub Sched_Click ()

 Dim rows As Integer, cols As Integer
 Dim twips As Integer

 rows = 100
 cols = 4
 twips = 1500

 Call Initgrid(Grid1, rows, cols, twips)
 Call Timesched(Grid1)

 cmdOK_bal.Enabled = False

End Sub
```

22 STRING AND MEMO HANDLING FUNCTIONS

The library includes many reusable routines to create memo handlers. These procedures read and write text files, check whether files are updated, cut, copy and paste blocks, find strings, merge documents and undo changes to text boxes.

In Visual Basic, you can pass a text box control to a function just as you would any other parameter. Many of the memo handling procedures of the library accept text boxes as arguments. To manage text files correctly, you must set the MultiLine property of the text box control to **True** before passing it to a library routine.

Function	Description
Edittext	Text file handler for cut, copy and paste operations
Findtext	Finds a string in a text box
Memowrite	Saves contents of text file to disk
Mergetext	Merges two text files
Readmemo	Reads contents of text file into a variable for editing
Undolast	Reverses the last edit operation in a text box
Upperword	Capitalizes the first letter of each word in a string (used to format proper names)

EDITTEXT

Handles cut, copy and paste operations

Syntax

```
Sub Edittext (<edit option> As Integer, <textctrl> As
          ⇨ Textbox)
```

Returns

Nothing

Arguments

edit option:

0 = cut selected text
1 = copy selected text
2 = paste selected text

textctrl - text box for cut, copy or paste operation

Module

TEXTOPER.BAS

Defaults

Cuts selected text

Remarks

Edittext cuts, copies and pastes text to and from the Clipboard. At design time, each possible operation is entered into a control array (using the Menu Design window). The value returned determines the action to perform.

See Also

Findtext, Memowrite, Mergetext, Readmemo

Example

TEXT.MAK demonstrates the use of Edittext. You can mark a range for an operation by dragging the mouse or by pressing:

```
   Ctrl-Del         (cuts text)
   Ctrl-Insert      (copies text)
   Shift-Insert     (pastes text)

Sub Ctrlarr_Click (index As Integer)

 ' Call text handler routine

 Call Edittext(index, text1)

End Sub
```

FINDTEXT

Finds a string in a text box

Syntax

```
Function Findtext (<textctrl> As Textbox, <search text>
  ⇨ As String, <start search> As Integer,<seek option>
  ⇨ As Integer, <case option> As Integer)
```

Returns

Character position of last match if successful, 0 if not

Arguments

textctrl - text box to search
search text - pattern to search for
start search - global variable indicating the character position where the search should begin each time

seek option:

1 = begin new search
2 = search next

case option:

1 = ignore case of search pattern
2 = make search case-sensitive

Module

TEXTOPER.BAS

Remarks

Findtext finds a string in a text box. After each search, it returns the position of the last match. Using this value, you can find the next match. By default, the search is case insensitive. That is, it treats John Smith and JOHN SMITH the same.

See Also

Edittext, Memowrite, Mergetext, Readmemo

Example

The following code, taken from TEXT.MAK, uses Findtext to locate string patterns in a text box. The Search menu contains the options:

Find first
Find next

To indicate a pattern, either enter it in the Search dialog box or mark it with a mouse. Optionally, you can change the ignore case option in the dialog box. Once it finds a match, the program remembers the query specifications for the next scan.

```
Sub Find_Click ()

 ' Search for first match

 seekfirst = True
 start_search = 1

 ' Paste text in Search dialog box if user marked it
 ' with mouse

 Clipboard.SetText Text1.SelText
 Searchform.Search.SelText = Clipboard.GetText()

 Searchform.Show
 Searchform.Search.SetFocus

End Sub


Sub OK_Search_Click ()

 ' Initiate search

 target_str = search.Text

 If option1.Value = True Then
    uppercase = False
 Else
    uppercase = True
 End If

 start_search = Findtext(Form1, text1, target_str,
           ⇨ start_search, seekfirst, uppercase)

 Unload Searchform

End Sub
```

```
Sub Findnext_Click ()

 ' Search for next match

 seekfirst = False

 start_search = Findtext(Form1.Text1, target_str,
           ⇨ start_search, seekfirst, uppercase)

 If start_search = 0 Then
    MsgBox "Pattern not found", 0, "SEARCH"
 End If

End Sub
```

MEMOWRITE

Saves a memo file to disk

Syntax

```
Function Memowrite (<file number> As Integer,
   ⇨ <file name> As String, <file variable> as String)
```

Returns

–1 if successful, 0 if not

Arguments

file number - number of file to update
file name - file to update
file variable - variable containing file information

Module

TEXTOPER.BAS

Remarks

Memowrite saves the contents of a text box to a file. It does this by assigning its value to a variable. It then passes the variable to the function with a file number and name. If the file does not exist, it is created. If it does, it is replaced.

See Also

Findtext, Mergetext, Readmemo

Example

When the user clicks the Save button in READMEMO.MAK, the contents of the text box are written to disk. If the text box is empty, a new file is created under the name UNTITLED.DOC. By default, this name appears in the title bar when the program loads. After a file is opened, its name appears there instead.

```
Dim fileno As Integer, filename As String
Dim filevar As String, err_switch As Integer


Sub Write_Click ()

 Const OK = 1

 fileno = 1: filevar = text1.Text
 err_switch = False

 ' Check if file exists before saving

 Do While Form1.Caption = "Untitled.doc" = True

  filename = InputBox("Save file as: ")

  If Fileexists(filename, err_switch) = False Then
     Form1.Caption = filename
  Else
       If filename <> "Untitled.doc" Then
          overwrite = MsgBox("File exists, overwrite",
                              ⇨ 33, "Warning")
          If overwrite = OK Then
             Form1.Caption = filename
          End If
       End If
  End If

 Loop

 retval = Memowrite(fileno, filename, filevar)
 Form1.Caption = filename

End Sub
```

MERGETEXT

Merges two text files

Syntax

```
Function Mergetext (<source file no.> As Integer,
                   ⇨ <source file name> As String,
                   ⇨ <textctrl> as Textbox)
```

Returns

String containing both files

Arguments

source file number - number of source file
source file name - source file
textctrl - text box control containing information to merge with (target file)

Module

TEXTOPER.BAS

Remarks

Mergetext provides an easy way to merge files. It adds a source file on disk to the bottom of another file previously read into a text box. It returns a string containing both files. You can later reassign the string to the text box for further editing.

See Also

Edittext, Findtext, Memowrite, Readmemo

Example

This example, taken from TEXT.MAK, uses Mergetext to concatenate text files. When the user selects the Merge files option from the File menu, an input box appears prompting for a file name. The program then appends its contents to the text box.

```
Sub Mergefiles_Click ()

  ' Read a file from disk and append it to one in text
  ' box

  Dim source_fileno As Integer
  Dim sourcefile As String
```

```
    source_fileno = 1
    sourcefile = InputBox("Enter name of file to merge")

    If source_filename <> "" Then
       text1.Text = Mergetext(source_fileno, sourcefile,
                              ⇨ text1)
       Close #source_fileno
    End If

End Sub
```

READMEMO

Reads contents of text file into a variable for editing

Syntax

```
Function Readmemo (<fileno> As Integer, <filename> As
             ⇨ String)
```

Returns

String variable containing file information

Arguments

file number - number of text file
file name - text file

Module

TEXTOPER.BAS

Remarks

Readmemo reads a text file into a variable for editing. It hides the details of the operation and thus provides an easy way of retrieving memos.

See Also

Edittext, Findtext, Memowrite, Mergetext

Example

When the user selects the Read button in READMEMO.MAK, the **InputBox** function prompts for a file. After entering the name, the contents of the file appears in a text box.

```
Dim fileno As Integer, filename As String
Dim filevar As String, err_switch As Integer
```

```
Sub Read_Click ()

 ' Open text file for editing

 fileno = 1

 file_OK = False

 Do While file_OK = False

   filename = InputBox("Enter file name", "File Open")

   file_OK = Valfile(filename)
   If filename = "" Then
      Exit Sub
   End If

 Loop

 ' Read file into text box

 text1.Text = Readmemo(fileno, filename)
 Form1.Caption = filename

End Sub
```

UNDOLAST

Reverses the last edit operation in a text box

Syntax

```
Sub Undolast (<textctrl> As Textbox)
```

Returns

Nothing

Arguments

textctrl - text box containing string to reverse

Module

TEXTOPER.BAS

Remarks

Undolast reverses the last edit operation in a text box. It is useful in memo handlers. Although Undolast will not debug your programs for you, it may save you from putting your fist through your monitor! Since nobody is perfect, it is a handy tool to have.

See Also

Edittext, Findtext, Memowrite, Mergetext, Readmemo, Upperword

Example

TEXT.MAK demonstrates the use of Undolast. When the user makes a mistake, the Undo option from the Edit menu reverses the operation.

```
Sub Undotext_Click ()

 ' Undo last edit

 Call Undolast(text1)

End Sub
```

UPPERWORD

Converts first character of each word in a string to uppercase and the rest to lowercase

Syntax

```
Function Upperword (<name> As String)
```

Returns

Formatted string

Arguments

name - string to format

Module

STR.BAS

Remarks

Upperword adds a nice touch to any program. It is useful in formatting proper names. For example, it turns thomas jefferson into Thomas Jefferson. You may wish to include it in all your data entry routines.

See Also

Valentry

Example

CUSTSCR.MAK demonstrates how to use Upperword. When the user selects the OK button, the program formats the entry in the text2 text box. The first letter of each part of the name appears in uppercase and the rest in lowercase.

```
Sub Format_name ()

 ' Capitalize first letter of each part of name

 Dim custname As String

 custname = text2.Text
 text2.Text = Upperword(custname)

End Sub
```

23 SCREEN AND PRINTER FUNCTIONS

Program appearance is a key issue in today's software industry. Visual Basic includes many tools that allow you to enhance the look of an application. The library contains several additional ones you can use. This chapter introduces these routines.

Function	Description
Bargraph	Displays a bar graph
Centerstr	Centers a string on a form in large characters
Checkfont	Returns **True** if a font is installed
Colorstr	Shows message with each letter in a different color
Delaytext	Prints a message with a delay and an optional shadow effect
Delaywin	Shows a pop-up window with a delay effect (window increases in size as it is drawn and then a message is printed inside it)
Fontlist	Creates a list of fonts available for the current display device and printer
Introscr	Shows a custom introductory screen
Shadowbox	Displays a window with a shadow border effect
Shadowtext	Displays a message with a shadow effect
Strwalk	Scrolls a message in picture box
Text3D	Displays a message with a 3D effect
Textblur	Displays a message with a blur effect
Textgrow	Shows a message growing on a form

BARGRAPH

Displays a bar graph

Syntax

```
Sub Bargraph (<formctrl> As Form, <pictctrl> As
  ⇨ PictureBox, <grid lines> As Integer, <max value>
  ⇨ As Single, <categories> As Integer, <bar groups>
  ⇨ As Integer, <data source>() As Single)
```

Returns

Nothing

Arguments

formctrl - form containing picture box
pictctrl - picture box on which to show graph
grid lines - number of grid lines to show on vertical axis
max value - highest value to graph
categories - number of categories to graph
bar groups - number of groups per category
data source - two dimensional array:

```
subscript 1 = category numbers
subscript 2 = graph data for each group within the
              categories
```

Module

SCR.BAS

Remarks

Bargraph charts information quickly and easily. Use it to graph sales figures, analyze trends and to make your presentations more effective. The data source is a two-dimensional array. Subscript 1 contains the numbers of each category. Subscript 2 holds the actual data. The following loop shows how to initialize it from a file:

```
Const BARGROUPS = 3: Const BARS_PERCAT = 3

Static Graph_data(BARGROUPS, BARS_PERCAT)

For i = 1 To BARGROUPS

    Input #fileno, column1, column2, column3
```

```
        Graph_data(i, 1) = column1
        Graph_data(i, 2) = column2
        Graph_data(i, 3) = column3

Next
```

Each category (or row in the file) contains three bar groups (columns). To increase the number of categories, change the BARGROUPS constant.

See Also

Scrblanker

Example

STAT.MAK uses Bargraph to chart the Northern, Southern and Western sales for a company that sells marine products (lorans, generators and depth finders). The graph provides an easy way to analyze and compare sales from each division. Figure 23.1 shows how the output appears.

```
Sub GraphStat_Click ()

 ' Show bar graph

 Const SCALEMAX = 10000: Const SCALES = 5
 Const BARS_PERCAT = 3: Const BARGROUPS = 3
 Const BAR1 = 1: BAR2 = 2: BAR3 = 3

 Static Graph_data(BARGROUPS, BARS_PERCAT)
```

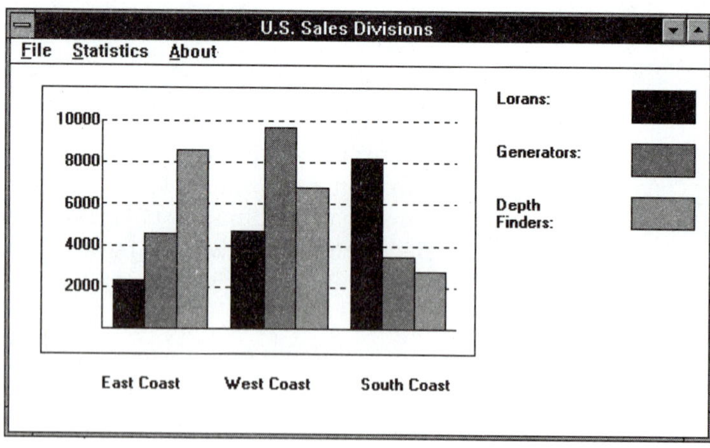

FIGURE 23.1 The STAT.MAK application

```
fileno = 1
filename = "sample.dat"

Open filename For Input As #fileno

' For each group, read values into array

For i = 1 To BARGROUPS

    Input #fileno, east, west, south

    Graph_data(i, BAR1) = east
    Graph_data(i, BAR2) = west
    Graph_data(i, BAR3) = south

Next

Close #fileno

' Show bar graph

picture1.Cls

Call Bargraph(Form1, picture1, SCALES, SCALEMAX,
      ⇨ BARGROUPS, BARS_PERCAT, Graph_data())

' Show bar graph labels

Form1.Caption = "U.S. Sales Divisions"
Call Showctrls

' Temporarily hide other controls on form

Loran_option.Visible = False
Gener_option.Visible = False
Depthfinder_option.Visible = False

End Sub
```

CENTERSTR

Centers a string in big bold letters on a form

Syntax

```
Sub Centerstr (<formctrl> As Form, <message> As String)
```

Returns

Nothing

Arguments

formctrl - form on which to show output
message - string to center and display

Module

STR.BAS

Remarks

Centerstr centers a string on a form in big bold letters. Use it to display important messages and to enhance the appearance of any program.

See Also

Colorstr, Strwalk, Upperword

Example

FONTTST1.MAK uses Centerstr to show a program credits screen. When the form loads, the following message appears centered on three lines:

PSEUDO PRODUCTIONS PRESENTS PC INSANITY

```
Sub Form_Load ()

 Show  ' Load and display form

 Dim message As String

 For i = 1 To 3
   Print
 Next

 Call Centerstr(Form1, "PSEUDO PRODUCTIONS")
 Print
 Call Centerstr(Form1, "PRESENTS")
 Print
```

```
 Call Centerstr(Form1, "PC INSANITY")

End Sub
```

CHECKFONT

Returns **True** if a font is installed

Syntax

```
Sub Checkfont (<formctrl> As Form, <font> As String)
```

Returns

–1 if True, 0 if not

Arguments

formctrl - name of current form
font - font to check

Module

SCR.BAS

Remarks

Checkfont returns **True** if a font is installed on a system. Use it before setting a font to ensure your application will have a fail-safe way of trapping font errors.

See Also

Fontlist

Example

The following code, taken from TEXT3D2.MAK, shows how to determine if a font is installed on a system. When the user clicks on the Redraw button, the program calls the library routine before attempting to change the default font.

```
Sub cmdFontGrow_Click ()

 ' Start 3D demo

 colpos = 200: rowpos = 150

 If Checkfont(Form1, "Times New Roman") = True Then
  picture1.FontName = "Times New Roman"
```

```
 End If

 timer1.Interval = 50

 cmdSave.Enabled = True

End Sub

Sub Timer1_Timer ()

 ' Show message growing with a 3D effect

 Dim colpos As Integer, rowpos As Integer

 Dim message As String

 message = "Welcome"

 Call Text3d(message, picture1, timer1, rowpos, colpos)

 If timer1.Enabled = False Then
  cmdFontGrow.Enabled = False
 End If

End Sub
```

COLORSTR

Shows a string with each character in a different color

Syntax

```
Sub Colorstr (<message> As String, <pictctrl> As
          ⇨ Picturebox)
```

Returns

Nothing

Arguments

message - string to print
pictctrl - picture box on which to display string

Module

SCR.BAS

Remarks

Colorstr shows a string with each character in a different color. It is useful in program introductory screens where appearance often matters most.

See Also

Centerstr, Strwalk

Example

COLORSTR.MAK demonstrates the use of the library routine. When the form loads, the following message appears with each letter in a different color:

PC Paint Blotchers Presents Point-By-Numbers

```
Sub Form_Load ()

 Show   ' Load and display form

 Dim message As String, countchar As Integer
 newline = Chr$(13) + Chr$(10)

 picture1.Print

 line1 = Space(8) + "PC Paint Blotchers" + newline
 line2 = Space(15) + "Presents " + newline

 message = line1 + line2

 picture1.FontSize = 17

 Call Colorstr(message, picture1)
 picture1.FontSize = 26

 picture1.Print Space(3);

 Call Colorstr("Point By Numbers", picture1)

End Sub
```

DELAYTEXT

Prints a message with a delay and an optional shadow effect

Syntax

```
Sub Delaytext (<formctrl> As Form, <timerctrl> As
        ⇨ Timer, <message> As String, <textcolor> As
        ⇨ Integer, <shadow_effect> As Integer)
```

Returns

Nothing

Arguments

formctrl - form on which to display message
timerctrl - timer control
message - string to display
textcolor - foreground color of text
shadow_effect:

0 = No shadow
1 = Near shadow
2 = Far shadow (default)

Module

SCR.BAS

Remarks

Delaytext prints a message on a form with a delay and an optional shadow background. To achieve this effect, you must place the call to Delaytext in the Timer procedure.

See Also

Shadowtext, Text3D

Example

TEXT3D.MAK Demonstrates how to use Delaytext. When the user clicks on the Delay Text button, the program shows a message with a delay and a shadow effect. Figure 23.2 shows how the form appears.

FIGURE 23.2 The Delaytext library routine

```
Sub cmdDelayText_Click ()

 ' Display text with a delay effect

 Const BRIGHT_CYAN = 11

 ForeColor = QBColor(BRIGHT_CYAN)

 timer2.Interval = 100

 Cls

End Sub


Sub Timer2_Timer ()

 Dim textsize As Integer, textcolor As Integer,
            ⇨ shadow_option As Integer
 Dim message As String, shadow_effect As Integer

 message = " Galactic Invaders"

 textcolor = 11: shadow_effect = 1

 ' Show message with a delay effect

 Call Delaytext(Form1, timer2, message, textcolor,
            ⇨ shadow_effect)
```

```
    If timer2.Enabled = False Then
        cmdDelayText.Enabled = False
    End If

End Sub
```

DELAYWIN

Shows a pop-up window with a delay and then displays a message inside it

Syntax

```
Sub Delaywin (<formctrl> as Form, <pictctrl> As
        ⇨ PictureBox, <message> As String)
```

Returns

Nothing

Arguments

formctr - form to draw window on
pictctrl - picture box to expand
message - string to print inside box

Module

SCR.BAS

Remarks

Delaywin draws a pop-up window with a delay effect that increases its size gradually. Afterwards, a message appears inside the window.

See Also

Introscr

Example

This example uses Delaywin to show credits for a program. When the user clicks the Delay Window button in SCR.MAK, the window appears with a message framed inside it.

```
Sub Delayw_Click ()

  ' Show message in a delayed pop-up window
```

```
 Dim line1 As String, line2 As String
 Dim line3 As String, line4 As String
 Dim newline As String, message As String

 Form1.Cls
 picture1.Cls

 newline = Chr(13) + Chr(10)

 line1 = Space(2) + "Software Enterprises " + newline
 line2 = Space(16) + "Presents" + newline + newline
 line3 = Space(8) + "Memory Manager" + newline
 line4 = Space(19) + "2010 " + newline

 message = line1 + line2 + line3 + line4

 Call Delaywin(Form1, picture1, message)

 Delayw.Enabled = False

End Sub
```

FONTLIST

Shows a pick list of fonts available for the current display device and printer

Syntax

```
Sub Fontlist (<listctrl> As Listbox)
```

Returns

Selected font

Arguments

listctrl - name of list box control

Module

TEXTOPER.BAS

Defaults

Uses primary printer (if installed)

Remarks

Fontlist creates a pick list of fonts available for the currently installed hardware. Use it to select the printing style.

See Also

Centerstr, Findtext, Upperword

Example

When the user selects the Choose Standard Font option in TEXT.MAK, a pick list appears. After a selection is made, the program saves the response in a configuration file.

```
Sub Chgfont_Click ()

 ' Show list of fonts

 Call Fontlist(pickfont.List1)
 pickfont.Show

End Sub


Sub cmdOK_Click ()

 font_picked = list1.Text
 rec1 = 1

 If list1.Text <> "" Then
    Form1.Text1.FontName = font_picked
 End If

 Unload pickfont

 ' Save new program configuration

 Open setup_file For Random As #setup_fileno Len
            ⇨ =Len(config)

 Get setup_fileno, rec1, config
 config.set_font = font_picked
 Put setup_fileno, rec1, config
 Close #setup_fileno

End Sub
```

INTROSCR

Shows a custom program introductory screen

Syntax

```
Sub Introscr (<formctrl> As Form)
```

Returns

Nothing

Arguments

formctrl - form on which to show output

Module

SCR.BAS

Remarks

Introscr produces a custom introductory screen by drawing a series of overlapping shadow boxes in different colors. Use it to enhance the appearance of any application.

See Also

Centerstr, Delaywin, Strwalk

Example

This example, taken from INTRSCR.MAK, uses Introscr to grab the user's attention at the start of a program. When the form loads, the output appears on Form1. Figure 23.3 shows how the welcome screen appears.

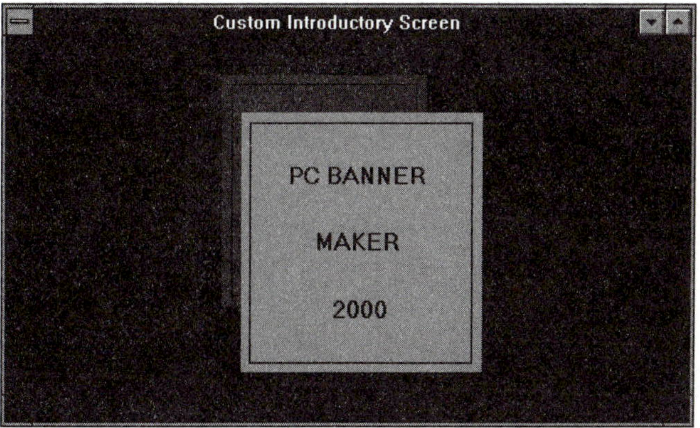

FIGURE 23.3 The Introscr library routine

```
Sub Form_Load ()

 ' Load and display form

 Show

 ' Show custom introductory screen

 Call Introscr(Form1)

 fontsize = 12

 Form1.CurrentX = 2850
 Form1.CurrentY = 1300
 Print "PC BANNER"

 Form1.CurrentX = 3250
 Form1.CurrentY = 2000
 Print "MAKER"

 Form1.CurrentX = 3400
 Form1.CurrentY = 2700
 Print "2000"

End Sub
```

SHADOWBOX

Draws a box with a shadow border effect

Syntax

```
Sub Shadowbox (<formctrl> As Form, <start row> As
  ⇨ Integer, <start column> As Integer, <end row> As
  ⇨ Integer, <end column> As Integer, <box color> As
  ⇨ Integer)
```

Returns

Nothing

Module

SCR.BAS

Arguments

formctrl - form on which to draw shadow box
start row - row position of upper left corner of box
start column - column position of upper left corner of box
end row - row position of lower right corner of box
end column - column position of lower right corner of box
boxcolor - **QBColor** color of box (1-15)

Defaults

Draws a white shadow box if color is left unspecified

Discussion

Shadowbox draws a box with a shadow background. Use it to display messages and to give your programs a unique and interesting look.

See Also

Delaytext, Introscr, Shadowtext, Text3D, Textblur

Example

The following code shows how to display a shadow box on a form. After drawing the box, a message is printed inside it. Figure 23.4 shows how the screen appears.

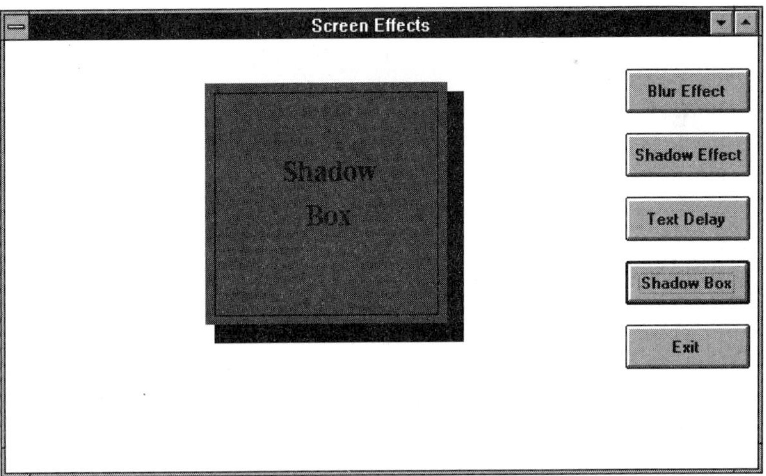

FIGURE 23.4 The Shadowbox library routine

```
Sub cmd_Drawshad_Click ()

 Dim x1 As Integer, y1 As Integer, x2 As Integer, y2
         ⇨ As Integer
 Dim boxcolor As Integer

 fontname = "Times New Roman"
 boxcolor = 3

 x1 = 600: y1 = 2400: x2 = 2800: y2 = 2700

 Cls

 ' Draw shadow box

 Call Shadowbox(Form1, x1, y1, x2, y2, boxcolor)

 Form1.ForeColor = QBColor(0)
 fontsize = 17

 x = 3200: y = 1300

 Form1.CurrentX = x
 Form1.CurrentY = y

 Print "Shadow"

 y = 1800: x = 3450

 Form1.CurrentX = x
 Form1.CurrentY = y

 Print "Box"

End Sub
```

SHADOWTEXT

Syntax

```
Sub Shadowtext(<formctrl> As Form, <message> As String,
  ⇨ <y> As Integer, <x> As Integer, <textsize> As
  ⇨ Integer, <textcolor> As Integer, <shadow_option>
  ⇨ As Integer)
```

Returns

Nothing

Arguments

formctrl - form to display message on
message - string to display
y - y coordinate of string to display
x - x coordinate of string to display
textsize - font size of string
textcolor - forecolor of string
shadow_option:

1 = near shadow (default)
2 = far shadow

Module

SCR.BAS

Default

Displays message using current font

Remarks

Shadowtext displays a message on a form with a shadow effect. By varying the <textsize> and <shadow_option> arguments, you can print the string at different pitches and with various degrees of shadows.

See Also

Text3D, Textblur, Textgrow

Example

The following example shows how to use Shadowtext. When the user clicks on the Shadow Effect button of TEXT3D.MAK, the program displays a message with a shadow background (see Figure 23.5). Notice how the program is able to trap and recover from an error if the selected font is not installed on the user's system.

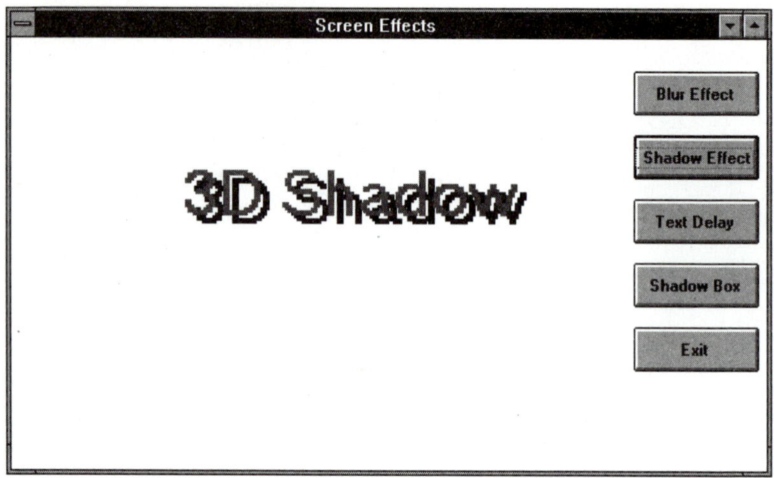

FIGURE 23.5 The Shadowtext library routine

```
Sub cmdShadow_Click ()

 Dim message As String, textsize As Integer
 Dim textcolor As Integer, shadow_option As Integer
 Dim font_to_check As String

 font_to_check = "MS Sans Serif"

 If Checkfont(Form1, font_to_check) = True Then
    Form1.FontName = "MS Sans Serif"
 End If

 picture1.Visible = False

 x = 2100: y = 1400

 Cls

 message = "3D Shadow"
 textsize = 36
 textcolor = 13
 shadow_option = 2

 ' Show message with shadow effect

 Call Shadowtext(Form1, message, y, x, textsize,
             ⇨ textcolor, shadow_option)

End Sub
```

STRWALK

Moves string in a picture box using a delay

Syntax

```
Sub Strwalk (<pictctrl> As Picturebox, <timer name> As
     ⇨ Timer, <message> As String, <moves> As Integer)
```

Returns

Nothing

Arguments

pictctrl - picture box to display message
timer name - timer for delay
message - string to move
moves - number of times to move string (measured in increments of 50 twips per move)

Module

SCR.BAS

Remarks

Strwalk scrolls a string in a picture box using a timer delay. Use it to create screen effects and to give your programs a custom look.

See Also

Centerstr, Colorstr, Upperword

Example

WALKSTR.MAK demonstrates the use of Strwalk. When the program starts, the title appears on the left edge in big bold letters. It then moves rightward across the screen. Afterwards, the credits for the application appear beneath the title.

```
Sub Timer1_Timer ()

 Dim moves As Integer, message As String

 ' Set total moves for string

 moves = 7

 message = "Intergalactic Airways"
```

```
    picture1.FontSize = 24

    Call Strwalk(picture1, timer1, message, moves)

    ' Print rest of introductory screen after
    ' scrolling title

    If timer1.Enabled = False Then

        picture1.Print
        picture1.CurrentX = 1650
        picture1.Print "Presents"
        picture1.Print
        picture1.CurrentX = 1200
        picture1.Print "PC Brilliance"

    End If

End Sub
```

TEXT3D

Displays a message with a three dimensional effect

Syntax

```
Sub Text3D(<message> As String, <pictctrl>
    ⇨ As PictureBox, <timerctrl> As Timer,
    ⇨ <rowpos> as Integer, <colpos> As Integer)
```

Returns

Nothing

Arguments

message - string to display
pictctrl - picture box control
timerctrl - timer control
rowpos - row to display message at
colpos - column to display message at

Module

SCR.BAS

Default

Displays message using current font

Remarks

Text3D shows a message in a picture box with a three dimensional effect. To display the message, you must be sure to set the timer Interval property before calling Text3D.

See Also

Shadowtext, Textblur

Example

TEXT3D2.MAK demonstrates how to use the library routine. When the user selects the Text 3D button, the program displays a message with a 3D effect (see Figure 23.6).

```
Sub cmdFontGrow_Click ()

 ' Start 3D demo

 colpos = 200: rowpos = 150

 If Checkfont(Form1, "Times New Roman") = True Then
    picture1.FontName = "Times New Roman"
 End If

 timer1.Interval = 50

 cmdSave.Enabled = True

End Sub
```

FIGURE 23.6 The Text3D library routine

```
Sub Timer1_Timer ()

 ' Show message growing with a 3D effect

 Dim colpos As Integer, rowpos As Integer
 Dim message As String

 message = "Welcome"

 Call Text3D(message, picture1, timer1, rowpos, colpos)

 If timer1.Enabled = False Then
    cmdFontGrow.Enabled = False
 End If

End Sub
```

Library routines that use timer delays may not perform adequately on some systems because of memory limitations. By saving screen images to a file, you can load graphics much faster than the time it would take to redraw a screen. Before an image in a graphics control can be saved, you must set the AutoRedraw property of the control to **True**. The following example shows how this is done:

```
Sub Form_Load ()

 ' Redraw graphics methods automatically

 picture1.AutoRedraw = True

End Sub


Sub cmdSave_Click ()

 ' Save screen image as a bitmap

 SavePicture picture1.Image, "C:\VB_LIB\TEST.BMP"

End Sub


Sub cmdLoad_Click ()

 ' Load saved image

 picture1 = LoadPicture("C:\VB_LIB\TEST.BMP ")

End Sub
```

NOTE: This same technique can also be applied to other library routines such as Colorstr, Textblur, Shadowbox and Shadowtext.

TEXTBLUR

Shows a message with a 3D blur effect

Syntax

```
Sub Textblur(<formctrl> As Form, <timerctrl> As Timer,
⇨ <message> As String, <x> As Integer, <y> As Integer,
⇨ <colorcode> As Integer, <textsize> As Integer)
```

Returns

Nothing

Arguments

formctrl - form to show message on
timerctrl - timer control to use
message - string to display
x - column position of message
y - row position of message
colorcode - **QBColor** value (1 - 15)
textsize - font size of message

Module

SCR.BAS

Remarks

Textblur shows a message with a blur effect by printing the message at various coordinates in contrasting colors. To achieve this effect, you must be sure to set the timer interval. The speed of the timer will determine how fast the message will appear.

See Also

ShadowText, Text3D

Example

TEXT3D.MAK demonstrates how to use Textblur. At run time, when you click on the Text Blur button, the program displays a message with a blur effect (see Figure 23.7).

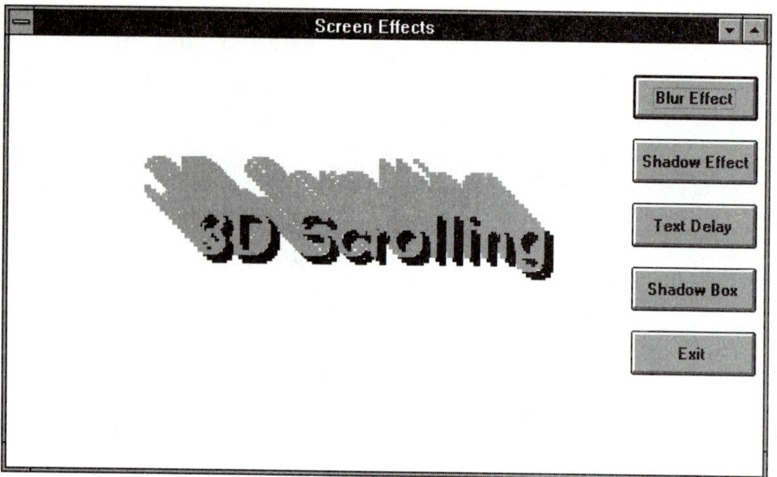

FIGURE 23.7 The Textblur library routine

```
Sub cmdBlur_Click ()

 picture1.Visible = False

 Dim font_to_check As String

 font_to_check = "MS Sans Serif"

 If Checkfont(Form1, font_to_check) = True Then
    Form1.FontName = "MS Sans Serif"
 End If

 x = 1600: y = 1200      ' Set print coordinates
 CurrentX = x: CurrentY = y

 timer1.Interval = 20    ' Activate timer control
 timer1.Enabled = True

 Cls

End Sub


Sub Timer1_Timer ()

 Const BRIGHT_WHITE = 15, TEXTSIZE = 36

 ' Call Textblur library routine
```

```
Call Textblur(Form1, timer1, "3D Scrolling", x, y,
        ⇨ BRIGHT_WHITE, TEXTSIZE)

End Sub
```

TEXTGROW

Shows a message growing on a form

Syntax

```
Sub Textgrow (<message> as String, <pictctrl> As
  ⇨ PictureBox, <timerctrl> As Timer, <rowpos>
  ⇨ As Integer, <colpos> As Integer)
```

Returns

Nothing

Arguments

message - string to display
pictctrl - picture box control
timerctrl - timer control
rowpos - row to display message at
colpos - column to display message at

Module

SCR.BAS

Default

Displays message using current font

Remarks

Textgrow shows a message growing on a form. Before calling Textgrow, you must set the Timer interval to activate the function.

See Also

Shadowtext, Text3D, Textblur

Example

This example, taken from TEXTGROW.MAK, shows how to make a message grow on a form.

```
Sub cmdTxtGrow_Click ()

 Dim font_to_check As String

 font_to_check = "Times New Roman"

 If Checkfont(Form1, font_to_check) = True Then
    picture1.FontName = "Times New Roman"
 Else
   picture1.FontName = "MS Sans Serif"
 End If

 ' Start demo

 timer1.Interval = 50

End Sub


Sub Timer1_Timer ()

 ' Show message growing on form

 Dim colpos As Integer, rowpos As Integer
 Dim message As String

 message = "Welcome"

 colpos = 150: rowpos = 200

 Call Textgrow(message, picture1, timer1, rowpos,
          ⇨ colpos)

 If timer1.Enabled = False Then
    cmdTxtGrow.Enabled = False
 End If

End Sub
```

24 SECURITY, VALIDATION AND UTILITY FUNCTIONS

Data validation and security are two prime issues in computer science. The library contains several routines that ensure the security and validity of information.

This chapter also introduces five utility procedures. These routines let you create calendars, clocks, custom data entry forms, conversion applications and screen blankers.

Security Functions	Description
Decrypt	Decrypts a string
Decryptfile	Decrypts a file
Encrypt	Encrypts a string
Encryptfile	Encrypts a file

Validation Functions	Description
Valentry	Validates input in a text box by filtering out non-numeric characters
Valfile	Validates a file name
Valtime	Validates a time argument

Utility Functions	Description
Chgfrac	Returns the fractional equivalent of a decimal
Moveto	Moves cursor to next or previous control on a form when user presses Enter or the up or down arrow keys
Scrblanker	Prevents burn-in by showing one of three pre-defined screen blankers
Showcalend	Displays a calendar
Showclock	Displays a digital clock

DECRYPT

Decrypts a string encrypted with Encrypt

Syntax

```
Function Decrypt (<string name> As String)
```

Returns

Decrypted string

Arguments

string name - string to decrypt

Module

SECURITY.BAS

Remarks

Decrypt decodes a string coded with Encrypt. Use it to decipher encrypted passwords or to prevent unauthorized users from seeing important messages over a network or telecommunication device.

Decrypt uses the following description method:

- Decrypts each character in the string by the value indicated by the global constant CODEVAL (17)
- Subtracts 1 if the ASCII value of the character is even and 3 if it is odd
- Optionally reverses string when the global constant REVERSE_STR is set to 1 (default)

Caution: Never change the value of the CODEVAL or REVERSE_STR constants after encrypting a string. In order to decrypt the message, the same encryption and decryption methods must be applied.

See Also

Decryptfile, Encrypt, Encryptfile

Example

SECURE.MAK uses the Decrypt function to decrypt a user's name and display it in the title screen of the program. When the security demo loads, the authorized user (rightful owner) of the software appears on the form. Figure 24.1 shows how the window appears.

FIGURE 24.1 The Decrypt library routine

```
Sub Show_user ()

 Dim secure_fileno As Integer, secure_filename As
     ⇨ String

 secure_fileno = 2: secure_filename = "userID.dat"

 Call Openfile(secure_fileno, secure_filename,
          ⇨ valid_user, 1)

 ' Read encrypted user's name

 retval = Getrec(secure_fileno, 1, valid_user)

 ' Decrypt name and show it

 If valid_user.userID <> 0 Then
  ownername = decrypt(valid_user.username)
  user_name.Caption = LTrim(ownername)
  Form2.getname.Enabled = False
 End If

 Close #secure_fileno

End Sub
```

DECRYPTFILE

Decrypts a file

Syntax

```
Function Decryptfile (<file number> As Integer,
                      ⇨ <file name> As String)
```

Returns

–1 if successful, 0 if not

Arguments

file number - number of file to decrypt
file name - file to decrypt

Module

SECURITY.BAS

Remarks

Decryptfile restores a file after it has been encrypted with Encrytfile. It uses the global constant CODENUM. This value determines how much to encrypt or decrypt a file. For more information on how it works, refer to the discussion of Decrypt.

See Also

Decrypt, Encrypt, Encryptfile

Example

Decode a file encoded with Encryptfile. When the user selects the Encrypt command from the File menu in SECURE.MAK, the program restores the records in the CUST.DAT file.

```
' File encryption/decryption program

Dim fileno As Integer
Dim file_name As String
Dim file_data As String
Dim total_bytes As Integer


Sub Form_Load ()

 Show   ' Show output as form loads
```

```
 fileno = 1: file_name = "cust.dat"

 Open file_name For Binary As #fileno

 ' Read contents of file to encrypt

 total_bytes = LOF(fileno)

 file_data = Input$(total_bytes, #fileno)
 text1.Text = file_data

End Sub


Sub Decode_Click ()

 ' Decrypt file

 If Filestatus(fileno, 0) = 0 Then
  Open file_name For Binary As #fileno
 End If

 retval = Decryptfile(fileno, file_name)

 Open file_name For Binary As #fileno

 total_bytes = LOF(fileno)
 file_data = Input$(total_bytes, #fileno)
 text1.Text = file_data

End Sub


Sub Encode_Click ()

 ' Encrypt file

 retval = Encryptfile(fileno, file_name)

 ' Reopen file if necessary

 If Filestatus(fileno, 0) = 0 Then
  Open file_name For Binary As #fileno
 End If

 total_bytes = LOF(fileno)
 file_data = Input$(total_bytes, #fileno)
 text1.Text = file_data
```

```
  Close #fileno

End Sub
```

ENCRYPT

Encrypts a string

Syntax

```
Function Encrypt (<string variable> As String)
```

Returns

String encrypted

Arguments

string variable - message to encrypt

Module

SECURITY.BAS

Caution

Always back up important information before experimenting with Encrypt or Encryptfile.

Remarks

Encrypt encrypts a string for security purposes. After encrypting the file, selecting the Decode button decrypts the file.

Encrypt uses the following encryption method:

- Adds 1 if the ASCII value of the character is even and 3 if it is odd.
- Encrypts each character in the string by the value indicated by the global constant CODEVAL (17).
- Optionally reverses string when the global constant REVERSE_STR is set to 1 (default).

See Also

Decrypt, Decryptfile, Encryptfile

Example

Make a string unreadable using Encrypt. SECURE.MAK uses the function to encrypt the user's name and save it to a file. For details on this example, refer to the discussion of Decrypt.

```
Sub Getname_Click ()

 ' Get software owner's name, encrypt it, and
 ' save it to a file

 Const IDOK = 1: Const IDCANCEL = 2

 Dim file_num As Integer, file_name As String
 Dim namestr As String

 file_num = 2: file_name = "userID.dat"

 line1 = "To demonstrate how you can discourage "
 line2 = "unauthorized users from making illegal "
 line3 = "copies of the software you create, this "
 line4 = "procedure will encrypt a name and save it "
 line5 = "to a file. Each time the program loads, "
 line6 = "the name will appear in the title screen. "
 line7 = "Please enter name: "

 message = line1 + line2 + line3 + line4 + line5 +
            ⇨ line6 + line7

 namestr = InputBox(message)
 namestr = Upperword(namestr)

 retval = IDCANCEL

 Do While retval <> IDOK
  retval = MsgBox("Is " + namestr + " correct?", 33,
             ⇨ "SECURITY DEMO")
  If retval <> IDOK Then
   namestr = InputBox(message)
  End If
 Loop

 ' Save name of user

 Call Openfile(file_num, file_name, valid_user, 1)

 Valid_user.valid_add = True
 namestr = Encrypt(namestr)
 Valid_user.username = namestr
 Valid_user.userID = 1

 retval = Replacerec(file_num, 1, valid_user)
```

```
    Close #file_num

    Getname.Enabled = False

End Sub
```

ENCRYPTFILE

Encrypts a file

Syntax

```
Function Encryptfile (<file number> As Integer,
                   ⇨ <file name> As String)
```

Returns

–1 if successful, 0 if not

Module

SECURITY.BAS

Arguments

file number - handle of file
file name   - file to encrypt

Caution

Always back up important information before experimenting with Encrypt or Encryptfile.

Remarks

Encryptfile encrypts a file for security purposes. It uses the global constant CODENUM. This value determines how much to encrypt or decrypt a file. For more information on how it works, refer to the discussion of Encrypt.

See Also

Decrypt, Decryptfile, Encrypt

Example

SECURE.MAK encodes a file using Encrytfile. When the user selects the Encrypt file option, the contents of the CUST.DAT file are encrypted. The Picture1 picture box then shows the encrypted document (see Figure 24.2). To restore the file, use Decryptfile.

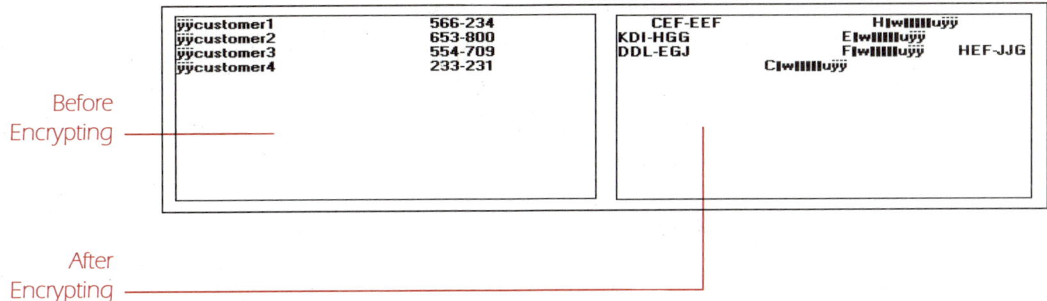

FIGURE 24.2 The Encryptfile library routine

```
Sub Encode_Click ()

 ' Encrypt file

 retval = Encryptfile(fileno, file_name)

 ' Reopen file if necessary

 If Filestatus(fileno, 0) = 0 Then
  Open file_name For Binary As #fileno
 End If

 total_bytes = LOF(fileno)
 file_data = Input$(total_bytes, #fileno)
 text1.Text = file_data

 Close #fileno

End Sub
```

VALENTRY

Filters out non-numeric characters

Syntax

```
Function Valentry (<key value> As Integer)
```

Returns

Valid characters (numbers and an optional decimal point)

Arguments

key value - single character to validate (KeyAscii)

Module

STR.BAS

Remarks

Valentry filters out non-numeric characters as they are typed using Visual Basic's Keypress procedure. After each character is entered, the system variable KeyAscii holds its value. If the input is valid (a number or decimal), the value appears in the text box.

See Also

Valfile, Valtime

Example

DATETIME.MAK demonstrates the use of Valentry. As the user types, each character is checked. Values that are not numeric are simply ignored.

```
Sub Vehicle_KeyPress (KeyAscii As Integer)

 ' Move cursor to next field when user presses Enter

 Const KEYENTER = 13

 If keyascii = KEYENTER Then
  driver.SetFocus
  KeyAscii = 0
 Else
  KeyAscii = Valentry(KeyAscii)
 End If

End Sub
```

VALFILE

Validates a file name

Syntax

```
Function Valfile (<file name> As String)
```

Returns

–1 if valid, 0 if not

Arguments

file name - file to check

Module

ENVIR.BAS

Remarks

Valfile validates a file name by breaking the string into several smaller components and checking each part. The following rules apply:

- The name must be 8 characters or less (plus an optional 3 character file extension).
- Valid characters include any numeric or alpha numeric combination except commas, spaces and backslash characters (\).
- A file name can contain only one extension.
- Names with file extensions must have a file prefix.

```
e.g., TEST.DAT
          |  |
 prefix _|  |_ extension
```

See Also

Valentry, Valtime

Example

READMEMO.MAK validates file names before saving and retrieving documents. If the file name is invalid or does not exist, the program prompts the user to reenter the name.

```
Sub Read_Click ()

 ' Open text file for editing

 Dim fileno As Integer
 Dim filename As String

 fileno = 1

 file_OK = False

 Do While file_OK = False

  filename = InputBox("Enter name of file", "File
                 ⇨ Open")

  file_OK = Valfile(filename)
  If filename = "" Then
```

```
      Exit Sub
     End If
    Loop

    ' Read file into text box

    text1.Text = Readmemo(fileno, filename)
    Form1.Caption = filename

End Sub
```

VALTIME

Checks if a time value is valid

Syntax

Function Valtime (<time value> As String)

Returns

–1 if valid, 0 if not

Arguments

time value - time to validate

Module

DATEFUNC.BAS

Remarks

Valtime validates a time. Arguments must be given in 24 hour format (military or international time). The time must also contain an hour/minute separator (:).

See Also

Valentry, Valfile

Example

DATETIME.MAK uses Valtime to check the time when a truck came in. The program reports if there is a problem when the record is saved.

```
Sub Time_In_KeyPress (keyascii As Integer)

 Const KEYENTER = 13
```

```
Dim time1 As String

If keyascii = KEYENTER Then

 If Len(time_in) = 0 Then
  time_in = Time           ' Enter time automatically
 Else
  time1 = time_in.Text     ' User typed time - so
                           ' validate it
  retval = Valtime(time1)
 End If

 retval = MsgBox("Save this record?", 33, "Record
             ⇨ Update")

 ' Save record if user chooses OK

 If retval = 1 Then
  Call cmdOK_click
 Else
  vehicle.Text = "": driver.Text = ""
  date_in.Text = "": time_in.Text = ""
 End If

 ' Move cursor to next field

 vehicle.SetFocus
 keyascii = 0              ' Turn off beep

End If

End Sub
```

CHGFRAC

Returns the fractional equivalent of a decimal

Syntax

```
Functions Chgfrac (<dec> As Single)
```

Returns

Fraction as a string

Arguments

dec - number to convert

Code Module

COMPUTE.BAS

Remarks

Chgfrac returns the fractional equivalent of a decimal. If the <dec> argument is greater than zero, Chgfrac returns only the fractional remainder as a string. If there is no remainder, the function returns a null string.

See Also

Showcalend

Example

The following example, taken from CONVERT.MAK, calculates the total number of five foot trim moldings for a house. When the user selects the Start button, the program computes the answer and uses Chgfrac to show the remainder as a fraction.

```
Sub cmdCalctrim_Click ()

 ' Compute trim moldings for house

 Const ICON_INFO = 64

 MOLDING_SIZE = 5   ' Feet

 Dim message As String, temp As Single

 totalfeet = InputBox("How many feet of trim
                    ⇨ molding?")

 temp = totalfeet / MOLDING_SIZE
 frac = Chgfrac(temp)

 ' Show answer - if remainder, print fractional
 ' equivalent

 If Int(temp) > 0 Then
  MsgBox "Moldings needed: " & Int(temp) & " " & frac,
        ⇨ ICON_INFO, "Conversion Demo"
 Else
  MsgBox "Moldings needed: " + frac, ICON_INFO,
        ⇨ "Conversion Demo"
 End If

End Sub
```

MOVETO

Moves cursor to the next or previous control on a form when the user presses Enter or the up/down arrow keys

Syntax

```
Function Moveto (<control1> As Control, <control2>
                ⇨ As Control, <key value> As Integer)
```

Returns

Nothing

Arguments

control1 - name of control directly above the current object on a form
control2 - name of control directly below the current object on a form
key value - name of key pressed:

NOTE: To get this value, place the call to Moveto in the KeyDown procedure of the control. Visual Basic automatically assigns the value of the key pressed to the KeyCode argument.

Module

STR.BAS

Remarks

Although Visual Basic allows you to move focus among controls using the Tab key or a mouse, it provides no built-in support for cursor navigation using the arrow keys. With Moveto, Visual Basic controls work like Get objects in a Clipper/xBase application - that is, you can move to the next/previous control on a form by pressing the up/down arrows key. You can also move to the next control by pressing the Enter key.

See Also

Valentry

Example

ORDERS.MAK demonstrates the use of Moveto. When the user presses the up arrow key, the cursor moves from the custname text box to the cmd_OK command button. Pressing the down arrow key or Enter key gives the next control focus. Notice the code in the KeyPress and Soundoff procedures. This turns off the beep that sounds when the user presses Enter.

```
Sub Custname_KeyDown (KeyCode As Integer,
                      ⇨ Shift As Integer)

 ' Move to next or previous control

 retval = Moveto(cmd_OK, street, KeyCode)

End Sub


Sub Custname_KeyPress (keyascii As Integer)

 ' Turn off beep

 Const KEYENTER = 13

 keyascii = Soundoff(keyascii)

End Sub


Function Soundoff (keyascii As Integer)

 ' Turn off beep when user presses Enter by
 ' setting value of key pressed to zero

 Const KEYENTER = 13

 If keyascii = KEYENTER Then
  keyascii = 0
 End If

End Function
```

SCRBLANKER

Prevents screen burn-in by displaying one of three pre-defined screen blankers

Syntax

```
Sub Scrblanker (<formctrl> As Form, <blanker_option>
              ⇨ As Integer, <startblanker> As Integer)
```

Returns

Nothing

Arguments

formctrl - form on which to display screen blanker
blanker_option:

1 = Show moving blocks
2 = Show connecting lines
3 = Show random circles

startblanker:

0 = True
1 = False

Module

SCR.BAS

Remarks

Scrblanker protects monitors from burn-in by displaying one of three predefined screen blankers. For best results, set the BorderStyle property of <formctrl> to 0 - None before calling Scrblanker. This property is available only at design time. You may wish to deactivate the mouse pointer while the blanker is active. To accomplish this, call the Windows API procedure ShowCursor. The definition for this routine is contained in SCR.BAS. By including this module in a project, you can enable/disable the mouse pointer the following way:

```
Call ShowCursor(False)          ' Hide mouse pointer
Call ShowCursor(True)           ' Show mouse pointer
```

See Also

Centerstr, Delaywin, Walkstr

Example

SCR.MAK shows how to implement the library routine. When the form loads, Scrblanker shows the moving blocks screen blanker. As the program runs, the pattern changes from blocks to lines and then to moving circles.

```
' Declare form level variable to indicate when screen
' blanker should be activated

Dim startblanker As Integer


Sub Form_Load ()

 ' Turn off mouse pointer

 Call ShowCursor(False)
```

```
    startblanker = 0

    ' Enable timer for screen saver

    timer1.Interval = 50

End Sub


Sub Timer1_Timer ()

    Const BLOCKS = 1, LINES = 2, BALLS = 3

    Static countrun As Integer, blanker_option As Integer

    countrun = countrun + 1

    ' Choose blanker pattern - clear screen when new
    ' pattern is selected

    Select Case countrun

       Case Is < 100
          If blanker_option <> BLOCKS Then
             Cls
          End If
          blanker_option = BLOCKS
       Case Is < 200
          If blanker_option <> LINES Then
             Cls
          End If
          blanker_option = LINES
       Case Is < 300
          If blanker_option <> BALLS Then
             Cls
          End If
          blanker_option = BALLS
       Case Else
          countrun = 0
    End Select

    ' Show screen blanker

    Call Scrblanker(BlankerFrm, blanker_option,
                 ⇨ startblanker)

End Sub
```

```
Sub Form_KeyPress (KeyAscii As Integer)

 Const ICON_INFO = 64

 ' Restore normal mouse pointer before quitting

 Call ShowCursor(True)

 MsgBox "Custom screen blanker", ICON_INFO, "Program
      ⇨ Information"

 End

End Sub
```

SHOWCALEND

Shows a calendar in a picture box

Syntax

```
Sub Showcalend (<formctrl> As Form, <picctrl>
            ⇨ As PictureBox, <month> As Integer)
```

Returns

Nothing

Arguments

formctrl - form on which to display calendar
picctrl - picture box to show calendar in
month - number of months to add or subtract from the current date

Module

DATEFUNC.BAS

Remarks

Showcalend prints a calendar in a picture box. It adds a fancy touch to any program. You may wish to incorporate it as part of an application or in a general utilities program.

See Also

Scrblanker, Showclock

Example

The Options menu in DATEDEMO.MAK demonstrates the use of Showcalend. When the user clicks on the Calendar option, the calendar appears in a picture box (see Figure 24.3).

```
Dim months As Integer


Sub Form_Load ()

 ' Load and display form with calendar

 Show

 Call Showcalend(Calend, picture1, months)

End Sub


Sub Next_month_Click ()

 ' Show next month

 picture1.Cls
 months = months + 1

 Call Showcalend(Calend, picture1, months)

End Sub


Sub Prev_Month_Click ()

 ' Show previous month
```

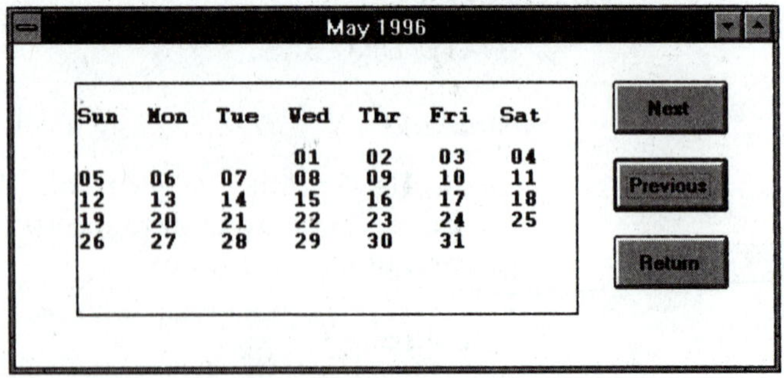

FIGURE 24.3 The Showcalend library routine

```
 picture1.Cls
 months = months - 1

 Call Showcalend(Calend, picture1, months)

End Sub


Sub cmd_Return_Click ()

 ' Unload form

 Unload Calend

End Sub
```

SHOWCLOCK

Shows a digital clock in a picture box

Syntax

```
Sub Showclock (<pictctrl> As Picturebox)
```

Returns

Nothing

Arguments

pictctrl - picture box on which to display clock

Module

DATEFUNC.BAS

Remarks

Showclock displays a digital clock inside a picture box. To initialize the clock, draw a timer control on a form and set its Interval property to 500 (milliseconds - approximately 1/2 of a second). Once the clock is active, it remains resident until either another window is given focus or the timer is disabled.

See Also

Scrblanker, Showcalend

Example

The following example demonstrates the use of Showclock. When the form loads, a digital clock appears in a picture box (see Figure 24.4).

```
Sub Form_Load ()

 ' Set timer interval and enable clock

 Const HALF_SECOND = 500

 Clock.Interval = HALF_SECOND
 Clock.Enabled = True

End Sub


Sub Clock_Timer ()

 ' Show time in picture box

 Call Showclock(Clockform.Picture1)

End Sub
```

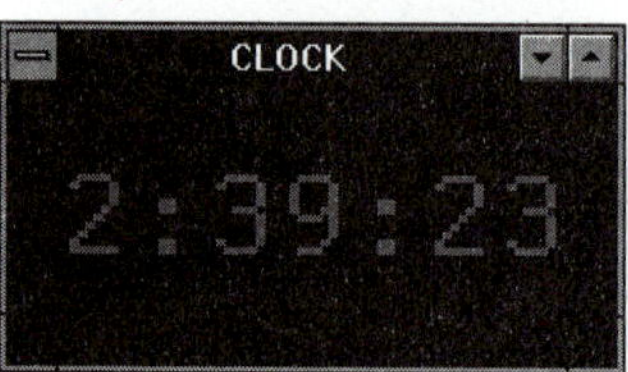

FIGURE 24.4 The Showclock library routine

25 STATISTICAL FUNCTIONS

With an array, you can perform quick statistical operations on a data set. Since it is faster to initialize an array once than it is to perform multiple disk reads from a file, you can dramatically increase your performance in data analysis using arrays.

The statistical procedures of the library, are all implemented using arrays. These routines work with both fixed size an dynamic arrays. Your programs will be more memory efficient, however, if you use dynamic arrays.

Function	**Description**
Arravg	Returns the average value of an array
Arrmax	Returns the maximum value of an array
Arrmedian	Returns the median value of an array
Arrmin	Returns the minimum value of an array
Arrmode	Returns the mode of an array
Arrneg	Counts negative elements in an array
Arrnonzero	Counts non-zero elements in an array
Arrsort	Sorts an array
Arrpos	Counts positive elements in an array
Arrstdv	Returns the standard deviation of an array
Arrsum	Sums an array of values
Arrvar	Returns the variance of an array

ARRAVG

Computes the mean of the values in an array

Syntax

```
Function Arravg (<array name> As Single, <option
            ⇨ switch> as Integer)
```

Returns

Mean

Arguments

array name - array of values
option switch:

1 = include zero values in average
2 = do not include zero values in average

Module

ARR.BAS

Remarks

Arravg computes the mean of a list of values in an array. When used in combination with some of the other array functions of the library, it provides a strong foundation for developing statistical applications. For example, you may wish to use it with Arrmedian, Arrmode, Arrstdv and Arrvar.

See Also

Arrmax, Arrmedian, Arrmin, Arrmode, Arrsum

Example

STAT.MAK demonstrates the use of Arravg. When the user selects the Compute option from the File menu, the program reads a list of values from the SAMPLE.DAT file into an array. It then calculates the average and shows the answer in the Picture1 picture box.

```
Sub Prtmean (Sample_Arr() As Single)

 ' Compute mean

 Dim avg_switch As Integer

 avg_switch = 1
```

```
    avg = Arravg(Sample_Arr(), avg_switch)

    ' Print mean if its menu selection is enabled

    If CompMean.Checked = True Then
       picture1.Print " Mean: "; avg
    End If

End Sub
```

ARRMAX

Returns the maximum element of an array

Syntax

```
Function Arrmax (<array name> As Single)
```

Returns

Maximum value

Arguments

array name - array to scan

Module

ARR.BAS

Remarks

Arrmax returns the maximum value of an array. Use it when you need to know what the highest element is. For example, you can use Arrmax to show the highest score on an exam.

See Also

Arrmin, Arrneg, Arrnonzero, Arrpos, Arrsum

Example

When the user selects the Compute option in STAT.MAK, the program generates statistics and uses Arrmax to show which product had the highest volume in sales.

```
Sub CompMax_Click ()

    ' Enable/disable menu option for printing maximum
    ' array value
```

```
 compmax.Checked = Not compmax.Checked

End Sub


Sub PrtMax (Sample_Arr() As Single)

 ' Get maximum array value and show it

 max = Arrmax(Sample_Arr())

 If CompMax.Checked = True Then
    picture1.Print " Max: "; max
 End If

End Sub
```

ARRMEDIAN

Returns the median value of an array

Syntax

```
Function Arrmedian (<array name> As Single,
                ⇨ <option switch> As Integer)
```

Returns

The median

Arguments

array name - array to use
option switch:

1 = round answer to next highest element if array contains an odd number of elements
2 = do not round answer up

Module

ARR.BAS

Remarks

Arrmedian computes the median value of an array. The median is the middle element (assuming the array has been sorted). The function automatically arranges the values in ascending order. It then returns the one at the midway point in the list.

See Also

Arravg, Arrmode, Arrstdv, Arrsum, Arrvar

Example

STAT.MAK demonstrates the use of Arrmedian. When the user selects the Compute option from the File menu, the program reads the values from the SAMPLE.DAT file into the array. It then computes the median and shows the answer in the Picture1 picture box.

```
Sub PrtMedian (Sample_Arr() As Single)

 ' Compute median

 Dim avg_option As Integer

 avg_option = 1

 med = Arrmedian(Sample_Arr(), avg_option)

 ' Show answer in picture box if its menu
 ' choice is enabled

 If CompMedian.Checked = True Then
    picture1.Print " Median: "; med
 End If

End Sub
```

ARRMIN

Returns the minimum element of an array

Syntax

```
Function Arrmin (<array name> As Single)
```

Returns

Lowest value

Arguments

array name - array to scan

Module

ARR.BAS

Remarks

Arrmin returns the minimum array element. Use it whenever you need to know what the lowest element is. For example, you can use Arrmin to determine the lowest age bracket of a sample population.

See Also

Arravg, Arrmax, Arrneg, Arrnonzero, Arrpos, Arrsum

Example

STAT.MAK demonstrates the use of Arrmin. The program uses the function to show which product had the lowest volume in sales.

```
Sub CompMin_Click ()

 ' Enable/disable menu choice for printing minimum
 ' value in array

 CompMin.Checked = NotCompMin.Checked

End Sub


Sub PrtMin (Sample_Arr() As Single)

 min = Arrmin(Sample_Arr())    ' Show lowest value
                               ' of array

 If CompMin.Checked = True Then
    picture1.Print
    picture1.Print " Min: "; min
 End If

End Sub
```

ARRMODE

Returns the mode of the values in an array

Syntax

```
Function Arrmode (<array name> As Single)
```

Returns

The mode

Arguments

array name - array of values

Module

ARR.BAS

Remarks

Arrmode returns the mode of a list of values in an array. The mode is the value with the most frequent occurrences. To account for multiple modes (when two or more values both occur the same number of times and appear more often than the other elements), the answers are saved in a temporary file called MODETEMP.DAT. You can read the values back in a loop like this:

```
Open "modetemp.dat" For Input As #filetemp

While Not EOF(filetemp)

 Input #filetemp, mode
 If mode <> 0 Then
    picture1.Print mode;
 End If

Wend
```

See Also

Arravg, Arrmax, Arrmedian, Arrmin, Arrsum

Example

When the user selects the Compute option in STAT.MAK, Arrmode calculates the mode and saves it to the MODETEMP.DAT file. Afterwards, the program reads the answers back and shows them in the Picture1 picture box.

```
Sub PrtMode (Sample_Arr() As Single)

 ' Compute and print mode

 retval = Arrmode(Sample_Arr())

 picture1.Print " Mode: ";

 filetemp = FreeFile

 Open "modetemp.dat" For Input As #filetemp

 While Not EOF(filetemp)

  Input #filetemp, mode
  If mode <> 0 Then
     picture1.Print mode;
    End If

 Wend

 picture1.Print
 picture1.Print

 Close #filetemp

End Sub
```

ARRNEG

Computes the total number of negative values in an array

Syntax

```
Function Arrneg (<array name> As Single)
```

Returns

Total negative elements

Arguments

array name - array of values

Module

ARR.BAS

Remarks

Arrneg returns the total number of negative elements in an array. Use it to determine how many cases of a sample population are valid or within a certain range.

See Also

Arrmax, Arrmin, Arrnonzero, Arrpos, Arrsum

Example

STAT.MAK shows how to use Arrneg. When the user selects the Compute option from the File menu, the program prints the answer along with various other statistics.

```
Sub CompNeg_Click ()

 ' Enable/disable menu choice for computing
 ' negative values in array

 CompNeg.Checked = Not CompNeg.Checked

End Sub


Sub PrtNeg (Sample_arr() As Single)

 ' Print total negative elements in array

 neg = Arrneg(Sample_arr())

 If CompNeg.Checked = True Then
    picture1.Print " Neg: "; neg
 End If

End Sub
```

ARRNONZERO

Returns total non-zero elements in an array

Syntax

```
Function Arrnonzero (<array name> As Single)
```

Returns

Total non-zero elements

Arguments

array name - array of values

Module

ARR.BAS

Remarks

Arrnonzero computes the total number of non-zero elements in an array. Use it to track valid responses given in a survey or to show missing data in a statistical analysis.

See Also

Arrmax, Arrmin, Arrneg, Arrpos, Arrsum

Example

STAT.MAK uses Arrnonzero to show sales progress for a company that sells marine products; lorans, generators and depth finders. When the user selects the Compute button from the File menu, the program reports the total number of divisions not making sales.

```
Sub PrtNonZero (Sample_arr() As Single)

 ' Calculate total non-zero elements in array

 zer = Arrnonzero(Sample_arr())

 ' Print answer

 picture1.Print "Divisions not making sales: "; zer

End Sub
```

ARRPOS

Computes positive elements in an array

Syntax

```
Function Arrpos (<array name> As Single)
```

Returns

Returns positive elements in array

Arguments

array name - array to use

Module

ARR.BAS

Remarks

Arrpos returns the total number of positive elements in an array. Use it to count the valid cases of a sample population.

See Also

Arrmax, Arrmin, Arrneg, Arrnonzero, Arrsum

Example

When the user selects the Compute option in STAT.MAK, the program reads the values in the SAMPLE.DAT file into an array. It then counts the positive elements and shows the answer in the Picture1 picture box.

```
Sub ComPos_Click ()

 ' Enable/disable menu choice for current statistic

 ComPos.Checked = Not ComPos.Checked

End Sub


Sub PrtPos (Sample_arr() As Single)

 ' Show positive elements in array

 pos = Arrpos(Sample_arr())

 If ComPos.Checked = True Then
    picture1.Print " Pos: "; pos
 End If

End Sub
```

ARRSORT

Sorts an array

Syntax

```
Function Arrsort (<array name> As Variant)
```

Returns

Nothing

Arguments

array name - array to sort

Module

ARR.BAS

Remarks

Arrsort sorts an array in ascending order using a bubble sort. By printing the array backwards, you can give the impression that the elements are arranged in descending order.

Since the <array name> argument is a variant, Arrsort can be used to arrange both numeric and string arrays. Note that it is also possible to arrange a list in order by:

- Setting the Sorted property of a list box or combo box
- Indexing a table with the Data Manager utility
- Printing a Crystal Reports report with group totals (indexes are created and handled automatically)

Alternately, you can use Arrsort to arrange elements where an array might be preferable to a list, table or report.

See Also

Arrmedian

Example

SORTDEM.MAK shows how to sort an array. At run time, when the Sort button is selected, the program reads a list of names from the CLUB.DAT text file, arranges them in ascending order and displays them in a picture box.

```
Dim Names(), member As String


Sub cmdSort_Click ()
```

```
Open "club.dat" For Input As #1

Dim current_name As Integer

' Fill dynamic array with names of club members

While Not EOF(1)
 current_name = current_name + 1
 Input #1, member
 ReDim Preserve Names(current_name)
 Names(current_name) = member
Wend

' Sort array

Call Arrsort(Names())

picture1.Cls

' Show sorted elements

For i = 1 To UBound(Names)
  picture1.Print Names(i)
Next

Close #1

End Sub
```

ARRSTDV

Calculates the standard deviation from a list of values in an array

Syntax

```
Function Arrstdv (<array name> As Single)
```

Returns

Standard deviation

Arguments

array name - array containing values to use

Module

ARR.BAS

Defaults

Bases answer on sample of population

Remarks

Arrstdv computes the standard deviation of a list of values in an array. Use it when you need to know how much an average deviates from the mean. Say what? For example, three students Moe, Larry and Curly each receive A's in Advanced Needlepoint. Their grades are:

Moe	Larry	Curly
190	100	83
92	84	100
88	84	85
90	92	90

If we relied solely on the mean, the average score for each student is 90. However, the standard deviation of Moe's grades is 1.6. This shows better performance overall than Larry and Curly whose scores deviated at 7.6 and 7.7. Moe always wins!

See Also

Arravg, Arrmedian, Arrmode, Arrvar

Example

Show which product has consistently sold the best throughout the sales period using Arrstdv. When the user selects the Compute option in STAT.MAK, the data in the SAMPLE.DAT file is read into an array. The program then calculates the standard deviation and shows the results in the Picture1 picture box.

```
Sub CompStdv_Click ()

 ' Enable/disable menu option for printing
 ' standard deviation

 CompStdv.Checked = Not CompStdv.Checked

End Sub


Sub PrtStdv (Sample_arr() As Single)

 ' Print standard deviation

 std = Arrstdv(Sample_arr())
```

```
 If CompStdv.Checked = True Then
    picture1.Print " Stdv.: "; std
 End If

End Sub
```

ARRSUM

Sums the values of an array

Syntax

```
Function Arrsum (<array name> As Single)
```

Returns

Array total

Arguments

array name - array containing a list of values to sum

Module

ARR.BAS

Remarks

Arrsum sums a list of values in an array. It is useful in reports that print group totals. Although the function is simple, it gets the job done and has built-in error checking to make programs fool proof (well almost).

See Also

Arravg, Arrmax, Arrmin, Arrmode, Arrnonzero, Arrpos

Example

Total a range of values in a grid. When the user selects the Sum option from the File menu in SUM.MAK, the program computes the Expenses column and prints the answer in row 7.

```
Sub Sum_Range_Click ()

 Const EXPENSES = 5

 Static Arr(EXPENSES) As Single
```

```
  For i = 1 To EXPENSES    ' Read values into array
    Grid1.Row = i
    Arr(i) = Val(Grid1.Text)
  Next

  total = Arrsum(arr())    ' Compute total expenses

  Grid1.Row = 7
  Grid1.Text = total

End Sub
```

ARRVAR

Computes variance of an array

Syntax

```
Function Arrvar (<array name> As Single)
```

Returns

Variance

Arguments

array name - array containing values to use

Module

ARR.BAS

Defaults

Bases average on a sample of the population

Remarks

The variance is the standard deviation squared. Arrvar computes this value using a list of numbers in an array. Like the standard deviation, the variance is more than just a simple measure of central tendency. It shows the range of values used in the average (and how much they deviate from the mean).

See Also

Arravg, Arrmedian, Arrmode, Arrstdv

Example

STAT.MAK demonstrates the use of Arrvar. For more information on this example, refer to the discussion of Arrstdv.

```
Sub CompVar_Click ()

 ' Enable/disable menu choice for computing
 ' variance

 CompVar.Checked = Not CompVar.Checked

End Sub


Sub PrtVar (Sample_arr() As Single)

 ' Print variance

 var = Arrvar(Sample_arr())

If CompVar.Checked = True Then
   picture1.Print " Var: "; var
 End If

End Sub
```

Appendix A

INSTALLING THE LIBRARY

The program disk included with this book contains sample applications, short examples and reusable code modules. Although it is not necessary to install these files to run the examples, the library modules require only about 100K of free disk space. To install all the examples, you need approximately 1.5 megabytes total disk space.

To Install the Library Modules (from DOS):

1. At the C:\ prompt, type MD VB_LIB <ENTER>.
2. Insert the disk with the library files into drive A:\.
3. Switch to the A: drive by typing A: <ENTER>.
4. Type COPY *.BAS C:\VB_LIB to install only the library modules.

To Install all the Files (from DOS):

1. At the C:\ prompt, type MD VB_LIB <ENTER>.
2. Insert the Program disk into drive A:\.
3. Switch to the A:\ drive by typing A: <ENTER>.
4. Type COPY *.* C:\VB_LIB <ENTER> to copy all the files on disk 1 to the hard drive.
5. Remove the first disk and insert the second disk into drive A:\.
6. Type COPY *.* C:\VB_LIB to install the remaining files.

Appendix B

CREATING EXECUTABLE PROGRAMS

After creating a program, you can compile the project so it will run as a stand alone application. When Visual Basic creates an executable file, it uses the default icon for the application. You can specify a different icon by setting the Icon property of the Startup form (the default is Form1).

Appendix B of the *Visual Basic Programmer's Guide* shows a list of icons you can use. Alternately, you can create your own icon using the ICONWRKS.MAK utility supplied with Visual Basic.

To Create an Executable File

1. From the File menu, choose Make EXE File...
2. In the File Name box, type the name of the project.
3. In the Application Title box, enter the name of application (this name will appear in the Program Manager under the icon).
4. Optionally, choose a different icon by selecting it from the Use Icon From drop-down list.

NOTE: This option does not allow you to change the Icon property of a form. It merely sets the default form used for the icon.

5. Click on OK to create the executable program (Visual Basic will assign a .EXE file extension to this file).

Before you can run the executable program, you must install the application on the machine it will be used on. The SetupWizard, supplied with Visual Basic, will correctly install all the files you need to run your application. For more information on installing programs, refer to Chapter 16, Writing Setup Programs.

Appendix C

ANSWERS TO ODD-NUMBERED REVIEW QUESTIONS

Chapter 1 Creating Interfaces

1. Visual Basic's sequential naming system for controls does little to document the purpose of objects. If you rename a control after writing code, you must also change the name of the event procedure. Otherwise Visual Basic will perform the wrong code block.
3. Answers to definitions:
   control - a graphical object placed on a form that responds to a user or system event.
   event procedure - a block of code linked to a control that executes when an event occurs.
   focus - when an object receives attention it is said to have focus.
   property - a control attribute.
   method - a keyword that causes an action to occur on an object.
5. The MaxLength property of a text box control determines the number of characters that can be entered into the text box.
7. The following example shows how to display a message in a modal dialog box when a command button called cmdOK is clicked:

```
Sub cmdOK_Click ()
    MsgBox ("This is a modal dialog")
End Sub
```

9. Display a message in a text box:

```
Sub Form_Load ()
    text1.Text = "Test string"
End Sub
```

11. Assign a string to a label control:

```
Sub Form_Load ()
  label1.Caption = "Test string"
End Sub
```

13. The ListCount property returns the total number of list elements.
15. At run time, you can select any number of check boxes. With option buttons, however, only one control per group can be selected.

To test if a check box is selected:

```
Sub Check1_Click ()

 Const CHECKED = 1

 If check1.Value = CHECKED Then
    MsgBox ("Check box is selected")
 End If

End Sub
```

To check if an option button is selected:

```
Sub Option1_Click ()

 If option1.Value = True Then
    MsgBox ("Option button is selected")
 End If

End Sub
```

17. To display a bitmap in an image control, you set the Picture property.

Example

```
image1.Picture = LoadPicture
          ⇨("C:\WINDOWS\PARTY.BMP")
```

19. The TabIndex property of a control allows you to change its tab order.

Chapter 2 Programming in Visual Basic

1. The following example shows how to send a message to a picture box or the **Printer** object. It assumes the form contains two option buttons, a picture box and a command button named cmdOK:

```
Sub cmdOK_Click ()

 ' Branch to appropriate routine

 If option1.Value = True Then
    Call PrtScreen
 Else
```

```
        Call PrtPrinter
    End If

End Sub


Sub PrtScreen ()

    ' Define new line character to format output on 2
    ' lines

    newline = Chr(13) + Chr(10)

    str1 = "The following message is directed to a
         ⇨ picture box."
    str2 = "The output should appear on 2 lines."

    picture1.Print str1 + newline + str2

End Sub


Sub PrtPrinter ()

    ' Define new line character to format output on 2
    ' lines

    newline = Chr(13) + Chr(10)

    str1 = "This message will be sent to the Printer
         ⇨ object and"
    str2 = "should also appear on 2 lines."

    printer.Print str1 + newline + str2
    printer.EndDoc

End Sub
```

3. Add 10 numbers using **For. . .Next** and a **Do. . .Loop**:

```
' For...Next loop

For i = 1 To 10
     tot_val = tot_val + i
Next

' Do...Loop
```

```
Do While i < 10
   i = i + 1
   tot_val = tot_val + i
Loop
```

5. Declare static array:

```
Sub testarr ()

 Static Products(1 To 3) As String

   .              .             .
   .              .             .

End Sub
```

7. The following procedure demonstrates how to declare, initialize and redimension a dynamic array. Notice that the array is first declared with no elements. Also notice that **Redim Preserve** is used to preserve the values of each element when the array is redimensioned:

```
Sub cmdOK_Click ()

 ' Declare dynamic array

 Dim DynArr() As String

 ' Redimension array

 ReDim DynArr(5)

 ' Initialize array

 DynArr(1) = "A": DynArr(2) = "B": DynArr(3) = "C"
 DynArr(4) = "D": DynArr(5) = "E"

 ' Redimension array and preserve other elements

 ReDim Preserve DynArr(6)

 DynArr(6) = "F"

 ' Print dynamic array

 For i = 1 To 6
    picture1.Print (DynArr(i))
 Next

End Sub
```

9. Copy contents of a label control to a text box control on another form:

```
Form2.Text1.Text = Form1.Label1.Caption
```

Chapter 3 Creating Menus

1. With shortcut keys, unlike access keys, you can perform menu operations without opening a menu.
3. To enable or disable a menu item, you set the Enabled property of the menu control to **True** or **False**.

Example

```
mnuFileOpen.Enabled = False
```

5. To define a menu control array, two or more menu items must share a common Name property and each menu definition must have a unique index.
7. If the **Show** method does not appear before the call to **PopupMenu** in the Form_Load procedure, the pop-up menu will appear before the form loads.

Chapter 4 Using Dialog Boxes

1. A custom control is a Visual Basic extension file that has an associated icon in the Toolbox.
3. To display a common dialog, you must set the Action property.

Example

```
CMDialog1.Action = 3   ' Displays Color dialog
CMDialog1.Action = 5   ' Displays Print dialog
```

5. The CancelError property of the common dialog custom control activates/deactivates error checking. The following example shows how it can be applied:

```
CMDialog1.CancelError = True
```

7. File controls are pre-defined objects in Visual Basic that allow you to interact with the system. The file list box control and the directory list box control are examples of file controls.
9. The following example shows how to display a list of files in a directory using a file list box control. Note that you could also accomplish the same task using the Open common dialog.

```
Sub Form_Load ()

  ' Set file list box pattern

  file1.Pattern = "*.FRM"

End Sub
```

11. The Copylist function of the library, copies a file list. To see a list of files recently updated in a directory, you can use the Fileschanged library routine. Before these functions can be used in an application, you must add the ENVIR.BAS module to the project.

Chapter 5 Error Handling & Debugging

1. The debugger can be activated in any of the following ways:
   - **Choose the Break command from the toolbar.**
   - **Press Control Break**
   - **Setup a watch expression**
   - **Define a breakpoint**
3. You can use the Immediate pane to monitor the values of variables, enter expressions and test execute code blocks.
5. By preceding **Print** methods with the **Debug** object, your projects can retain debugging code between sessions.
7. The output does not appear on the form because the **Show** method was not included before the **Print** method. With single stepping or procedure stepping, you can determine if these lines are executing.
9. The following code shows how you can write the error handler:

```
Function Checkfile (filename As String)

 On Error Goto Err_Handler:

 ' Test if file exist   trap error if it doesn't

 filedat = FileDateTime(filename)

 Checkfile = -1 '  Return -1 if file exist

 Exit Function

Err_Handler:
 MsgBox ("File does not exist")

 Checkfile = 0  ' Return 0 and exit procedure -
                ' file does not exist
 Exit Function

End Function
```

11. To test for the existence of a directory, you can try switching to the directory using the **ChDir** statement. If no error occurs, it means the directory exists.

Chapter 6 Database Access

1. To bind a text box to the data control:

Example

Control	Property	Setting
Data1	DatabaseName	"C:\VB\CUST.MDB"
Data1	RecordSource	cust_table
text1	DataSource	Data1
text1	DataField	custname

3. The Jet database engine creates databases in Microsoft Access format.
5. To deactivate auto-commit mode, you use the **BeginTrans** method (or statement) to begin a transaction. Afterwards, you use either **CommitTrans** to save the transaction or **RollBack** to cancel the change.
7. The **MoveFirst**, **MoveNext**, **MovePrevious** and **MoveLast** methids allow you to move the record pointer around a recordset.
9. The Options property of the data control lets you achieve multi-user access in a database. By adding its various property settings, you can achieve more than one form of database access.

In Windows for Workgroups, it is not necessary to run SHARE.EXE (and it will cause conflicts if you do attempt to run this program).

Chapter 7 Dynamic Grids

1. The grid control is a spreadsheet-like custom control that allows you to display text, numbers and graphics in tabular format.
3. If a grid contains more columns or rows than will fit on one screen, Visual Basic automatically adds scroll bars. If you click the left or right arrows on the horizontal scroll bar, the fixed columns of the grid, unlike the non-fixed columns, do not scroll. The same principle holds true for fixed rows and non-fixed rows. When you click the up or down arrows on the vertical scroll bar, the non-fixed rows scroll and the fixed rows do not.
5. The ColAlignment property controls the alignment of non-fixed columns. The FixedAlignment property controls the alignment of fixed columns.
7. To add a row to a grid, you use the **AddItem** method. To remove a row, you use the **RemoveItem** method.
9. The following code sets the column width of a range of cells:

```
For i = 1 to 10
     Grid1.ColWidth(i) = 1200       ' Twips
Next
```

11. When you click on a cell once, a Click event occurs. When you click on a cell twice, a DblClick event occurs.
13. To use the grid functions of the library, you must add the GRIDFUNC.BAS module to a project.

Chapter 8 Memo Handling

1. Before you can edit multiple lines in a text box, you must set the MultiLine property to **True**.
3. The Undolast function of the library reverses changes in a text box.
5. This example shows how to extract a file name from a string. It assumes that the string has been padded in the first 12 characters:

```
MsgBox (Left(list1.Text, 12))
```

   If you are unsure of the string length, you can use the **Len** function to get the length and **Instr** function to find the position of a string pattern within another string.
7. Save a text box to a file:

```
' Save document
```

```
fileno = FreeFile
filevar = text1.Text

filename = InputBox("File Name:")

retval = Memowrite(fileno, filename, filevar)

Close fileno
```

NOTE: This example assumes that <fileno>, <filename> and <filevar> have been properly declared in the Declaration section of the form.

9. The New MDI Form command from the File menu in Visual Basic allows you to create a new MDI container.
11. True: In a MDI application, only one parent window can be defined.

Chapter 9 Dynamic Data Exchange

1. DDE (Dynamic Data Exchange) is a technology that allows you to share information with other Windows-based applications. DDE, however, is not limited to just information exchange. You can use DDE to send commands to applications for them to perform.

   Three examples of DDE uses:

   - To access a spreadsheet.
   - To link a text box to a word processor.
   - To communicate among Visual Basic projects.

3. To specify the topic of a conversation, you must set the LinkTopic property. Chapter 9 shows several examples of how this can be done.
5. The three types of DDE links you can create are automatic, manual and link notify.
7. For a Visual Basic form to be declared as a source, you must set the LinkMode property of the form to 1 - Source.
9. The following code fragment shows how to send a command to a source for it to execute. It assumes that a valid link has already been established between a Visual Basic control and a Word for Windows document:

```
text1.LinkExecute "[FileClose 1]"
```

11. To poke information into a source, you use the **LinkPoke** method.
13. Significant events for DDE conversations:

    LinkOpen, LinkClose, LinkError, LinkNotify, LinkExecute

15. In DDE, an error can occur when an application appears to be inactive. A source can attempt to supply data in an invalid format or that is too large for a Visual Basic control to accept. You can monitor DDE events and use the LinkError procedure to determine the status of a conversation.
17. The following code shows how to trap DDE errors:

```
Sub Form_LinkError (LinkErr As Integer)
```

```
Const TIME_OUT_ERR = 282, MB_ICONEXCLAMATION = 48
Const NO_LINK = 6, NO_UPDATE = 8, LOW_MEMORY = 11

Select Case link_err
    Case LOW_MEMORY
        errmsg = "Low memory - unable to perform
            ⇨ DDE operation"
    Case NO_LINK
        errmsg = "Destination unable to connect"
    Case NO_UPDATE
        errmsg = "Destination unable to poke data"
    Case TIME_OUT_ERR
        DoEvents
    Case Else
        errmsg = Error
End Select

' Show DDE error message

MsgBox errmsg, MB_ICONEXCLAMATION, "DDE Error"

End Sub
```

Chapter 10 Creating Linked and Embedded Objects

1. Object linking and embedding (OLE) is a technology that allows you to share information with other Windows-based applications. It differs from dynamic data exchange in that your applications can control the views of other programs.
3. A linked object is a reference to an object stored and maintained by another Windows application. With an embedded object, a program must have a way of maintaining the object.
5. At run time, you create objects by setting the Class, SourceDoc and Action properties.
7. You can get the class name of an application by consulting the program's documentation or by creating a test link at design time and displaying the Class property with **MsgBox**.
9. The following example shows how to create a linked object at run time:

```
Sub Form_Load ()

' Create link to Word

OLE1.Class = "Word for Windows"
OLE1.SourceDoc = "C:\Winword\Temp.Doc"
OLE1.Action = 1

End Sub
```

11. See Table 10.1.

Chapter 11 Producing Charts and Graphs

1. The following properties are used to display legends, labels, ticks and grid lines:

Property	Description	Example
LegendText	Displays legends	Graph1.LegendText = "USA"
LabelText	Displays labels	Graph1.LabelText = "NY"
Ticks	Displays x, y ticks	Graph1.Ticks = 1
GridStyle	Displays grid lines	Graph1.GridStyle = 3

3. Display a pie chart:

```
Sub Form_Load ()

  ' Draw a two dimensional pie chart

  Const PIE_2D = 1, DRAW_GRAPH = 2

  Graph1.GraphType = PIE_2D
  Graph1.DrawMode = DRAW_GRAPH

End Sub
```

5. When the AutoInc property of the graph control is set to 1, you can quickly initialize a graph. AutoInc automatically advances the value of ThisPoint and ThisSet, making it possible to fill a graph with actual figures instead of test data.
7. To erase a graph, Drawmode must be set to 0.

Example

```
Graph1.DrawMode = 0
```

9. Although you can print a graph using the **PrintForm** method, DrawMode produces a higher quality image of the graph.

Example

```
Graph1.DrawMode = 5
```

11. To display a transparent graph, the Visible property of the graph control must be initially set to **False**. Then, at run time, you set this property to True (after setting the SeeThru property).

Chapter 12 Designing Reports

1. Database fields are most often placed in the Details section of a report.
3. The Grand Total. . . command from the Insert menu allows you to add a grand total field to a report.
5. To add database fields to a report, you use the Insert Database Field dialog. This dialog is automatically available when you create a new report.

7. For a file link to be successful, both tables must be indexed by a common field which must also be identical in structure.
9. To insert the date, page number and report title, the following options are available through the Insert menu in Crystal Reports:

Text Field. . .	**Inserts a text field**
Print Date Field	**Inserts a date field**
Page Number Field	**Inserts a page number field**

11. Print a report from Visual Basic:

```
Sub cmdPrint_Click ()

 Const WINDOW = 0

 Const PRINT_REPORT = 1

 Report1.Destination = WINDOW
 Report1.DataFiles(0) = "C:\VB_LIB\EMPLOY.MDB"
 Report1.ReportFileName = "C:\VB_LIB\EMPLOY.RPT"
 Report1.Action = PRINT_REPORT

End Sub
```

Chapter 13 Game Programming in Visual Basic

1. To reposition a picture box or image control on a form, you use the **Move** method—e.g., car.Move x,y.
3. Animation with the Left and Top properties produces an unsteady effect as the image must move left first and then up (assuming the Left property is set first).
5. Since the default value of the Enabled property is **True**, you only need to set the Interval property to enable a timer.
7. Setting the Interval property of a timer too fast can cause a time-out error (error 282).
9. The **Point** method returns the **RGB** color of a pixel on a form. You can use this method to determine the boundaries of screen objects during animation.

Chapter 14 Professional Features and Third Party Extensions

1. The following example shows how to prepare the communications control for a transmission:

```
Comm1.CommPort = 1
Comm1.Settings = "2400,N,8,1"
Comm1.PortOpen = True
```

3. Display an outline:

```
' Create list of distributors

Outline1.List(0) = "Distributors"
Outline1.List(1) = "A-Z Distributors"
Outline1.List(2) = "Bargain Express"
Outline1.List(3) = "Fast Buck"


Set index level for each item

Outline1.Indent(0) = 0
Outline1.Indent(1) = 1
Outline1.Indent(2) = 2
Outline1.Indent(3) = 3
```

5. The following special symbols are reserved by the masked edit control:

 # = Digit place holder
. = Decimal place holder
, = Thousands separator
: = Time separator
/ = Date separator
\ = Set next character to a literal - used to over-ride the default meaning of special mask characters (#.,:/&A?)
& = Place holder for character (ANSI characters between the ranges 32-126 and 128-255)
? = Place holder for letter - a-z or A-Z

NOTE: The actual symbols that are used as time, date and currency separators will depend on your international settings configuration (in Windows).

7. The 3D group push button might be preferable to a 3D command button when you want to remind the user that an operation is in effect. For example, you can display a picture of an inverted clipboard during a cut/paste operation (while the button is in the down position).
9. Display a status indicator on a panel:

```
Sub Form_Load ()

  ' Initialize status indicator

  Panel3d1.FloodType = 1
  hscroll1.Min = 1: hscroll1.Max = 100
```

```
End Sub


Sub HScroll1_Change ()

 ' Flood panel area according to scroll bar's value
 Panel3d1.FloodPercent = hscroll1.Value

End Sub
```

11. With Motion Works MediaShop, you can perform true animation in Visual Basic. The product also includes a sound wave editor and video image editor.

Chapter 15
Exposing the Power of the Windows API

1. When working with strings, you must be sure to specify the length of each variable or the DLL may corrupt memory.
3. With *call by reference*, parameters are given access to the addresses of variables and can change their values. *With call by value*, this is not possible. By default, Visual Basic uses *call by reference*. To pass an argument by *value*, you must include the **ByVal** reserved word before the argument in the parameter list.
5. Call GetActiveWindow procedure:

```
Sub Form_Load ()

 ' Show handle of the current form

 Show

 curwin = GetActiveWindow()

 MsgBox ("The handle of the current window is " +
      ⇨ Str(curwin))

End Sub
```

7. With DLLs written for Visual Basic, you can pass an entire array by including the name of the array in the parameter list followed by empty parenthesis. If the DLL was not exclusively designed for use with Visual Basic, you can still pass an entire array if the array is numeric by passing the first element of the array. This technique fails with string arrays and could corrupt memory.

Chapter 16
Writing Setup Programs

1. In pre-installation, the files that the setup program itself needs to install an application (e.g., DLLs and VBXs) are copied to the customer's machine. These files are not the same as the actual program files your application requires. During the installation, all other necessary files required to use the application are then copied to the hard drive.

NOTE: The installed application may also require other DLLs and VBX files not required by the pre-installation.

3. Custom setup programs are necessary when you need to:

   - Install only part of the application.
   - Use custom controls or other DLLs not already used by the setup program.
   - Use your own compression utility.

5. The Windows API VER.DLL contains procedures that return the version stamp or time and date of a file. With programs not written in Visual Basic, VER.DLL can detect the version stamp to prevent a newer version of a file from being overwritten by an older version of the same file (during an installation). In Visual Basic, VER.DLL cannot detect the version stamp, so it uses the time and date of the file's creation instead.

WORKING WITH SEQUENTIAL ACCESS, RANDOM ACCESS, AND BINARY ACCESS

USING SEQUENTIAL ACCESS

Sequential access is a method of accessing file information where records are stored sequentially to plain text files. Thus if there are ten records in a text file, to read the last record, you must read every record in the file that comes before it.

Although sequential access has its drawbacks, in some cases it can be very useful. For example, you can use sequential access to retrieve text files for a memo handler. To open a file for sequential access, you use the following syntax:

```
Open <filename> For [Input | Output | Append] As
                    ⇨ [#]<filenumber>
```

Once a file is open, you can save variables to it using **Print** and **Write**. The difference between **Print** and **Write** is that **Write** surrounds variable items with commas and strings with quotes. These separators must be included in order for Visual Basic to correctly read variables from a file. The following example shows how to save a list of names and phone numbers using sequential access:

```
Sub cmdSave_Click ()

 filename = "temp.dat"
 filenumber = 1

 ' Open text file

 Open filename For Output As #filenumber
```

```
 Write #filenumber, "Customer 1", "(435)235-4356"
 Write #filenumber, "Customer 2", "(653)535-6319"
 Write #filenumber, "Customer 3", "(905)112-3217"

 Close filenumber

End Sub
```

After saving the list, you can read the records back in a loop like this:

```
Sub cmdRead_Click ()

 picture1.FontName = "Courier"
 filename = "temp.dat"
 filenumber = 1

 Open filename For Input As #filenumber

 While Not EOF(filenumber)
  Input #filenumber, cust_name, phone
  picture1.Print cust_name, phone
 Wend

 Close #filenumber

End Sub
```

CLOSING A FILE

To prevent the possibility of data loss, you must close a file each time it is opened. Once a file is closed, all system resources are made available again to Visual Basic.

Syntax

```
Close [[#]<filenumber>][,[#]<filenumber>]...
```

USING RANDOM ACCESS

Random access is a method of accessing files that are assumed to be composed of fixed length records. In random access, you can quickly retrieve any record by specifying the *relative position* of the record in the file. For example, if a file contains 5 records, the relative position of the last record is 5.

The following example shows how to open a file for random access. Notice that the **Len** clause *must* be included in order to correctly read records from the file.

```
' Define user type

Type Filestruc
 client As String * 25
 phone As String * 13
End Type

Global typevar As Filestruc


Sub cmdOpenfile_Click ()

 ' Open file for random access

 Open "test.dat" For Random As #fileno Len =
        ⇨ Len(typevar)

End Sub
```

Filestruc is the name of a user type that indicates the structure of each record. In this case, the record contains two fields, <client> and <phone>. The definition for the user type must appear in the Declaration section of a module (.BAS file). <Typevar> is a global variable of the user type.

Once a file is opened for random access, you can quickly read and write records using the **Get** and **Put** statements. **Get** reads a record from a file. **Put** allows you to save and update records.

Syntax

```
Get [#]<fileno>, [<recno>], <uservar>

Put [#]<fileno>, [<recno>], <uservar>
```

Example

```
' Read third record in file

Get #fileno, 3, typevar

' Overwrite second record in file

Put #fileno, 2, typevar
```

ADDING RECORDS TO RANDOM ACCESS FILES

R_ACCESS.MAK shows how to add new records using random access. The **Type** definition for this example is defined in R_ACCESS.BAS. To determine how many records are in the file, the file size is divided by the total number of bytes of a fixed length record. The program then adds the new record at the end of the file:

```
' Define user type

Type Filestruc
 client As String * 25
 phone As String * 13
End Type

Global typevar As Filestruc

Sub cmdSave_Click ()

 Dim fileno As Integer

 fileno = 1

 Open "test.dat" For Random As #fileno Len =
        ⇨ Len(typevar)

 ' Calculate total number of records in file

 total_records = LOF(fileno) / Len(typevar)

 typevar.client = text1.Text
 typevar.phone = text2.Text

 ' Add new record

 Put #fileno, total_records + 1, typevar

 Close #fileno

End Sub
```

In the preceding example, the global variable <typevar> is of type Filestruc (the name of the user type). Using this definition, you can access the values of each field of the record.

Example

```
MsgBox (typevar.client + " " + typevar.phone)
```

UPDATING RECORDS IN RANDOM ACCESS FILES

To update a record in a random access file, the contents of the record buffer are overwritten with the current values of each field. The following example shows how this is done:

```
fileno = 1
record_num = 2

Open "test.dat" For Random As #fileno
         ⇨ Len = Len(typevar)

' Read second record in file

Get #fileno, record_num, typevar

typevar.client = "Sally Smith"
typevar.phone = "(456)547-4321"

' Update the record

Put #fileno, record_num, typevar

Close #fileno
```

DELETING RECORDS FROM RANDOM ACCESS FILES

To delete a record from a random access file, each record in the file following the one being removed is copied down one position. The following code fragment demonstrates how to do this:

```
' Calculate total number of records in file

lastrecord = LOF(fileno) / Len(typevar)

For i = delrec To lastrecord

 ' Read each record

 Get fileno, i + 1, typevar

 ' Rewrite each record 1 position higher

 Put fileno, i, typevar

Next
```

This system has one problem. When a record is deleted from a random access file, a blank record is left at the bottom of it. To remove the blank record, you could write a routine to handle this yourself or call the library function Delnull. Delnull removes bad or inaccessible records from random access files. Table D-1 shows a list of other library routines you can use to simplify file handling.

Function	Purpose
DBEngine	Adds, updates or removes records using the database engine.
Deleterec	Removes a record from a random access file.
Delnull	Removes inaccessible records at the end of a random access file.
Initscroll	Initializes a scroll bar for browsing records in a random access file.
Lastrec	Calculates the total number of records in a random access file.
OLEread	Reads an OLE object from a file.
OLEsave	Saves an OLE object to a file.
Replacerec	Updates a record in a random access file.
Saverec	Appends a record to a random access file.
Scrollupdate	Reads a record into memory each time the scroll bar is clicked.

TABLE D-1 DATABASE AND FILE HANDLING ROUTINES OF THE LIBRARY

USING BINARY ACCESS

Binary access is a form of file access that allows you to store and access file information in a non-fixed record format. In binary access, you can directly edit any byte position in a file. Since records can be of variable length, however, an application must have a way of keeping track of where information is stored in a file in order to correctly read records back.

Because of the difficulties of dealing with binary access, you should consider using random access or the database engine instead when working with records. There are, however, some practical applications of binary access that would not be possible otherwise. For example, you can use binary access to save a picture created in Microsoft Paintbrush using code like this:

```
Const OLE_UPDATE = 11

Open filename For Binary As #fileno

OLE1.FileNumber = fileno
OLE1.Action = OLE_UPDATE

Close #fileno
```

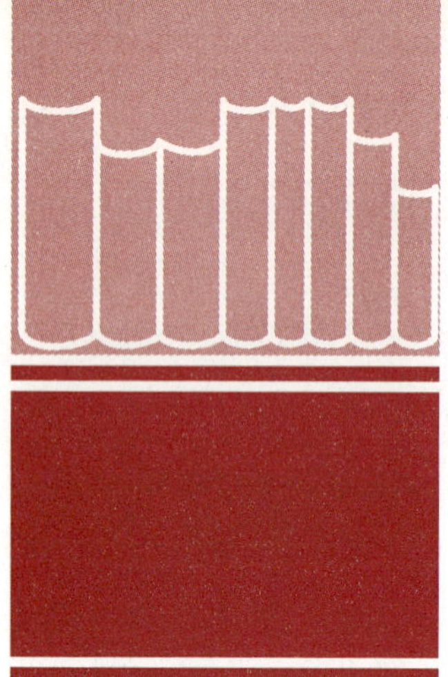

INDEX

A

B

C

D

E

F

G

H

I

L